COMPLETE ENCYCLOPEDIA OF
FORMULA 1

Tim Hill and Gareth Thomas

Edited by Kate Santon and Sarah Rickayzen

PaRragon

Bath · New York · Cologne · Melbourne · Delhi
Hong Kong · Shenzhen · Singapore · Amsterdam

This edition published by Parragon Books Ltd in 2014

Parragon Books Ltd
Chartist House
15–17 Trim Street
Bath BA1 1HA, UK
www.parragon.com

Copyright © Parragon Books Ltd 2009–2014

Produced by Atlantic Publishing

Photographs © LAT except those on pages 1, 2, 4, 6,10, 12, 19, 26, 28, 38,
45, 49, 50, 53, 60, 64, 76, 77, 87, 88, 92, 98, 101, 105, 108, 110, 116, 119, 124, 134, 138,
140, 141, 143, 145, 147, 235, 237, 239, 240, 242© Getty Images

ISBN 978-1-4723-7506-3
Printed in China

CONTENTS

INTRODUCTION

When the internal combustion engine was developed in the late nineteenth century, there were those who viewed it purely in utilitarian terms, as simply another means of getting from A to B. And there were those who wanted to test their vehicles – and themselves – to the absolute limit: to get from A to B quicker than anyone else.

More than a century has passed since the days of the spectacular inter-city races, which launched a new field of sporting endeavour. But the raw appeal remains the same: man and machine operating as one in high-risk, high-reward gladiatorial combat.

The chase for the victors' laurels gained fresh momentum in 1950, when the Fédération Internationale de l'Automobile launched the world championship. The 32 men who have held the coveted title to date include legendary names who would feature in any list of all-time greats: Fangio, Brabham, Clark, Stewart, Senna, Prost, Schumacher. Others came agonisingly close to gaining a seat at the top table. Stirling Moss missed out narrowly on several occasions, Wolfgang von Trips was killed when the 1961 title lay within his grasp, while team orders robbed the mercurial Gilles Villeneuve of the crown in 1979.

This highly illustrated book chronicles the history of the world championship, from Giuseppe Farina's victory for Alfa Romeo at Silverstone on 13 May 1950 to the present day. All the top drivers are profiled, and there is a wealth of information on the major marques and championship venues, while the comprehensive statistics section will settle many an argument. It is a story of ingenuity and endeavour, rivalry and camaraderie, triumph and tragedy, in pursuit of the greatest prize in motor sport.

TIMELINE

1950

The first world championship is contested under the jurisdiction of the FIA.

Alfa Romeo, Cooper, Ferrari and Maserati take part.

The Spa-Francorchamps circuit in Belgium, Silverstone in Britain, Autodromo Nazionale di Monza, Italy, Bremgarten in Switzerland, Reims-Gueux in France and the Monaco circuit all host races. The Indianapolis 500, United States, is included as a round.

The first race of the world championship is the British GP at Silverstone. Giuseppe (Nino) Farina wins in an Alfa Romeo.

Giuseppe Farina is the first world champion.

1951

First race at the Nürburgring.

Argentinian José Froilán González wins the British GP Silverstone – Ferrari's first world championship victory.

25 out of the 33 starters at the Indianapolis 500 fail to finish, the largest number of retirements in any F1 race.

Luigi Fagioli wins the French GP, the oldest winner ever at 53 years and 22 days.

1952

Ferrari win all rounds in the contest apart from the Indianapolis 500.

1953

The first South American GP is held at Autódromo Oscar Alfredo Gálvez, Buenos Aires.

1955

Ascari is killed when a tyre deflates on his Ferrari sports car at Monza.

Louis Chiron is the oldest man to take part in a GP, entering the Monaco race at nearly 55 years old.

1957

A Vanwall, shared by Tony Brooks and Stirling Moss, gives British constructors their first win at the British GP, Aintree.

Juan Manuel Fangio wins his fifth world championship.

1958

Luigi Musso is killed during the French GP after crashing his Ferrari.

Peter Collins is killed during the German GP at the Nürburgring when his Ferrari crashes and hits a tree.

Stuart Lewis-Evans dies from injuries and burns received after crashing at the Morocco GP.

1959

After retiring from racing the previous year, Mike Hawthorn dies in a road accident.

Jack Brabham is the first driver to win the title in a rear-engined car.

1960

British drivers Chris Bristow and Alan Stacey die at the Belgian GP. Stirling Moss breaks both legs in a practice accident.

The Italian GP is held on the banked track at Monza. British teams boycott the race on safety grounds.

1961

Watkins Glen hosts its first GP.

Engine size restricted to 1.5-litre.

Ferrari dominate the season with the classic 'sharknosed' rear-engined car.

Giancarlo Baghetti wins in a Ferrari at Reims, the only driver ever to win a GP on his debut.

Wolfgang von Trips and several spectators are killed at the Italian GP.

1962

Stirling Moss suffers a career-ending crash at a pre-season Goodwood meeting.

Lotus introduce ground-breaking new model, the 25, with a monocoque chassis.

Jack Brabham enters German GP with a car of his own construction.

1963

The first of Graham Hill's five victories at Monaco.

1964

Jim Clark wins the first GP to be held at Brands Hatch.

John Surtees secures the Drivers' title and so becomes the first (and only) man to win world titles on both two and four wheels.

1965

Tyre supplier Goodyear's first win is at the Mexican GP.

1966

Bruce McLaren forms his own team.

Rules change to allow the 3-litre engines.

Jackie Stewart is trapped in his car after crashing at the Belgian GP, leading him to campaign and eventually transform the sport's attitude to driver safety.

Jack Brabham wins his third world championship title and Brabham-Repco win the Constructors' title.

1967

Kyalami GP Circuit, South Africa, hosts its first GP.

Italian Lorenzo Bandini dies of the injuries sustained after crashing while leading the Monaco GP in his Ferrari.

The ground-breaking Lotus 49 wins on debut at the Dutch GP.

The first Canadian GP is held at Mosport Park.

1968

Sponsorship makes its first appearance in F1, ending the use of national racing colours.

Wings appear on GP cars to aid down force.

Jim Clark is killed in a Formula Two race at Hockenheim.

1969

Jackie Stewart wins by a 2-lap margin at the Spanish GP, the joint biggest winning margin in GP history.

1970

The Hockenheimring hosts the German GP for the first time.

The wedge-shaped Lotus 72 debuts.

Piers Courage is killed in the Williams' de Tomaso at the Dutch GP.

Bruce McLaren is killed at Goodwood while testing a Can-Am car.

Jochen Rindt is killed during qualifying for the Italian GP. He later becomes the first posthumous F1 champion.

1971

The French GP moves to Paul Ricard and the Canadian GP moves to Mosport Park.

Peter Gethin wins Italian GP by 0.01s from Ronnie Peterson – the narrowest winning margin ever.

Slicks are introduced to F1 racing.

Jo Siffert dies from smoke inhalation at Brands Hatch.

1972

Bernie Ecclestone takes over at Brabham.

Jo Bonnier is killed at Le Mans.

1973

The Interlagos circuit hosts its first GP.

Ex-champion Graham Hill sets up his own Embassy Hill racing team.

The Ford DFV engine wins every GP of the season.

Mike Hailwood saves Clay Regazzoni's life by pulling him from his burning BRM at the South African GP. Hailwood is awarded the George Medal for valour.

Roger Williamson is killed at the Dutch GP. David Purley attempts to save his life and is awarded the George Medal.

The pace car is used for first time in F1 during the Canadian GP but it is not successful.

Jackie Stewart becomes champion for a third time but withdraws from the US GP after François Cévert is killed during qualifying.

1974

Peter Revson is killed during testing.

1975

Lella Lombardi is the first woman to score points in an F1 GP, taking 0.5 points in the Spanish GP.

The Brazilian GP is Graham Hill's 176th and last race. Later that year, he and Tony Brise, together with other team members, are killed in a plane crash.

Five spectators are killed at the Spanish GP when Rolf Stommelen's Hill-Ford crashes into the crowd.

Mark Donohue dies of injuries sustained during practice at the Austrian GP.

1976

Niki Lauda is severely burned in an accident at the Nürburgring.

Mario Andretti wins the first Japanese GP at Mount Fuji.

Tyrrell introduce a six-wheeled car.

1977

Patrick Head joins Frank Williams' team.

Tom Pryce is killed after hitting a track marshal at the South African GP.

Jody Scheckter scores the 100th GP victory for the Ford DFV engine, at Monaco.

Renault's RS01, the first turbo powered car, makes its debut at the British GP.

Spectators are killed when Gilles Villeneuve's Ferrari crashes during the Japanese GP.

1978

Circuit Gilles Villeneuve, Montreal, hosts its first GP.

The Williams team introduce their first own car, the FW06.

Ronnie Peterson dies from injuries inflicted at a crash in the Italian GP.

Niki Lauda wins the last Swedish GP with the controversial Brabham BT46B 'Fan Car'.

Bernie Ecclestone becomes chief executive of the F1 Constructors' Association. Brabham introduce carbon brakes.

1980

Autodromo Enzo e Dino Ferrari circuit, San Marino, makes its F1 debut.

Patrick Depailler is killed in a testing accident at Hockenheim prior to the German GP.

Imola hosts its first GP, temporarily replacing Monza as the Italian GP venue.

1981

Ron Dennis takes over McLaren, and the team introduces a carbon-fibre chassis.

First Las Vegas GP, held in the car parks of Las Vegas casinos.

1982

BMW debut their turbo engine in the Brabham.

Canadian Gilles Villeneuve is killed during qualifying for the Belgian GP at Zolder, when he lost control of his Ferrari after making contact with Jochen Mass's March.

Riccardo Paletti dies when he crashes into the stalled Ferrari of Didier Pironi during the start of the Canadian GP.

Didier Pironi is seriously injured after a collision with the Renault of Alain Prost during qualifying at Hockenheim.

1983

The first race is held at the remodelled Spa-Francorchamps.

Michele Alboreto's Tyrrell chalks up the 155th and last win for the Cosworth DFR/DFY engine at the United States GP in Detroit.

Ferrari win the championship for the last time until 1999.

1984

First race composed entirely of turbo-charged cars is held at the Osterreichring, Austria.

Tyrrell is disqualified for the entire 1984 season after allegations of technical infringements.

Niki Lauda wins his third title by half a point from team-mate Alain Prost.

1985

Renault and Ligier boycott the South African GP at the request of the French government, in protest over apartheid.

Rosberg wins the first Australian GP.

Renault are the first constructor to log car data on computers.

1986

Frank Williams is paralysed in a road accident driving back from Paul Ricard.

The Hungarian GP at Hungaroring, Budapest, becomes the first F1 race to be held behind the 'Iron Curtain'.

1987

The FIA announce turbo engines are to be banned from 1989.

Nelson Piquet wins his third world championship.

1988

McLaren win 11 consecutive races and end the season with 15 victories in 16 races.

1989

Alain Prost wins his third world championship.

1990

The 500th F1 GP is held in Adelaide.

1991

Circuit de Nevers Magny-Cours, France, and Circuit de Catalunya, Barcelona, host their first Grands Prix.

The Australian GP in Adelaide is stopped after 14 laps due to rain. It is the shortest race in F1 history.

McLaren win their seventh title in eight years while the Honda engine makes it the fifth in a row.

Ayrton Senna wins his third world championship.

1992

Nigel Mansell wins the first five races of the season, a record equalled by Michael Schumacher in 2004.

1993

Ayrton Senna wins European GP at Donington by more than a minute.

The safety car is reintroduced. The first to be used was a Fiat Tempra.

1994

Rubens Barrichello crashes in Friday practice at Imola; Simtek's Roland Ratzenberger is killed in the Saturday practice; JJ Lehto and Pedro Lamy crash, sending debris into the crowd and injuring eight people. After the restart, Ayrton Senna is killed after going off at Tamburello.

Karl Wendlinger is in a coma after crashing at Monaco.

1995

Damon Hill wins by a 2 lap margin at the Australian GP, the joint biggest winning margin in GP history.

1996

McLaren announce the end of the longest sponsorship association, with Marlboro, signing instead with West.

Only 3 cars finish at Monaco, the lowest number of finishers ever.

1997

Five principals from the Williams team are charged with manslaughter after the death of Senna. They are subsequently cleared of the charges.

Bridgestone enters F1.

Michael Schumacher is disqualified from the 1997 championship, but retains his wins and points. Williams and McLaren are cleared of allegations that they colluded in the result of the Jerez GP.

1998

Sidepod 'X-wings' banned despite being used for a year.

1999

Sepang International Circuit hosts its first F1 race.

Ferrari win the Constructors' title, their first in 16 years.

2000

Michael Schumacher is Ferrari's first Drivers' champion for 21 years.

2001

Michael Schumacher wins his fourth world championship, equalling the achievements of Alain Prost.

2002

Schumacher and Barrichello amass more points than the rest of the constructors put together.

2003

The fastest average race speed (247.585km/h) was recorded at the Italian GP.

Shanghai International Circuit opens

Ferrari win the Constructors' title for the sixth consecutive year.

2004

Michael Schumacher wins a record seventh title.

2005

Istanbul Park, Turkey, hosts its first GP.

The fastest top speed (372.6km/h) was recorded by Juan Pablo Montoya at the Italian GP.

2008

Singapore hosts its first GP.

First Valencia GP is held.

Lewis Hamilton wins the Drivers' title by a point, overtaking Toyota's Timo Glock at the final corner of the final GP of the season.

2009

Abu Dhabi hosts its first GP.

The German GP is Mark Webber's 130th race and his first win.

Nelson Piquet Jr is dropped by Renault and announces that he deliberately crashed in 2008 to help his team-mate.

Brawn GP become the first constructor to win the title in their debut season. The team is renamed Mercedes for the beginning of the new season.

2010

Red Bull's Sebastian Vettel becomes the youngest driver to win the world championship in the sport's history at the age of 23 years and 134 days.

Ferrari start their 800th GP in Turkey.

Rubens Barrichello celebrates his 300th GP start.

South Korea hosts its first GP.

2011

Inaugural Indian GP.

The rain-interrupted Canadian GP becomes longest-ever F1 race at 4 hours 4 minutes.

2012

Sebastian Vettel becomes youngest triple world champion at the age of 25 and also the third driver to win three consecutive titles.

Austin hosts the first US Grand Prix since 2007.

2013

Vettel equals Alberto Ascari's 60-year-old record of nine consecutive victories in lifting a fourth successive crown. His 13 wins also matches Schumacher's best haul for a season in 2004.

THE DRIVERS

FERNANDO ALONSO

Born:	29 July 1981, Oviedo, Spain
Grand Prix starts:	217*
Grand Prix victories:	32*
Points total:	1606*
World Champion:	2005, 2006

*TO END OF 2013 SEASON

TWO-TIME WORLD CHAMPION

In 2005, Fernando Alonso completed a hat-trick of records: the youngest-ever pole-sitter (2003), race winner (2003) and now world champion, the latter breaking Fittipaldi's long-standing record of 1972.

The son of an amateur kart racer, Alonso first climbed into the cockpit at the age of three, later competing successfully in competitions, firstly in his native Spain, then internationally.

By 2000 he had graduated to F3000, earning fourth place in that year's championship. He made his F1 debut with Minardi the following year at the Australian GP, at the age of 19. No points that season, but the Spaniard's potential was spotted and he signed as test driver for Renault for 2002. 2003 saw Alonso promoted into a race seat and the start of his determined efforts to reach the very top of the tree. His maiden victory came in Hungary, taking three more podiums that year to finish with 55 points and sixth place.

By contrast, the early part of 2004 was disappointing with team-mate Jarno Trulli out-racing him. As the season progressed Alonso's performance improved, and he finished the year in fourth place.

Teamed with Giancarlo Fisichella in 2005, Alonso's first win of the campaign came in Malaysia, followed by victories in Bahrain and at San Marino. Battling against the improving form of McLaren in the shape of Kimi Raïkkönen, he clinched the world title in Brazil, finishing third that day. He added 7 wins, 15 podiums and 133 points to his score-sheet, having led the championship from the second race of the season.

Alonso moved to McLaren in 2007, ceding his crown to Ferrari's Raïkkönen in a final-round thriller. He tied for the runner-up spot with rookie team-mate Lewis Hamilton. Relations were strained between the two and it was little surprise when Alonso rejoined Renault at the end of the year. After two disappointing campaigns, in which he finished fifth and ninth and added two wins to his tally, Alonso moved to Ferrari for the 2010 season.

He made a winning debut in Bahrain and sent the Ferrari fans wild with victory at Monza, results that helped him to an 8-point lead going into the final round. Sebastian Vettel's victory there denied him a third world crown.

Alonso regularly outdrove his machinery over the next three seasons, twice more ending the year runner-up to Vettel. There was a gulf between him and the champion in 2013, when relations between driver and team became very strained.

MARIO ANDRETTI

Born:	28 February 1940, Montona, Italy
Grand Prix starts:	128
Grand Prix victories:	12
Points total:	180
World Champion:	1978

AMERICA'S GREATEST WORLD CHAMPION

Mario Andretti wasn't America's first world champion, but his record makes him the greatest to emerge from that country. Andretti's family emigrated to the US when he was in his mid-teens. Barely a decade later he had won a hat-trick of IndyCar titles. He made his F1 debut at Watkins Glen in 1968 for Lotus, a team still reeling from Clark's death. He took pole first time out in an unfamiliar car. After a few more outings for Lotus in 1969, Andretti appeared for the STP March team, with whom he scored his first points. He finished third at Jarama, but generally the car was uncompetitive.

On joining Ferrari in 1971, he won first time out at Kyalami, but didn't concentrate on F1 full-time until 1975, with Parnelli. After a couple of indifferent seasons the team folded and he returned to Lotus. In the Lotus 78 Andretti drove to four victories in 1977 and third place in the championship. His performance continued to improve in 1978, winning six races; he was helped along the way by team-mate Ronnie Peterson, who acted as the perfect foil, following him home four times.

By the time they reached Monza, Lotus had the championship won, though either driver could have claimed the crown. Peterson was injured in a shunt and Andretti went on to win yet again. The title was his when the news came through that Peterson had died from complications.

Lotus lost its way over the next two years. Andretti's move to Alfa Romeo produced a disappointing 3 points. In 1982 Andretti returned to IndyCars, taking yet another title in 1984.

ALBERTO ASCARI

Born:	13 July 1918, Milan, Italy	
Died:		26 May 1955
Grand Prix starts:	31	
Grand Prix victories:	13	
Points total:	140.64	
World Champion:	1952, 1953	

THE LAST ITALIAN WORLD CHAMPION

Alberto Ascari and his father Antonio had careers which followed an eerily similar path. Ascari Snr – one of the premier drivers of the post-WWI era – was killed at the age of 36 while competing at the 1925 French GP. Thirty years later Alberto lost his life on the track at the age of 36.

Ascari began his racing career with motorbikes before moving to four wheels with Ferrari in 1940 in the famous Mille Miglia road race, but it was not until 1947 that he made his Grand Prix debut. Having moved to Maserati, he and team-mate and mentor Luigi Villoresi started from the back of the grid at the 1948 British GP as a result of arriving late. They carved their way through the field to finish first and second. Villoresi took top honours, but Ascari was recognised as a driver with enormous potential.

By the end of the following season, with wins at the Swiss and Italian GPs, Ascari was back with Ferrari. He finished fifth in the inaugural world championship of 1950. A year later he won in Germany and Italy, but it wasn't quite enough to take the title from Fangio and Alfa Romeo. In 1952 he won at Spa and the following five Grand Prix races, assuring him the world championship for that year. Ascari's victory at Spa in June 1953 completed a run of nine successive wins in a 12-month period and he retained his title with a win at Bremgarten.

Ascari's move to Lancia in 1954 resulted in a disappointing Championship Series that year. In 1955 he walked away unscathed from a dramatic crash into the harbour at Monaco, only to be killed four days later while testing a Ferrari sports car at Monza. He remains the last Italian to win the world championship.

RUBENS BARRICHELLO

Born:	23 May 1972, São Paulo, Brazil
Grand Prix starts:	325*
Grand Prix victories:	11*
Points total:	658*

*TO END OF 2011 SEASON

RECORD FOR GRAND PRIX STARTS

In 2004 Rubens Barrichello completed his fifth season as foil to Michael Schumacher's perennial assault on the championship. His efforts helped Ferrari lift the Constructors' title in each of those seasons. Runner-up to Schumacher in 2002 and 2004, Barrichello has shown on numerous occasions that he has the talent to beat anyone on his day. Indeed, in Austria 2002 Barrichello led until the final lap before team orders forced him to allow Schumacher through. The bad publicity this attracted led to the banning of such practices.

Barrichello went to Europe after winning five national kart titles in his teens. He immediately won the GM Lotus Euroseries, then beat Coulthard to the 1991 British F3 title, driving for West Surrey Racing. He made his F1 debut for Jordan in 1993. In only his third race, the European GP at Donington, he was running second before retiring, while his first points came at Suzuka, where he finished fifth.

He began 1994 strongly, including a podium finish at the Pacific GP, but suffered a big spill during practice at Imola. Deeply affected by Senna's death, he showed great fortitude in taking a brilliant pole at Spa. He was sixth that year, and having failed to improve on that in the next two seasons, left to join the Stewart team in 1997.

Finishing second to Schumacher at Monaco was that year's highlight. After a disappointing 1998, his loyalty to Stewart was rewarded with three podiums and seventh in the 1999 championship, though it was team-mate Johnny Herbert who gave the team its first victory. In 2000 he replaced Irvine as Ferrari no. 2, scoring his maiden win from 18th on the grid at a wet Hockenheim. After six years as Ferrari's no. 2, 33-year-old Barrichello took up a fresh challenge with Honda. The next three seasons yielded just 41 points, though the 2008 Turkish GP, his 257th, did see him pass Riccardo Patrese's record for F1 starts. Barrichello went into the 2009 season, his 17th in F1, driving for the new Brawn GP team. He scored his first victories for five years and took third place in the championship, switching to Williams for the 2010 campaign.

Released by the Grove-based team after a disastrous 2011 season in which he accumulated just 4 points, Barrichello moved to IndyCars, bringing to an end the F1 career of the only man to compete in 300 grands prix.

GERHARD BERGER

Born:	27 August 1959, Worgl, Austria
Grand Prix starts:	210
Grand Prix victories:	10
Points total:	386

200 FORMULA ONE RACES IN 14 YEARS

Gerhard Berger is one of only a handful of drivers to compete in over 200 F1 races, a consistent performer in his 14-year career at the top level. He made his debut at the 1984 Austrian GP for ATS, finishing sixth in only his second race. A move to Arrows yielded 3 points in 1985, but his career then took off. He joined the newly-formed Benetton team, which had just evolved from Toleman, scoring both his and the team's maiden victory in Mexico. Ferrari came calling, and Berger embarked on the first of two stints at Maranello. He won the final two races to secure fifth place in 1987; only the 'big four' – Prost, Senna, Piquet and Mansell – finished ahead of him. A year later only the runaway McLarens of Senna and Prost got the better of him, and his one victory came in the best place of all for a Ferrari man, Monza. New team-mate Mansell outscored him in 1989, though in an indifferent season he enjoyed a huge slice of luck: escaping a big accident at Imola with minor injuries.

Three years at McLaren followed, a period where he was naturally in Senna's shadow. He was a regular on the podium, but scored just three wins. At Suzuka in 1991 Senna moved over on the last lap to let him taste victory. And in Montreal a year later he inherited the lead after Senna retired with electrical trouble.

Berger returned to Ferrari in 1993, a period when Maranello was playing second fiddle to Williams and Benetton. He did win at Hockenheim in 1994 to break Ferrari's longest winless streak, a season in which he finished third yet again, a position he would never be able to improve upon.

His final two campaigns were back at Benetton. With team bosses hinting that his days were numbered, Berger announced his retirement before Hockenheim, then won the race in brilliant style again.

JACK BRABHAM

Born:	**2 April 1926, Hurstville, Australia**
Grand Prix starts:	126
Grand Prix victories:	14
Points total:	261
World Champion:	1959, 1960, 1966

THREE TIMES WORLD CHAMPION

Jack Brabham moved from the dirt-track circuits of his native Australia to Britain in 1955 to test himself against the cream of Europe. He joined the Cooper Car Company team and made his F1 debut at the British GP that year. He gave the works team its first success at Monaco in 1959, going on to win the championship title ahead of Moss.

In 1960 Brabham retained his title with two rounds to spare. When he slipped down the rankings in 1961, he set up his own team, and before the 1962 season was out, had become the first man to notch championship points in his own car.

The fledgling team achieved its first victory with Dan Gurney, in the 1964 French GP. Two years later Jack matched that achievement, followed by three more victories in 1966, to win his third world championship. He remains the only man to lift the crown in a car bearing his name.

Brabham competed for four more years, claiming his 14th and final victory at Kyalami in 1970. He retired after finishing fifth in that year's championship, and sold the team to Bernie Ecclestone the following year.

TONY BROOKS

Born:	25 February 1932, Dukinfield, England
Grand Prix starts:	38
Grand Prix victories:	6 (1 shared)
Points total:	75

CHAMPIONSHIP RUNNER-UP FOR FERRARI

Tony Brooks gave up a career in dentistry to concentrate on motor racing. 1955 was his breakthrough year when he moved to single-seaters, winning the non-championship Syracuse GP in a Connaught on his F1 debut. The following year Brooks contested his first world championship, with BRM, but it was to prove a false dawn as he was thrown from his car during practice at Silverstone, and spent the rest of the year competing in sports car events.

Having signed for Vanwall in 1957, he finished fifth in the championship that year. Brooks won three times in 1958 – in Belgium, Germany and Italy – but a number of retirements meant that he had to settle for third place overall, behind Hawthorn and Moss.

Vanwall withdrew at the end of the year and Brooks moved to Ferrari where he finished the season runner-up, 4 points behind the formidable Jack Brabham. In his final two seasons he slipped down the rankings, garnering a total of just 13 points. Having joined the Yeoman Credit team in 1960, Brooks moved back to BRM for his final campaign. He retired at the end of 1961 to concentrate on his garage business.

JENSON BUTTON

Born:	19 January 1980, Frome, England
Grand Prix starts:	249*
Grand Prix victories:	15*
Points total:	1072*
World Champion:	2009

*TO END OF 2013 SEASON

BRITAIN'S 10TH WORLD CHAMPION

Having starred in Cadet Karts at the age of eight, Button won the British championship in 1990 and 1991, finishing runner-up in the world championship in 1995. In 1997, at the age of 17, he became the youngest winner of the European Super A championship, and was seen as one of motor sport's rising stars.

In 1998 he continued his upward surge, taking the British Formula Ford title, and third place in the F3 championship. In late 1999, Button finally signed with Williams, finishing sixth in only his second GP, Interlagos 2000, and becoming the youngest Briton to notch a championship point. He ended the year in eighth place.

Button spent the next two seasons with Benetton-Renault. In 2002 he scored in seven races and finished seventh in the final table. He moved to BAR in 2003, regularly outperforming team-mate Jacques Villeneuve, a former world champion. In 2004 only the Ferraris got the better of Button, who stood on the podium ten times and scored 85 points.

Button started 2005 poorly, with a disqualification at the San Marino GP, and hence a three-race ban. His performance improved with third places at both Hockenheim and Francorchamps, ending the season with 37 points and in ninth place overall.

A number of contractual controversies during 2004 and 2005 between Button, Honda and Williams led to speculation that he would be leaving BAR. In fact, he remained with the Honda team during 2005 and went on to win his first race with them at the Hungaroring in 2006.

Button notched just 9 points over the next two seasons, and went into the 2009 campaign under the new Brawn GP banner, following Ross Brawn's buy-out of the Honda team. Jenson made the most of the highly competitive Mercedes-powered BGP 001, winning six of the first seven races and scoring in all 16 of the races he finished. He secured the title with a storming drive at

Interlagos, finishing fifth after lining up fourth on the grid. Button also contributed the lion's share of the points as Brawn captured the Constructors' title in its single year in existence. Britain's tenth world champion signed for McLaren to partner the compatriot whose crown he had taken: Lewis Hamilton. He notched two early-season victories in 2010 and remained in contention for most of the year before finishing in fifth place, just behind his McLaren team-mate.

2011 saw him finish runner-up to Vettel, splitting the mighty Red Bulls and coming out on top in the intra-team battle with Lewis, the first man to do so. Button also signed a deal committing his long-term future to McLaren, and became the team leader following Hamilton's departure for Mercedes at the end of the 2012 season. 2013 was a dire year for McLaren and a podium-free season for Jenson, who just scraped into the top 10 in the final standings.

JIM CLARK

Born: 4 March 1936, Kilmany, Scotland	
Died:	7 April 1968
Grand Prix starts:	72
Grand Prix victories:	25
Points total:	274
World Champion:	1963, 1965

TRAGIC END FOR SUPREME RACER

Famous for his smoothness, effortless control and computer-like brain, Jim Clark inherited the mantle of supreme champion from Fangio. Having joined Lotus in 1960, he spent his whole career there, forging a formidable partnership with team boss Colin Chapman. His GP debut came at Zandvoort in 1960 picking up a respectable 8 points by the end of the season. The following year, he gained eighth place overall but the campaign was overshadowed by his involvement in the crash at Monza in which several spectators were killed and Ferrari's Wolfgang von Trips lost his life.

Clark's maiden victory came at the 1962 Belgian GP and he went into the final round in South Africa with a chance at the championship. He was heading for the victory which would have snatched the crown from Graham Hill when his Lotus failed.

Brushing aside disappointment, Clark took the championship the following year, winning seven of the ten rounds. His chances of retaining his title in 1964 were lost when the Lotus failed on the penultimate lap of the final race in Mexico. He took his second world crown in 1965 with another maximum haul from the six races where he reached the line. Victory in the Indy 500 made it a notable double.

1966 was a relatively lean season but early in 1967 the new Cosworth DFV engine arrived and Clark was immediately back in contention. Four more wins put him third in the championship behind the two powerful Brabhams.

His first victory in 1968 came at Kyalami, giving him his 25th career success, and putting him one ahead of Fangio in the all-time list. Clark was 31 and at the height of his powers when he competed in a F2 race at Hockenheim on 7 April. His car left the track and hit a tree, killing him instantly.

PETER COLLINS

Born:	6 Nov 1931, Kidderminster, England
Died:	3 August 1958
Grand Prix starts:	32
Grand Prix victories:	3
Points total:	47

TRAGIC END FOR GENEROUS ENGLISHMAN

Peter Collins graduated to Formula One as a 20-year-old, making his championship debut with HWM at the 1952 Swiss GP. He struggled to make any impression in what was an unreliable car, a pattern that was to be repeated over the next three years. In that time he drove for Vanwall and BRM as well as HWM, but his main successes came in sports cars with Aston Martin's works team.

When the hardware allowed, Collins was certainly quick, a fact not lost on Ferrari, who signed him for 1956. He played the supporting role to Fangio, notably at Monaco, where he handed his Lancia-Ferrari over after the three-time champion's car failed. Back-to-back victories at Spa and Reims showed that Collins was a serious contender in his own right.

Both Collins and Jean Behra went into the final race, Monza, knowing they could snatch the title from Fangio with a victory and fastest lap, provided the Argentine failed to score. With Behra and Fangio out of the race, Collins allowed Fangio to take over his car, sacrificing his own championship ambitions. Fangio duly took the title, while Moss won the race relegating Collins to third in the final championship table.

1957 was something of an anticlimax, Collins recording just two third places in a season dominated by Fangio and Maserati. 1958 augured well as Ferrari fielded the new 246 Dino. Collins registered two top-six finishes before beating team-mate Mike Hawthorn into second place at Silverstone. Collins lay third in the championship as the circus moved to the Nürburgring. There, vying for the lead with Tony Brooks's Vanwall, Collins crashed and was fatally injured when he was flung from his car. He was 26. Collins finished a posthumous fifth in that year's championship, but it was for his magnanimous act of sportsmanship in helping Fangio claim his fourth world crown that he is best remembered.

DAVID COULTHARD

Born:	27 March 1971, Twynholm, Scotland
Grand Prix starts:	247
Grand Prix victories:	13
Points total:	535

SCOT'S RECORD RACE HAUL WITH MCLAREN

From winning a string of Scottish karting titles in the mid-1980s, David Coulthard progressed through the ranks of Formula Ford, F3 and F3000, with top three finishes in each of those championships. He was the inaugural winner of the McLaren Autosport BRDC award in 1989 on the back of his success in the Formula Ford. In 1991 he just missed out on the British F3 title, beaten narrowly by another rising star, Rubens Barrichello. He tested for Williams in 1993, but it was not until 1994, and Senna's death at San Marino, that he got his chance in the F1 team, partnering Damon Hill. From eight races he amassed 14 points, but was replaced by the returning Nigel Mansell for the final three races. Even so, Coulthard was offered the drive for the 1995 season, and earned third place with eight podiums in that year's title race.

He joined McLaren in 1996, and remained there for nine years, driving 150 races: a record for a driver with one team. Initially, Coulthard's ranking slipped to seventh in 1996, but two wins at Melbourne and Monza the following year helped him to equal third in that season's title race. Over the next two years his team-mate Mika Häkkinen dominated the championship, winning both the 1998 and 1999 titles, with Coulthard managing just third and fourth respectively.

By 2001 he had emerged from Häkkinen's shadow, but Schumacher's time had come and Coulthard finished a distant second in the championship. By 2003 Kimi Raïkkönen had taken over as McLaren's front runner, and at the end of the following year Coulthard left to sign for the Red Bull Racing Team. Although not managing any podiums, he ended the season with 24 points and 12th place overall. He continued racing with Red Bull in 2006 and achieved the team's first podium finish at Monaco, where he came in third. He ended the 2007 season in tenth place after amassing 14 points. Coulthard announced that he would retire at the end of the 2008 season. He got into the points only twice in his swansong

year, but there was a final flourish at the Canadian GP, where he made it onto the podium for the 62nd time. He remained in the sport as a media pundit and consultant to Red Bull.

NINO FARINA

Born:	30 October 1906, Turin, Italy
Died:	30 June 1966
Grand Prix starts:	33
Grand Prix victories:	5
Points total:	127.33
World Champion:	1950

ITALIAN BECOMES FIRST FORMULA ONE CHAMPION

Giuseppe (Nino) Farina was a protégé of Tazio Nuvolari in the 1930s, becoming Alfa Romeo's no. 1 driver when Nuvolari left to join Auto Union in 1937. He won a hat-trick of Italian championships prior to the outbreak of WWII, and afterwards drove Maseratis and Ferraris, but returned to Alfa on the eve of the new Drivers' championship in 1950. Farina won the very first race, held at Silverstone on 13 May 1950, and snatched the title by 3 points.

The following year the tables were turned: Farina won just once and slipped to fourth in the title race, 12 points behind Fangio. Farina moved to Ferrari for 1952, where he was a regular runner-up to team-mate Alberto Ascari, and finished second and third in the championship for 1952 and 1953 respectively.

Ascari departed Ferrari in 1954 leaving Farina the team's no. 1 driver, but his season was blighted by injury. He sustained a broken arm in the Mille Miglia, then suffered terrible burns during a sports car race at Monza. He returned in 1955 to finish fifth in that year's championship, retiring at the end of the season. He was killed in a road accident while on his way to watch the 1966 French GP.

JUAN MANUEL FANGIO

Born:	24 June 1911, Balcarce, Argentina
Died:	17 July 1995
Grand Prix starts:	51
Grand Prix victories:	24
Points total:	277.14
World Champion:	1951, 1954, 1955, 1956, 1957

VETERAN ACE BECOMES FIVE TIMES WORLD CHAMPION

In 1949 at the age of 37 Juan Manuel Fangio left his native Argentina to try his hand on the racetracks of Europe. He was an unknown quantity, but six wins in ten starts changed all that. Alfa Romeo quickly signed him for the inaugural world championship in 1950. With team-mates Farina and Fagioli – 'The Three Fs' – Alfa dominated the series. Having ceded the championship title to Farina that year, in 1951 Fangio went into the final round, the Spanish GP, holding the advantage and won easily to claim the first of his five world titles.

A broken neck put him out of the title race for 1952. He returned the following year with Maserati, but it was Ascari and Ferrari's year. At the beginning of the 1954 season, with two wins for Maserati, Fangio moved to Mercedes to drive the W196. He gave it a maiden victory at Reims, followed by three more wins and the world title.

1955 brought four more victories, and a third championship title, in a season truncated by the tragedy at Le Mans, where over 80 spectators were killed. Fangio's fourth world title was with Ferrari in 1956 and is best remembered for the magnanimity of team-mate Peter Collins, who twice gave him his car; the second time Collins himself had a chance of lifting the title. His generosity allowed Fangio a shared second behind Moss, giving him the championship by 3 points.

He returned to Maserati for 1957, and four wins in the first five European rounds set up his fifth world title. Fangio retired midway through the 1958 campaign, with a victories-to-starts ratio of almost 50 percent.

EMERSON FITTIPALDI

Born:	12 December 1946, São Paulo, Brazil
Grand Prix starts:	144
Grand Prix victories:	14
Points total:	281
World Champion:	1972, 1974

WORLD CHAMPION AT 25

In becoming world champion at the age of 25 years and 298 days, Emerson Fittipaldi became the youngest world champion F1 had known. This record stood until 2005 when the honour passed to Fernando Alonso, world title-holder at 24 years and 59 days.

Son of a motor sport commentator, Emerson Fittipaldi and his brother Wilson drove karts in their native Brazil, Emerson becoming Brazilian champion at the age of 18. In 1969 the young Emerson left Brazil for Britain and began competing in Formula Ford. Within two years he had impressed enough to earn an F1 berth with Lotus. He finished fourth behind team-mate Jochen Rindt at Hockenheim in 1970, despite running an outdated model. Following Rindt's death, Fittipaldi drove the superior Lotus 72 to victory at the US GP. His maiden win came in only his fourth start.

The Brazilian enhanced his reputation in 1971, despite managing just 16 points. A year later Lotus fielded an upgraded version of the Lotus 72 – the John Player Special – and Fittipaldi swept to the championship with five victories. The last of those, at Monza, gave him the crown with two races to spare. Former champion Jackie Stewart won both of those races for Tyrrell to finish runner-up, and the following year their positions were reversed. Fittipaldi won three races but had to settle for runner-up to the Scot.

Fittipaldi moved to McLaren for 1974, and Stewart's retirement meant that his chief rival of the past two seasons was off the scene. Three wins took Fittipaldi into a final-race showdown at Watkins Glen with Ferrari's Clay Regazzoni. The two were locked together in the points table, with Tyrrell's Jody Scheckter also in contention. Fourth place gave Fittipaldi his second championship, both of his rivals failing to score.

After finishing runner-up again in 1975, this time to Niki Lauda, Fittipaldi joined his brother's Copersucar team. There were a couple of podiums over the next five years but the cars were off the pace compared with the top F1 teams. He came out of retirement to take the IndyCar title in 1989, winning the Indy 500 that year and in 1993.

ROMAIN GROSJEAN

Born:	7 April 1986, Geneva, Switzerland
Grand Prix starts:	45*
Grand Prix victories:	0*
Points total:	228*

*TO END OF 2013 SEASON

'READY TO BE ONE OF THE BEST'

Romain Grosjean came of age in 2013. He put behind him the cavalier moves and dramatic shunts that prompted Mark Webber to label him a 'first-lap nutcase' in 2012, the Aussie having been on the receiving end of one of those early-race collisions laid squarely at Grosjean's door. A year on, Romain displayed admirable control and maturity to match his undoubted rapidity behind the wheel, and as Vettel closed in on his fourth championship it was the Franco-Swiss who gave him the best run for his money.

Following the usual baptism in karting, Grosjean took the 2003 Formula Renault title in his native land. A couple of years in the French series of the Renault championship were enough for him to get the measure of that competition; he won it at the second attempt. The pattern repeated itself in the Formula 3 Euroseries: victory in the sophomore year. Next up, in 2008, came GP2, where it took him a little longer to claim the title. It came in 2011, when he also picked up the GP2 Asia Series laurels for good measure, his second success in the latter competition. Add in his 2010 victories in the FIA GT1 World Championship and Auto GP, and it meant a curriculum vitae in which he had a winning record in every division of motor sport where he had pitched up.

Grosjean's first taste of the big league came with test-driving duties for Renault in 2008, and a handful of races the following year when Renault dispensed with Nelson Piquet Jr's services mid-term. He had to wait two years for his next chance, by which time the team had been reincarnated as Lotus. He delivered three podiums in 2012, very much the junior partner to the returning Kimi Raikkonen but playing his part in pushing the team to fourth in the constructors' championship. Wayward and erratic were common epithets applied to Grosjean in his early days in F1 – Webber went a step further with his withering comment – though he was clearly a speed merchant. Monaco 2013 saw another round of metal-bashing, inviting more questions as to whether he could drive fast and eliminate the errors. He proved the doubters wrong in style, not simply emerging from the Finn's

shadow but eclipsing the former champion in the second half of the campaign. He added six podiums to his tally without quite making it onto the top step. At the Nurburgring and Suzuka he was exceptional, and in India made up 14 places from his grid slot to take third. After holding off Webber to go one better than that in Austin, the Aussie praised the man who split the Red Bulls with a measured performance. 'Now it's a different ball game,' said Mark. Different, too, in terms of expectation, following Raikkonen's departure to Ferrari. Having begun to repay the faith Lotus had in him, Grosjean became the Enstone-based outfit's No. 1 for 2014. "I feel ready to lead the team," he said. 'Ready to be one of the best.'

MIKA HÄKKINEN

Born:	28 September 1968, Helsinki, Finland
Grand Prix starts:	165
Grand Prix victories:	20
Points total:	420
World Champion:	1998, 1999

DOUBLE WORLD CHAMPION

Mika Häkkinen took over from Keke Rosberg as Finland's F1 star. He won the British F3 title in 1990, graduating to F1 with Lotus the following season. Indeed, by the time he lifted the British F3 title in 1990, Häkkinen was being managed and mentored by the 1982 world champion. The following year he graduated to F1 with a Lotus team in decline. The Judd-engined car was well off the pace, though he did bring it home fifth at Imola to register his first points. He scored in six races in 1992, to finish a highly creditable 8th in the championship. Fourth place at Magny-Cours took the eye, and it was clear that with a better car Häkkinen had the ability to challenge the best.

In 1993 he joined McLaren, though initially had to kick his heels behind Senna and Michael Andretti. It was only after the latter was fired that Häkkinen got his chance. He outqualified Senna on his debut in Portugal, then, in his second start, at Suzuka, finished third behind his team-mate and Prost.

After Ayrton Senna moved to Williams in 1994, Häkkinen took over as McLaren's no. 1 driver. 1994 yielded six podiums, earning Häkkinen fourth place in the championship. He sustained life-threatening head injuries at the 1995 Australian GP, but recovered to finish fifth in the next two seasons. He got his long-awaited victory at Jerez, the final round of the 1997 championship, though he was helped by Villeneuve, who reined in his Williams knowing that third was enough for him to win the title.

Having waited so long for a victory, they then came thick and fast. Häkkinen topped the podium eight times in 1998 to claim the crown, then won five times in 1999 in defence of the title. In both years it went to the final race: he held off Ferrari's Michael Schumacher's challenge in 1998, then when injury forced the German out of the running in 1999, Häkkinen had the edge on his Ferrari team-mate Eddie Irvine.

There were four wins in 2000, one of them after a dazzling 320-km/h battle with Schumacher at Spa, but this

time he finished runner-up to the German. His swansong F1 season yielded two more victories, in Britain and the US, a year in which he slipped to fifth in the title race.

LEWIS HAMILTON

Born:	7 January 1985, Stevenage, England
Grand Prix starts:	129*
Grand Prix victories:	22*
Points total:	1102*
World Champion:	2008

*TO END OF 2013 SEASON

RECORD-BREAKING FIRST SEASON

After winning the British Cadet championship in 1995, 10-year-old Lewis Hamilton went to the Autosport Awards ceremony, a star-struck youngster keen to fill his autograph book. Among the luminaries of the sport he approached that evening was Ron Dennis, who added 'Call me in nine years' time' next to his signature. He was responding to Lewis's bold statement of intent that he wanted to drive in F1 for McLaren, following in the footsteps of his hero, Ayrton Senna. In fact, just three years went by before Dennis's team took the karting prodigy under its wing. It was a huge relief for the Hamilton family, who for years had scrimped and saved to fund Lewis's racing.

The honours continued to come thick and fast: European Champion and World Cup Champion in Formula A in 2000; Formula Renault UK Champion in 2003, winning 10 out of 15 races; and F3 Euroseries Champion in 2005, with 15 wins and 13 poles. For 2006 it was on to GP2 with the ART team, where he took the title after battling with Nelson Piquet Jr. That autumn, McLaren confirmed his F1 seat for 2007, alongside double world champion Fernando Alonso. Elated but not overawed, Hamilton made a blistering start to his rookie year at the top table, with nine straight podium finishes, including back-to-back wins in Canada and the USA. He headed the championship race from Round Three until the final twist at Interlagos, where Kimi Räikkönen's victory was enough to snatch the crown by a single point. Hamilton was philosophical about the defeat, which he took with great humility. At 22 he had become the youngest driver to lead the championship, breaking Bruce McLaren's record, and knew his talent and extraordinary focus would give him many more tilts at the title. Hamilton had to wait just one year to put the disappointment of 2007 behind him. It was another championship that went to the wire, a last-gasp overtaking manoeuvre at Interlagos securing him fifth place, enough to snatch the title from Ferrari's Felipe Massa by one point. At 23 years 301 days he

became the youngest-ever Formula One champion, taking the record from Fernando Alonso. McLaren struggled in 2009, and Lewis's reputation was tarnished following an unseemly incident at Melbourne, where he was disqualified for misleading the stewards. He recovered impressively to score two late-season wins.

Hamilton added three more victories in 2010 and led mid-season, though during the run-in couldn't quite hang onto the coat tails of Alonso's Ferrari and the Red Bulls.

Another trio of wins followed in 2011, but a series of crashes and errors blighted a season in which he finished behind a team–mate – Jenson Button – for the first time in his career. Lewis took seven poles and notched four wins in a frustrating 2012 season in which McLaren were bedevilled by gremlins and ill fortune. He ended the year just outside the top three, having already announced that he was leaving Woking for Mercedes.

He added just one win in another Vettel-dominated season, but with five poles on his way to fourth in the championship, the prospects for the Hamilton-Mercedes marriage looked highly promising.

MIKE HAWTHORN

Born:	10 April 1929, Mexborough, England
Died:	22 January 1959
Grand Prix starts:	45
Grand Prix victories:	3
Points total:	127.64
World Champion:	1958

BRITAIN'S FIRST WORLD CHAMPION

The blond, flamboyant Mike Hawthorn cut a dashing figure on the racing scene in the 1950s. Although he invariably competed in a cap and bow tie, his dapper appearance belied his fierce competitiveness and the fact that he served a long apprenticeship before winning the world crown.

By 1952, when he made his GP debut at Spa, Hawthorn was already seen as a rising star. He enhanced his reputation by finishing third at Silverstone on the way to taking joint fourth place in the championship. He drove for a team run by father Leslie, but for 1953 he was snapped up by Ferrari. His first GP victory came at Reims that year, Hawthorn outbraking Fangio at the final corner in a breathtaking manoeuvre. He again finished fourth, having shown great consistency as well as courage and skill.

The 1954 campaign was blighted by an accident at the non-championship Syracuse GP, but Hawthorn recovered to win the Spanish GP and finish third overall. He briefly joined Vanwall in 1955 a decision prompted by his father's death and the need to oversee the family business – before rejoining Ferrari. The championship races proved fruitless, but he did win at Le Mans in a Jaguar. Victory was tainted by an accident which resulted in 82 deaths, Hawthorn coming in for criticism for the manoeuvre that precipitated the tragic incident.

After a forgettable 1956 season Hawthorn returned to form, reunited once again with Ferrari. He finished fourth in 1957 but 1958 was the crowning glory. He won only once, the French GP, but scored consistently to pip Moss for the title by a single point.

Hawthorn announced his retirement almost immediately. He was deeply affected by the death of team-mate Peter Collins and was also suffering from a debilitating kidney condition. He was killed in a road accident near Guildford on 22 January 1959, just three months after becoming Britain's first world champion.

DAMON HILL

Born:	17 September 1960, London, England
Grand Prix starts:	116
Grand Prix victories:	22
Points total:	360
World Champion:	1996

EIGHT VICTORIES CLINCH TITLE

Despite the inevitable comparisons with his father, Damon Hill overcame media scrutiny to make his own mark, emulating Graham's achievement by taking the world title in 1996. Moving from motorcycles, his first love, to four wheels was not, initially, a resounding success. Between 1986 and 1988 Hill competed in the British F3 championship, improving each year to finish third in his final campaign. Three years in F3000 followed, where he showed himself to be a genuine racer, despite mediocre hardware. His performances landed him a test-driving contract at Williams, where he helped develop the car that swept Mansell to glory in 1992.

Hill made his F1 debut with a declining Brabham team that year, struggling even to qualify in a poor Judd-powered car. Mansell's departure to IndyCars in 1993 opened the door at Williams, and Hill found himself partnering three-time champion Alain Prost. After a series of podium finishes, Hill recorded his first win in Hungary, and added two more to take third in the title race. It might have been even better had he not suffered engine failure while leading the British GP, and a puncture when he was within sight of victory at Hockenheim.

Senna replaced Prost at Williams in 1994, but after the Brazilian's death at Imola, Hill became Williams' lead driver. He rose to the challenge, his battle with Benetton's Michael Schumacher ending with a controversial clash in the Adelaide decider. Hill lost out by a single point, though six wins helped Williams complete a hat-trick of Constructors' titles.

Hill was again runner-up to Schumacher in 1995, but in the following season he took the crown, scoring eight victories in the 16-race series to see off the challenge of team-mate Jacques Villeneuve. Williams had already decided he was surplus to requirements, and Hill spent a year with Arrows, followed by two seasons at Jordan. These yielded a single victory, Spa 1998 marking Jordan's maiden success. Hill retired in 1999, having carved his place in the record books as the only son of a champion to take the title.

GRAHAM HILL

Born:	15 February 1929, London
Died:	29 November 1975
Grand Prix starts:	176
Grand Prix victories:	14
Points total:	289
World Champion:	1962, 1968

BRITAIN'S BLUE RIBAND CHAMPION

Graham Hill was an outstanding driver whose extrovert character was very different from that of his great rival, Jim Clark, although the two shared a steely resolve. As Clark signed for Lotus in 1960, Hill left for BRM, accumulating just 7 points in his first two seasons with them. By 1962 both the car and Hill's results had improved: his maiden victory in the opening race at Zandvoort was followed by wins in Germany and Italy, snatching the title from Clark in

the final race that season. In the next three championship series Hill finished runner-up: to Clark in 1963 and 1965, and to Ferrari's John Surtees in 1964, losing the title by a single point that year. In 1966 Hill had a disappointing championship, although he did win the Indy 500 driving a Lola-Ford. In 1967 he rejoined Lotus, now with the new Cosworth DFV engine, and looked set for an assault on the 1968 championship. Team-mate Clark's death at Hockenheim early in the season and the loss of Mike Spence at Indianapolis shattered the morale of the Lotus camp; Hill restored it with three victories in Spain, Monaco and Mexico, on the way to a second world title.

He slid down the rankings in 1969, although he took his fifth Monaco victory. A crash at Watkins Glen left him with severe leg injuries and it was clear that his best days were behind him. He retired in 1975 and remains the only driver to complete the blue riband treble: the world championship, the Indy 500 and Le Mans (1972).

After retirement, Hill concentrated on establishing his own team, Embassy Hill. He and five team members were killed in November 1975 when the plane he was piloting crashed in fog near Elstree.

PHIL HILL

Born:	**20 April 1927, Miami, USA**
Died:	**28 August 2008**
Grand Prix starts:	**48**
Grand Prix victories:	**3**
Points total:	**98**
World Champion:	**1961**

AMERICA'S FIRST WORLD CHAMPION

Having enjoyed success in sports cars and winning Le Mans, Phil Hill made his debut at the 1958 French GP, finishing seventh. He had already caught the eye of Ferrari and was soon signed; he spent the next four years with the team. His progress was steady: two second places, in France and Italy, moved him to fourth in the 1959 championship; in 1960 he dropped one place though he took a victory at Monza.

Having lagged the field in 1960, Ferrari introduced the new 1.5-litre formula in 1961, and by the penultimate race, Monza, the title was up for grabs between Ferrari team-mates Phil Hill and Wolfgang von Trips. The German clashed with Jim Clark's Lotus on the first lap of the race and was killed, along with 12 spectators. Hill won the race and with it the title, but his achievement was deeply overshadowed by the tragedy.

In 1962 Ferrari fell behind the British teams, and the following year Hill joined a Ferrari breakaway team which left to set up ATS. He failed to gain a single point, and a season with Cooper was scarcely better, yielding only a sixth place at Brands Hatch. After that Hill concentrated on sports car racing, and retired in 1967 due to ill health. He died in 2008.

DENNY HULME

Born:	18 March 1936, Nelson, New Zealand
Died:	4 October 1992
Grand Prix starts:	112
Grand Prix victories:	8
Points total:	248
World Champion:	1967

HULME EDGES OUT BRABHAM

Denny Hulme travelled to Britain in 1960 to compete in Formula Junior, and a year later was working as a mechanic for Jack Brabham's fledgling outfit. Having driven works Brabhams in Formula Junior, the Tasman series and F2, Hulme was promoted to F1 in 1965. Replacing Dan Gurney, who was competing at Indianapolis, he made his debut at Monaco, finishing eighth. Two races later, Brabham made way for the New Zealander at Clermont-Ferrand, and he repaid his boss with fourth place.

In 1966 Gurney's departure left Hulme as official no. 2. Brabham won his third title that year, and Hulme made the podium four times to secure fourth place in the championship. A year later it was his turn. At Monaco he took the lead after the fatal crash of Ferrari's Lorenzo Bandini, and went on to score his maiden victory. Victory at the Nürburgring, and third place in the final race, the Mexican GP, was enough to give Hulme the title.

In 1968, Hulme joined McLaren, taking two more victories to finish third in that year's championship. There were just four more wins over the next six years, 1972 being his best, with a 39-point haul giving Hulme third behind Fittipaldi and Stewart. He remained at McLaren until his retirement in 1974. Hulme died from a heart attack while competing in Australia's Bathurst touring car race in 1992.

JAMES HUNT

Born: 29 August 1947, Belmont, England	
Died:	15 June 1993
Grand Prix starts:	92
Grand Prix victories:	10
Points total:	179
World Champion:	1976

THRILLING HUNT 'THE SHUNT' LIFTS WORLD CROWN

James Hunt's early forays into motor racing began with a humble Mini, moving on to Formula Ford and F3, signing for the March F3 team in 1972. Within a year he had departed to join forces with Lord Hesketh's maverick outfit and a step-up to F2 and Hunt showed he had the speed to handle the step up in class.

Having made his F1 debut in 1973, Hunt finished second behind Ronnie Peterson in the final race of the year at Watkins Glen. This gave him a highly respectable eighth place in the championship and the following season saw him match that performance, this time in the team's own car. In 1975 improvements to the car saw him finish fourth in the table, having beaten eventual champion Niki Lauda into second place at Zandvoort to score his maiden victory.

Hesketh's withdrawal from the GP circuit at the end of 1975 saw Hunt replacing Emerson Fittipaldi at McLaren. 1976 was a thrilling season, with Hunt and Ferrari's Niki Lauda battling for the crown to the finish. His first win for McLaren came in Spain, but at Silverstone his victory points were expunged following an infringement of the rules governing the car's dimensions. With Lauda out following his horrific accident at the Nürburgring, Hunt was back in contention, and he went into the final race, the Japanese GP, 3 points behind Lauda. Lauda withdrew in appalling weather conditions and Hunt went on to secure third place and the title.

Despite three more victories in 1977, McLaren was in decline, and by the following year Hunt appeared to lose motivation and enthusiasm. He quit mid-season in 1979 and went on to become a F1 TV commentator until his death from a heart attack in 1993.

JACKY ICKX

Born:	1 January 1945, Brussels, Belgium
Grand Prix starts:	116
Grand Prix victories:	8
Points total:	181

BELGIUM'S BRIGHT YOUNG TALENT

Emerging as one of motor racing's brightest young talents in the 1960s, Jacky Ickx progressed from trials riding and hill climbs to saloon cars in rapid succession. In 1965 he signed for Tyrrell and was given his world championship debut in the 1966 German GP, albeit in an F2 Matra-Ford.

In 1967 the young Belgian divided his time, winning the European F2 title while making the occasional F1 appearance. He qualified his F2 car at the Nürburgring, and made his way from the back of the grid through to fourth before his suspension gave out. Two races later, driving for Cooper at Monza, he finished sixth to gain his first championship point.

There followed a move to Ferrari where he finished fourth in the title race, outpacing team-mate Chris Amon and giving Ferrari their only win of the season, at Rouen. When Rindt left Brabham for Lotus, Ickx was drafted in as replacement and had a fine year, winning in Germany and Canada to finish runner-up to Stewart, and adding a Le Mans victory to his achievements.

He returned to Ferrari and remained there for the next four years, adding five more wins over the first three seasons. After 1970, the car became increasingly uncompetitive and Ickx quit midway through the 1973 series to join Lotus, scoring 15 points in two seasons. Outings for Williams, Ensign and Ligier between 1976 and 1979 were not noteworthy and from then on he concentrated on sports cars, winning Le Mans for a sixth time in 1982.

ALAN JONES

Born:	**2 November 1946, Melbourne, Australia**
Grand Prix starts:	**116**
Grand Prix victories:	**12**
Points total:	**206**
World Champion:	**1980**

FIRST CONSTRUCTORS' TITLE FOR WILLIAMS

Unlike his racing driver father, Alan Jones travelled to Europe from Australia to compete on the biggest stages. Having spent five years in the junior ranks, his F1 debut came in a privately entered Hesketh in 1975. He also drove that year for Graham Hill's fledgling Embassy Racing, and gained a fifth place in Germany. The deaths of Hill and five of his team in a plane crash at the end of the year left Jones looking for a new challenge.

He then spent a year with John Surtees, notching up 7 points in his one season there. By the fourth race of the 1977 series he was driving for Shadow to replace Tom Pryce, who had been killed at Kyalami. Jones scored a stunning success in Austria, giving him and the team their first podium finish, and beating Lauda into the bargain. In 1978 he linked up with Williams and towards the end of the 1979 season, Jones took four wins in five starts to finish third in the championship. With more than five wins in 1980, he took the crown, staving off the challenge of Brabham's Piquet, and Williams had their first Constructors' title. Jones scored two more wins to make third in the 1981 championship, then announced his retirement. He made two comebacks but failed to do justice to his talent.

HEIKKI KOVALAINEN

Born:	19 October 1981, Suomussaimi, Finland
Grand Prix starts:	112*
Grand Prix victories:	1*
Points total:	105*

*TO END OF 2013 SEASON

LOTUS'S FLYING FINN

Heikki Kovalainen spent a long apprenticeship on the karting scene in his homeland, culminating in his becoming Nordic champion in 2000. He took the Elf Masters title the same year, his last before making the step up to car racing in the British Formula Renault series. He finished fourth in the 2001 championship, not quite as impressive as compatriot Kimi Raïkkönen, who won the event the preceding year, but two wins did help bring him the Rookie of the Year award.

In 2002 Kovalainen competed in the British F3 championship, taking third place to confirm his reputation as one of the sport's rising stars. He played second fiddle to experienced team-mate Franck Montagny in the 2003 World Series by Nissan championship, but lifted the title the following year, driving for Pons Racing. 2004 also saw him win the individual title at the Race of Champions, beating David Coulthard and Michael Schumacher en route to victory in Paris. He was edged into second place by Nico Rosberg in a thrilling inaugural GP2 championship in 2005.

The following year he became Renault's main test driver, and when Fernando Alonso departed to McLaren at the end of a second title-winning campaign, Kovalainen was promoted to the vacant race seat in 2007. He scored 30 points in his debut season in the elite division, the highlight coming at Fuji Speedway, where he fended off Raïkkönen's attentions to take second behind Lewis Hamilton in a race run in appalling conditions. It was the Finn's first podium and Renault's best result of the year. Kovalainen outpointed team-mate Giancarlo Fisichella.

When Renault welcomed Alonso back for the 2008 campaign, Kovalainen was on the move, taking Alonso's McLaren berth. He was the junior partner as Lewis Hamilton mounted a successful title charge, but he did notch three more podium finishes, including a maiden victory at the Hungarian GP. Comfortably outscored by Hamilton again the following season, Button's arrival in 2010 meant he was on the move again, this time to the new Lotus outfit. They were the pick of the three debutants, and Kovalainen regularly outgunned his team-mate Jarno Trulli during the first two seasons, albeit without adding to his points haul.

He remained with the team rebranded as Caterham in 2012, but lost his seat the following year. A couple of late-season appearances for Lotus in 2013, following Raikkonen's early departure, yielded no points.

NIKI LAUDA

Born:	**22 February 1949, Vienna, Austria**
Grand Prix starts:	**171**
Grand Prix victories:	**25**
Points total:	**420.5**
World Champion:	**1975, 1977, 1984**

REMARKABLE COMEBACK FROM THE THREE TIMES CHAMPION

Niki Lauda's return to F1 racing just six weeks after the horrific fireball accident at the Nürburgring is one of sport's most remarkable comebacks. His determination and self-belief were evident from the start, working his way from F2 into F1 with constructors March by 1970. A season at BRM in 1973 produced just 2 points for a fifth place at Zolder. The following year Lauda began his four-season association with Ferrari, teaming up with Clay Regazzoni. In their first season, Regazzoni out-pointed him, the duo finishing second and fourth respectively in the championship, although Regazzoni had won just once, and Lauda twice – but he had suffered a number of retirements.

But in 1975, Lauda won five races to clinch the world crown with a race to spare, and give Ferrari its first title since Surtees 11 years earlier. 1976 saw epic battles with Hunt and McLaren, and that crash at the Nürburgring, where Lauda received the last rites. Terribly scarred, he returned to the fray at Monza six weeks later. He pulled out of the final race at Suzuka owing to appalling conditions, allowing Hunt to take the title by one point.

Despite roaring back in 1977 to take a second title with Ferrari, Lauda had a difficult year with the team and quit to join Brabham in 1978. This move produced a respectable 44 points and fourth place, but 1979 proved disastrous, and the Austrian announced his retirement.

Three years later he returned, with McLaren, topping the podium in just his third race, and finishing fifth overall in the 1982 championship. 1983 was disappointing, but a year later he blew away his competitors, taking the title from his team-mate Alain Prost by half a point, the closest championship finish ever.

Lauda is the only man to come out of retirement to reclaim the world title. He won his twenty-fifth and final GP at Zandvoort in 1985, retiring at the end of that season.

NIGEL MANSELL

Born:	8 Aug 1953, Upton-on-Severn, England
Grand Prix starts:	187
Grand Prix victories:	31
Points total:	482
World Champion:	1992

FIERCE COMPETITOR – FIFTH ON ALL-TIME LIST

Mansell's championship-winning season of 1992 was the crowning glory of more than two decades in competitive motor sport. It was a year of outstanding achievement, as he took pole in all but two of the races and won nine of them to become the first man to rack up over a century of points. His nearest rival, Riccardo Patrese, finished a staggering 52 points behind. Having made his F1 debut for Lotus in 1980, at the Austrian GP, Mansell spent four more seasons with the team. Moving to Williams in 1985 transformed his career, with two victories, at the European and South African GPs, helping him to sixth place in the championship.

In 1986 and 1987 he was runner-up; first to Prost when he blew a tyre in the final race, allowing Prost to snatch the crown. In the second, he lost out to team-mate Nelson Piquet, despite scoring six wins that year. Over the next three years Mansell was out of contention for the title. Lured back to Williams in 1991, he finished runner-up for the third time, a tally of five wins not being quite enough to outdo Senna.

After his victory in 1992 Mansell turned to IndyCars, winning five races and the 1993 championship. He made a dramatic return to F1 and Williams following Senna's death in 1994, recording his 31st and final win at the Australian GP in Adelaide. Hill and Coulthard were confirmed as drivers for Williams for 1995, and Mansell began the season with McLaren, but quit for permanent retirement after two races. He stands fifth in the all-time list for GP victories, behind Schumacher, Prost, Senna and Piquet.

FELIPE MASSA

Born:	25 April 1981, São Paulo, Brazil
Grand Prix starts:	192
Grand Prix victories:	11*
Points total:	816*

*TO END OF 2013 SEASON

FERRARI'S BRAZILIAN ACE

For a few brief moments at Interlagos on 2 November 2008 the Ferrari camp thought Felipe Massa had secured the world crown, and the passionate home fans were ready to acclaim their first champion since Ayrton Senna in 1991. Lewis Hamilton spoiled the party with his last-gasp manoeuvre that saw him pass Timo Glock to snatch fifth place, and with it the title by a single point. Massa hid his disappointment and congratulated the new champion in a display of magnanimity that was a fitting template for all sportsmen. 'I know how to lose and I know how to win,' said the Brazilian ace. He certainly showed the winning mentality in 2008, outgunning Hamilton 6–5 in terms of top-of-the-podium finishes, and he had the consolation of helping Ferrari to yet another Constructors' title. Perhaps more significantly, after three successive top-four finishes in the Drivers' championship, the pre-eminent individual award was getting ever closer.

São Paulo-born Massa had seven years in karting before stepping up to Formula Chevrolet at the age of 17. He took just one season to adjust before lifting that title, after which he moved to Europe to compete in Formula Renault, following in the footsteps of such luminaries as Alain Prost and René Arnoux. In 2000 he won both the European and Italian Formula Renault titles, at a time when future Ferrari team-mate Kimi Raïkkönen was taking the laurels in the British equivalent. The Euro F3000 series was the next port of call, and six wins out of eight brought him that championship. It also earned him an invitation from Sauber to join the F1 ranks in 2002, replacing the departing Raïkkönen. That proved a steep learning curve, and he had his share of spins when pushing hard. Four points and 13th place was not the kind of return the Brazilian was used to for a season's efforts. He spent the following year as a Ferrari test driver, and he was older and wiser when he returned to Sauber in 2004, helped by the fact that the team was using Ferrari power. He garnered 12 points, with a best-place finish of fourth in an accident-ridden race at Spa. There was a similar return in 2005, the year in which Peter Sauber sold out to BMW, after which Massa moved to

Ferrari to take over Barrichello's long-held no. 2 berth to Michael Schumacher. Schumacher and Alonso fought a ding-dong battle in 2006, but Massa was the best of the rest, albeit 41 points adrift of his team-mate. That campaign was notable for his first two victories, scored in Istanbul and in his home race. It was Schumacher's swansong year, and Massa found himself partnering Raïkkönen in 2007. There were three more victories, though he eventually finished fourth in a Ferrari–McLaren duel won by Kimi. A year later, Massa thought he had matched his team-mate's achievement when he took the chequered flag in Brazil, but Hamilton had done just enough to secure the crown. His 2009 campaign ended with a freak accident during qualifying for the Hungarian GP, Massa sustaining injuries that required a metal plate to be fitted to his skull.

He was back for 2010, though had to play second fiddle to new team-mate Alonso. Things came to a head in Germany, where he was told to allow the Spaniard through, sparking a team orders row reminiscent of the Schumacher–Barrichello debacle at the 2002 Austrian GP.

He finished no higher than fifth in 2011, while Alonso recorded ten podiums, a disparity that cast doubts over his future at Maranello. 2012 brought glimpses of his best form and a contract extension, but there was little surprise when the axe fell a year later. Signed for Williams for 2014.

BRUCE McLAREN

Born: 30 August 1937, Auckland, New Zealand	
Died:	2 June 1970
Grand Prix starts:	101
Grand Prix victories:	4
Points total:	196.5

McLAREN FOLLOWS BRABHAM'S LEAD

Bruce McLaren won a scholarship in New Zealand which allowed him to travel to Europe to compete in F2, and within a year he had won his first GP. Having made his F1 debut at the Nürburgring in 1958 for Cooper, he launched a full campaign the following year. McLaren won at Sebring to become the youngest-ever Grand Prix winner at 22 years and 104 days old. That took him to sixth place in the championship, and in 1960 he finished runner-up to his mentor, Jack Brabham. McLaren stayed with Cooper for the next five seasons, his best being 1962, when he won in Monaco and ended the year third behind Hill and Clark. In 1966, McLaren followed Brabham's lead to set up on his own with the Robin Herd-designed car, but he struggled to find a decent engine for his car. By 1968, the car had Cosworth DFV power and he had lured reigning champion Denny Hulme from Brabham. McLaren's fourth GP win, at Spa, was the first for the marque and it helped him to finish fifth in the championship.

Consistent scoring put him third in the table for 1969, though there were no victories. McLaren contested three rounds of the 1970 series – finishing second in the Spanish GP at Jarama – before he was killed while testing one of his CanAm cars at Goodwood.

JUAN PABLO MONTOYA

Born:	20 September 1975, Bogotá, Colombia
Grand Prix starts:	95
Grand Prix victories:	7
Points total:	307

AUDACIOUS COLOMBIAN

Juan Pablo Montoya's audacious style and brilliance throughout his four seasons with Williams has won him legions of fans, though his combative nature cost him dearly on occasions. He signed on as test driver for Williams in 1997, and fully expected to be awarded an F1 seat for 1999, after winning the F3000 title the previous season, but Williams opted for the Ralf Schumacher–Alex Zanardi pairing instead. Montoya finally got his chance in 2001, taking three poles that year, and converting one of them, Monza, into a famous maiden victory. A year later, on the same track, he broke Keke Rosberg's 1985 record for the fastest qualifying lap, averaging 161.17mph. His seven poles that year clearly reflected his aptitude for raw speed. In 2002, Montoya was on the podium seven times, finishing third overall behind Schumacher and Barrichello. Taking two wins at Hockenheim and Monaco in 2003, he finished third again, this time behind Schumacher and Raïkkönen in a tight title race. Montoya slipped to fifth in 2004, and before the season was out it was announced that he would be replacing Coulthard at McLaren.

Teaming with Raïkkönen, 2005 proved to be a mixed year for Montoya: early hopes thwarted by bad luck, interspersed with brilliant moments. Overcoming the unpredictability of his new McLaren, he took three wins and five podiums to finish fourth overall in the championship, more than 50 points behind team-mate Raïkkönen. He continued to drive for McLaren in 2006, but consistent underperformance put his future with the team in jeopardy. The announcement that the reigning champion, Alonso, would join McLaren for the 2007 season made Montoya's future with the team more uncertain. Eventually he decided to call it a day mid-season, in favour of NASCAR racing.

STIRLING MOSS

Born:	17 September 1929, London, England
Grand Prix starts:	66
Grand Prix victories:	16 (1 shared)
Points total:	186.64

GREATEST DRIVER NEVER TO WIN WORLD CROWN

Despite never winning the world title, Stirling Moss was nevertheless acclaimed as one of the greatest of his generation. His competitiveness and supreme professionalism ensured him rapid progress through the junior ranks to make a F1 debut with HWM in 1951.

In 1954 he ran a privately entered Maserati, and secured a fine third at Spa. Having signed for Mercedes for 1955, Moss scored his maiden victory in the British GP, finishing runner-up to team-mate Fangio in the championship that year. He was second behind Fangio for the next two seasons, rejoining Maserati in 1956 and missing out on the title by 3 points. A year later, having signed with Vanwall, Moss scored three more victories – one of which came at the British GP at Aintree – but again they weren't enough to stop Fangio. Moss came closest to winning the world crown in 1958. In the title showdown race, the Moroccan GP, Moss crossed the line ahead of Mike Hawthorn's Ferrari, but lost the title to him by a single point.

The following year, Moss joined the Walker outfit and once again had a chance of taking the crown going into the final race, the US GP at Sebring, but mechanical failure meant he had to settle for third overall. He drove the new Lotus 18 for Walker in 1960 and gave the car its maiden victory, at Monaco, but finished a distant third overall behind Brabham and McLaren when a crash during practice for Spa put him out for four rounds. Moss won at Monaco and the Nürburgring the following year, despite Ferrari's dominance, but in 1962 he sustained horrific injuries in a non-championship race at Goodwood, which ended his career in top-level motor sport. He had, however, already established himself as one of motor racing's legendary names and received a knighthood in 2000 for his contribution to the sport.

RICCARDO PATRESE

Born:	**17 April 1954, Padua, Italy**
Grand Prix starts:	**256**
Grand Prix victories:	**6**
Points total:	**281**

FORMULA ONE RECORD-BREAKER

Having won the European F3 title the previous season, Riccardo Patrese made his F1 debut for Shadow in 1977, scoring his first championship point in the final race, the Japanese GP.

He followed members of the Shadow team when they left to form Arrows in 1978. Encouraging results that season were overshadowed by the accident at Monza which resulted in Ronnie Peterson's death. Patrese was barred from the next race though later investigations exonerated him from any blame for the Monza accident.

The next three seasons yielded a total of just 19 points, and in 1982 he moved to Brabham, where he took his first win at Monaco and came tenth in the championship that year. Playing second fiddle to Piquet in 1983, he won the final race of the season in South Africa.

Following two disastrous years with Alfa Romeo, Patrese returned to a Brabham team in decline. In 1988 he moved to Williams where his career began to improve, twice finishing third and taking runner-up slot behind Mansell in 1992. His final victory came 11 years after his first, a F1 record. He retired after a season with Benetton, playing support to Michael Schumacher. Patrese's record of 256 races stood for 15 years, Rubens Barrichello overhauling his tally midway through the 2008 season.

SERGIO PÉREZ

Born: 26 January 1990, Guadalajara, Mexico

Grand prix Starts:	**57***
Grand Prix victories:	**0***
Points total:	**129***

*TO END OF 2013 SEASON

MEXICAN FLYER

When Lewis Hamilton announced he was leaving McLaren at the end of the 2012 campaign, the Woking-based team turned to a 22-year-old with less than two seasons under his belt to fill the shoes of the 2008 world champion. Opinion was divided on the appointment. Those who thought it a shrewd move pointed to some star performances for Sauber in 2012, notably Malaysia, Montreal and Monza, where he converted lowly grid positions into podiums. 'The most exciting young talent in Formula One,' said new boss Martin Whitmarsh. 'A racer', was Bernie Ecclestone's verdict on the first Mexican to line up on the grid since the days of Hector Rebaque in the early 80s. The doubters said fortune favoured him in those eye-catching performances. They also referred to an unimpressive run at the back end of his sophomore season – a single point gained from his last seven races, by which time the McLaren deal was done. The raw talent was undoubtedly there, but the young driver needed to show greater consistency to prove himself a worthy successor to Lewis.

'Checo' Pérez stepped up to single-seaters in 2004, competing in the US Skip Barber series for a Telmex-sponsored team. The backing of the telecoms giant and billionaire Carlos Slim made him an attractive proposition as he made his way up the pyramid. At 15 Pérez moved to Germany to compete in Formula BMW, then moved on to the British F3 championship, winning the national class. Next came a spell in GP2 – the Asia Series, then Europe – finishing runner-up to Pastor Maldonado in 2010.

Pérez joined Ferrari's academy and was widely touted as a replacement for Massa, but Maranello decided to pass and it was Sauber who gave him his break into the big time in 2011. He crossed the line seventh on debut, only to be robbed by a technical breach. At the year end he had accumulated just 14 points, but had shown enough promise to be retained for 2012. That decision was vindicated as he broke into the top 10 in the drivers' championship, more than quadrupling his points haul.

A confident Pérez headed to Woking with the world championship in his sights. He arrived at the most inopportune moment, McLaren left competing with the midfield division. Even so, a season's best of fifth and a 49-point tally – both bettered by team-mate Button – didn't convince the bosses and Pérez departed to Force India at the end of the campaign.

RONNIE PETERSON

Born:	14 February 1944, Orebro, Sweden
Died:	11 September 1978
Grand Prix starts:	123
Grand Prix victories:	10
Points total:	206

TRAGEDY FOR TWO TIMES RUNNER-UP

Twice a world championship runner-up, Swede Ronnie Peterson made his F1 debut in 1970, the year Jochen Rindt was killed at Monza. Many felt that he was Rindt's natural successor.

After his stunning performances in F3 and F2, Max Mosley signed Peterson for the new March outfit in 1970.

He was promoted to the works team in 1971, and took four second places, one of them being Monza, which provided the closest F1 finish ever, when the Swede ended the race 0.01 seconds behind Peter Gethin's BRM. He ended the year as runner-up to Stewart.

Peterson switched to Lotus in 1973, scoring his maiden victory at Paul Ricard, and winning in Austria after team-mate Fittipaldi retired from the race. Four victories in all gave him third in the championship that year.

Peterson stayed with Lotus for the next two seasons and scored three wins, but the car lagged behind the competition. Back with March in 1976 he chalked up a victory at Monza; a year with Tyrrell followed, and 1978 saw his return to Lotus, supporting Mario Andretti. Peterson suffered serious leg injuries in a crash at the start of the Italian GP at Monza, and died the next day from complications. He finished the year as posthumous runner-up in the championship.

NELSON PIQUET

Born:	17 February 1952, Rio de Janeiro, Brazil
Grand Prix starts:	204
Grand Prix victories:	23
Points total:	485.5
World Champion:	1981, 1983, 1987

A HAT-TRICK OF WORLD TITLES

Nelson Piquet is in the all-time top ten for race victories, poles and fastest laps, and in 1987 he became only the fifth man to win a hat-trick of world titles. Piquet made his F1 debut with Ensign at Hockenheim in 1978, had three outings in a privately entered McLaren then joined Brabham for the final race of the season. 1979 was a disappointing year. When team-mate, Lauda left to join McLaren in 1980, Piquet became the team's no. 1, and finished runner-up to Alan Jones in the championship. In 1981, Piquet went into the final round, Las Vegas, trailing Reutemann by one point, but fifth place was enough to give him the crown, as Reutemann failed to score. 1982 proved unsuccessful for Piquet, but he and Brabham roared back in 1983, clinching his second title with third place at Kyalami. Piquet won just three races over the next three seasons, switched to Williams in 1986 and took his third world title the following year. Two indifferent years at Lotus saw him move to Benetton, where he ended his F1 career winning three final GPs. His 485.5 point career haul puts him eight in the all-time list.

ALAIN PROST

Born:	24 February 1955, St Chamond, France
Grand Prix starts:	199
Grand Prix victories:	51
Points total:	798.5
World Champion:	1985, 1986, 1989, 1993

MASTER TACTICIAN WINS FOUR WORLD CROWNS

Alain Prost became only the second man to win the world championship four times, following Fangio into the record books. Michael Schumacher has since joined them.

His smooth and calculated driving style and mastery of tactics earned him his nickname: 'The Professor'. He made his F1 debut in 1980 for McLaren, taking a poor car to sixth place on his debut in Buenos Aires, and showing his enormous potential. This was confirmed when he moved to Renault in 1981, winning three races to finish fifth, just

7 points behind champion Piquet. A third place in 1982 was improved to that of runner-up behind Neson Piquet the following year.

On returning to McLaren in 1984 Prost won a remarkable seven races, but he again had to settle for the runner-up spot, half a point behind team-mate Niki Lauda.

Prost took the 1985 championship with two races to spare and retained the title after getting the better of the Williams pair Mansell and Piquet in a three-way showdown in Australia in 1986. Mansell's tyre blew and Piquet was brought in for a precautionary stop, leaving Prost to win both the race and the title.

The Williams team dominated 1987, but McLaren hit back in 1988, with Prost and new team-mate Senna between them winning 15 of the 16 races, and Senna taking the title by 3 points. The positions were reversed in 1989, their crash at Suzuka settling the championship in Prost's favour, but he was again consigned to runner-up spot behind Senna in 1990. A poor season followed, after which he took a year's sabbatical. Driving for Williams in 1993, he replaced reigning champion Mansell, and added seven more victories to his tally to claim his fourth world crown before retiring.

KIMI RAÏKKÖNEN

Born:	17 October 1979, Lappeenranta, Finland
Grand Prix starts:	194*
Grand Prix victories:	20*
Points total:	969*
World Champion:	2007

*TO END OF 2013 SEASON

FERRARI'S FINNISH WINNER

First there was Rosberg, then Häkkinen, and as the curtain was drawing down on the latter's illustrious career, Finland hailed the emergence of a new F1 star: Kimi Raïkkönen. Raïkkönen had a long line of successes in karting before turning to single seaters in 1999, and it was his outstanding seven wins in ten outings in the 2000 British Formula Renault series that brought him to the attention of F1 bosses. In September 2000 he tested for Sauber, making his championship debut a few months later at the Australian Grand Prix, finishing in sixth place. Taking over from Mika Häkkinen at McLaren in 2002, Raïkkönen was their no. 2 to David Coulthard, finishing the year sixth overall. Within a year, he was not only McLaren's front-runner but also its title contender. His only victory in 2003, and his maiden one at that, was at Sepang, but he backed it up with ten podiums to finish only 2 points behind the perennial champion, Michael Schumacher.

In 2004 Raïkkönen scored a second win, at Spa, and notched up 45 points but problems with the new car early in the season saw him slip to seventh overall, more than 100 points behind Schumacher.

2005 saw him emerge as a genuine championship winner, taking seven victories, including Spain, Monaco, Canada and Japan. However, reliability problems, yet again, meant that he was unable to lift the crown, finishing runner-up, 20 points adrift of Fernando Alonso. After winning no races and finishing fifth overall in 2006, Raïkkönen made the switch from McLaren to Ferrari. Six wins helped him lift the 2007 title, pipping McLaren duo Hamilton and Alonso by a single point. He set the fastest lap in ten races in 2008, equalling Michael Schumacher's record and putting him third on the all-time list, but could finish only third in the championship. A fourth victory at Spa was his sole success in 2009, after which he left Ferrari to compete in the World Rally Championship. After two years away, in which he struggled to make an impact in

rallying, Raïkkönen returned to the fray with the new Lotus F1 team that emerged from the ashes of Lotus Renault. An impressive comeback year yielded points in every round bar one, a clutch of podiums and a late-season victory that put him third in the championship.

He kicked off his 2013 campaign with a brilliant win in Melbourne and accumulated points with metronomic efficiency in the first half of the year. Outshone by team-mate Grosjean thereafter, Kimi missed the final two races through injury, by which time his return to Ferrari was already sealed.

DANIEL RICCIARDO

Born:	1 July 1989, Perth, Australia
Grand Prix starts:	50*
Grand Prix victories:	0*
Points total:	30*

*TO END OF 2013 SEASON

AUSTRALIA'S RISING STAR

Mark Webber vacated one of the most desirable seats in Formula One when he departed for new pastures at the end of 2013. His replacement was a fellow Aussie, whom he predicted would soon justify his elevation to a leading outfit. Daniel Ricciardo had all the hallmarks of a first-rate driver, maybe even a champion in the making. 'He's earned his stripes,' said Webber, 'and now he's in a top team where he can show everybody, including himself, what he's really capable of.'

Ricciardo hails from Perth, Western Australia, where he cut his teeth on the karting circuit and went on to compete in national championships. In his mid-teens he progressed to Formula Ford, then Formula BMW, where he took third in the Asian series in 2006. From there it was on to Formula Renault 2.0, but 2009 was a key period in his development: landing the British F3 title – as his boyhood hero Ayrton Senna had done – and impressing in a young driver test for Red Bull. Ricciardo was now firmly on the radar of the Milton Keynes-based outfit; all he needed was scope to hone his skills and a suitable opening in the senior ranks when the time was right. STR was the obvious proving ground, but with no slot available there in 2010, Ricciardo combined test-reserve duties for Red Bull with the Renault 3.5 series, in which he narrowly missed out on overall top spot. He also tested again for Red Bull, this time at Abu Dhabi, where he eclipsed Vettel and Webber's best times set a few days earlier in the grand prix.

Red Bull secured him a seat among the elite in 2011, albeit in the back division with the HRT minnows. His debut came at Silverstone, and he showed enough in the second half of the season to be handed a drive at Red Bull's sister outfit the following year. Two seasons with STR yielded some highly respectable top-10 finishes, and in his second full campaign he doubled his points tally and climbed four places up the Drivers' Championship ladder. He outshone team-mate Jean-Eric Vergne, especially with his raw speed in qualifying. The pick of those performances came at the British GP, where he lined up fifth before slipping to eighth by the time the chequered flag came out. It was one thing to outperform the car over one lap, quite another to do it over full race distance. That would not be a problem once he stepped into Webber's shoes, running with the team that had dominated the championship for four years. 2014 thus provided the opportunity for Ricciardo to show that promise and potential could be converted into podiums. His compatriot was confident he would do just that.

JOCHEN RINDT

Born:	**18 April 1942, Mainz-am-Rhein, Germany**
Died:	**5 September 1970**
Grand Prix starts:	60
Grand Prix victories:	6
Points total:	109
World Champion:	1970

POSTHUMOUS CHAMPION

As soon as Jochen Rindt swapped hill climbs and rallies for circuit racing in the early 1960s his speed and style marked him out as a man to watch. He made his championship debut at Zeltweg in 1964 for Brabham, failing to finish that day, but the following year he raced for Cooper alongside Bruce McLaren. His first championship points came in 1965.

Rindt took three podiums in 1966, but then struggled the following season due to an uncompetitive Cooper. This was followed by an unsuccessful year with Brabham, suffering reliability problems. Rindt moved to Lotus in 1969 to partner reigning champion Graham Hill, whom he outscored in a season which produced his maiden victory at Watkins Glen.

Hill's leg injuries in a crash at the 1969 US GP ended his time at the top of F1, and in 1970 Fittipaldi was drafted in to support Rindt. Rindt won five races out of six in mid-season to lead the title race comfortably, but was tragically killed during practice for Monza. With four races still to run, Jacky Ickx, the only man who could catch him, was unable to bridge the gap. Rindt thus became the first posthumous world champion.

KEKE ROSBERG

Born:	6 December 1948, Solna, Sweden
Grand Prix starts:	114
Grand Prix victories:	5
Points total:	159.5
World Champion:	1982

CONSISTENT FINN BECOMES WORLD CHAMPION

The 'Flying Finn' spent four seasons with unheralded teams in the F1 basement, scoring an aggregate of just 6 points between 1978 and 1981. It was thus an inspired decision on the part of Williams to choose Rosberg as the man to replace Alan Jones in 1982, one which was vindicated as he reclaimed the crown that the team had lost to Nelson Piquet and Jack Brabham the previous year.

Rosberg struggled to qualify his Theodore in the 1978 F1 series, though he drove the car to an outstanding victory in the International Trophy at a rain-soaked Silverstone. He had a few outings for ATS, and also returned to Theodore, this time running a Wolf. Nor did he make much impact in 1979, when he took over from James Hunt at Wolf. By 1980 Walter Wolf had had enough and the team merged with Fittipaldi, and Rosberg found himself partnering the 1972 and 1974 world champion. Third place in the Argentinian GP at Buenos Aires helped the Finn to outscore Fittipaldi, albeit by a single point. Fittipaldi moved upstairs in 1981, and Rosberg was joined by Brazilian Chico Serra. However, once again the battle was in qualifying rather than trying to get into the points.

Moving from Fittipaldi Automotive to Williams in 1982 gave Rosberg his big chance, the first time he had competitive hardware, and he grabbed it with both hands. He received a further boost when Carlos Reutemann quit after two races and he was elevated to team leader. Rosberg won only once, the Swiss GP at Dijon-Prenois, but was consistently in the points, scoring ten times in a season when the best 11 finishes counted. He held off the challenge of John Watson to secure the title with fifth place at Caesar's Palace.

Rosberg won twice in the next two seasons: firstly hampered by the late arrival of the Williams turbo unit, and then, struggling to come to terms with it. He finished third in the 1985 championship, but slipped to sixth the following season with McLaren, his swansong F1 campaign.

NICO ROSBERG

Born:	27 June 1985, Wiesbaden, Germany
Grand Prix starts:	147*
Grand Prix victories:	3*
Points total:	570.5*

*TO END OF 2013 SEASON

YOUNGEST DRIVER TO SET FASTEST LAP

The son of the 1982 champion, Finland's Keke Rosberg, Nico was born in Wiesbaden and holds dual nationality, though he races under a German flag.

Rosberg took up karting at the age of 11, and just six years later, in 2002, won the inaugural German Formula BMW championship. He competed in the Formula Three Euroseries for his father's team in 2003 and 2004, finishing eighth and fourth, respectively. He had already tested for Williams, and after an outstanding 2005, when he won the inaugural GP2 championship for the ART Grand Prix team, he joined the Grove-based outfit, replacing BMW Sauber-bound Nick Heidfeld. Williams had seven Drivers' championships and nine Constructors' titles to its name, but the last of those had come in 1997, so it was always going to be a testing F1 baptism for the then 20-year-old Rosberg.

There was a highly promising start as he and partner Mark Webber both got into the points at the Bahrain curtain-raiser. Rosberg immediately went into the record books, taking over from Fernando Alonso as the youngest driver to set the fastest lap in a Grand Prix. The rest of the season was something of an anticlimax, Rosberg and Webber between them suffering 20 retirements. Rosberg's only other scoring race was the European GP, where he again took seventh place.

Williams adopted Toyota power in 2007, and Rosberg's fortunes took a turn for the better. He was among the points in seven races, a fine late-season run culminating in fourth place at Interlagos. He couldn't quite improve on his 20-point haul the following season, but 2008 did see Rosberg on the podium for the first time. He finished third in the season-opener in Melbourne, and went one better in F1's first-ever floodlit race around the streets of Singapore. Rosberg ended his four-year spell at Williams in 2009, joining compatriot Michael Schumacher at the new Mercedes GP team. In 2010 he scored three podiums and

finished seventh, best of the rest in a year dominated by Red Bull, Ferrari and McLaren. Rosberg's 142-point haul was double that of team-mate Michael Schumacher, and he got the better of the seven-time champion again in 2011 and 2012. The latter season also saw him convert his first pole into a maiden victory in China.

Nico acquitted himself well against new team-mate Lewis Hamilton in 2013, taking two victories to the Briton's one. In Monaco, one of a hat-trick of poles, he converted his grid spot into a sparkling win, 30 years after his father's victory at the same circuit.

JODY SCHECKTER

Born:	29 January 1950, East London, S Africa
Grand Prix starts:	112
Grand Prix victories:	10
Points total:	255
World Champion:	1979

FERRARI RELIABILITY BRINGS THE WORLD CROWN

Jody Scheckter was initially seen as scintillatingly quick but something of a liability. Rising through the ranks on his home turf, he made his name driving on the edge – and sometimes beyond it. On one occasion he was black-flagged for dangerous driving, but by 1970 he had won the South African Formula Ford championship and Europe beckoned.

More thrills and spills followed in Formula Ford and F3, and in 1972 McLaren decided that if they could exploit the former and curb the latter, they could have a serious contender on their hands. Scheckter had five outings in 1973 as back up to Hulme and Revson. Four ended in retirement, one of which – Silverstone – witnessed an opening-lap 20-car pile-up triggered by the South African. There were calls for him to be banned, and McLaren decided he had no future there. Ken Tyrrell recognised the positive – a driver who had led at Paul Ricard for 41 of the 54 laps in only his third F1 start before tangling with reigning champion Fittipaldi – and signed him in 1974 to replace the retired Jackie Stewart.

Victories in Sweden and Britain plus a couple of second places put him in with an outside chance of the title, but he failed to score in the decider, Watkins Glen, and had to settle for third behind Fittipaldi and Regazzoni. Success in his home GP was the highlight of 1975, when he slipped to seventh in the overall rankings. Tyrrell then unveiled its six-wheeled P34. Scheckter drove it to second place in only its third outing, Monaco, then went one better at Anderstorp. It would be the car's sole success.

In 1977 Scheckter gave another car its only taste of victory. He joined the new Wolf team, won first time out in the WR1 in Buenos Aires, and also crossed the line first in Monaco and Canada. Scheckter stayed in contention with Lauda's Ferrari for most of the year but had to content himself with runner-up to the Austrian.

After a disappointing second season with Wolf, Scheckter joined Ferrari. Reliability proved key, and three

wins plus a string of points finishes helped the South African take the title from team-mate Villeneuve, who was under orders to play the supporting role. The 1980 car, by contrast, was a disaster, with Scheckter picking up just 2 points all year. He retired at the end of that campaign.

RALF SCHUMACHER

Born:	30 June 1975, Kerpen, Germany
Grand Prix starts:	180
Grand Prix victories:	6
Points total:	329

SCHUMACHER ENDS FOUR-YEAR WILLIAMS DROUGHT

Ralf Schumacher rose to prominence in the German F3 championship of 1994, taking third place and then runner-up the next season. A move to Formula Nippon saw him take the title at the first attempt.

He was offered his F1 break in 1997 with Jordan, where he paired with Giancarlo Fisichella. In his second season, alongside Damon Hill, he managed just 14 points, then left to join Williams. He emerged from his brother's shadow in 1999, making the podium at Melbourne – his Williams debut, from eighth on the grid – and taking second place at Monza. Teamed with Jenson Button in 2000, he managed fifth overall in the title race.

He scored his maiden win at Imola in 2001, thus ending a 54-race barren run for Williams. Winning at Montreal, he and Michael became the first siblings to finish one-two in a championship race. His third win that year came on home soil at Hockenheim.

The next two seasons saw him take three wins to give him fourth and fifth in the championship, outscored on both occasions by team-mate Montoya. He slipped to ninth overall in 2004 and announced his intention to drive for Toyota the following season.

For the first 12 races of 2005, he was outraced by team-mate Jarno Trulli, but showed some promise towards the end, taking a third at the Chinese GP. He ended the season sixth overall, 2 points ahead of Trulli. Having totalled just 25 points in the 2006 and 2007 seasons, Schumacher quit F1 to compete in the German touring car series.

MICHAEL SCHUMACHER

Born:	3 January 1969, Kerpen, Germany
Grand Prix starts:	308
Grand Prix victories:	91
Points total:	1566
World Champion:	1994, 1995, 2000, 2001, 2002, 2003, 2004

SEVEN TIMES WORLD CHAMPION REWRITES THE RECORD BOOKS

Michael Schumacher, in a league of his own, has rewritten the record books. He is the only driver to have taken five championships in a row, surpassing Juan Manuel Fangio. His Formula One debut came at Spa in 1991, driving for Jordan. He retired before the end of the first lap, but in qualifying seventh he'd already proved that he had talent. Benetton quickly signed him and he rewarded them with a fifth at Monza two weeks later. In his first full season in 1992, he was regularly on the podium, and this, together with a maiden win at Spa, put him third in the championship that year. 1993 gave him another win, plus eight podiums.

1994 saw him take his first title, albeit amid controversy with Hill in the final race at Adelaide. He retained the title in 1995 with nine wins, casting aside all doubts as to his championship abilities.

In 1996 he moved to Ferrari, whose car was not as fast as Williams, and suffered a temporary setback. He began his dominance of F1 in 2000, taking five consecutive championship titles, his best year being 2004 when he won 12 of the first 13 rounds.

At the beginning of 2005, rule changes were introduced to try to level the playing field and make the racing more competitive. Whether as a result of this or not, Schumacher had a disappointing season, taking just one victory – at the US GP in Indianapolis – and making five podiums. He finished the season third behind Fernando Alonso and Kimi Raïkkönen.

2006 was to be Schumacher's final season in Formula One and his chances of winning one last championship were slim with Alonso dominating at the beginning of the season. However, in a thrilling reversal of fortunes, Schumacher began to catch up and eventually he and Alonso were neck and neck with just two races to go. Sadly, engine trouble forced Schumacher out of the penultimate race in Japan, which pushed Alonso too far out of his grasp. However, after three years on the sidelines, he made a dramatic return to F1 with the new Mercedes GP team, joining forces once again with Ross Brawn. The then 41-year-old's best return of the 2010 season was fourth, and he ended the year almost 200 points down on the new world champion Vettel. Even team-mate Nico Rosberg outscored him two to one, and an eighth world crown looked a distant prospect.

He closed the gap on Rosberg considerably in 2011 and on half a dozen occasions was the first man home behind the big three of Red Bull, McLaren and Ferrari. Schumacher, who celebrated the 20th anniversary of his F1 debut at Spa, geared up for his third season back on the grid, insisting that he could fight for wins given the right hardware package. He might have claimed his 92nd win at Monaco 2012 had a penalty not robbed him of pole. Ultimately, it was another midfield finish in the championship, again well behind Rosberg, after which F1's most successful driver bowed out for the second time.

After a glittering career spanning more than two decades in a sport fraught with danger, Schumacher sustained serious head injuries in a skiing accident in December 2013, news that shocked F1 fans the world over.

AYRTON SENNA

Born: 21 March 1960, São Paulo, Brazil	
Died:	1 May 1994
Grand Prix starts:	161
Grand Prix victories:	41
Points total:	614
World Champion:	1988, 1990, 1991

FORMULA ONE'S GREATEST TALENT

With 65 pole positions, 41 wins, 80 times on the podium, and 614 points, Ayrton Senna was to many F1 aficionados the greatest ever talent in F1.

After winning a string of karting titles, Senna moved to Britain in 1981 to further his career in four-wheeled competition. Within three years he had won the British F3 title, holding off the challenge of Martin Brundle. In 1984 he made his F1 debut, testing for Brabham and Williams, between them winners of the previous four world championships, but choosing instead to join the smaller Toleman outfit.

His first point came at Kyalami, and by his sixth race, Monaco, he was chasing race-leader Prost when the race was stopped due to bad weather conditions. Before the end of the season he had signed for Lotus, scoring his first wins at Estoril and Spa, in 1985, and taking a fourth overall in the title race that year.

The next two seasons saw him elevated to third in the championship both times, but Senna wanted more and joined McLaren in 1988. He was teamed with twice-champion, Prost, and a bitter rivalry soon developed. Senna won his first championship in 1988 by 3 points from Prost, but the following season Prost relegated him to runner-up after their clash at Suzuka. Prost then left for Ferrari but the rivalry continued, culminating in yet another clash in Japan at the 1990 championship, and Senna taking the title. He later hinted at his responsibility for the crash.

His third title was won with a comfortable 24-point margin over Mansell, but the Williams car began to dominate after that. Despite this, Senna won three GPs in 1992. In 1993, five wins earned him the runner-up spot to Prost.

Senna joined Williams in 1994, taking pole in the first two rounds but retiring in each. He was on pole again at San Marino, when he crashed fatally at Tamburello, aged 34.

JACKIE STEWART

Born:	**11 June 1939, Milton, Scotland**
Grand Prix starts:	**99**
Grand Prix victories:	**27**
Points total:	**360**
World Champion:	**1969, 1971, 1973**

FLYING SCOTSMAN WINS THREE WORLD CROWNS

Jackie Stewart was a natural behind the wheel, and quickly attracted the attention of some of the sport's major players. Ken Tyrrell signed him for his F3 team in 1964, but it wasn't long before he was offered F1 contracts and he signed for BRM at the end of the season.

His championship debut came at the 1965 South African GP, where he took sixth place, winning his first race at Monza before the season was out. He finished a stunning third in his debut season behind Jim Clark and team-mate Graham Hill. He remained at BRM for two more years, but with an uncompetitive and unreliable car, he won just once in that time, at Monaco in 1966.

Stewart was reunited with Tyrrell in 1968, a partnership that would yield three world titles. He missed two races in 1968 through injury and finished runner-up to Graham Hill's Lotus. But the following season, in a Matra MS80, he swept away the opposition, taking the title 26 points clear in the final table. A disappointing 1970 season was followed by Stewart taking his second world title in 1971, winning six of the eleven rounds. Despite four more victories in 1972, Fittipaldi went one better and Stewart had to settle for the runner-up spot.

He added five more victories to his tally the following year to take his third championship before the season was out. He planned to retire at the US GP, but the death of team-mate François Cévert during qualifying led Tyrrell to withdraw, and Stewart retired with immediate effect. His 27 wins set a new world record that was to stand for 14 years.

JOHN SURTEES

Born:	11 February 1934, Tatsfield, England
Grand Prix starts:	111
Grand Prix victories:	6
Points total:	180
World Champion:	1964

CHAMPION ON TWO WHEELS AND FOUR

John Surtees is still the only man ever to win world championships on both two wheels and four. He landed his first motorcycling world title in 1956 and followed it up with six more championships over the next four years.

He was offered an F1 drive with Lotus in 1960, finishing second to reigning champion Jack Brabham at Silverstone on only his second outing. Surtees joined Yeoman Credit Cooper in 1961, winning just 4 points in a car of variable quality. Rejecting an offer from Ferrari, he remained with Cooper to finish fourth in the 1962 championship, but when Ferrari asked again, he judged the time to be right, and signed up.

1963 gave Surtees his first victory at the Nürburgring, and a fourth place overall. Two more wins the following year took him into the final race, the Mexican GP, in contention for the crown against Hill and Clark. Luck went his way, as they hit problems. Team-mate Lorenzo Bandini allowed him through to take second place, enough to win the championship by a single point.

He sustained severe injuries in a CanAm sports car race in 1965, and in the middle of the following season joined Cooper to finish runner-up. He then spent two years at Honda, followed by a disappointing year with BRM, before forming his own team in 1970. He retired from GP racing in 1972 to manage the business, but results were indifferent and the team folded in 1978.

SEBASTIAN VETTEL

Born:	3 July 1987, Heppenheim, Germany
Grand Prix starts:	120*
Grand Prix victories:	39*
Points total:	1451*
World Champion:	2010, 2011, 2012, 2013

*TO END OF 2013 SEASON

TRIPLE WORLD CHAMPION

Lewis Hamilton took the accolades for becoming the youngest-ever world champion in 2008, but he was not the only record-breaker among the young bloods that year. It was easy to overlook the enormous strides made by Sebastian Vettel, in his first full season in the elite division.

Vettel was a junior karting star, who swept the board when he stepped up to the German Formula BMW Championship in 2004. He locked horns with Hamilton in the Formula 3 Euroseries in 2005, finishing fifth that year and runner-up the next. He went into 2007 as BMW Sauber test driver, while also competing in the Renault World Series. Vettel made his F1 debut at the US Grand Prix, replacing the injured Robert Kubica. Fellow test driver Timo Glock had had a spell with Jordan in 2004, but the team's decision was vindicated as the 19-year-old finished in eighth place, taking over from Jenson Button as the youngest driver to score a championship point.

Vettel was contracted to Red Bull from the end of 2007, but BMW Sauber released him early so that he could join Red Bull's sister outfit Scuderia Toro Rosso, which had lost Scott Speed. He finished fourth in Shanghai in the penultimate race of the year, but it was in 2008 when he really began to show his mettle. He scored in seven of the last nine races, including a maiden victory from pole at Monza. With that success he displaced Fernando Alonso as F1's youngest race winner.

Vettel finished eighth in the championship with a highly creditable 35 points, and it was no surprise when he was named in the Red Bull line-up for 2009, replacing David Coulthard. He ran champion Jenson Button closest that year, notching four more wins on his way to the runner-up spot. DNFs proved costly, but the 'new Schuey' had continued his meteoric rise.

The march continued all the way to the top in 2010, Vettel becoming F1's youngest champion. There were ten poles and five wins, though he didn't top the leader board until the final race.

There was no such late drama in 2011, Vettel taking 15 poles – breaking Mansell's record – and 11 wins to retain the crown with four rounds to spare and at 24 years 98 days become F1's youngest double world champion. He didn't have things all his own way in 2012, but a brilliant late-season run helped him pip Alonso and add youngest three-time championship winner to his record collection. Vettel became only the third driver to take the crown in three consecutive years.

Title number four was delivered at a canter in 2013, courtesy of an unbroken nine-win sequence in the second half of the year. 13 victories in all put him over 150 points clear of runner-up Alonso. Vettel joined Fangio and Schumacher as a member of the quadruple club, at 26 by far the youngest of that select group.

GILLES VILLENEUVE

Born:	18 January 1950, Saint-Jean-sur-Richelieu, Canada
Died:	8 May 1982
Grand Prix starts:	67
Grand Prix victories:	6
Points total:	107

NATURAL RACER A SAD LOSS TO FORMULA ONE

Gilles Villeneuve's early forays into four-wheeled motor sport began with Formula Ford, winning an invitation race in 1976, and a year later retaining his Canadian Formula Atlantic title.

At his F1 debut in the 1977 British GP he competed well, despite an ageing McLaren, and finished eleventh.

McLaren chose to lose him and he was driving for Ferrari before the season was out, replacing Lauda.

Villeneuve's maiden victory came on home soil in the final round of the 1978 championship. The following year he took two victories at Kyalami and Long Beach, and added a third in the final race at Watkins Glen. Team-mate Scheckter already had the title in the bag by then, Villeneuve having to follow team orders, and he finished runner-up to him in the championship.

The 1980 Ferrari was a disaster, with Villeneuve scoring only 6 points, and his team-mate and reigning champion scoring just a couple. The 1981 model showed little improvement, but Villeneuve managed wins in Monaco and Spain to finish seventh overall.

At San Marino in 1982, Villeneuve was furious when his then team-mate Didier Pironi broke an agreement and passed him on the last lap. At the qualifiers for Zolder two weeks later, the feeling of resentment between the two was palpable. Villeneuve was determined to take pole and in so doing, struck Jochen Mass's March. He was hurled from his Ferrari and killed.

JACQUES VILLENEUVE

Born:	**9 April 1971,**
	Saint-Jean-sur-Richelieu, Canada
Grand Prix starts:	165
Grand Prix victories:	11
Points total:	235
World Champion:	1997

CANADIAN WINS 1997 SHOWDOWN WITH SCHUMACHER

Jacques Villeneuve experienced a meteoric rise to become world champion, a feat his father never achieved. He became the youngest ever winner of the IndyCar championship in 1995 and secured a two-year deal with Williams as a result. His maiden victory at the European GP at the Nürburgring in 1996 was followed by three more wins, and he emerged as the only rival to team-mate Damon Hill. Crashing out at Suzuka ended his slim chance of taking the title, Hill winning when he needed a single point.

The championship title came in 1997, where there were seven wins, and a showdown in the final race at Jerez. Michael Schumacher led the title race by a point and attempted to shunt Villeneuve out of the race, but the Canadian recovered to finish third and take the title.

Villeneuve signed up with BAR at the end of a disappointing 1998, where he had made the podium just twice. The team did not pick up a single point in 1999, Villeneuve suffering 12 DNFs. The next four years saw him make a total of 40 points, and at the end of 2003 BAR dispensed with his services.

After a short time with the Renault team at the end of the 2004 season, Villeneuve moved to Sauber-Petronas for another attempt at the title. The 2005 Championship saw him score just 9 points with a fourth at San Marino being his best finishing position. He continued to race under the newly-named BMW Sauber in 2006, but a crash in the German Grand Prix left him with injuries, which forced his team to bring in a replacement, Robert Kubica. Villeneuve was being edged out of the team as Kubica put in several impressive performances, finishing on the podium in only his third race. As a result the former champion decided to retire from the sport during the middle of the season.

MARK WEBBER

Born:	27 August 1976, Queanbeyan, Australia
Grand Prix starts:	217*
Grand Prix victories:	9*
Points total:	1047.5*

*TO END OF 2013 SEASON

AUSTRALIA'S FIRST WINNER FOR 28 YEARS

The son of a New South Wales motorcycle dealer, Mark Webber gravitated towards four-wheeled competition, as his father was not keen for him to take up bike racing. He served his apprenticeship in karts and Formula Ford in his native country before departing to try his hand in the bigger European arena.

Webber took second place in the British Formula Ford championship in 1996, and fourth in the British F3 series the following year. He turned to sports cars in 1998, accepting an offer from Mercedes to compete in the FIA GT series. Partnering Bernd Schneider, who had won the inaugural championship the previous year, Webber took second place, but his sports car career came to an abrupt end after a spectacular 290km/h crash at Le Mans in 1999. He spent the next two years competing in the F3000 series, finishing in the top three on both occasions.

While competing in F3, Webber was also on the F1 fringe as a test driver, for Arrows in 2000 and Benetton in 2001. When Benetton morphed into Renault in 2002, Fernando Alonso was given the test-driver berth, on the back of a good showing with Minardi, and Webber moved in the opposite direction. Compatriot Paul Stoddard had just taken over at Minardi, and he must have been delighted as Webber finished fifth on his F1 debut in Melbourne. It was Minardi's first points for three years; unfortunately, the rest of the season was a blank for Webber and the team.

There followed two seasons with the ailing Jaguar team, and 11 scoring races represented a decent return in the final throes before Red Bull took over the concern. Webber joined Williams in 2005 and had his best return to date, 36 points, 6 of those coming at Monaco, where he scored his first podium finish. After a disappointing 2006 – ten retirements and a mere 7-point haul – Webber moved to Red Bull. He gained another podium at the 2007 European GP, but remained anchored in the midfield division of the Drivers' championship. It was a different story in 2009,

where Red Bull battled it out with Brawn for the major honours. Webber scored his maiden victory in Germany and also won in Brazil on his way to fourth place in the championship. It marked the first success for an Australian since Alan Jones in 1981.

He claimed his first two wins in 2009 – the first victory for an Aussie driver since Alan Jones in 1981 – and four more in the first half of the 2010 campaign to lead the title race. He lost out in a four-way decider, ending the year third behind team-mate Vettel and Alonso.

2011 suggested 35-year-old Webber's chance of title glory had slipped through his fingers. While Vettel blew the field away in the RB7, Webber had to wait until the final race of the year for a consolation victory that left him a distant third in the championship. He led the Red Bull charge at the halfway mark in 2012 before falling away to finish the year in sixth place, over 100 points shy of Vettel's haul.

It was a similar story in Webber's final season in F1. 199 points was good enough for third in the 2013 championship, but amounted to only half of Vettel's title-winning total, reflecting the fact that once again his team-mate exploited prime Red Bull hardware that much better.

THE
CONSTRUCTORS

ALFA ROMEO

Country:	**Italy**
Foundation:	**1910**
Years in Formula One:	**1950–51, 1979–85**
Constructors' Title victories: 0	

WINNERS OF THE INAUGURAL MANUFACTURERS CHAMPIONSHIP

Alfa Romeo was founded in 1907 by Milanese aristocrat Cavaliere Ugo Stella, in partnership with the French automobile firm of Alexandre Darracq. After that collaboration ended, Stella set up a new company, Anonima Lombarda Fabbrica Automobili, in the Portello suburb of his home town.

The first Alfa appeared in 1910, a 24hp model designed by Giuseppe Merosi. Within a year the company also turned its thoughts to motor sport, Franchini and Ronzoni competing in the 1911 Targa Florio in an Alfa.

Alfa takes on Romeo's name

Nicola Romeo bought the company in 1915, and after helping to support the war effort, Alfa reverted to car production. In 1920 the name of the company was changed to Alfa Romeo, the Torpedo being the first car to bear the famous badge.

In 1923 Alfa driver Enzo Ferrari was instrumental in luring renowned designer Vittorio Jano from Fiat. The first Jano-designed car was the P2, in which Giuseppe Campari and Antonio Ascari enjoyed enormous success. In 1925 Alfa Romeo won the inaugural manufacturers' world championship with the same model.

First monoposto racing car

In 1932 Jano unveiled the Tipo B P3, the first monoposto racing car. It made a victorious debut at that year's Monaco GP, with Tazio Nuvolari at the wheel, and went on to dominate the Grand Prix arena for the next two years. In 1933 Alfa was nationalised by a Mussolini government keen to showcase the best in Italian design and technology, and the company withdrew from racing. For the next five years Alfa Romeos did compete, Enzo Ferrari running a semi-works team. Auto Union and Mercedes were dominant in this period, though Alfa did enjoy some stunning successes, notably at the Nürburgring in 1935. Nuvolari beat the German powerhouses in their own back yard with the now-outdated P3. So confident had the organisers been of a home victory that the German national anthem was cued up ready to acclaim the victor. Nuvolari promptly produced his personal copy of the Italian anthem for the post-race honours.

The rise of the Alfetta

Jano was sacked in 1937, and after Alfa regained control of its racing affairs the following year, the marque turned its attention to the voiturette class. Giocchino Colombo designed the famous 158 'Alfetta'. This was a 1.5-litre model, and in 1939 the Italians decided to hold all their races to a 1500cc formula to stave off the German onslaught. Mercedes did produce a one-off car to win that season's Tripoli GP, but in the postwar period the Alfetta was the car to beat. Not that

following year, with the famous 'Three Fs' dominating the championship series. Giuseppe Farina pipped Fangio for the title, with Luigi Fagioli third. A year later Fangio lifted the first of his five world crowns in an Alfa 159, essentially the same car but with a two-stage compressor.

Lack of funds causes Alfa to quit

Although Alfa had squeezed home in the 1951 title race, the team bosses knew that without a major injection of funds, it would lose out to Ferrari the following season. No money was forthcoming, so Alfa announced its immediate withdrawal from the sport.

Alfa Romeo did return to Grand Prix racing in 1976, supplying engines to Bernie Ecclestone's Brabham team. In 1978 Niki Lauda scored two wins, one of which was in the famous 'fan car' in its only outing before it was banned. Alfa ran under its own name once again for the next seven years, but failed to recapture the heady successes of the early 1950s. The best return came in 1983, when Andrea de Cesaris scored 15 points to finish eighth in the championship.

that happened too often, the Alfa enjoying a 26-race winning streak in the late 1940s.

Alfa withdrew from racing in 1949, following the double blow of losing ace driver Jean-Pierre Wimille – killed during practice for the Buenos Aires GP in January that year – and team-mate Count Trossi, who lost his fight against cancer. The marque was back for the inaugural world championship the

OPPOSITE: **1983 Brazilian Grand Prix, Jacarepagua, Rio de Janeiro. Andrea de Cesaris (Alfa Romeo 183T).**

ABOVE: **From left: Baconin Borzacchini, Enzo Ferrari, Tazio Nuvolari in front of an Alfa Romeo 8C 'Monza' (c.1931–32).**

BELOW: **1951 French Grand Prix, Reims. Race winner Juan Manuel Fangio (Alfa Romeo 159A).**

AUTO UNION

Country:	Germany
Foundation:	1932
Years in Formula One:	0
Constructors' Title victories: 0	

REVOLUTIONARY NEW DESIGN BY FERDINAND PORSCHE

Along with Mercedes, Auto Union dominated motor racing in the 1930s, a period in which Adolf Hitler actively promoted track success and speed records as a means of demonstrating to the world the fruits of German design and engineering.

Auto Union was formed in 1932, an amalgamation of four companies: Audi, Horch, Wanderer and DKW.

Spurred on by the intense domestic rivalry, the company produced a revolutionary new racing car in 1934, designed by Ferdinand Porsche. The 4.4-litre, 16-cylinder engine was mounted behind the driver, and with an output of 300bhp it made a mockery of the new 750kg formula, introduced in an attempt to curb the manufacturers' penchant for increasing engine size year on year.

First win for rear-engined car

At the 1934 German GP at the Nürburgring, Hans Stuck became the first man to drive a rear-engined car to victory in

a championship race. Stuck was a favourite of the new German Chancellor, and although not in the first rank of drivers, he was good enough to cross the line first in the inaugural Swiss GP at Bremgarten, and at the Czech GP. Mercedes undoubtedly boasted the stronger line-up, prompting Auto Union to sign Achille Varzi. Varzi had had a stellar year with Alfa Romeo in 1934 but didn't achieve the same heights with Auto Union. Victory in the 1935 Tunis GP was one of the highlights, but by 1936 his career was on the wane. However, Auto Union unearthed a new star. Bernd

Rosemeyer claimed his first victory in the 1935 Czech GP, and a year later – his first full Grand Prix campaign – he won six races, including the German Swiss and Italian GPs, to become European champion, the most prestigious title in motor sport at that time.

Death of Rosemeyer

By the end of 1937, Rosemeyer had notched ten wins in 31 Grand Prix starts. He was killed during an attempt to recapture the world speed record from Mercedes in January 1938, and as his replacement Auto Union signed the legendary Tazio Nuvolari. Nuvolari had wanted to join the team three years earlier, but it is said that neither Varzi nor Stuck wanted the greatest driver of the era alongside them. Nuvolari won the Italian and Donington GPs in 1938, while team-mate Hermann Muller drove an Auto Union to victory in the 1939 French Grand Prix.

As Auto Union's base was the East German town of Zwickau, it proved impossible to resurrect the marque as a racing outfit after WWII. Its legacy in the modern era is the four-ring logo – representing the merger of the original four companies – which Audi continues to use.

OPPOSITE ABOVE: **1938 Donington Grand Prix, Donington Park, England. Tazio Nuvolari (Auto Union D-typ) on his way to first position.**

OPPOSITE BELOW: **Hermann Müller attained fourth position at the 1937 Donington Grand Prix, driving this Auto Union C-typ.**

BELOW: **Hans Stuck's Auto Union A-typ in the pit lane at the 1934 French Grand Prix, Montlhery, Paris.**

BAR/HONDA

BAR Country:	United Kingdom
Foundation:	1997
Years in Formula One:	1999–2005
Constructors' Title victories:	0
HONDA Country:	Japan
Foundation:	1964–68, 2006–08
Years in Formula One:	0
Constructors' Title victories:	0

VILLENEUVE SIGNS FOR FLEDGLING BAR TEAM

Tobacco giant BAT entered F1 after buying the Tyrrell team in 1997. British American Tobacco took to the grid as British American Racing, making its debut at the Melbourne curtain-raiser in 1999. One of the team's prime movers was Craig Pollock, whose close association with Jacques Villeneuve helped secure the services of the 1997 world champion. It proved to be a difficult baptism, but things improved with the arrival of Honda power in 2000, Villeneuve finishing fourth on four occasions. His 17 points put him seventh in the championship, ahead of Button's Williams and both Jordans.

In 2001 Villeneuve finally got BAR onto the podium, in Spain and Germany, and there were changes at the top as Dave Richards took the helm. After a hugely disappointing 2002 campaign, Richards drafted in Jenson Button from Renault. Button regularly outperformed the former champion, whose loss of interest and patience culminated in a dramatic walk-out just before the final race at Suzuka.

Runner-up to Ferrari

Button scored ten podium finishes in 2004, his 85-point haul taking BAR to the runner-up spot behind Ferrari in the Constructors' race. The Briton was somewhat unlucky in 2005, his third place at Imola chalked off for a technical infringement, which also earned him a two-race ban. He scored 37 points for ninth place, Takuma Sato adding just one to the team effort as BAR slipped to sixth overall.

The highlight of the 2005 season for BAR didn't occur on the track – that was something of a disappointment following the great strides the team had made in the previous campaign. Rather, it was the change of heart on the part of Jenson Button, who committed his future to a team he said offered him the best chance of fulfilling his ambition of becoming Britain's ninth world champion. That decision came with a hefty price tag, Button reportedly having to stump up some £10 million to buy himself out of the contract which should have seen him rejoin Williams in 2006.

Honda buy out BAT

Honda bought out BAT's majority stake at the end of 2005, and the Honda Racing F1 team took its place on the grid the following season. It was the first time since 1968 that Honda had lined up on the constructors' roster. Rubens Barrichello joined from Ferrari, replacing Sato, and predicted great things for the new concern. He finished seventh in 2006, one place behind Button, who put the team on top of the podium at the Hungarian GP. A combined total of 86 points placed Honda a creditable fourth in the Constructors' Championship. Fortunes dipped dramatically over the following two seasons, the same drivers accumulating just 20 points between them. In December 2008 Honda announced that it was quitting the sport and put the team up for sale. Following an 11th-hour buy-out, the new Brawn GP team debuted at the Australian GP.

LEFT: **BAR team principal Dave Richards, under whose direction BAR took second place in the 2004 Constructors' Championship.**

OPPOSITE: **Rubens Barrichello, BAR Honda 007 (Formula One testing, Jerez, Spain, January 2006).**

BELOW: **Olivier Panis, BAR Honda 003. (Formula One testing, Silverstone, England, January 2001).**

BENETTON

Country:	**United Kingdom**
Date of foundation:	**1986**
Years in Formula One:	**1986–2001**
Constructors' Title victories: 1995	

FASHIONING A GEAR CHANGE IN MOTOR SPORT

The famous fashion house entered Formula One as a sponsor to Tyrrell in 1983. Just two years later it decided to take the plunge into team ownership, buying out Ted Toleman's outfit. Toleman had hardly set the F1 world alight in its five years at the top, its main claim to fame being a couple of podium finishes for the young Ayrton Senna in 1984.

Toleman designer Rory Byrne stayed on with the new concern, and his BMW-powered B186 was competitive from the outset. In the penultimate round of the 1986 season Gerhard Berger, helped by a shrewd tyre strategy, gave Benetton its maiden success on a bumpy Mexico City track.

1987 saw the beginning of a long-term deal with Ford. Thierry Boutsen finished fourth in the 1988 title race, Alessandro Nannini taking sixth the following year. The Italian won the controversial 1989 Japanese GP, inheriting maximum points after Senna was disqualified for chopping a chicane following a clash with Prost. Flavio Briatore took over as team principal that year, and with three-times champion Nelson

Piquet spearheading the line-up, Benetton had their best season to date in 1990. The Brazilian won the last two races of the season for a share of third in the title race.

Schumacher snatched from Jordan

Piquet stayed on for 1991, and performed creditably again, but more significant was the arrival of Michael Schumacher. His signature infuriated Eddie Jordan, for whose team the German wunderkind had made an impressive debut at Spa, qualifying seventh.

Schumacher hung onto Williams' coat-tails in 1992, but the active suspension of the FW14B made Mansell unstoppable. He did take his maiden win at Spa, though, and with another victory plus eight podiums in 1993, Benetton continued to narrow the gap on Williams.

Following Senna's death at Imola in 1994, Schumacher pipped the Brazilian's Williams team-mate Damon Hill for the title. It wasn't plain sailing: there was a ban for ignoring a black flag at Silverstone; disqualification at Spa for skidblock wear which infringed the rules; and the clash with Hill at the Adelaide decider which took both men out and preserved the German's 1-point advantage.

Nine wins brings championship double

Benetton switched to Renault power in 1995 and Schumacher delivered a more emphatic, less controversial second championship, winning nine races. With Johnny Herbert playing a useful supporting role, Benetton won its only Constructors' Title that year.

The team slipped after Schumacher departed to Ferrari in 1996, and the loss of technical wizards Rory Byrne and Ross Brawn to Maranello was also a severe blow. The withdrawal of Renault in 1997 also impacted on performances. In 2000, however, Renault decided to return to F1 as a full works team, and to that end purchased Benetton. Fisichella and Button picked up 10 points between them in the 2001 Benetton-Renault, the last campaign before Renault assumed total control and the Benetton name disappeared.

OPPOSITE ABOVE: **Jarno Trulli (Benetton), Formula One testing at the Circuit de Catalunya, Barcelona, Spain, January 2002.**

OPPOSITE BELOW: **Michael Schumacher (Benetton-Renault), first position, and team boss Flavio Briatore celebrate taking his second successive Drivers' Championship on the podium at the 1995 Pacific Grand Prix, Tanaka International, Aida, Japan.**

BELOW: **Thierry Boutsen (Benetton B187-Ford) during the 1987 French Grand Prix (Paul Ricard, Le Castellet).**

BRABHAM

Country:	United Kingdom
Date of foundation:	1962
Years in Formula One:	1962–87, 1989–92
Constructors' Title victories: 1966, 1967	

THE DETERMINED AUSTRALIAN

After winning successive world titles with the rear-engined Cooper, Jack Brabham's thoughts turned to running his own team. He left Cooper at the end of 1961 and, with friend and fellow Antipodean Ron Tauranac as chief engineer, entered the fray at the Nürburgring the following season. The Climax-powered BT3 failed to go the distance that day, but within two years Jack was back on top of the podium, this time as a team boss. Dan Gurney gave the marque its maiden success, at Rouen in 1964, and also took victory in Mexico that year.

When Gurney competed in the 1965 Indy 500, Brabham drafted Denny Hulme into the team for the Monaco GP, the Kiwi having competed in Formula Junior events for Brabham. Following Gurney's departure to set up his Eagle team, Hulme took the no. 2 seat on a permanent basis.

Repco deal

There were no wins in 1965, a Lotus-BRM-dominated season, but with the introduction of the new 3-litre formula for 1966, the Brabham team came to the fore. Jack cut an engine deal

with an Australian company which supplied parts under the Repco name. Brabham became the first man to take a Grand Prix victory in a car bearing his own name when he crossed the line first at Reims. Three more wins brought him his third world crown, and Hulme's valuable contribution helped the team lift the Constructors' Title. Brabham had just turned 40, and at Zandvoort he took time out to poke fun at himself by appearing with false beard and walking stick. He won the race.

Denny Hulme retained the title for the stable, despite the arrival of the new Cosworth DFV to power the Lotus cars. Hulme won just twice, Monaco and Germany, but consistency put him ahead of his boss and Clark in the final table.

Belgian Jacky Ickx gave Brabham the runner-up spot in 1969, albeit a long way off the pace set by Stewart in the Matra-Ford. Jack called it a day the following season. He should have signed off with a fourth victory in the British GP, heading the Lotus 72 of ex-Brabham driver Jochen Rindt by a street at Brands Hatch. But his BT33 died and he coasted through for second. It was later found that the engine had been left to run rich after starting from cold, and thus used four gallons more than it should. The mechanic who no doubt got it in the neck that day was none other than future McLaren supremo Ron Dennis.

'Fan car' banned

Tauranac bought the company – Motor Racing Developments – but it soon changed hands again, former F3 driver Bernie Ecclestone stepping up to the role of team boss. Gordon Murray was promoted from assistant to Brabham's chief designer. The Murray-designed BT44 scored three wins in 1974, with Carlos Reutemann at the wheel. Reutemann's third place in 1975 was Brabham's best effort of the decade, and the team hoped that switching from Cosworth to Alfa Romeo power, and signing Lauda from Ferrari, would put it on top again. The Austrian joined in 1978, the year of the BT46B, the famous 'fan car'. It swept to victory on its debut in Sweden – and was then promptly banned by the FIA, who ruled that the fans were there to suck air from underneath the car rather than cool the engine.

Brazilian tyro Nelson Piquet made his debut for Brabham that year, and it was he who gave the team their final two championships, in 1981 and 1983. Brabham reverted to Cosworth power, while Murray was again producing innovative designs. For 1981 he devised an ingenious hydraulic system whereby the car sank during the race – improving ground-effect and cornering speed – but complied with the regulation 6cm height between ground and bottom of the car for the mandatory tests. Piquet edged Williams duo Reutemann and Jones that season, and two years later pipped Renault and Prost, Brabham by now running a BMW unit.

In 1986 Piquet joined Williams and Riccardo Patrese notched just two points in a miserable campaign. To compound the misery, Murray departed to McLaren. Ecclestone withdrew at the end of 1987, though Brabham reappeared on the grid two years later, having been bought by Swiss financier Joachim Luithi. He was soon in jail for tax evasion. The team struggled on until 1992, when the Brabham name finally disappeared for good.

OPPOSITE ABOVE: **Jack Brabham celebrating victory in the 1966 French Grand Prix at Reims.**

OPPOSITE BELOW: **Niki Lauda wins the 1978 Swedish Grand Prix at Anderstorp in the controversial Brabham Alfa fan car, making its debut and last outing before being banned.**

ABOVE: **Jack Brabham (Brabham BT3-Climax) competes in the German Grand Prix at the Nürburgring, August 1962.**

BRAWN

Country:	United Kingdom
Date of foundation:	2009
Years in Formula One:	2009
Constructors' Title victories:	2009

A SPARKLING DEBUT

Honda's decision to pull out of Formula One in December 2008 left the Brackley-based outfit in turmoil, and drivers Button and Barrichello unsure of a place on the grid for the new season. An 11th-hour management buy-out saved the day, Ross Brawn stepping into the breach as team principal. There were job losses as the operation had to be slimmed down, but some hasty sponsorship deals were done, Mercedes provided the power and the team lined up at Melbourne for the season opener, just three weeks after Brawn GP officially came into existence.

Anyone who thought Brawn was there simply to make up the numbers was disabused of the notion in Australia, where Button and Barrichello scored a remarkable one-two. Not since the days of Fangio and Kling driving for Mercedes in 1954 had a new entrant made such an immediate impact on the sport. A protest regarding the design of the rear diffuser was dismissed, and while others feverishly redesigned their own pieces of aerodynamic kit, Brawn forged relentlessly ahead. Button won six of the first seven races, while Barrichello weighed in with two victories in the second half of the season. The gap did close, Red Bull mounting the strongest challenge, but Button continued to accumulate points and secured the championship in Brazil, the penultimate round. Vettel pipped Barrichello for the runner-up spot, but it wasn't enough to prevent Brawn from adding the Constructors' Title. That was a first for a team making its debut, since the Constructors' Cup hadn't been introduced until 1958. A fairytale double meant that Ross Brawn had added to the string of driver and team championships he helped mastermind with Benetton and Ferrari, though he had worn his technical director's hat for those successes.

Brawn GP became a one-season wonder as Mercedes bought a majority stake in the team at the year's end, heralding a return to the sport it had left in the wake of the tragic events at Le Mans in 1955. Brawn and Nick Fry remained to oversee the new Mercedes GP team's quest for honours. It meant that Brawn left the stage having captured both titles in its single season in existence, while eight wins in 17 races translated to a 47 percent success rate. It was a proud record that looked set to stand for a considerable time.

Above: **Jenson Button is congratulated by Ross Brawn after clinching the Drivers' Championship at Interlagos on 18 October 2009.**

Opposite: **Jenson Button leads during the Turkish GP, chalking up his sixth win from the first seven races of the 2009 season.**

BRM

Country:	**United Kingdom**
Date of foundation:	1948
Years in Formula One:	1951, 1956–77
Constructors' Title victories:	1962

LONG WAIT FOR FIRST VICTORY

The roots of BRM go back to the early 1930s, when Raymond Mays and Peter Berthon founded English Racing Automobiles, a concern which sought commercial backing for its racing ventures. Mays and Berthon left ERA in 1939, but the same idea underpinned their new project: to attract sponsors and fund a British Grand Prix car capable of taking on the world's finest. British Racing Motors was born.

To comply with the Grand Prix regulations of the day, the car was fitted with a V-16 1.5-litre supercharged engine. Launched in December 1949, the BRM was hailed as a world-beater – which made the subsequent fall from grace the more dramatic. The teething troubles were endless, but under pressure from the backers, Mays was forced to enter the car for the 1950 International trophy meeting at Silverstone. It was an unmitigated disaster, Raymond Sommer being left on the grid with a broken driveshaft.

Figure of fun

BRM became a figure of fun, something Reg Parnell's fifth place in the 1951 British GP couldn't reverse. Retirements made that result somewhat flattering. The final straw came

with a change in the Grand Prix formula, which rendered the car effectively obsolete. In 1952 a sorry chapter was closed when the BRM Trust was sold to industrialist Sir Alfred Owen for a knockdown price.

Over the next six years rival British marques Cooper, Connaught, HWM – and particularly Vanwall – all outperformed BRM in championship races. Harry Schell and Jean Behra both got on the podium at Zandvoort in 1958, easily BRM's best day thus far, and a year later on the same circuit, Jo Bonnier gave the marque its maiden success.

The 1960s were BRM's heyday, particularly the 1.5-litre era which ran from 1961 to 1965. There was a championship double in 1962, with BRM finishing runner-up in the Constructors' race for the following three seasons too. The team began the 1962 campaign still looking for a second victory, and under severe pressure from Owen to deliver. Graham Hill had amassed just 7 points from the previous two championships, but the development of a new mid-engined V-8 unit promised much.

Four wins for Hill

Hill scored three victories and two second-places with the best five scores to count. Even so, he went to Kyalami in December knowing that a Jim Clark victory could still rob him of the title. That proved academic as the Lotus fell by the wayside and Hill took his fourth win of the year.

In 1964, another final race shoot-out, Hill went to Mexico City leading Ferrari's John Surtees by 5 points, and Clark by 9. Hill was cruising in third when he tangled with Surtees' team-mate, Lorenzo Bandini. Clark's engine gave out, and Bandini allowed Surtees through to take second place and the 6 points he needed to snatch the crown for Ferrari.

Debut for Stewart

BRM gave Jackie Stewart his first taste of F1 in 1965. The Scot won at Monza, and Hill added two more wins to the BRM tally, but Clark ended the year with a perfect score from his best six races.

The introduction of the 3-litre formula in 1966 marked the beginning of a long slow decline for BRM. There were four more wins for the stable in the early 1970s. One of those fell to Jo Siffert in Austria in 1971, helping him to a share of fourth place in the championship. That would be the best return in the post-Hill era, and BRM made its swansong appearance six years later, at Kyalami.

OPPOSITE ABOVE: **Niki Lauda (BRM P160E) in action during the 1973 Swedish Grand Prix, Anderstorp.**

LEFT: **Raymond Mays, one of the co-founders of BRM, pictured at the 1951 British Grand Prix, Silverstone.**

BELOW: **Joakim Bonnier (BRM P25) driving to victory in the 1959 Dutch Grand Prix at Zandvoort. This was the first Grand Prix win for BRM.**

COOPER

Country:	United Kingdom
Date of foundation:	1946
Years in Formula One:	1950, 1952–68
Constructors' Title victories:	1959, 1960

THE REAR-ENGINE REVOLUTION

John Cooper made his name making low-cost cars with chain-driven motorcycle engines for the budget Formula 500 series of the postwar era. He competed in such events, along with the likes of Moss and Ecclestone, but it would be as an innovative manufacturer that Cooper would scale the heights.

The natural home for the 500cc engine was behind the driver, and when Cooper turned his thoughts to competing against Ferrari, Maserati and the other giants, he decided to apply the same principle. The Cooper garage in Surbiton would be the launchpad for the rear-engined revolution.

1955 was a key year, not so much for a breakthrough on the track but for Jack Brabham's arrival from Australia to try his hand against the best drivers in the business. He gravitated towards the Cooper stable and this combination

Five wins for Brabham

The marque was even more dominant the following year, winning six out of nine, Brabham reeling off five straight victories mid-season. He duly claimed his second crown, McLaren taking the runner-up spot. Cooper comfortably retained the Constructors' Cup.

Cooper struggled with the introduction of the new 1.5-litre formula in 1961, and although McLaren took third in the 1962 championship, and Jochen Rindt matched that four years later, the Surbiton stable fell behind the pace set by other marques. Pedro Rodriguez gave the marque its final victory in South Africa, the opening round of the 1967 championship, but the Maserati engine was no match for the Brabham-Repco, and Lotus upped the stakes even further by rolling out the Cosworth DFV that season. Cooper withdrew the following year, though the lineage of F1 success continued through the teams set up by Brabham and McLaren.

would go on to dominate the field. Brabham stole the show at Monaco in 1957, running third in his underpowered Cooper-Climax before suffering a fuel pump problem. He pushed the car over the line for sixth place.

Moss provides maiden victory

Stirling Moss had the honour of giving Cooper its first victory, at the 1958 Argentina GP, though this was for Rob Walker's stable. Maurice Trintignant then gave Cooper its second win, in Monaco, for the same privateer outfit. At that season's Nürburgring race Cooper and Brabham noted the performance of Kiwi Bruce McLaren – winner of the F2 race and fifth overall – and signed him to the F1 team for 1959. Another piece of the jigsaw was thus slotted into place.

Brabham gave the latest T51 model a winning debut at the 1959 Monaco GP. A new 2.5-litre Climax engine finally gave the car the power it needed to compete with the best, and at 458kg it had a considerable weight advantage over the front-engined opposition. Brabham also won at Aintree, and in the decider at Sebring had to resort to muscle power once again, pushing the T51 across the line for fourth place. He took the title by 4 points from Brooks's Ferrari. Moss had given Rob Walker two wins that year in a T51, and McLaren's victory in the US meant a Cooper had taken the chequered flag in five of the eight European rounds.

OPPOSITE ABOVE: **John Cooper, founder of the marque.**

OPPOSITE BELOW: **Alan Rees (Cooper T81-Maserati) achieved ninth position in the 1967 British Grand Prix at Silverstone.**

ABOVE: **Stirling Moss driving a Cooper Alta in the 1953** Daily Express **Meeting, also at Silverstone.**

DELAGE

Country:	France
Date of foundation:	1905
Years in Formula One:	0
Constructors' Title victories:	0

SETTING THE STANDARDS

Delage enjoyed huge success in the 1920s, a period in which French marques were in the vanguard of motor sport. The company was founded by ex-Peugeot engineer Louis Delage in 1905, and within a few years it was building its own engines and body parts, and competing in Grand Prix events. René Thomas won the 1914 Indianapolis 500 in a Delage, averaging over 82mph. A decade later the same man drove a Delage to a new world record of over 143mph, eclipsing the previous mark by 10mph.

Hot work for Benoist

Delage virtually swept the board at the two prewar British Grands Prix, run at Brooklands in 1926 and 1927. Robert Senechal and Louis Wagner shared the spoils in the inaugural race, with Robert Benoist also needing temporary respite on his way to taking third. One of the reasons for the shared drives was a design problem which had the exhaust pipe running too close to the drivers' feet. Trays of iced water were kept on hand to cool the scorched and blistered soles.

In 1927 Delage fielded the 15-S8, which not only had a superb straight-eight engine, but also gave the drivers

considerably more comfort as the exhaust system had been rerouted. There was a clean sweep at Brooklands, Benoist this time coming out on top. It was a golden year for both driver and manufacturer, as they also won the French, Spanish and Italian Grands Prix. Benoist received the Légion d'Honneur for his remarkable achievements.

By the 1930s, Italian and German marques had taken over, and Delage, in financial difficulties, withdrew from motor sport. The company went into liquidation in 1935, though the name lived on until the early 1950s, produced by Delahaye.

TOP: **Edmond Bourlier (Delage 15S8), driving to second position in the 1927 French Grand Prix, Montlhery, Paris.**

ABOVE: **1926 British Grand Prix, Brooklands. Robert Senechal/Louis Wagner (Delage 15S8) lead Albert Divo (Talbot 700) (Senechal/ Wagner finished in first position).**

OPPOSITE ABOVE: **1932 British Empire Trophy, Brooklands, Great Britain. The winner was John Cobb, seen here at the wheel of the Delage V12/LSR that he drove.**

OPPOSITE BELOW: **1936 Junior Car Club 200 mile race, Donington Park, England. Dick Seaman, the winner, driving a Delage 15S8.**

FERRARI

Country:	Italy
Date of foundation:	1946
Years in Formula One:	1950–

Constructors' Title victories: 1961, 1964, 1975, 1976, 1977, 1979, 1982, 1983, 1999, 2000, 2001, 2002, 2003, 2004, 2007, 2008

THE STANDARD BEARERS OF F1

No marque encapsulates the glamour, style and thrill of Grand Prix racing like Ferrari. It is the only constructor to have contested every world championship, but the magic of Ferrari is not based on mere longevity, or even success on the track. When Michael Schumacher lifted the title in 2000, the beginning of a five-year period of domination, it ended a 21-year barren streak in the Drivers' championship; yet even when Ferrari found race victories, let alone championships, hard to come by, it remained the brand with the greatest cachet in motor sport.

Enzo Ferrari enjoyed moderate success as a driver with Alfa Romeo in the 1920s. At a race in Ravenna in 1923, an Italian couple presented him with a badge which their fighter pilot son had carried with him during WWI. It bore the famous prancing horse motif – an emblem of spirit and power – which would become synonymous with Ferrari.

Split with Alfa

Enzo Ferrari's first foray into team ownership came in the 1930s, when he began running semi-works Alfas from a base in Modena. With the legendary Tazio Nuvolari at the wheel he enjoyed some success against the mighty German marques which dominated that era. By 1939 Ferrari harboured plans to go his own way, but the outbreak of war deferred the appearance of the first true Ferrari for almost a decade. The debut came at the 1948 Monaco GP, Ferrari running a remodelled V12 sports car.

In 1949 Ferrari signed Alberto Ascari and Luigi Villoresi from rivals Maserati, further strengthening a driver line-up that already included Raymond Sommer and Giuseppe

Farina. Farina departed to Alfa for the inaugural world championship the following year and lifted the title. Ascari finished fifth in what was a transitional season, Ferrari moving from the supercharged 125 to an unblown 4.5-litre unit. By the end of the year it was on the pace with the dominant Alfa 158, and being less thirsty than the supercharged Alfetta, things looked good for 1951. Alfa squeezed home in that title race too, but this time with Ascari and José Froilán González breathing down their necks. The 'Pampas Bull' gave Ferrari its first championship win that year, at Silverstone. Ascari won the next two rounds to complete a hat-trick for the marque.

Ascari dominant

Alfa's withdrawal left the way clear, and a Ferrari crossed the line first in every European round of the 1952 championship, Ascari becoming the team's first world champion. Five more victories in 1953 saw him retain his crown.

Ferrari fell behind when the 2.5-litre formula was introduced in 1954, but the arrival of Fangio two years later gave the marque its third championship. That was with a modified version of the Vittorio Jano-designed Lancia D50, Ferrari having taken the car over when Lancia withdrew from F1 in 1955. Lancia-Ferraris also appeared in 1957, but it was in the new Dino 246 that Mike Hawthorn pipped Stirling Moss to lift the 1958 title.

'Sharknose'

Ferrari was one of the last to embrace the rear-engined revolution, but in 1961, with the introduction of the 1.5-litre formula, it ruled the roost with the new V6 'sharknose'. Phil Hill and Wolfgang von Trips fought a thrilling championship duel, which the American won after von Trips' fatal accident in the penultimate round at Monza. That took the gloss off Ferrari's first Constructors' title, three years after the introduction of that award.

John Surtees snatched the title from Graham Hill and Jim Clark in Mexico, the climax of the 1964 season, but when the 3-litre era arrived in 1966, Ferrari struggled. In 1970 Jacky Ickx gave Ferrari the runner-up spot when he failed to overhaul Jochen Rindt's points total, the Austrian having lost his life at Monza. Clay Regazzoni finished third that year, and four years later it was the Swiss's turn to narrowly miss out as Fittipaldi got the better of him in a final-race decider.

OPPOSITE ABOVE: **2006 Scuderia Ferrari 248 F1 launch, Mugello, Italy, 24 January 2006.**

OPPOSITE BELOW: **Scuderia Ferrari boss Enzo Ferrari stands with his chief designer Mauro Forghieri, as they look over the Ferrari 312 chassis at the 1967 Italian Grand Prix, Monza.**

BELOW: **Luigi Villoresi (Ferrari 375) competing at the 1951 French Grand Prix, Reims-Gueux.**

The Lauda era

Niki Lauda was Ferrari's unheralded second-string at the start of that year, by the end he had established his racing credentials, and in 1975 he cruised to the title, Ferrari's first in 11 years. Lauda lost out by a single point to James Hunt in the famous 1976 Ferrari-McLaren battle, in which the Austrian recovered from the horrific fireball crash at the Nürburgring. Consistency brought Lauda and Ferrari another championship in 1977, and two years later the team scored a championship one-two, emulating the successes of 1952 and 1961. This was the dawn of the ground-effect era, and although the Ferrari 312T4 wasn't at the head of the new game, it was strong and reliable, and in Gilles Villeneuve and Jody Scheckter the team boasted a hugely talented driver line-up. The South African took the championship, garnering four more points than his Canadian team-mate.

Enzo's death

There were two Constructors' titles in the 1980s, but by the time Enzo Ferrari died – in 1988 at the age of 90 – McLaren and Williams were enjoying greater success. Alain Prost did win five races in 1990, the year in which he clashed with former McLaren team-mate Senna at Suzuka, an incident that handed the crown to the Brazilian. Prost was driving the John Barnard-designed Ferrari 641 that year, but it was over the next decade that the team would lay the groundwork, which

would put Ferrari back to the forefront of F1. Frenchman Jean Todt, who had led Peugeot to a string of sports car titles, joined as team principal in 1993. A trio of ex-Benetton men, who had won back-to-back world championships in 1994 and 1995, were then recruited to the Maranello cause. Rory Byrne took over from Barnard as chief designer, Ross Brawn was installed as technical director, and in Michael Schumacher the team had the man who had succeeded Prost and Senna as the best in the business.

Five-year juggernaut

In 1997 Schumacher went a step too far in trying to secure his first title with Ferrari, failing in his attempt to take Jacques Villeneuve out in the decider at Jerez. Three years later Schumacher won nine races as Ferrari edged McLaren into the minor placings. There was yet another Constructors' title, too, Maranello's first double for 21 years. For the next four years Ferrari pulverised the opposition. Apart from 2003, when the team's winning margin was 2 points in the Drivers'

BELOW: **Niki Lauda (Ferrari 312T) on his way to winning the 1975 Monaco Grand Prix, Monte Carlo.**

OPPOSITE LEFT: **Fernando Alonso celebrates on the podium after finishing third at the Brazil Grand Prix in 2013.**

OPPOSITE RIGHT: **Alonso (front) leaves the pit lane during practice for the Korean Grand Prix, October 2010.**

Championship and 14 in the Constructors' race, the gaps were enormous. In 2002 Schumacher notched a record 144 points to take the title in the shortest time ever, and Ferrari became the first team to break the 200-point mark. Two years later the team raised the bar still further as the champion scored 148 points and Ferrari 262, more than double the total of runner-up, BAR. After ceding the crown to Renault for two years, Ferrari was back on top in 2007, Kimi Räikkönen's championship victory helping Maranello secure yet another double. Celebrations began when Felipe Massa took the chequered flag in the final race at Interlagos in 2008, but the champagne went flat as the team learnt that Lewis Hamilton had snatched fifth place at the death, and with it the title by a single point. A 16th Constructors' Championship softened the blow, Ferrari stretching its lead over Williams to seven in the all-time list. 2009 was a major disappointment, Räikkönen finishing sixth in the championship, while Massa's season was cut short by a serious injury. Ferrari dropped to fourth in the Constructors' race, its worst showing since the early 1990s, but there were hopes for improved fortunes in 2010 as Massa regained full fitness and two-time champion Fernando Alonso arrived to replace Räikkönen. The decision to favour title-chasing Alonso over Massa, notably at the German GP,

sparked a team orders row and landed Ferrari with a $100,000 fine. Alonso had been gifted seven points at Hockenheim; when he lined up for the Abu Dhabi decider his lead was eight. A narrow win would have left a sour taste in the mouth. In the event, Ferrari blew the title with a tactical error, bringing Alonso into the pits on Lap 15 when he was lying fourth. Shadowing Mark Webber's move backfired as Alonso got stuck in midfield and crossed the line seventh. Race winner Sebastian Vettel had turned a 15-point deficit over the Spaniard into a 4-point advantage. Instead of building on that near-miss, Ferrari fell off the pace. Heads rolled when the 2011 F150° failed to deliver, ex-McLaren man Pat Fry taking over as technical director, having only joined the backroom team in the off-season. Ferrari, he said, had become too conservative, and a more creative, innovative approach would be needed to compete with Red Bull and his former Woking-based employer. The runner-up spot in both championships in 2012 was a forward step, and for many Alonso was the pick of the drivers in getting within a whisker of championship winner Vettel in a car that was lagging in the development race. Alonso was again Vettel's closest challenger in 2013, a distant second this time, while the team was pipped for the constructors' runner-up spot by Mercedes.

FORCE INDIA

Country:	United Kingdom
Date of foundation:	2008
Years in Formula One:	2008–
Constructors' Title victories:	0

PUTTING INDIA ON THE F1 MAP

The genesis of Force India can be traced back to the team Eddie Jordan fronted in the 1990s. It morphed into MF1 Racing when acquired by the Russian-backed Midland Group, and appeared briefly under the Spyker banner in 2006 and 2007 when the Dutch sports car company took a controlling interest. The following year saw the birth of Force India, billionaire industrialist Vijay Mallya heading the team that drew a blank in its first campaign. Mallya assumed the principal's role in 2009, when a new deal with Mercedes helped power Giancarlo Fisichella to take pole at Spa. Force India had its first podium, Fisichella immediately following his second place in Belgium with a highly creditable fourth at Monza. They were the only scoring races, an aggregate haul of 13 points for the season showing that the curve was upward, if modestly inclined. 'Every little step forward in this challenging environment is a gigantic step forward for India,' said Mallya, determined to put the country on the map as a Formula One team as well as grand prix host.

In 2010 the team just lost out to Williams for sixth spot in the constructors' race, with Adrian Sutil responsible for the lion's share of the 68-point haul. He delivered three top-six finishes. Force India consolidated its midfield position in 2011, Sutil again leading the way, this time ahead of rookie Paul di Resta, who was promoted from test-reserve duties. The team ended the year four points shy of fifth-placed Renault. Nico Hulkenberg took Sutil's berth for 2012, another internal promotion that gave the outfit a duo of exciting young bloods. Each recorded a best finish just outside the podium places – Hulkenberg in Belgium, di Resta in Singapore – and together they cracked the 100-point barrier, though a strong showing by Sauber meant they dropped a place in the final constructors' standings. The loss of Hulkenberg to Sauber at the end of that campaign was a blow, following the departure of technical director James Key to the same rival. Andrew Green, once of Red Bull, had taken Key's place in 2011. His third season in charge of the backroom team saw the returning Sutil this time having to play second fiddle to di Resta. Their combined 77-point haul represented the first retrograde step, and both drivers were dropped for 2014. Hulkenberg was welcomed back into the fold, partnering Sergio Pérez, whose rising-star status had taken a knock in his one-season spell with McLaren.

The distinctive orange, green and white livery makes Force India readily identifiable on race day, and this still relatively young, Silverstone-based outfit has ambitions to build on that solitary podium gained in 2009. 'I have always been crazy about Formula One,' says Vijay Mallya, adding: 'The more passion, the better the performance.'

BELOW: **British driver Paul di Resta pictured during qualifying for the Korean Formula One Grand Prix in October 2013.**

JAGUAR

Country:	United Kingdom
Date of foundation:	1999
Years in Formula One:	2000–04
Constructors' Title victories: 0	

SHORT-LIVED PERIOD AS F1 TEAM

In 1997 three-times world champion Jackie Stewart entered F1 as a team boss, partnered, unsurprisingly, by Ford, with whom he had enjoyed such spectacular success three decades earlier. The highlight for the fledgling team came with Johnny Herbert's victory at the 1999 European GP. A year later Ford bought Stewart out and entered the 2000 championship rebranded as Jaguar, which was a Ford subsidiary. There were high hopes for the Milton Keynes-based team as the blue-and-white livery of Stewart-Ford gave way to the green of Jaguar, but the next five years were to be fraught with disappointment. Personnel changes – including Stewart's departure as team principal before the start of the 2000 season – didn't help.

Irvine delivers first podium

Eddie Irvine, runner-up to Schumacher in 1999, arrived from Ferrari, but his 4 points represented the entire haul for the debut season. Irvine did give the team its first podium finish, at Monaco in 2001, and the Ulsterman repeated that achievement at Monza a year later, but the successes were few and far between; Jaguar's return for those two campaigns was just 17 points.

Mark Webber and Christian Klien between them could manage just five sixth-place finishes in the following two seasons. That meant a five-year haul of just 49 points from 85 races. In September 2004 it was announced that the team was being sold to one of its sponsors, Red Bull, the energy drink company owned by Austrian billionaire Dietrich Mateschitz.

ABOVE: **Eddie Irvine gave Jaguar their first podium finish by coming third at the 2001 Monaco Grand Prix.**

BELOW: **Johnny Herbert (Jaguar R1) during qualifying for the 2000 Belgian Grand Prix. He completed the race in eighth position.**

JORDAN

Country:	United Kingdom
Date of foundation:	1981
Years in Formula One:	1991–2005
Constructors' Title victories: 0	

THE CHARISMATIC IRISHMAN

A number of top drivers got their big break with Eddie
Jordan's team, including Barrichello, Irvine, and both
Schumacher brothers. Jordan entered F1 in 1991, a decade
after the enterprising, charismatic Irishman established his
outfit. It was a respectable debut, with Andrea de Cesaris and
Bertrand Gachot both getting in the points in Montreal, in
what was only the fifth outing for Gary Anderson's impressive
Jordan 191. When Gachot was jailed following an altercation
with a taxi driver, Jordan fielded a new young tyro at Spa,
Michael Schumacher. The future champion retired after
outqualifying de Cesaris, and was soon being wooed by
Benetton, much to the annoyance of the Jordan boss.

Yamaha power proved underwhelming in 1992, and a
Hart V-10 unit was secured for the following season, as was
Rubens Barrichello. With better luck the Brazilian might have
garnered more than the 2 points for fifth at Suzuka. Just

behind him that day was Eddie Irvine, who marked his F1 debut by trading blows with Senna as well as scoring a point.

Barrichello puts Jordan on podium

Only drivers from the big four – Benetton, Williams, McLaren and Ferrari – finished ahead of Barrichello in 1994, his 19-point haul including third place at the Pacific GP, Jordan's first podium finish. He also gave the team its first pole, at Spa, where he had a spell in front before spinning off. Irvine might have been up with his team-mate had he not been hit with a three-race ban for his part in a pile-up at the season's curtain-raiser at Interlagos.

Peugeot provided the power for the next three years, but it was when Jordan switched to a Mugen-Honda unit in 1998 that the team registered its first victory. Damon Hill won an accident-littered race at Spa, with team-mate Ralf Schumacher making it a famous one-two. It would be Hill's 22nd and final victory, while Jordan's first had come at the 259th attempt.

Frentzen takes third in title race

Things got even better in 1999 as Heinz-Harald Frentzen arrived from Williams, with Schumacher going in the opposite direction. Frentzen won at Magny-Cours and Monza and finished third in the championship, behind Häkkinen and Irvine. Only McLaren and Ferrari headed Jordan in the Constructors' race.

1999 was to be Jordan's high watermark. The team's only other victory came in the 2003 Brazilian GP, where in the confusion of a red-flagged race Fisichella was awarded second place to Räikkönen. A subsequent FIA inquiry reversed that decision, and the Finn did the presentation honours at the next race. It was Fisichella's maiden success.

Early in 2005 it was announced that the team was being taken over by the Midland Group. It continued to run as Jordan for the duration of that season, but a colourful 15-year chapter was brought to an end as MF1 Racing took its place on the grid at the start of the 2006 series.

OPPOSITE ABOVE: **Nick Heidfeld, Jordan Ford EJ14. Formula One testing Imola, Italy, February 2004.**

OPPOSITE BELOW: **Eddie Jordan sits in the cockpit of an EJ13 as the team celebrated its 200th Grand Prix at the 2003 Brazilian Grand Prix, Interlagos, São Paulo.**

BELOW: **Heinz-Harald Frentzen, (Jordan 199 Mugen-Honda) driving to victory in the 1999 French Grand Prix, Magny-Cours.**

LOTUS

Country:	**United Kingdom**
Date of foundation:	1956
Years in Formula One:	1958–94, 2010–

Constructors' Title victories: 1963, 1965, 1968, 1970, 1972, 1973, 1978

CHAPMAN THE GREAT INNOVATOR

It is rare for an F1 marque to rise to the top of the sport, then, after a period in the doldrums, sweep all before it once again. That is exactly what Lotus did in the 1960s and '70s, though it actually competed at the top level in five decades.

The man behind Lotus was Colin Chapman, one of the greatest innovators in the history of motor sport. In 1954, two years after founding Lotus, he drove a Mark 8 model to victory on the undercard to the British GP. With its spaceframe chassis, the Lotus 8 was beautifully engineered, a sign of things to come when Chapman made his bow in F1 four years later.

The debut season saw Graham Hill and Cliff Allison compete in the Lotus 12, Chapman's first single-seater. Allison outshone the future champion, taking fourth at Spa, then, in the new Lotus 16, vying for the lead at the Nürburgring when his radiator sprang a leak.

Chapman follows Cooper's lead

Hill and new partner Innes Ireland suffered a string of retirements in 1959, but the next generation model, the Lotus 18, became a serious contender. Chapman, noting Cooper's success, saw that rear-mounted engines represented the way forward. It was Moss who gave the marque its maiden win, however, driving a Rob Walker Lotus

18 to victory at Monaco in 1960. Team Lotus fielded a number of drivers that year, and although Ireland earned plaudits for 18 points and fourth in the championship, it was a young Scot, with 8 points from six outings, who would have a much greater impact on Lotus and F1. Over the next eight years, until his death in an F2 race at Hockenheim in 1968, Jim Clark and Lotus formed a formidable partnership. Apart from winning the title in 1963 and 1965, on both occasions with perfect scores, Clark might also have won in 1962 and 1964 had his car been more reliable.

First monocoque

Chapman consistently produced vehicles worthy of the greatest driver of the era. In 1962 he introduced the Lotus 25, the first F1 car with a monocoque chassis. It was both lighter and more rigid and, unsurprisingly, was soon copied by other

chassis designers. Its arrival signalled the death-knell for the spaceframe chassis.

In 1967 the Lotus 49, with a new Ford engine, was unveiled. With a little prodding from Chapman, Ford had agreed to add some glamour to their brand by producing a racing engine. For one year it was agreed that Lotus would have exclusive use of the Cosworth DFV unit, and at Zandvoort 1967 Clark gave the engine the first of over 150 victories. After the Scot's death the following year, Graham Hill gave Lotus its third championship, and the 49 was also the vehicle for the last privateer GP victory, Jo Siffert winning at Brands Hatch for Rob Walker.

Chapman was at the forefront of experiments with wings and stalk-mounted aerofoils. There were safety concerns over the earliest modifications, but it was the birth of the downforce era that would soon become common F1 currency.

Jochen Rindt became the sport's first posthumous champion in 1970, taking five wins in the wedge-shaped Lotus 72 before losing his life at Monza. Chapman was already grooming a new young star, Emerson Fittipaldi, and two years later the Brazilian became F1's youngest champion in the latest incarnation of the 72 model.

Ground-effect revolution

The final golden period came six years later, when the Lotus 79 came on stream and Mario Andretti and Ronnie Peterson took a championship one-two. Chapman's design created a vacuum, which literally sucked the car onto the track; soon all F1 marques were studying the 'ground-effect' principle. Chapman gave Nigel Mansell his debut in 1980, but succumbed to a heart attack before his latest protégé topped the podium. Elio de Angelis and Ayrton Senna brought Lotus some respectable results in the mid-1980s, but the marque never recaptured the heights it had attained under its inspirational leader, and folded in 1994.

Lotus return

Lotus made a surprise return to the sport in 2010, though this was a brand new team formed by a Malaysian consortium led by Tony Fernandes. The backers included car giant Proton – Lotus' owners – which made naming the new outfit a simple task. Jarno Trulli and Heikki Kovalainen were signed to spearhead Lotus' assault on the championship in its new incarnation. There were no points finishes, but Lotus was the pick of the three new entrants.

In 2011 Lotus F1 Racing became Team Lotus as Fernandes sought to break the shackles of a licensing agreement with Group Lotus. That led to a messy row as Group Lotus bought into Renault's F1 team, the latter seeking to scale back its role to engine supplier only. It meant Team Lotus – running on Renault power – lined up against Lotus Renault in 2011, with both outfits crying foul and calling their lawyers. The matter resolved itself as Fernandes acquired another famous name in motor sport, Caterham, and announced that his F1 team for 2012 would run under that name. Meanwhile, the Lotus team – minus the Renault appendage – recruited returning former champion Kimi Raïkkönen for its 2012 campaign, and his consistency helped the team to a creditable fourth in the constructors' battle. Raikkonen and Grosjean combined to match that in 2013 – just 35 points behind runner-up Mercedes – but there were serious concerns about the team's financial health. Kimi claimed he hadn't been paid and left for Ferrari, and the choice of Maldonado as his replacement – a driver bearing considerable sponsorship money – provided further evidence that all was not well at Enstone.

OPPOSITE ABOVE: **Romain Grosjean during practice for the Brazilian Grand Prix in November 2013.**

OPPOSITE BELOW: **Jim Clark (Team Lotus) with team boss Colin Chapman pictured at the 1963 Dutch Grand Prix, Zandvoort.**

BELOW: **Cliff Allison in a Lotus 12-Climax at the 1958 Belgian Grand Prix, Spa-Francorchamps.**

MASERATI

Country:	Italy
Date of foundation:	1926
Years in Formula One:	1950–58
Constructors' Title victories:	0

THE FAMILY BUSINESS

One of the most famous names in motor sport was born in 1914 when Alfieri Maserati, along with brothers Ernesto and Ettore, founded a garage business in Bologna. It would be 12 years before the company built its first racing car, the Tipo 26, which sported an 8-cylinder, 1.5-litre supercharged engine. It made its debut at the 1926 Targa Florio, with Alfieri himself at the wheel. He finished ninth overall in what was a Formula Libre event, winning the 1500cc class. This race also saw the famous trident badge, a design inspired by a statue of Neptune in the main square at Bologna, adorn a Maserati for the first time.

Alfieri Maserati died in 1932, aged 44. This was a decade in which the marque scored a number of Grand Prix victories, with the likes of Nuvolari and Varzi at the wheel, though the era was dominated by Alfa Romeo, Mercedes and Auto Union.

OSCA founded by Maserati family

Financial pressures caused the remaining brothers to sell out to the Orsi family in 1937, though they secured a contract to continue working for the company for the next decade. The company relocated to Modena and focused its attention on building road cars, though Maseratis did win the Indianapolis 500 in 1939 and 1940. When the contract expired, the brothers were keen to return to racing in their own right and a new company, OSCA, was formed in 1947.

The Maserati 4CLT won on its first outing, the 1948 San Remo GP, with Alberto Ascari at the wheel. Ascari and Luigi Villoresi were the works drivers, and they dominated that year's British GP, despite arriving late and having to start from the back of the grid. Maserati suffered a huge blow when Enzo Ferrari signed both drivers for 1949. That year Baron Emmanuel de Graffenried won at Silverstone with a privately entered Maserati, and in the early years of the world championship Maseratis would be the popular choice for privateers keen to slug it out with the works teams. Stirling Moss was among those who took this route.

Fangio scores maiden win

Ferrari dominated the 1952 and 1953 championship races, which were run to an F2 formula, but by the back end of the latter season Fangio, Gonzalez and Marimon were pushing hard for Maserati. The marque finally scored its maiden victory at Monza, Fangio coming out on top after a thrilling duel with Ascari, though the latter already had his second title in the bag.

Fangio won the first two rounds of the 1954 championship in the famous 250F, one of the most successful cars of the 2.5-litre era, but he was merely biding his time until his new employers, Mercedes, were ready with their new hardware.

For the 1957 season Maserati managed to re-sign the four-times world champion. It would be a glorious F1 swansong for both driver and manufacturer. Fangio won four of the seven European races to relegate Stirling Moss to second place in the title race for the third year running. But within a year a funding crisis led Maserati to withdraw from F1 and concentrate on its road car operation.

OPPOSITE ABOVE: **Juan Manuel Fangio (Maserati 250F) en route to victory in the 1957 German Grand Prix, Nürburgring.**

OPPOSITE BELOW: **Juan Manuel Fangio (Maserati), first, and Mike Hawthorn (Ferrari), second, on the podium at the 1957 German Grand Prix.**

BELOW: **José Froilán González (Maserati A6GCM), competing in the 1952 Italian Grand Prix, Monza.**

MATRA

Country:	France
Date of foundation:	1964
Years in Formula One:	1968–72
Constructors' Title victories: 1969	

FRANCE MAKES ITS MARK

Matra takes its name from French aerospace company Mécanique Avion Traction. Matra boss Marcel Chassagny provided hardware and financial support for the racing ventures of a friend, René Bonnet. When the latter got into financial difficulties in 1964, company executive Jean-Luc Lagardere saw it as an opportunity to go down the works path. Matra Sport was formed.

After a brief flirtation with F3 and F2, Matra, with backing from Elf, took the step up to the top division in 1968. The team ran its own V12-powered car, Jean-Pierre Beltoise heading the Matra Sports entry. The company also supplied a car to Ken Tyrrell and his young star, Jackie Stewart, who operated as Matra International. Stewart, running on Cosworth power, fared much the better, though his three wins weren't enough to wrest the title from Graham Hill and Lotus.

Championship at second attempt

For 1969 Matra concentrated on sports cars, leaving Tyrrell and Stewart to fly the company flag in F1. The Scot took six victories to give Matra the championship at only the second attempt. Beltoise, Stewart's team-mate that year, provided able support, his contribution helping put Matra well clear of Brabham and Lotus in the Constructors' race.

At the end of the year Matra's automotive division was sold to Chrysler France, and politics dictated that Matra

couldn't compete with the Ford DFV. The company's insistence on using its own V12 unit was enough to end the deal with Tyrrell. Matra immediately went on the slide, Beltoise only just making the top ten in 1970.

Powering Ligier to victory

Chris Amon spearheaded Matra's next two campaigns. The New Zealander won first time out in 1971, in Argentina, though this was a non-title race as a precursor to that country's return as a championship venue. Third place in Spain was his best effort when it counted. On top of the podium that day was the man Matra had let go and who was now on his way to a second title with Tyrrell.

There was another lone podium for Amon in 1972, when the team wound down its F1 operation by fielding just one car. Matra disappeared from the grid at the end of the year, concentrating its efforts on sports cars. That brought a return to winning ways, Henri Pescarolo and Graham Hill winning at

OPPOSITE ABOVE: **Jackie Stewart (Matra MS10-Ford) leaves the podium after the 1968 Dutch Grand Prix. He won despite wearing a plaster cast on his right hand.**

OPPOSITE BELOW: **Chris Amon (Matra-Simca MS120C) in action during the 1972 South African Grand Prix at Kyalami.**

ABOVE: **Jackie Stewart (Matra MS10-Ford) on his way to winning the 1968 Dutch Grand Prix, Zandvoort.**

Le Mans, Matra retaining the 24-hour classic title in the following two years. In 1973 and 1974 Pescarolo was partnered by Gerard Larrousse.

In 1974 Matra announced it was quitting the sport and designer Gérard Ducarouge joined the new Ligier team, which also took over the Matra V12 engines. Matra powered Jacques Laffite to Ligier's maiden victory, at Anderstorp in 1977, and the Frenchman also won in Austria and Canada four years later.

McLAREN

Country:	United Kingdom
Date of foundation:	1966
Years in Formula One:	1966–
Constructors' Title victories: 1974, 1984, 1985, 1988, 1989, 1990, 1991, 1998	

DENNIS BUILDS ON McLAREN'S DREAM

Bruce McLaren was F1's youngest-ever race winner until Fernando Alonso's victory in Hungary in 2003. A protégé of fellow Antipodean Jack Brabham, McLaren followed in the footsteps of the three-times champion by establishing his own team in 1966. It was the start of the 3-litre era, and McLaren struggled to find a unit that would do justice to the Robin Herd-designed M2B. While 'Black Jack' won his third world crown with the superb Brabham-Repco, the Kiwi had just 3 points to show for his season's efforts.

It was an inauspicious start, but better times lay ahead. In 1968 he signed reigning champion and compatriot Denny Hulme – from Brabham. Although Hulme would win in Italy and Canada, and finish third to McLaren's fifth in the championship, it was the team boss who gave the team its maiden victory, at Spa. He was helped by the fact that Jackie Stewart's Matra-Ford ran out of juice with the line almost in sight, but McLaren was on its way. Hulme scored the only victory of 1969, though McLaren's consistency put him third behind Stewart and Ickx in the title race.

McLaren killed at Goodwood

McLaren had contested just three rounds of the 1970 championship – finishing second at Jarama – when he was killed while testing one of his CanAm cars at Goodwood. He was 33. Hulme battled on for fifth place in the championship.

Teddy Mayer, with whom McLaren had formed Bruce McLaren Motor Racing Ltd in 1963, took the reins for the next decade, and it was under his leadership that the team won its first Drivers' and Constructors' titles. In 1972 the team, now backed by Yardley, was competitive again, the pick of the bunch apart from Fittipaldi in the Lotus 72D and Stewart's Tyrrell-Ford. It was a similar story in 1973, though Gordon Coppuck's M23, which made its debut at Kyalami, looked a winner. And with Fittipaldi at the wheel in 1974, it was. Now running as Marlboro Team Texaco, McLaren did the double, edging Regazzoni and Ferrari in both championships. The Brazilian won only three races but was consistently in the points.

Ferrari got their revenge in 1975, but a year later the M23 was still the car to beat, this time in James Hunt's hands. Hunt's third place in torrential conditions in Japan was enough to pip Lauda by a single point.

Dennis takes over

McLaren was behind the game in the ground-effect era, and it would be eight years before the team was back on top. Ron Dennis and designer John Barnard were the key men in McLaren's spectacular run of success in the 1980s. Dennis had been running Marlboro's F2 team, Project 4, and in 1980 the sponsor brokered the deal which saw the two outfits merge. Dennis brought Barnard with him, and the latter produced MP4/1, F1's first carbon-fibre monocoque. Lauda was coaxed out of retirement, TAG-Porsche came on board to provide the turbo unit, and in 1984 this combination took the title. Lauda won by half a point from team-mate Prost, with the rest nowhere, the duo between them winning 12 races.

Prost made it a McLaren hat-trick by winning in 1985 and 1986, though in the latter season the Williams-Honda, which ran away with the Constructors' Championship, was the class act of the field. By 1988 McLaren had the benefit of Honda power, and went on to win four successive titles, Senna lifting three of them, Prost the other.

Mercedes deal

Honda's withdrawal in 1992 put McLaren on the back foot for a couple of seasons, though Senna still managed five wins and the runner-up spot with Ford power in 1993. A new era dawned in 1995, when Mercedes, back in F1 as an engine supplier, agreed a deal with Dennis's team. It would be two years before the new partnership registered a win, Coulthard's victory in the 1997 curtain-raiser ending a four-year barren spell. But Mika Häkkinen won 13 races in the following two campaigns to win back-to-back titles, Coulthard weighing in with three victories as he finished third and fourth.

McLaren came closest to halting the Schumacher-Ferrari five-year juggernaut when Kimi Räikkönen lost out by just 2 points in 2003. In 2005 the 'Iceman' was dogged by ill-luck, yet still managed seven wins in the MP4/20. McLaren won ten of the 19 races but missed out to Alonso and Renault in both championships.

It was all change in 2007, Räikkönen moving to Ferrari and team-mate Juan Pablo Montoya quitting F1 altogether.

The team paired double world champion Fernando Alonso with rising British star Lewis Hamilton, and looked set to record a famous double. Räikkönen spoiled the party by snatching a dramatic 1-point victory in the final race, while a spying scandal cost the team the Constructors' Cup. A frosty relationship between Alonso and Hamilton resulted in the two-time champion returning to Renault after just one year, with Heikki Kovalainen travelling in the opposite direction. A dramatic finale to the 2008 season saw Hamilton snatch the title from Ferrari's Felipe Massa. It brought McLaren a twelfth Drivers' title, putting the team three wins behind Ferrari in the all-time list. In the close season Ron Dennis announced that he was stepping down from the role of team principal, handing over to Martin Whitmarsh after 27 years at the helm.

It was a difficult baptism for the new man, for it wasn't until the second half of the season that Hamilton wrung two victories from the MP4/24. Things looked more promising for 2010 as Button joined the team, giving McLaren the two most recent champions in its line-up. The team still finished a distant second to Red Bull in both championships in 2011, and McLaren's challenge was to catch the team whose design genius Adrian Newey once worked his magic at Woking. 2012 was a curate's egg, seven wins and eight poles, but also a number of gaffes and reliability issues. Hamilton and Button ended the year a distant fourth and fifth, Ferrari bumped the team down to third in the constructors' race, and long before the prizes were handed out Whitmarsh learned that Hamilton was off to pastures new. Whitmarsh's own position appeared under threat following a dire 2013 campaign, when the team failed to register a single podium and ended the year a lot nearer to Force India and Sauber than fourth-placed Lotus. It was bad news for Sergio Pérez, dispensed with after one season in favour of Danish rookie Kevin Magnussen. Former Lotus team boss Eric Boullier was brought in to restore McLaren's fortunes, while Ron Dennis returned to his old CEO role in Whitmarsh's stead.

MERCEDES

Country:	Germany
Date of foundation:	1901
Years in Formula One:	1954–55, 2010–
Constructors' Title victories:	0

SHORT-LIVED BUT SPECTACULAR

In the early years of the 20th century, Austrian Daimler dealer Emil Jellinek raced the imported cars under his daughter's name – Mercedes. The famous marque appeared at the birth of Grand Prix racing, the 1906 French GP, staged at Circuit de la Sarthe. Although there was no German victory that day, it wasn't long before the famous three-pointed star, symbolising mastery of land, sea and air, made its mark on motor sport's premier events.

Daimler employee Christian Lautenschlager was the first Mercedes star, winning the 1908 French GP at Dieppe. He kept his factory job and raced only sporadically, which made his celebrated victory in the 1914 French GP – a seven-hour marathon staged at Lyon – all the more remarkable.

Rivalry with Auto Union

After Hitler's rise to power in 1933, Mercedes took up the challenge laid down by the Führer to build world-beating racing cars. It was a propaganda war that also sparked intense internal rivalry between Mercedes and Auto Union.

The two German marques dominated Grand Prix racing from 1934 to the outbreak of WWII, and also vied with each other for the land-speed record.

The new era began when the Hans Nibel-designed W25 was unveiled at the 1934 Eifel GP at the Nürburgring. It transgressed the new 750-kg weight limit and team boss Alfred Neubauer is said to have ordered the paintwork to be stripped, leaving the gleaming aluminium bodywork on show; the legend of the 'Silberpfeile' – Silver Arrows – was born.

Caracciola takes three European titles

The undoubted star of this era was, like Lautenschlager, a former company employee. Rudolf Caracciola was crowned

European champion three times between 1935 and 1938, losing out to Auto Union's Bernd Rosemeyer in 1936. Caracciola's CV included five victories in his home Grand Prix. So disenchanted were the Italians with being reduced to also-rans that in 1939 they ran their races to a 1500cc formula. Mercedes responded by building a scaled-down version of their Grand Prix car and scored a one-two victory. This model never raced again.

Neubauer still the mastermind

Mercedes made a dramatic return to Grand Prix racing in 1954, four years after the inception of the world championship. Neubauer was still at the helm, and Fangio was recruited to head the driver line-up, though the 1951 champion had a couple of outings for Maserati as the new W196 wasn't quite ready for action. Fangio and Karl Kling made it a triumphant return, finishing first and second when the W196 made its debut at Reims. Fangio went on to win three of the next four races, the W196 appearing both in streamlined and open-wheeled form during the course of the season. Silverstone was the only circuit which didn't suit the car, and even here Fangio picked up points for fourth place.

Withdrawal follows Le Mans tragedy

Fangio was joined by Moss in 1955, and the season developed into a two-horse race. Maurice Trintignant's win for Ferrari at Monaco prevented a clean sweep for Mercedes. The British GP at Aintree saw the W196 at its most dominant, Karl Kling and Piero Taruffi following Moss and Fangio home to give Mercedes the top four finishers. The lustre of that triumph was tarnished by events at Le Mans a month earlier, where Pierre Levegh's Mercedes 300 SLR ploughed into a spectators' enclosure, causing over 80 fatalities. Four F1 races were cancelled as a result, and although Fangio comfortably retained his crown, Mercedes withdrew from racing at the end of the year.

Mercedes returned to the sport as engine supplier to the fledgling Sauber team in 1993, switching to McLaren two years later. It was the beginning of a highly successful partnership, which brought Mika Häkkinen successive world championships in 1998 and 1999, and Lewis Hamilton the crown in 2008. A year later, Mercedes was back in business as a team in its own right when it bought a majority stake in Brawn GP, having powered that outfit to both the Drivers' and Constructors' Championships in 2009. If a return to racing after 55 years wasn't dramatic enough, Mercedes GP grabbed the headlines for coaxing 41-year-old Michael Schumacher out of retirement to lead the charge. The first two seasons were steady, rather than spectacular. Mercedes collected a few podiums, courtesy of Schumacher's team-mate Nico Rosberg, and consolidated its place as the fourth best team on the grid behind Red Bull, McLaren and Ferrari. Shanghai 2012 saw Rosberg deliver Mercedes' first victory since 1955. The team struggled to build on that success and slipped to fifth in the constructors' race, but were buoyed by news of Lewis Hamilton's arrival for the new season. He replaced Schumacher, whose three-year comeback yielded but a single podium. Three wins, nine podiums and eight poles represented an excellent return in the first Hamilton-Rosberg season, enough to put Mercedes second in the constructors' standings. A backroom shift for 2014 saw Ross Brawn depart and ex-McLaren man Paddy Lowe arrive to share team principal duties with Toto Wolff. Many people's tip for a serious tilt for the title in 2014.

OPPOSITE ABOVE: **Winner of the 1955 British Grand Prix at Aintree was Stirling Moss, driving a Mercedes Benz W196.**

OPPOSITE BELOW: **The team boss from the 1930s, Alfred Neubauer, was still at the head in 1955, the year that the Mercedes team withdrew from F1.**

BELOW: **Lewis Hamilton in front at the Abu Dhabi Grand Prix in November 2013.**

MINARDI

Country:	Italy
Date of foundation:	1985
Years in Formula One:	1985–2005
Constructors' Title victories: 0	

THE SMALL POPULAR TEAM

Giancarlo Minardi's Faenza-based team was held in high regard during the 20 years in which it competed, F1 fans recognising the achievements of the tiny Italian outfit in a sport dominated by teams with telephone-number budgets.

In 1979 Minardi began building its own cars for the European Formula Two championship, and six years later, as F2 was superseded by F3000, Minardi made the decision to step up to the top table. Pierluigi Martini gave the team its first outing at the 1985 curtain-raiser in Brazil. Minardi ran an outdated Cosworth engine to begin with, and even the introduction of must-have turbo power failed to improve matters significantly.

Martini was dropped from the team, but both he and the Cosworth unit were reinstated for 1988 and they gave Minardi its first point, at the 1988 Detroit GP. A year later Martini and Spain's Luis Perez Sala both scored at Silverstone, and Minardi squeezed into the top ten in the Constructors' race.

OPPOSITE ABOVE: **Paul Stoddart marks the last race for the Minardi F1 team at the Chinese Grand Prix, October, 2005.**

OPPOSITE BELOW: **Christijan Albers (Minardi-Cosworth PS05), in action at the 2005 USA Grand Prix, Indianapolis.**

ABOVE: **Pierluigi Martini (Minardi M185 Motori Moderni) attempting to qualify for the 1985 Monaco Grand Prix, Monte Carlo, during the team's maiden F1 season.**

Martini on front row

On the opening round of the 1990 series, in Phoenix, Martini put the M189 on the front row of the grid, alongside the McLaren of pole-sitter Gerhard Berger. A year later he took M191, now using Ferrari power, to fourth place at both San Marino and Estoril. That helped Minardi to finish seventh in the Constructors' Championship, which would be its best showing.

The next decade saw a succession of changes, both in engine suppliers and drivers, and Minardi became a perennial also-ran, though Christian Fittipaldi did match Martini's achievement by taking fourth at Kyalami in 1993. When Hungarian driver Zsolt Baumgartner finished eighth at Indianapolis in 2004, Minardi fans cheered their first point since Mark Webber's fifth spot at Albert Park two years earlier.

Stepping stone for future stars

Minardi was an early stepping stone for a number of top drivers, including Giancarlo Fisichella, Jarno Trulli and 2005 world champion Fernando Alonso. Financial constraints have always impinged on track performances, however, something not even the deep pockets of airline boss Paul Stoddart, who bought Minardi in 2001, managed to reverse.

In September 2005 the team was sold to Red Bull, which announced it would race two teams in 2006. Die-hard fans petitioned the new owners to retain the Minardi name, but commercial imperatives meant that the new outfit would take to the grid as Scuderia Toro Rosso – Team Red Bull – signalling the end of an era for a much-loved F1 minnow.

RED BULL

Country:	United Kingdom
Foundation:	2004
Years in Formula One:	2005–
Constructors' Title victories:	2010, 2011, 2012, 2013

THE CHARGE TO THE TOP

The rise of Red Bull has arguably been the story of the last decade. Over the years many teams have entered the sport hoping to take on the established outfits. Red Bull is one of the few to have done just that, not merely running with the likes of McLaren and Ferrari but regularly leaving them and the rest of the field trailing in their wheeltracks.

Its roots lie in the team operated by Jackie Stewart and his son in the late 90s. That was reincarnated as Jaguar at the turn of the century, and in 2005 Red Bull was born from those ashes. The name of the famous energy drink company appeared on the grid for the first time that season, and its magnate backer Dietrich Mateschitz, soon showed he was not content with simply making the step up from sponsor to owner. Red Bull made an immediate impact, David Coulthard proving there was life after McLaren by finishing fourth at the Melbourne opener. DC ended the year with a creditable 24 points, Christian Klien providing able support as Red Bull finished the season in seventh spot, ahead of the more established Sauber, Jordan and Minardi outfits.

At the end of the year Red Bull showed their intent to break into the top echelons by recruiting Adrian Newey. The designer of a string of world championship-winning cars with Williams and McLaren ended his eight-year association with Ron Dennis's team, seeking fresh pastures with a smaller but no less ambitious player. Newey's arrival was a major coup as Red Bull geared up for the new 2.4-litre, V8 era. Delighted team boss Christian Horner said the pieces were falling into place for the team to be a race winner within two years. They looked on course as Coulthard gave the team its maiden podium at the 2006 Monaco GP. An aggregate points haul of 24 in 2007 was nothing spectacular, but that season did witness the beginning of Red Bull's productive relationship with Renault as engine supplier, the team having run on Cosworth and Ferrari

power in its first two years. Mark Webber was in the points in nine races in 2008, though fourth was his best return. Coulthard stepped onto the podium in Montreal, one of just two rounds where he registered. Sebastian Vettel starred for Red Bull's sister outfit Toro Rosso that season and was promoted to the senior team for 2009. He pushed Brawn and Jenson Button all the way for the title, putting Red Bull on the top step for the first time in Shanghai. Webber picked up a couple of wins to add to Seb's four; second and fourth respectively in the drivers' championship left Red Bull runner-up to the Ross Brawn-led one-season wonder in the constructors' race.

Red Bull was the car to beat in 2010. The constructors' crown was secured with a race to spare, Vettel clinching the coveted double with victory in the Abu Dhabi finale. Between them he and Webber headed the grid in 15 of the 19 rounds, converting nine of those into maximum points. It was clear that both titles were heading back to Milton Keynes long before the end of the 2011 campaign, and although the constructors' battle was again wrapped up with room to spare the following year, the driver's championship went down to the wire. Vettel ended the season three points clear of Alonso. 2013 brought a fourth double, Vettel and the RB9 proving irresistible in the second half of the season. His 13 wins took Red Bull to 47 victories in its nine-year history.

Webber's departure at the end of 2013 opened the door for compatriot Daniel Ricciardo, promoted from STR five years after Vettel was similarly elevated. The German was the undoubted star, something that caused some spiky moments in his time partnering Webber, and with the Horner-Newey axis driving the team forward, there was no indication that Red Bull was about to surrender its top-dog status any time soon.

OPPOSITE ABOVE: **David Coulthard, Red Bull Racing Cosworth RB1, at the 2005 Japanese Grand Prix, Suzuka.**

OPPOSITE BELOW: **Red Bull boss Dietrich Mateschitz and then team manager Tony Purnell chat by the side of the RB01 during Formula One Testing, November 2004, Barcelona, Spain.**

ABOVE: **Sebastian Vettel celebrates victory at the 2013 Brazilian Grand Prix with team-mate Mark Webber in the background.**

BELOW: **Mark Webber drives during a test run in Spain in 2011.**

RENAULT

Country:	France
Date of foundation:	1898
Years in Formula One:	1977–85, 1989–97, 2002–11
Constructors' Title victories:	2005, 2006

BUILDING ON A LEGEND

The Renault brothers manufactured and raced cars in the great city-to-city spectaculars that predated the Grand Prix era. Marcel Renault was among those who lost their lives in the infamous Paris-Madrid race of 1903, one of several tragic incidents that helped usher in the age of circuit racing. It was a Renault that crossed the line first in the inaugural Grand Prix, staged at Le Mans in 1906. Only 11 of the 32-car field went the distance in the two-day race, Ferenc Szisz's 90hp Renault coming out on top.

Renault departed the racing scene for almost 70 years, the team not making its F1 debut until 1977. Jean-Pierre Jabouille had a few fruitless outings that season, failing to take the turbo-charged RS01 the distance in an era dominated by 3-litre, normally aspirated units. Jabouille and the team notched just 3 points in 1978, but the breakthrough was only one year away. After a few unsuccessful outings for the old RS01, the new RE10 appeared. Jabouille won from pole

position at the team's home GP, at Dijon, team-mate René Arnoux taking third. Although there were no further victories, a Renault headed the grid on four more occasions; it was the dawn of a new era as rival manufacturers took another look at the potential of turbo power.

Prost's maiden victory

Alain Prost came within 7 points of champion Nelson Piquet in 1981, giving Renault another success at the French Grand Prix in Dijon – his maiden victory – and also crossing the line first at Zandvoort and Monza. Two years later the same drivers fought the title race to the wire. Prost went into the final race, Kyalami, with a 2-point cushion, but his turbo blew up and third place for the Brazilian's Brabham was enough to snatch the crown.

Prost was openly critical of the team's failure to maintain the advantage it had enjoyed over its rivals. He departed for a highly successful stint at McLaren, while Renault, after two indifferent seasons, quit the sport. It did continue as an engine supplier, however, and its units powered Williams and Benetton to a string of world titles in the 1990s.

Benetton buy-out

Renault returned as a works team after buying out Benetton in 2000, with Flavio Briatore heading the new enterprise. Jenson Button and Jarno Trulli were feeding off scraps in 2002, a year dominated by Ferrari, but in 2003 Fernando Alonso became the youngest-ever pole-sitter, at Sepang, then in Hungary took over from Bruce McLaren as F1's youngest winner.

Jarno Trulli won at Monaco in 2004, but was dropped at the end of the season, Giancarlo Fisichella arriving to partner Alonso. 2005 was a season of glorious triumph: 15 podiums, including seven wins, helped Alonso become F1's youngest champion in the 56-year history of the event. The last of those, at Shanghai, clinched the Constructors' title for Renault, who edged McLaren by 9 points. The reigning champions continued to dominate the table in 2006, although Ferrari began to close the gap and even inched ahead late in the season. The competition went down to the last race in Brazil, but Renault managed to retain its title by just five points. The team slipped down the rankings in 2007, when Alonso left to join McLaren, but he returned a year later and gave Renault two more wins in 2008.

2009 was a disaster on and off the track. The team scored just one podium finish all year, and also had to face the fall-out from race-fixing allegations arising from Nelson Piquet Jr's crash at the 2008 Singapore GP. The Brazilian maintained that it was a premeditated spill, orchestrated to bring out the safety car and give team-mate Alonso victory. Briatore initially denied the charge – made by a driver who had just been sacked – but Renault later accepted culpability. Briatore and Pat Symonds, the team's director of engineering, departed in a damage-limitation exercise. Renault was put on probation, but pre-empted further sanctions by selling a majority holding of its racing division to Luxembourg-based investment group Genii Capital, the new owners retaining the Renault name for the 2010 campaign.

Group Lotus came on board and the team ran as Lotus Renault in 2011, a season in which it had to contend with the loss of lead driver Robert Kubica to injury. Renault had by now relinquished its remaining stake and in 2012 its name disappeared from the list of constructors, though it continued to power several cars on the grid, including the all-conquering Red Bull and those running under the rebranded Lotus F1 name.

OPPOSITE ABOVE: **Robert Kubica takes part in a training session at Ricardo Tormo racetrack in Cheste, near Valencia, February 2011.**

OPPOSITE BELOW: **Fernando Alonso celebrates Renault's Constructors' Championship victory with Flavio Briatore. Briatore left Renault – and F1 – in 2009 in the wake of a race-fixing scandal surrounding the previous year's Singapore Grand Prix**

BELOW: **British Grand Prix, Silverstone, England, July 1977. Jean-Pierre Jabouille in Renault's debut race.**

BMW SAUBER

Country:	Switzerland
Date of foundation:	1970
Years in Formula One:	1993–
	(as BMW Sauber)
Constructors' Title victories: 0	

THE SWISS SEARCH FOR A BREAKTHROUGH

Peter Sauber's Mercedes-backed team made the step up to F1 in 1993, after a highly successful period in sports cars, which culminated in a world championship-Le Mans double in 1989. The team was in the points on its very first outing, Kyalami 1993, where Finnish driver JJ Lehto brought the Sauber C12 home fifth, albeit two laps behind Senna and Prost. Lehto took a fine fourth at Imola, and team-mate Karl Wendlinger matched that at Monza, helping Sauber to a share of sixth place in the Constructors' Championship. It would set the pattern for the next 13 years: solid midfield consolidation without really threatening to make a major breakthrough.

Heinz-Harald Frentzen took Lehto's seat in 1994, and in his two spells with the team the German would become its most successful driver, notching 48 points in five seasons.

Switch to Ferrari power

In 1997, after running a works Ford engine for two years, Sauber began using Ferrari power, rebadged as Petronas for sponsorship reasons. It was during this long association that Sauber had its best return, Nick Heidfeld and Kimi Räikkönen between them scoring 21 points in 2001. That lifted Sauber to fourth in the table, ahead of Jordan, BAR and Benetton, although the gap between the big three and the rest of the field was immense. Indianapolis 2003 saw Sauber lead a Grand Prix for the first time in its history, Frentzen eventually finishing third to equal the team's best showing.

In the summer of 2005 Peter Sauber sold out to BMW, the latter bringing to an end its partnership with Williams and giving F1 a new name on the grid for 2006. It was also announced that Ferrari were taking up their long-term option on Felipe Massa, who would be replacing Barrichello at Maranello. Having promoted the careers of Räikkönen, Heidfeld and Massa, Sauber proved to be a shrewd judge of new talent in its 13-year involvement with the sport.

A new young star, Robert Kubica, partnered Nick Heidfeld as BMW Sauber led the charge to catch front-runners Ferrari and McLaren in 2007. The team took second in the Constructors' Championship, following a spying row that saw McLaren's points haul expunged. The duo carried on in the same vein in 2008. Kubica got on the podium seven times and topped it in Montreal, the team's maiden success. Heidfeld recorded four second-place finishes, including following his team-mate home in Canada. Kubica ended the season level with Räikkönen, edged out of third place on race wins, while 135 points put the team third behind Ferrari and McLaren in the Constructors' Championship.

BMW quit the sport at the end of a disappointing 2009 season and sold the team back to Peter Sauber, who returned to the front line at the age of 66. The team was registered as BMW Sauber for 2010, though that was an administrative detail as the new cars were Ferrari-powered.

A sponsorship deal with Mexican industrialist Carlos Slim, the world's richest man, gave Sauber a welcome boost going into the 2011 season. It also paved the way for exciting young rookie Sergio Pérez to take his place at motor-sport's top table, the first Mexican driver to compete in the world championship for 30 years. Some scintillating drives in 2012 saw Pérez break into the top 10, and helped Sauber climb to sixth in the constructors' race, trebling their previous year's points tally. It was a mixed blessing, however, as the emerging star was recruited by McLaren as replacement for the departing Hamilton. 2013 was a tale of woe until a mid-season tweak to the C32 allowed new recruit Nico Hulkenberg to show what a fine prospect he is. 50 points in the last eight rounds helped secure seventh spot, but Hulkenberg's return to Force India at the end of the year was a blow.

OPPOSITE ABOVE: **Sauber's Nico Hulkenberg drives in front of Kimi Raikkonen in a Lotus at the 2013 Indian Grand Prix.**

OPPOSITE BELOW: **Peter Sauber, who regained ownership of the team in November 2009.**

BOTTOM: **Karl Wendlinger (Sauber C12 Ilmor) on the way to finishing fourth at the 1993 Italian Grand Prix, Monza.**

BELOW: **Nick Heidfeld, Sauber Petronas C22, leads the pack during the 2003 United States Grand Prix, Indianapolis.**

TORO ROSSO

Country:	Italy
Date of foundation:	2005
Years in Formula One:	2006–
Constructors' Title victories: 0	

JUNIOR TEAM WIN INDEPENDENCE

Just one year on from the 11th-hour deal that saw Red Bull take over Jaguar's F1 berth, the company's billionaire boss Dietrich Mateschitz went on the acquisition trail once again. His purchase of struggling Italian outfit Minardi in 2005 gave him two entrants for the following year's competition. Much to the chagrin of Minardi fans, who had to hoped to see preserved a name that had featured on the grid for two decades, it was announced that the latest phoenix-like transformation would operate under the banner Scuderia Toro Rosso. For the die-hards there was at least consolation in the fact that the new enterprise retained Minardi's old base at Faenza.

Putatively the junior sibling to the main Red Bull division, Toro Rosso registered but a solitary point in its debut season, courtesy of Vitantonio Liuzzi. That was far from discouraging as the cars were running on restricted V10 engines when the front runners had moved to V8 power. Liuzzi's partner, Scott Speed, was dropped midway through the 2007 campaign, paving the way for Sauber reserve Sebastian Vettel to take the seat in the back half of the season. The highlight was a fourth place in China, and Vettel was duly signed full-time for 2008. The German scored in nine outings, capped by a maiden pole and victory for the team – its sole win to date – at a wet Monza. The Ferrari-powered, junior member of the Red Bull stable thus topped the podium before the main division of Mateschitz's F1 empire. STR also took the honours in the constructors' battle between the siblings with sixth place, one ahead of Red Bull.

Vettel had been responsible for 35 of the 39-point haul and was immediately plucked for A-team duty. Toro Rosso fielded three drivers in 2009, Buemi, Bourdais and Alguesuari, none of whom could prevent STR from finishing bottom of the heap. The following two seasons appeared better largely because of the arrival of HRT, Virgin and Lotus, who failed to register a single point between them. The same year also marked STR's debut as an independent constructor, a severing of the Red Bull apron strings that was bound to have an effect. Too strong for the minnows, not strong enough to make an impact on the midfield division; that has been the recent story for Toro Rosso, who also lost Daniel Ricciardo to Red Bull at the end of 2013.

BELOW: **Daniel Ricciardo drives in for a pitstop during practice for the 2013 United States Grand Prix.**

TOYOTA

Country:	Japan
Date of foundation:	2001
Years in Formula One:	2002–09
Constructors' Title victories: 0	

CORPORATE GIANT ENTERS THE FRAY

The world's third biggest motor manufacturer had a proud record in rallying, with a string of world championships to its name, when it entered the F1 fray in 2002. Like Ferrari, Toyota manufactured its own chassis and engines, yet even with the backing of such a huge corporation, there was no guarantee of success in such a specialised field.

Mika Salo got the team off to an excellent start, finishing sixth at Melbourne, Toyota's very first F1 outing. He and Allan McNish were dropped for 2003, Olivier Panis and Cristiano da Matta taking over the driving duties for the next two seasons. In 2003 the duo accumulated 16 points, enough to put Toyota ahead of Jordan in the final shake-up.

Breakthrough season

2004 was targeted as the breakthrough year, the team confidently predicting regular points finishes. In fact, Panis and da Matta garnered just 9 between them; the prediction was a year out. For it was 2005 which saw Toyota really start to come good. Ralf Schumacher and Jarno Trulli were signed, and they scored an aggregate 88 points in the TF105. That put them sixth and seventh respectively in the title race; only the McLaren and Renault men, plus seven-times champion Michael Schumacher, finished ahead of them. Toyota failed to get into the points in just two races, but a maiden victory was

still proving elusive. Although the new TF106 was unveiled early in 2006, it failed to help Toyota achieve its aim to end the competition as one of the top three constructors. Schumacher and Trulli fared little better in 2007, managing just 13 points between them. GP2 champion Timo Glock was drafted in to replace Schumacher for 2008, and he recorded the team's best result of the year, second place at the Hungarian GP.

There were a few podiums in 2009, but fifth in the Constructors' race wasn't enough to prevent Toyota from bowing out of F1 at the end of the year, citing the difficult economic climate.

ABOVE: **Jarno Trulli, Toyota TF105, celebrates taking second position at the 2005 Malaysian Grand Prix, Sepang, Kuala Lumpur.**

BELOW: **Jarno Trulli at the wheel of the new Toyota TF106 during Formula One testing, Jerez, Spain, January 2006.**

TYRRELL

Country:	United Kingdom
Date of foundation:	1960
Years in Formula One:	1970–98
Constructors' Title victories:	1971

BREAKING INTO THE BIG TIME

Ken Tyrrell was among the crop of young drivers to come to prominence in the 500cc Formula Three era of the 1950s, a shoestring class which brought racing within the reaches of the likes of Stirling Moss and Peter Collins. Tyrrell founded his own team in 1960, but the key date came four years later, when his long association with Jackie Stewart began. Although Stewart made his F1 debut with BRM in 1965, he continued to drive for Tyrrell when commitments allowed. In 1968 the two embarked on their first joint F1 adventure, in a Matra-Ford. Matra were new to the sport, and as well as running their own V-12 powered car, they supplied one to Tyrrell. The works car, driven by Jean-Pierre Beltoise, fared much worse than the Tyrrell version, which had been fitted with the Ford Cosworth DFV. Stewart missed out to Graham Hill in the title race, though at the Nürburgring that year he finished four minutes ahead of his rival, the biggest margin of victory in championship history.

Six wins brings championship double

Stewart and Matra-Ford swept the board the following year, winning six of the 11 rounds for a championship double. 1970 saw Matra receive backing from Chrysler France, making it politically impossible for the cars to use Ford power.

With that door closed, Tyrrell ran a March that season, an interim arrangement while its own car was being developed. The Tyrrell 001 was on the grid before the end of the year, but it was 1971 when it came into its own. Stewart added six more wins to his tally, while second-string François Cévert took what would be his only career victory in the final round, Watkins Glen. Tyrrell also took the Constructors' Title in what was its first full season running its own car.

Clark's record broken

There were four more wins in 1972 but Stewart was hampered by an ulcer and had to be satisfied with the runner-up spot behind Fittipaldi and Lotus. Those positions were reversed in 1973, a season in which the Scot set a new mark of 27 victories, beating Jim Clark's record. Watkins Glen would have been Stewart's 100th Grand Prix, and thoughts of bowing out at the top were crystallised as Cévert was killed during qualifying.

Having lost both his star and the heir apparent, Tyrrell gave Jody Scheckter and Patrick Depailler their first full season in F1. They finished third and fourth in the 1976 title race – the year of the famous P34 six-wheeler – with a one-two at Anderstorp the crowning moment. It was soon back to a conventional arrangement, but over the next 20 years successes were sporadic. Depailler did win at Monaco in 1978, a welcome victory after eight second-places, while Michele Alboreto had the honour of giving the Cosworth DFV its final victory at Detroit in 1983. But Tyrrell was consigned to a midfield position, and in 1997 the team was bought by British American Tobacco, who joined the circus as BAR two years later.

Opposite above: **Jody Scheckter at the controls of his six-wheeled Tyrrell P34-Ford in the 1976 Swedish Grand Prix, Anderstorp. This was to be the car's only GP win.**

Opposite below: **Ken Tyrrell with Jackie Stewart, a formidable partnership for the Tyrrell team.**

Below: **Michele Alboreto (Tyrrell 01-Ford) gives Tyrrell their final Grand Prix win at Detroit, Michigan, USA, June 1983.**

VANWALL

Country:	United Kingdom
Date of foundation:	1949
Years in Formula One:	1954–60
Constructors' Title victories: 1958	

INAUGURAL CHAMPIONS

Vanwall took its place in the history books as winner of the inaugural Constructors' Cup in 1958, and ran Mike Hawthorn's Ferrari mightily close in that year's Drivers' Championship.

Team owner Tony Vandervell was an industrialist and fervently patriotic racing fan who was one of the early backers of the ill-fated BRM project. His frustration with that, and determination to see a British racing car take on the world, led him to acquire a Ferrari 125 in 1949. In adapted form, these 'Thinwall Specials' – the name taken from the revolutionary bearings made by Vandervell's company – took to the track, Reg Parnell finishing fourth at Reims in the 1951 French GP.

'Vanwall Special'

By then Vandervell decided to sever all links with BRM and Ferrari and build his own car. Norton, with some input from Rolls-Royce, worked on a new engine, Cooper was commissioned to provide the chassis. Unveiled in 1954 and dubbed the 'Vanwall Special', the car made its debut at the prestigious International Trophy meeting, held at Silverstone. It was running in fifth place in the final when an oil pipe broke, but the signs were encouraging.

Peter Collins was behind the wheel at that year's British Grand Prix. It was another retirement, but once again, there had been much to commend the performance.

A 2.5-litre Vanwall – the 'Special' had now been dropped – appeared in 1955, but neither Mike Hawthorn, Ken Wharton or Harry Schell got into the points in a Mercedes-dominated year. A frustrated Hawthorn decamped mid-season.

'C'est une bombe!'

Stirling Moss, open to offers after Mercedes' withdrawal from the sport, tested a Vanwall but opted to join Maserati for 1956. Vandervell also tried to sign Fangio, but in the end Harry Schell was retained and Maurice Trintignant joined the team for a two-pronged attack. Colin Chapman was brought in to improve the chassis, which became a spaceframe layout, and Frank Costin designed new bodywork with better aerodynamics. Trintignant's verdict when he saw the new car: 'Ça alors, c'est une bombe!'

Moss, not on Maserati duty, gave the car a victorious debut at the 1956 International Trophy, outclassing the much-vaunted Lancia D50s run by Ferrari. The rest of the season didn't match that standard, but it was a shot across the bows of the rivals.

Victory at Aintree

The teething troubles addressed, Vandervell turned his thoughts to the driver line-up for 1957. Schell and Trintignant were both released; in came Moss, along with Tony Brooks, the cream of British talent. Moss finished runner-up – again – to Fangio, with Brooks taking fifth in the title race. The highlight was the British GP at Aintree. Moss took pole, Brooks third, with new young star Stuart Lewis-Evans making it three Vanwalls in the first six on the grid. Moss was running well until a technical glitch occurred. Brooks, still recovering

from injury, gladly handed over his car and Moss tore through the field from ninth to become the first Briton to win the home Grand Prix in a British car. With better luck, Lewis-Evans might have made it a Vanwall one-two.

Moss also won the two Italian races, Pescara and Monza. In the latter, Brooks set the fastest lap and Lewis-Evans took pole. 1958 couldn't come quickly enough.

Lewis-Evans killed in fireball crash

Vanwall again gave the curtain-raiser in Argentina a miss, Moss winning in a Rob Walker Cooper. He and Brooks then shared six victories in the European races to take the title race to the wire. Mike Hawthorn, with just a single win to his name, pipped Moss by a point in a championship decided by the best six scores. That disappointment paled beside the death of Lewis-Evans, who died from burns suffered in the Moroccan GP, where Hawthorn's fifth second place of the season clinched the crown for Ferrari.

For Vandervell, who was not in the best of health, this was a crushing blow, and in January 1959 it was announced that Vanwall was withdrawing from competition.

Opposite Above: **Tony Vandervell celebrates winning the 1957 British Grand Prix, at Aintree, England.**

Opposite Below: **Stirling Moss (Vanwall) won the 1958 Moroccan Grand Prix, Ain-Diab, Casablanca.**

Above: **Harry Schell leads Stirling Moss (both Vanwall) in the 1956 International Trophy, Silverstone, Great Britain. Moss finished in first position.**

WILLIAMS

Country:	United Kingdom
Date of foundation:	1968
Years in Formula One:	1973–
Constructors' Title victories: 1980, 1981, 1986, 1987, 1992, 1993, 1994, 1996, 1997	

FRANK WILLAMS' TEAM THIRD ON ALL-TIME LIST

Frank Williams first made his mark on Formula One as a privateer, running a Ford-powered Brabham for his friend Piers Courage in the 1969 championship. In only the car's second outing, at Monaco, Courage followed home the reigning champion and Monaco king Graham Hill to give Williams his first points at the sport's top table. There was another podium finish at Watkins Glen, and the team also collected points at Silverstone and Monza to round out a fine debut season.

Williams was deeply affected by Courage's death in a fireball accident at Zandvoort in 1970. The next few years were somewhat thin, Williams' drivers scratching for the odd championship point against the powerhouse works teams. In 1974 he ran his own chassis for the first time, his driver line-up that year including rookie Jacques Laffite. The Frenchman's second place at the Nürburgring in 1975 gave Williams his first podium as a constructor. The team was struggling to keep its head above water, however: a situation that led to a collaboration with Austrian oil magnate Walter Wolf in 1976. That quickly disintegrated, and Williams re-entered the fray the following year, founding Williams Grand Prix Engineering. More significantly, he brought in Patrick Head as chief designer; thus was born a partnership, which would go on to win seven Drivers' Championships and nine Constructors' titles.

First championship

After a transitional year, the new Williams FW06 was soon in the points, with Alan Jones at the wheel. In 1979 Jones was a title contender, though it was team-mate Clay Regazzoni who gave Williams its first win, at Silverstone. This was in Head's superb FW07, the class act in the field in the new ground-effect era. Jones went on to win four of the next five races. Had the FW07 been available for the early rounds, Jones may well have beaten Jody Scheckter, who took the title with just 11 more points than the Australian.

Williams' first championship was deferred only one year, Jones picking up in 1980 where he left off the previous season, taking the chequered flag five times on his way to the

title. Had Jones and Carlos Reutemann played a cannier team game, Williams might have won in 1981, but their frosty relationship helped Nelson Piquet lift the crown. Williams at least retained the Constructors' Title. Consistency brought Keke Rosberg the 1982 championship, the last hurrah for the Cosworth engine.

Williams entered the turbo era with Honda engines, and by 1986 the car was the pick of the bunch, winning nine of the 16 rounds. Unfortunately, those were shared between Mansell and Piquet, to Alain Prost's advantage.

That year the team was left reeling as Frank Williams was involved in a car crash, which left him confined to a wheelchair. The team boss returned as committed and indefatigable as ever, and saw Piquet and Mansell at the top of the tree in 1987.

Record for Mansell as Williams dominate

The loss of the superb Honda unit brought a dip in fortune, but a deal with Renault in 1989 put Williams back on top. Mansell, returning from a spell at Ferrari, finished runner-up to Prost in 1991; a year later, the FW14, now with active suspension, was unstoppable. Mansell scored a record-breaking nine wins, and had the title sewn up with five races to spare.

Nigel Mansell departed to IndyCars, and Prost ended a year's sabbatical, returning to Formula One with Williams and claiming his fourth world crown. The Professor's no. 2 that year was Damon Hill, promoted from test driver. In 1994 Hill found himself carrying the fight after Senna's spell with the Didcot team was so tragically cut short at Imola. Hill missed out by a single point to Schumacher, following the controversial clash that took them both out of the Adelaide decider. In 1996 the championship developed into a Williams two-horse race, Hill edging out Jacques Villeneuve. The Canadian went one better than his mercurial father by winning the 1997 title, nursing his FW19 to the line despite Schumacher's best efforts to prevent him from doing so.

In 2000 Williams began using BMW engines, and over the following four seasons Juan Pablo Montoya and Ralf

Schumacher added ten more victories to the team's roll of honour. It currently lies third in the all-time list of Drivers' and Constructors' Championships. Only Ferrari and McLaren – both active in F1 for considerably longer – have delivered more titles than Frank Williams' team. A move to Toyota power in 2007 had little impact, the team scoring just 93.5 points over the next three seasons. Williams renewed its relationship with Cosworth for 2010, and it was also all change in the driver line-up as Barrichello lined up alongside newcomer Nico Hulkenberg, fresh from his triumph in the GP2 championship.

There were some encouraging signs, but it proved another false dawn as sponsorship money dried up. Williams suffered its worst-ever return in 2011, Barrichello and rookie Pastor Maldonado garnering just five points between them. Mike Coughlan, who was embroiled in the 2007 Spygate row while at McLaren, returned to F1 as Williams' chief engineer, quickly promoted to technical director for 2012, when the team returned to Renault power, the combination that had delivered many of its greatest triumphs. Bruno Senna took Barrichello's seat, 18 years after his uncle died at the wheel of a Williams, and the changes at Grove also saw Patrick Head sever his ties with the F1 arm of the company after 34 years. The team showed it was heading in the right direction as Maldonado put them back on top of the podium for the first time since 2004. An aggregate 76 points represented a vast improvement, and with the internal promotion of highly-rated Valtteri Bottas as Senna's replacement for 2013, Williams looked to make further progress through the midfield division.

OPPOSITE ABOVE: **Valtteri Bottas drives during the first practice session at the Spa-Francorchamps circuit in August 2013.**

OPPOSITE BELOW: **Frank Williams in 1971.**

BELOW: **Jacques Villeneuve in the Williams FW19-Renault, forging ahead to win the Luxembourg Grand Prix at the Nürburgring.**

THE
CIRCUITS

ARGENTINA

Track: Autódromo Oscar Alfredo Gálvez Buenos Aires	
Track length:	4259m
Total distance:	306.54km (72 laps)

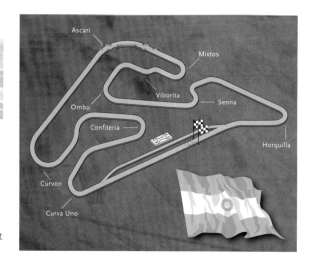

Although the Argentine Grand Prix no longer features as part of the Formula One world championships, the last having taken place in 1998, 20 such races were held, somewhat intermittently, from 1953 until that time. All were staged near Buenos Aires at the Autódromo Oscar Alfredo Gálvez, or the Autodrome, as it is perhaps more commonly known.

Situated on a flat expanse of former marshland, the circuit was constructed in 1952 with the blessing of Argentine president Juan Perón, on the back of the success of native countryman Juan Manuel Fangio, who had taken the world championship title the previous year. He would go on to do so on four consecutive occasions during the 1950s, taking first place in the Argentine Grand Prix three times in the process.

Fangio was also to win the inaugural race held at the Autodrome in 1952, the Perón Cup, but it would be the Italian Alberto Ascari who would triumph in the first Formula One race to be held there in 1953, which was in fact also the first Formula One competition ever to be staged outside Europe. Having completed 36 laps, Fangio had been forced to retire his Maserati due to transmission failure.

However, Fangio was to win at home in 1954, 1955 and 1957, with first place being claimed by the Italian Luigi Musso in 1956. Following a highly distinguished career, Fangio was to retire at the age of almost 50, and his last appearance at his home circuit took place in 1958, when the win would be taken by Britain's Stirling Moss.

Following the exile of president Perón in 1955, the political climate in Argentina became increasingly unstable, and 1960 was to bear witness to the last Argentine Grand

Prix for over ten years until its return in 1972. The world champion, Jackie Stewart, would take top place on the podium on that occasion, but the race marked the emergence of a new homegrown talent, Carlos Reutemann, who made his auspicious world championship debut by taking pole position.

With the exception of 1976, the Argentine Grand Prix continued to be a regular fixture until the 1980s, with Reutemann seeing second place success at the Autodrome in 1979 and 1981, but the outbreak of the Falklands War in 1982, and Reutemann's retirement, would ensure that he was never to win at home.

By the time the race returned to Argentina in 1995, the circuit had been purchased by a private consortium, and in the wake of Ayrton Senna's death in 1994, a process of safety-conscious modernisation had been set in motion throughout Formula One. For the Autodrome, this meant the replacement of many of its high-speed, sweeping curves with a tightly twisting infield section, but the circuit remained exciting, and as Jean Alesi and Michael Schumacher proved in 1995 and 1997 respectively, with costly mistakes at the first corner, it could still be a challenging circuit for the drivers.

Damon Hill took the win for Williams in 1995, and again in 1996, during what would become his championship season, and the following year, that team's success was continued at the Autodrome by Canadian Jacques Villeneuve.

At the start of the 1998 season, with Reutemann a state senator, it was hoped that the future of the Argentine Grand Prix was secure, but with the organisers of the race facing increasing financial difficulties, 1998 would herald the last championship race to be held at the Autodrome, which was won by Michael Schumacher.

LEFT: **1979 Argentinian Grand Prix, Buenos Aires, Argentina.**

AUSTRALIA

Track:	Albert Park, Melbourne
Track length:	5303m
Total distance:	307.57km (58 laps)

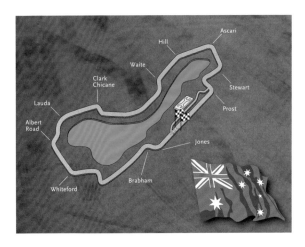

Located just south of central Melbourne, the Albert Park circuit has been home to the Australian Grand Prix for the past 15 years. The circuit, which is essentially street-based, and which is situated around a small man-made lake in Albert Park, was opened in 1996 after considerable expense and improvement of the road sections, resulting in a smooth and rather picturesque course. However, it has not been without its detractors, notably local residents who have objected to the encroachment of the race on a public park, and the disruption that the event causes to their lives each year. However, the government and the race organisers have claimed that the improved amenities and economic benefits far outweigh such perceived costs, and it remains something of a favourite amongst drivers and fans alike.

In the inaugural race in 1996, the Canadian Jacques Villeneuve caused a sensation by coming incredibly close to securing a win on his debut – a feat only achieved once before, in 1961 by Giancarlo Baghetti – but he was forced to slow by a drop in oil pressure, allowing Williams team-mate Damon Hill to take the first win in what was to become his world championship year. That race was also notable for a spectacular first-lap crash by Martin Brundle.

After qualifying by a huge margin in 1997, Villeneuve once more looked set to dominate, but at the first corner he was sent out of the race by Eddie Irvine. Heinz-Harald Frentzen, who had been looking strong in second, crashed in the final stages, and technical problems for Damon Hill meant that he didn't even start the race, all of which provided the opportunity for David Coulthard to secure victory for McLaren.

McLaren's success continued at Albert Park in 1998, with a win from Mika Häkkinen, who would become world champion that year, but from 1999 to 2002, Ferrari would dominate the event, first with a win from Eddie Irvine, and then with three consecutive victories by Michael Schumacher.

The race was marred by tragedy in 2001, when a marshal was killed by a flying tyre following a crash between Ralf Schumacher and Jacques Villeneuve, but in 2002 there was cause for celebration amongst the crowd, with Australian Mark Webber putting in a performance which saw him finish a surprising fifth in his Minardi, a result, which in Australia at least, eclipsed Michael Schumacher's win.

Coulthard interrupted Schumacher's winning run for a year by securing his second victory at Albert Park in 2003, and Italian Giancarlo Fisichella took first place for Renault in 2005. A year later, Melbourne lost its curtain-raiser slot to avoid clashing with the Commonwealth Games. It returned to its usual place until 2010, when Bahrain took over and Australia was moved to second on the calendar. Button won for McLaren, having given Brawn GP its maiden success there the previous year. Since 2011 it has resumed its place as the season's curtain-raiser, Button making it three wins in four in 2012. Raïkkönen's 2013 win for Lotus was his sole victory of the year.

Despite being constrained within a city park, the Albert Park circuit is amongst the longest and most distinctive in Formula One, and with 16 corners, several chicanes and only one major straight, there is often little room for overtaking, but the venue still offers the opportunity for both high-speed action and impressive cornering manoeuvres.

BELOW: **2005 Australian GP, Albert Park, Melbourne.**

AUSTRIA

Track: Spielberg Circuit, Zeltweg	
Track length:	4326m
Total distance:	307.15km (71 laps)

The first Austrian Grand Prix was held in 1964 at Zeltweg Airfield, but despite its success, the course was deemed to be unsafe, and the race was removed from the Formula One calendar until 1970 and the completion of a purpose-built circuit: the now legendary Osterreichring, which was also located close to Zeltweg. The Austrian Grand Prix was staged at that venue consecutively for 18 years until 1987, when it became regarded as too dangerous. For a decade, the race was once more to disappear from the world championships, but following major modernisation, which included several changes to the layout of the track, the circuit reopened as the A1-Ring, and went on to host the Austrian Grand Prix from 1997 to 2003.

Straddling the municipalities of Zeltweg and Spielberg, set high in the Styrian mountains, the Osterreichring was notable for both its dramatic scenery and changes in elevation, but was perhaps best known for its speed and sweeping curves.

The circuit was a real test of a driver's mettle and abilities, with the first curve, Hella-Licht, being approached up a long steep gradient, so as to render the apex invisible until it was reached, at speed. Tragically, in 1975, it was to claim the life of American driver Mark Donohue, who despite remaining conscious after crashing, was to die of his injuries in hospital. That year, driving conditions had been made all the more difficult by torrential rain, turning the race into something of a lottery, and the win was claimed by Vittorio Brambilla, who had been leading the field when the race was cut short. However, even his win was not without incident, as he was to crash into the barriers after seeing the chequered flag.

Throughout the 1970s, the Osterreichring became known for producing unpredictable results, with several first-time winners, including Jo Siffert in 1971, and in the years between 1975 and 1977, Vittorio Brambilla, John Watson, and Alan Jones. In 1979, Jones would triumph there again, the year before he would become world champion. Another surprise result came in 1982, with one of the closest ever finishes in Grand Prix history, with just 0.08 seconds separating Keke Rosberg and the winner, Elio de Angelis. Frenchman Alain Prost notched up three wins at the circuit during the 1980s, first in 1983, and then again during his championship seasons of 1985 and 1986, with Niki Lauda

taking the win in 1984, in what was his championship year. The last Austrian Grand Prix to be held at the majestic Osterreichring, in 1987, was won by Briton Nigel Mansell.

The circuit was then abandoned for almost ten years, mainly due to concerns over its safety, before being rebuilt during the mid-1990s and reopened as the A1-ring, named after A1, the mobile phone company that was its sponsor. In order to be reaccepted by Formula One, the circuit's length had been reduced, the sweeping curves had been cut short or bypassed, and a slower, twisting infield section inserted.

From the outset, the circuit seemed to many to be a shadow of its former self, but the inaugural race was to throw up a number of surprises. Jacques Villeneuve, who required the win to stay in the running for the title, began in pole position and went on to win the race by three seconds from David Coulthard after Schumacher was penalised for failing to notice a safety flag and Häkkinen, Trulli, Irvine and Alesi failed to finish.

Coulthard succeeded in winning at the A1-Ring in 2001, with Michael Schumacher victorious in the subsequent final two competitions held there in 2002 and 2003, although in 2002 the Austrian Grand Prix was shrouded in controversy after the Ferrari team ordered Rubens Barrichello to hand victory to Schumacher.

The seven-year revival ended in 2003, when Austria was dropped from the schedule. Under Red Bull's ownership, the Spielberg circuit received a much needed facelift and reopened its doors in 2011, now bearing the name of the energy drink company that had breathed new life into it. The Red Bull Ring returned to the calendar in 2014, and there is little doubt that Dietrich Mateschitz, the Austrian entrepreneur whose team has made such an impact on the sport in the last decade, would cherish a victory on his native soil.

BAHRAIN

Track:	Bahrain International Circuit, Sakhir
Track length:	5417m
Total distance:	308.52km (57 laps)

The Bahrain Grand Prix is amongst the most recent to have been added to the world championships, and was the first Formula One event to take place in the Middle East. Its home is the Bahrain International Circuit at Sakhir, which is also amongst the most recently constructed of venues, and is remarkable not only for its impressive, world-class facilities, but also for the feat of engineering involved in its construction, which took little more than a year to complete. Designed by Formula One's favoured architect, Hermann Tilke, the man behind new tracks in Malaysia, China and Turkey, the venue has a capacity of some 50,000 spectators, incorporates six individual tracks (two of which are configured to Formula One standard), media and medical centres, and the striking eight-storey Sakhir Tower, which incorporates the Bahrain Motor Federation, International Circuit Management offices, a restaurant and several hospitality suites, and provides views of the entire circuit.

The project was a national concern for Bahrain, which fought off competition from other Middle Eastern countries such as Egypt, and was instigated and backed by the Honorary President of the Bahrain Motor Federation, Crown Prince, Sheikh Salman bin Hamad al-Khalifa. Despite fears that the circuit would not be ready in time for 2004, the inaugural Bahrain Grand Prix took place on 4 April that year, and the FIA awarded it the 'Best Organised Grand Prix'.

Although there were concerns over the dusty conditions, which had been blamed for causing spins during practice, 17 cars finished the race in 2004, with only three retirements. Ferrari took the top two places on the podium, with Michael Schumacher in first, and Rubens Barrichello second, while young Briton, Jenson Button took third place in his BAR. Another first followed, with the celebratory champagne replaced with lemonade and rosewater, this being a Muslim country.

The 2005 race saw the highest-ever temperatures at a Grand Prix, with an air temperature of 42°C, and track temperatures reaching 56°C, which no doubt accounted for several of the eight retirements.

Fernando Alonso and Michael Schumacher, starting the race in pole and second positions, respectively, battled it out in the opening laps, until Schumacher was forced into the pits after overshooting a corner, which remarkably made this his first technical retirement since 2001.

Alonso went on to take victory, bringing Renault their 100th Grand Prix win, while amazingly Ferrari were left without points for the first time in almost two years. Alonso repeated his success in 2006, and another win in 2010 made the Spaniard the most successful driver in the race's short history.

The track itself comprises 12 corners and an impressively long straight that provides plenty of opportunities for overtaking, and although some detractors have commented that the layout does not live up to some of the other new courses, such as Sepang in Malaysia for example, it remains an interesting and impressive venue, which is enhanced by its unique desert location and Arabian flavour.

2010 saw Bahrain host the season's curtain-raiser once again, and with an expanded grid the organisers inserted an extra loop that would add around 0.9km to the lap distance although It was announced that the race would revert to its original length for 2011. In the event, a volatile political situation meant that race didn't take place. It was initially postponed and later cancelled from the schedule, but returned to its usual early-season slot in the calendar for 2012.

BELGIUM

Track:	Spa-Francorchamps
Track length:	7004m
Total distance:	308.17km (44 laps)

Widely regarded as the greatest Formula One circuit of all time, Spa-Francorchamps, the home of the Belgian Grand Prix, is also amongst the most historic of the world championship venues, having been constructed in 1921 and first used for Grand Prix racing in 1925. Although it has undergone various transformations over the years, its reputation as a classic circuit has remained largely unscathed.

The long, flowing track is set in the wooded hills of the Ardennes, and was originally a very fast course, comprising mainly slender public roads that left little room for error. Despite having been reduced to about half its original length, from over 14km to almost 7km, it remains the longest circuit in F1.

Several corners have also been inserted, making for a slower, but perhaps more demanding course. But the one thing that has always posed a major difficulty for drivers at Spa is the weather, for while conditions may be dry on one part of the track, it can be pouring with rain on another; at one time, the Belgian Grand Prix had seen rain on 20 consecutive occasions. All this, coupled with several changes in elevation, combines to make Spa probably the most challenging circuit on the Formula One calendar.

As if to illustrate this point, only a handful of drivers have ever won at Spa more than twice, and all of them have been championship drivers. Juan Manuel Fangio secured three victories, in 1950, 1954 and 1955, and during the 1960s, Briton Jim Clark won on four consecutive occasions, from 1962 to 1965. However, in spite of his triumphs there, Clark hated Spa, and with good reason. In 1958, on his first outing to the circuit, he had witnessed the death of Archie Scott-Brown, and two years later, during his first Grand Prix at the course, he narrowly avoided collision with wreckage after Chris Bristow's fatal crash, and also lost his team-mate, Alan Stacey.

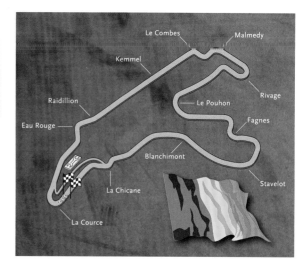

The great Jackie Stewart also famously loathed Spa, and following a terrifying accident on the first lap in 1966, when rain had caused eight cars to spin, resulting in Stewart finding himself upside-down in a ditch with petrol leaking onto him and requiring rescuing by fellow drivers Bob Bondurant and Graham Hill, he began a lifelong campaign to improve safety in F1. After 1970, it was decided that it was too dangerous to continue hosting Formula One events at Spa, and the Belgian Grand Prix instead alternated between Zolder and Nivelles.

Following a major overhaul of the track, which included the addition of several chicanes, wider run-off areas and an improved surface, the race returned to Spa in 1983, and after being held once more in Zolder in 1984, it has remained at Spa since 1985. Ayrton Senna was victorious on that occasion, the first of his five wins at the circuit, the remaining four being achieved in the consecutive years between 1988 and 1991. Only Michael Schumacher has won more times at Spa-Francorchamps, claiming six wins from 1992 to 2002.

The historic circuit was omitted from the 2006 calendar because upgrades were not completed on time. The local government, keen to maintain Spa's place on the Formula One circuit, completed the renovations and the course was reinstated for 2007. The 2011 race marked the 20th anniversary of Michael Schumacher's F1 debut. He couldn't add to his victory tally – Vettel and Webber scored a Red Bull clean sweep – but fifth place from the back of the grid showed that Schuey was still a force to be reckoned with. Vettel, who made it two wins in three years in 2013, said Spa was one of his favourite venues, offering 'every type of racing corner'. He added: 'The difference in altitude and the unpredictable weather really make the track a big challenge.'

Left: Nico Hulkenberg drives in the wet, August 2010.

BRAZIL

Track:	Interlagos, São Paulo
Track length:	4309m
Total distance:	305.91km (71 laps)

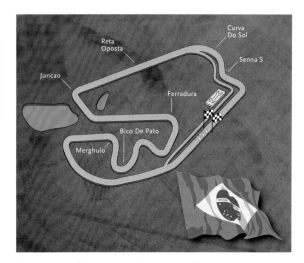

With a carnival atmosphere that is perhaps unmatched in the world championships, with the possible exceptions of Monza and Imola, the Brazilian Grand Prix holds a special place in the hearts of Formula One fans, and no doubt the drivers too, but it is also regarded as one of the most challenging events on the calendar, and the Interlagos circuit presents drivers with a unique combination of difficulties.

In addition to the extreme heat and humidity, Interlagos is one of the few circuits to be raced in an anti-clockwise direction, meaning that most of the corners are left-handed, and the drivers are subjected to sustained G-force on the left side of the body that can be rapidly draining, and despite improvements, the track is also notoriously bumpy, creating problems for both drivers and their cars alike. In addition, there are several changes in elevation, tricky corners, and only two real opportunities for overtaking; at the end of the pit straight, and at the end of the long back straight, the Reta Oposta.

Although constructed in the late 1930s, the first world championship Brazilian GP was held at Interlagos in 1973, the year after native Emerson Fittipaldi claimed the first of his two world championships, the second coming in 1974, and he was to secure victory in the first two Formula One Grand Prix races at Interlagos. Brazilian success was continued in 1975 by Carlos Pace, after whom the circuit would become officially named following his tragic death in a plane crash just two years later.

At the end of the 1970s, the Brazilian Grand Prix moved to Jacarepaguá in Rio de Janeiro, home of another Brazilian

champion, Nelson Piquet, where it would remain until returning to a modernised Interlagos in 1990. By that time the circuit had been shortened to a little over half its original length, and the incredibly fast opening section moderated by the addition of 'Senna's S' curve.

Further home victories were assured in 1991 and 1993 by Ayrton Senna. Then, from 1994 to 2000, a pattern emerged whereby whoever won at Interlagos went on to become world champion, with wins from Michael Schumacher in 1994, 1995 and 2000, Damon Hill in 1996, Jacques Villeneuve in 1997 and Mika Häkkinen in 1998 and 1999. 2001 was notable for the dramatic arrival of Colombian Juan Pablo Montoya, who would go on to win at Interlagos in 2004 for Williams and 2005 for McLaren, and in 2005 Fernando Alonso made history there, with his third place enough to secure his position as the youngest Formula One world champion of all time. Felipe Massa won at Interlagos in 2006, the first Brazilian to win on home ground since Senna in 1993. He might have won in 2007 too, but allowed team-mate Kimi Räikkönen to take victory, and with it, the championship. The 2008 race eclipsed previous dramatic finales as Lewis Hamilton snatched fifth place in the closing seconds to take the title from race winner Massa. Webber gave Red Bull victory in 2009, but Button and Barrichello did enough for Brawn GP to clinch a championship double.

Interlagos witnessed yet another showdown in 2012. Button took the flag, while sixth-placed Vettel did enough to secure his third consecutive title, edging Ferrari's Alonso. It lost its traditional season-closing spot in 2014, moved to the penultimate round where Red Bull would be looking to build on its impressive record of four wins in five years.

LEFT: **2003 Brazilian Grand Prix, Interlagos.**

CANADA

Track:	Circuit Gilles Villeneuve, Montreal
Track length:	4361m
Total distance:	305.27km (70 laps)

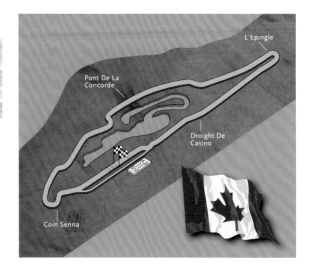

Following the first Canadian Grand Prix in 1967, which was held at Ontario's Mosport Park, the event alternated between that venue and Quebec's Mont Tremblant until 1971, when safety concerns about the latter saw it moved back to Mosport Park until 1977. The race was then moved to its current location on the Île Notre-Dame, a man-made island in the St Lawrence River, Montreal.

Designed by Roger Peart, the circuit presents a combination of long, fast straights and tight, slow corners and chicanes. Although it is not an over-demanding course for drivers, with good opportunities for overtaking at the hairpin and last chicane particularly, it can be hard on the cars, and after Monza it is regarded as the most hardwearing on the brakes.

The race therefore often becomes a battle of attrition, but that is not to say that it is not capable of producing some exciting, action-packed encounters, or that the drivers always have an easy time of it, and many experienced drivers have been caught out at Montreal.

The first Canadian Grand Prix held there, in 1978, was won by Gilles Villeneuve, the home-grown talent and former snowmobile racer who had single-handedly ignited interest in

Formula One in Canada during the late 1970s, and it also provided the first Grand Prix win of his career. It was fitting then, after his tragic death in qualifying for the 1982 Belgian Grand Prix, that the venue was renamed the Circuit Gilles Villeneuve in his memory.

Sadly, a terrible accident also occurred during the Canadian Grand Prix that year when Villeneuve's team-mate, Didier Pironi, stalled and was crashed into by Riccardo Paletti, who would later die from his injuries in hospital.

The course has changed relatively little over the years although, in an attempt to improve safety, the early 1990s saw the addition of a new corner in front of the pits and also a chicane, but in 1997 the race was brought to an early conclusion after Oliver Panis spun from the track, breaking both his legs; and in 1999, the wall after the final chicane, which famously bears the slogan 'Welcome to Quebec', put former world champions Michael Schumacher, Damon Hill and Jacques Villeneuve, son of Gilles, out of the race.

However, between 1994 and 2004, Schumacher dominated the circuit, notching up a total of seven victories there. Robert Kubica's victory for BMW Sauber in 2008 brought to an end Montreal's 31-year run as a Formula One venue. The Circuit Gilles Villeneuve was dropped from the schedule to accommodate the new Abu Dhabi GP for 2009. With backing from the Canadian government, the Grand Prix returned to the roster in 2010. The following year, Montreal witnessed one of the most dramatic races in F1 history. A lengthy rain break meant it took over four hours to complete – a championship record – and it was also notable for the last-lap error by Sebastian Vettel that allowed Jenson Button to snatch victory.

LEFT: **1997 Canadian Grand Prix, Montreal, Canada.**

CHINA

Track:	**Shanghai International Circuit**
Track length:	**5451m**
Total distance:	**305.26km (56 laps)**

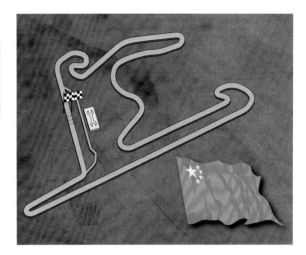

Like the Bahrain Grand Prix, the inaugural Chinese Grand Prix became a new addition to the Formula One world championships in 2004, and the event took place at a brand new, state-of-the-art circuit, where no expense had been spared in its development and construction. It announced China's arrival as a player on the Formula One world stage.

As at Bahrain, the Shanghai International Circuit was designed by renowned architect Hermann Tilke, who is also responsible for Sepang in Malaysia and Istanbul Park in Turkey. It boasts superlative facilities for both spectators and teams alike, with approximately half of the venue's area occupied by a superb track, and the remainder home to a complex that houses entertainment and commercial areas, with provision for exhibitions and conventions.

A delight for fans, the circuit boasts a capacity of 200,000, with permanent seating for almost 50,000 spectators, some 29,000 of which are located in the grandstand, from where around 80 percent of the track is visible. The course itself comprises 14 corners, divided equally into right and left hand turns, and two major straights, providing plenty of opportunities for overtaking, but also requiring rapid changes between acceleration and deceleration that are demanding for both the drivers and their cars.

Rubens Barrichello won the Inaugural Chinese Grand Prix in 2004 for Ferrari, his second successive victory of the season, having led for most of the race, with young Briton Jenson Button keeping the pressure on to finish just over a second behind in his BAR, while Michael Schumacher failed to secure any points for only the second time that year.

Then in 2005 the race brought an end to the season and a double triumph for Fernando Alonso and his Renault team, with Alonso having won the FIA Formula One Drivers' World Championship, and clinching the Constructors' title for Renault. In an impressive performance, Alonso led for the entire 56 laps. Lewis Hamilton might have become rookie world champion in 2007 had he not gone into the gravel in Shanghai, opening the door to Räikkönen, who won the race and went on to pip the Briton for the title. Lewis made up for it a year later with a crucial win in China that helped propel him to the championship.

Built at a cost of US$240 million – at the time the most expensive circuit ever constructed – Shanghai International Circuit is certainly a spectacular venue. The layout has also received a generally positive response from drivers, mainly for the variety it offers but, in spite of this, it has its critics, who claim that no amount of money could have transformed what was formerly flat marshland into a classic circuit such as Suzuka in Japan or Belgium's Spa-Francorchamps.

BELOW: **Shanghai, China, 2004: one end of the impressive complex that spans the start/finish straight at the Shanghai circuit.**

FRANCE

Track:	**Circuit de Nevers Magny-Cours**
Track length:	**4411m**
Total distance:	**308.59km (70 laps)**

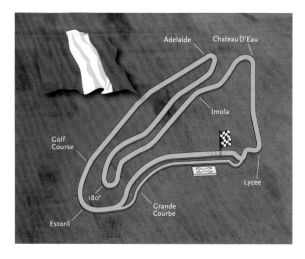

As the birthplace of Grand Prix motor racing, France can lay claim to the oldest international race, with the first French Grand Prix having taken place in 1906. The race was then included in the first world championships in 1925, and has been part of the annual Formula One competition since its inception in 1950, apart from 1955. The French Grand Prix has been held at numerous venues throughout the country since that time, but its home since 1991 has been the Circuit de Nevers Magny-Cours.

Formerly known as the Circuit Jean Behra, the Circuit de Nevers Magny-Cours, or simply Magny-Cours as it is more commonly known, was first constructed in 1959, and was home to a racing school that spawned drivers such as Jacques Laffite and François Cévert. However, the track fell into disrepair, and it was not until it was modernised during the 1980s, at the behest of President Mitterrand, that the circuit began to attract the attention of the Fédération Internationale de l'Automobile (FIA) and international racing events began to return.

As part of the process of redesign and redevelopment, inspiration was drawn from many of the existing major circuits, particularly regarding corners, and most are named after other circuits, such as the Adelaide hairpin and Estoril corner.

The track is renowned for its smooth, fast surface, and the layout offers a mixture of long straights and both fast and technical turns, demanding rapid transitions between acceleration and deceleration, which are testing for even experienced drivers. Despite this, many within the Formula

One community, drivers and fans alike, regard the circuit as rather average, with few overtaking opportunities, and a somewhat lacklustre atmosphere and facilities, which is no doubt due in part to the remote location of the venue.

In recent years, however, there has been something of an improvement in both facilities and the quality of racing at Magny-Cours, although it is has often been poor weather that has made for the more interesting encounters.

British legend Nigel Mansell took victory in the first two races at Magny-Cours in 1991 and 1992, the latter being his world championship season, followed by French hero Alain Prost in 1993, Michael Schumacher in 1994 and 1995, and Damon Hill in 1996, all of which were championship years for the drivers in question. Schumacher has since repeated the pattern in 2001, 2002 and 2004, and has notched up a total of seven wins at the circuit.

In 2002 the length of the pit lane was reduced due to changes at the final corner and chicane, which were designed to increase overtaking, and although it had little effect in that respect, the shorter pit stop times enabled Schumacher to win in 2004 with a strategy of four pit stops. Economic reasons were cited for the omission of Magny-Cours from the 2009 calendar. It meant that there would be no French Grand Prix for only the second time in the championship's 60-year history. After four years on the sidelines, it was mooted that the French Grand Prix would return in 2013, possibly at the Paul Ricard circuit in a race-sharing arrangement with Spa. That failed to materialise, but there were signs in 2014 that France might soon be back on the schedule. Bernie Ecclestone revealed that talks had taken place with a view to bringing Formula One back to Magny-Cours if guarantees about the hosting fee could be delivered.

LEFT: Fernando Alonso (Renault R25) crosses the line in 2005.

GERMANY

Track:	The Hockenheimring
Track length:	4574m
Total distance:	306.46km (67 laps)

Hockenheim, or the Hockenheimring, to give it its full title, was originally constructed in 1936 as a test track for Mercedes-Benz. It was nearly 8km in length, and comprised simply two long straights connected by two long bends, but following WWII, a new Hockenheim was built, with a tightly twisting stadium section, where the grandstands are situated, and a long, fast, forested 'country' section, composed of long straights separated by chicanes. Further modifications were made for safety reasons in 2001, reducing the track's overall length to around 4.5km.

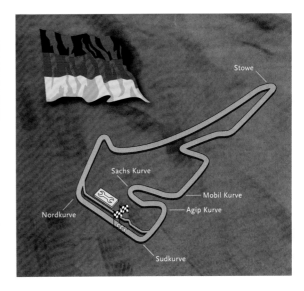

Hockenheim first hosted a Formula One race in 1970, two years after the legendary Jimmy Clark lost his life there during a F2 event. A memorial marks the spot and a corner, the Jim Clark Kurve, was later dedicated in his honour. The 1970 race was won by Austrian Jochen Rindt on his way to immortality as the sport's first posthumous champion. In 1977 Hockenheim took over from the Nürburgring as the home of the German GP, hosting every race for the next 30 years apart from 1985. The 1977 race also went to an Austrian who went on to take the championship, the great Niki Lauda.

After the 2001 German Grand Prix, with safety in mind, well-known circuit architect Hermann Tilke was brought in to redesign the course, focusing on the fast forested sections, where drivers had previously powered past the trees at over 320km/h (200mph), and which were particularly dangerous in wet conditions. This section was truncated, and new corners were added, reducing the circuit's overall length, which required an increase in laps from 45 to 67.

The modifications have been criticised by some, who believe that they detract from Hockenheim's character, but it is largely agreed that they were necessary, and the addition of a hairpin, with opportunities for overtaking, has no doubt placated some disgruntled fans.

Regardless of the changes, the German Grand Prix at Hockenheim remains one of the highest-attended races on the Formula One calendar. Hockenheim missed out in 2007 as the FIA ushered in a new era in which the circuit would alternate with Nürburgring for Germany's championship round.

LEFT: **1979 German Grand Prix, Hockenheim, Germany. Alan Jones (Williams FW07-Ford) leads into the Nordkurve at the start.**

GERMANY

Track:	**The Nürburgring**
Track length:	**5148m**
Total distance:	**308.86km (60 laps)**

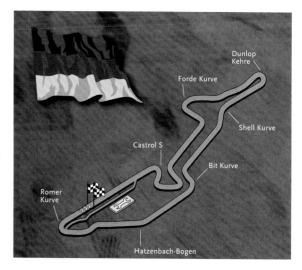

The original Nürburgring was an awesome circuit, which wound its way through the Eifel Mountains, around the village and castle of Nürburg, for a distance of over 28km, and was the setting for the first German Grand Prix in 1927. However, today's Nürburgring, which was constructed in the 1980s and is now the home of the European Grand Prix, is a meagre shadow of that former classic track.

The ADAC Eifelrennen road races began in the region in the early 1920s and the construction of a purpose built racing track got underway in 1925. The result was the first incarnation of the Nürburgring, an immense circuit with 174 bends, which could be divided into two sections; the Nordschleife, or Northern Loop, which was over 22km in length, and the shorter Südschleife, or Southern loop, of almost 8km. There was also a much shorter track around the pit area that could be used for small events and practice.

The first German Grand Prix was held at the circuit in July 1927 and utilised the full Ring, but after 1929, only the Nordschleife would be used for such events, while minor races and motorcycle competitions were primarily confined to the Südschleife.

Following WWII, motor racing returned to the Nürburgring and the Nordschleife section became home to the German Grand Prix, which was now included in the F1 world championships, featuring such greats as Ascari, Fangio, Jackie Stewart, Moss and Surtees.

Throughout the 1960s, as F1 cars became increasingly powerful, and the sport more dangerous, there was mounting pressure to improve the safety of circuits, and in 1970 drivers

decided to boycott the German Grand Prix, with the result that it was moved to Hockenheim that year. Improvements were made, and the race returned to the Ring until 1976.

Ironically, Nicky Lauda, who had been attempting to organise a boycott of the 1976 German Grand Prix due to safety concerns, crashed on the second lap of that race and was lucky to survive. As a result, it would be the last Formula One Grand Prix to be held at the old Nürburgring, and construction of the new circuit began in 1981.

The new, shorter Nürburgring was built around the old pits area, and opened in 1984 to hold the European Grand Prix. It returned in 1995 and 1996, and began a nine-year run on the calendar in 1999, when Briton Johnny Herbert was to seize Stewart's first and only win before their sale to Ford.

Although incomparable to the old Nürburgring, the GP-Strecke, as today's circuit is also known, is regarded as a fairly challenging and technical course, with few over-taking opportunities, a slippery surface, and a first corner that is notorious for having ended many a driver's race on the first lap.

The European Grand Prix was to have been discontinued at the end of the 2006 season, with just one race taking place in Germany each year, at Hockenheim and Nürburgring alternately. It was the latter's turn to host the 2007 event, but as Hockenheim held the naming rights to the German Grand Prix, the race went ahead under the European GP banner. The 2013 race at the Nurburgring, where Vettel recorded his first home victory, marked the 73rd time that Germany had hosted a grand prix: 59 under its own name, plus 12 editions of the European GP and two under the Luxembourg GP banner in the late 90s.

LEFT: **2001 European Grand Prix, Nürburgring.**

GREAT BRITAIN

Track:	Silverstone, Northampton
Track length:	5891m
Total distance:	306.32km (52 laps)

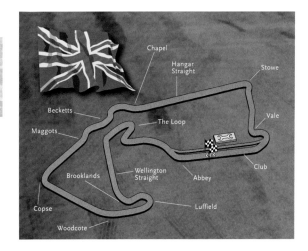

The Silverstone circuit is located at a former WWII airfield, RAF Silverstone, and it is known as 'The Home of British Motor Racing'. But Silverstone occupies a unique position, not only in terms of British motor sport, but indeed in the history of Formula One, for it was the venue for the first-ever Formula One world championship Grand Prix in 1950. Before the construction of a dedicated circuit, organisers made use of the perimeter track around the airfield, and for the inaugural race, spectators were held back by rope, and corners were marked by oil drums. The British Grand Prix was held at the circuit from 1950 until 1954, before alternating with Aintree, best known as a horse-racing course and home of the Grand National, until 1964 when it instead began to alternate between Silverstone and Brands Hatch. But from 1987, Silverstone has been the permanent home of the British GP.

In 1950, every Grand Prix was won by Alfa Romeo, as team-mates Juan Manuel Fangio and Giuseppe Farina battled it out, but Ferrari quickly emerged as challengers, winning their first championship Grand Prix at Silverstone in 1951 and the next three consecutive races there, thanks to the skills of José Froilán González and Alberto Ascari and the fuel economy of the Ferrari 375.

During the 1960s, British legend Jim Clark was to win the British Grand Prix five times for Lotus, with three of those victories achieved at Silverstone, but McLaren were to dominate the circuit in the 1970s, with wins from Peter Revson, Emerson Fittipaldi and James Hunt.

The first major changes to the established layout came in 1987, when the British Grand Prix moved to Silverstone for good, with the addition of Bridge Bend before the final Woodcote kink, and the removal of the chicane for reasons of safety; and the race that year was won by local hero Nigel Mansell, following an epic battle with team-mate Nelson Piquet.

Mansell would triumph again in 1991 and 1992, the latter being his championship year. In 1991 further modifications had been made, with the notorious Maggotts and Stowe corners being eased. Several further changes were made during the 1990s, including improved access and facilities for spectators but, despite this, in recent years the track has come under criticism, and the 2005 event came close to being removed from the Formula One calendar.

The wrangling between Silverstone's owners, the British Racing Drivers Association and the F1 executive was settled amicably on that occasion, but the future of the race was guaranteed only until 2009. Midway during the 2008 season it was announced the contract would be awarded to Donington Park, which would take its place on the schedule from 2010. In the event, the East Midlands circuit defaulted and Silverstone was restored to the calendar, part of a new 17-year deal. The 2010 race was run over the 'Arena' layout, which added around 750 metres to the track length and, the organisers hoped, offered more overtaking opportunities. Red Bull's Mark Webber was the first winner on the newly configured track. The 2011 race hit the headlines for a short-lived regulation amendment curtailing the use of off-throttle blown diffusers. The change hit Ferrari less than its rivals, and Fernando Alonso recorded the team's sole victory of the year. The 2013 race, won by Rosberg, was dramatic for its spate of spectacular blowouts, which brought Pirelli rubber under the microscope and led to a change of tyre construction for the remainder of the season.

LEFT: **1994 British Grand Prix, Silverstone.**

GREAT BRITAIN

Track:	Brands Hatch
Track length:	4206m
Total distance:	319.66km (76 laps)

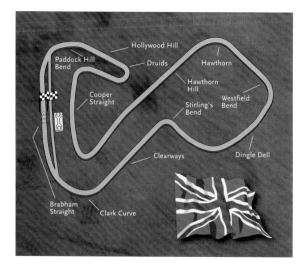

Although Silverstone claims the title as 'The Home of British Motor Racing', Brands Hatch has played host to a number of world championship events, including both the British and European Grand Prix, and whereas the circuit at Silverstone is flat and, some have said, characterless, Brands Hatch is situated within a natural amphitheatre that offers both excellent views for spectators, and a more varied course for the drivers.

During the 1920s and 1930s, the fields at Brands Hatch were used by cyclists, cross-country runners and motorcyclists, and a rudimentary circuit was developed, but the land was used as a depot for military vehicles during WWII, and was heavily bombed.

However, after the war, there was still a desire to see the land used as a racing circuit, and in 1947, Brands Hatch Stadium Ltd was established, with the result that by 1950, a track suitable for car racing had been created, and Formula Three events began to be held. In 1953 a motor racing club and school was formed, and throughout the 1950s, there were further developments, including the lengthening of the track, the creation of Druid's Bend, and the addition of pits, banks for spectators and a grandstand.

The first non-championship Formula One event was held in 1960 and was won by Jack Brabham, before the circuit was purchased by Grovewood Securities and placed under the management of John Webb, who successfully negotiated to host the British Grand Prix, alternating with Silverstone. So, in 1964, the first world championship Formula One race was held at Brands Hatch, which was won by Jim Clark. Brabham took

victory two years later and Jo Siffert in 1968. However, by that time, the circuit had claimed the lives of three drivers, and after Siffert tragically lost his life in 1971, a major overhaul took place.

The British Grand Prix continued to alternate between Brands Hatch and Silverstone up until 1986, and Brands Hatch was also to play host to the European Grand Prix in 1983 and 1985. On the first of these occasions, the event was hurriedly scheduled to replace the cancelled New York Grand Prix, but was nevertheless highly successful, and in 1985, the race would return, providing Nigel Mansell with his first Grand Prix win.

The following year, Mansell would triumph again, taking first place in the last British Grand Prix to be held at Brands Hatch before the event moved permanently to Silverstone.

In 1986, Brands Hatch was sold to John Foulston, and Brands Hatch Leisure was created, but sadly Foulston was to die soon afterwards while testing an IndyCar at Silverstone, and John Webb took over the running of the company until 1990.

During that time, the track saw further modifications, including the addition of a chicane and Dingle Dell Corner, and the tightening of Westfield and Graham Hill Bend, and in the late 1990s trackside facilities were also improved.

In 1999 it was announced that Brands Hatch would hold the 2002 British Grand Prix, but the company was sold once more, and unfortunately the new owners failed to secure planning permission to bring the circuit up to the required standard. Although not staging the British Grand Prix, Brands Hatch continues to host several notable events, such as the World Superbike Championships, the A1 Grand Prix and touring car series, and also holds testing and public track days.

LEFT: **1986 British Grand Prix, Brands Hatch. Nelson Piquet leads away from Nigel Mansell.**

HUNGARY

Track: Hungaroring, Budapest

Track length: 4381m

Total distance: 306.67km (70 laps)

The first Hungarian Grand Prix was held in 1936, but the political climate of Eastern Europe ensured that the event would not return for 50 years, and therefore, when it did so in 1986, it represented a major coup for the Formula One world championships and Bernie Ecclestone. It was also the first Formula One Grand Prix to be held behind the Iron Curtain. The race has since become a regular fixture on the Formula One calendar however, with its home at the Hungaroring, near Budapest.

The circuit was constructed in just eight months in 1985, in a natural amphitheatre in the rolling Hungarian hills, which offers spectators with probably the best visibility of any track in the championships. However, there is relatively little change in elevation in the track itself, and the tightly twisting layout offers few opportunities for overtaking, which has frequently resulted in rather processional events.

The race is also held at the height of summer, and the circuit is little used for the rest of the year, ensuring that conditions are invariably hot and dusty, turning racing into something of an endurance test for both the drivers and their vehicles. Despite all this, the Hungaroring has produced some memorable races and some important results.

Nelson Piquet won the first race for Williams in 1986, beating fellow Brazilian Ayrton Senna in his Lotus, with the two well ahead of the rest of the pack. Piquet would claim victory again the following year, in his third and final world championship season, but Senna would stand at the top of the podium in 1988 for McLaren, after beating team-mate Alain Prost by just half a second.

In 1989, Nigel Mansell put in an impressive performance to win, having started the race from 12th place on the grid, and then 1990 saw another incredibly close finish, with Thierry Boutsen keeping Senna at bay to win by 0.288 seconds.

Senna won again in 1991 and 1992, but Mansell's second place was enough to secure him the 1992 world championship title.

Damon Hill won in 1993 and 1995 for Williams, the former being his first Grand Prix victory, and then almost pulled off a surprise win for the Arrows team in 1997, after qualifying in third and taking the lead from Michael Schumacher, before suffering gearbox problems that pushed him back to second place and saw former team-mate Jacques Villeneuve snatch the win for Williams in the final lap.

Other notable races include Schumacher's third win at the Hungaroring in 2001, which provided his fourth world title and equalled Alain Prost's record of 51 Grand Prix wins, and then in 2003, after some modifications to the circuit which were designed to improve overtaking, Fernando Alonso became the first Spaniard to win a Grand Prix and the youngest driver ever to do so, at the age of 22 years and 26 days. The 2006 race saw Jenson Button record his maiden F1 victory for Honda, a stunning drive in the wet from 14th on the grid. Hamilton and Button shared six wins between 2006 and 2013, Lewis's 2013 victory putting him on a par with Schumacher as the most successful drivers at the circuit, with four wins apiece.

BELOW: **1997 Hungarian Grand Prix. Damon Hill at Turn 12, followed by Eddie Irvine.**

INDIA

Track: Buddh International Circuit, Greater Noida	
Track length:	5125m
Total distance:	307.5km (60 laps)

2011 saw the realisation of a ten-year dream to bring Formula One to India. There had been plans to build a circuit that could stage a championship race in Calcutta, Hyderabad and Bangalore, while a group championing Mumbai's cause had also thrown its hat into the ring. But in the end the Jaypee Group ploughed £250 million into the Buddh International Circuit, part of its Sports City complex in Greater Noida, a 30-mile expressway ride from Delhi. The Hermann Tilke-designed track was built on land where rice and wheat once grew, a symbol of extravagant wealth surrounded by pockets of grinding poverty. The development was not without its critics. Felipe Massa said a similar situation once pertained in Brazil, and hoped high-profile events such as a visit from the F1 circus would help to promote the kind of growth his homeland had enjoyed. Force India boss Vijay Mallya, one of the driving forces behind the campaign to bring top-level racing to the country, said it was not just a sporting coup but would showcase 'a vibrant young nation at its best'.

The track runs clockwise with 16 as yet unnamed turns, nine right-handers, seven left. Features include a kilometre-long straight bookending hairpins at Turns 3 and 4, and a long, sweeping right through turns 10 and 11. Some

ABOVE: **Force India's Adrian Sutil finished the inaugural Indian GP in ninth position, four places ahead of his team-mate Paul di Resta.**

interesting elevation changes were included to spice things up, and with construction going right to the wire, drivers had to beware the perils of dust lying on a green track.

The race was slotted in at Round 17 of the 2011 championship, by which time both the Drivers' and Constructors' titles had been decided. It witnessed one landmark, however: Vettel's pole was a record 16th of the year for Red Bull. 60 laps later, he had converted his grid placing into an 11th win of the year, and in a late flourish set a lap record of 1 min. 27.249 sec. Button and Alonso took the minor placings. Force India squeezed into the points, Adrian Sutil finishing ninth, while the partisan crowd were able to cheer on Narain Karthikeyan, who brought his HRT home in 17th. Karthikeyan, who became the first Indian driver to make it into the elite division when he debuted for Jordan in 2005, said: 'Having a high profile event like this gives the country a boost…it is fantastic to have F1 here.' India's only other man to compete in F1, Karun Chandhok, missed out on the historic race, his sole outing for Team Lotus that year coming in Germany. But as the consensus view of the inaugural Indian GP was extremely positive, it looked set to remain a fixture on the calendar for some time, giving both men further opportunities to bid for glory on home turf. In 2013 Vettel chalked up his hat-trick, and maintaining his 100 percent success rate at the circuit also delivered a fourth world title. His chance to make it four wins in a row disappeared when India was axed for 2014. Tax was one issue; F1 was classed as entertainment rather than a sport. Initially, a return to the calendar in 2015 was mooted, though with other new venues in the pipeline it now seems India may have to wait rather longer to host its fourth grand prix.

ITALY

Track: Autodromo Enzo e Dino Ferrari, San Marino	
Track length:	4933m
Total distance:	305.61km (62 laps)

The circuit at Imola hosted its first championship race in 1980, and quickly became one of the best loved on the Formula One calendar, largely on account of the Italian Ferrari fans, or tifosi, who guaranteed a supercharged race day atmosphere. However, the tragic events of 1994, when Roland Ratzenberger and Ayrton Senna lost their lives at Imola on consecutive days, has had lasting implications both for the circuit and the whole of Formula One.

Although most commonly referred to as Imola, after the nearby town of that name, the circuit is actually named the Autodromo Enzo e Dino Ferrari, in honour of Ferrari founder Enzo Ferrari, who passed away in 1988, and his son Dino, who died at a tragically young age during the 1950s. The circuit is fairly close to the Ferrari factory at Maranello, and the surrounding area is also home to the car manufacturers Maserati and Lamborghini, and so the construction of a test track for prototypes, which incorporated some public roads, was begun in 1950, to be first used in 1952 by Ferrari.

Motorcycle racing began at the circuit in 1953, and then car racing the following year, but it was not until 1963 that the venue first played host to Formula One, with a non-championship event that was won for Lotus by Jim Clark. The circuit was notoriously fast and flowing, and in 1973 and 1974, chicanes were added as a safety measure, before Formula One returned in 1979 with another non-championship race, which was won on this occasion by Niki Lauda in a Brabham-Alfa Romeo.

The first championship event was held in 1980, as Imola hosted the Italian Grand Prix, which had been moved from its usual home at Monza due to a pile up at the start line in 1978, in which Sweden's Ronnie Peterson had been killed. The race was won by Nelson Piquet, also in a Brabham.

Formula One returned to Imola in 1981 with the San Marino Grand Prix, which is named after the nearby principality of San Marino, and the race has remained an annual fixture ever since, providing Italy with two Grand Prix events each year, much to the delight of Ferrari fans, who regard Imola as their team's home circuit.

Unusually, the race is run in an anti-clockwise direction, forcing drivers to endure increased G-forces on the opposite side of the body to that which they are used to, and changes in gradient present a further difficulty. Until recently however, the greatest challenge faced by drivers at Imola came in the form of demanding corners such as Tamburello, Tosa and Piratella. However, this was to change as the dangers of the track and the need for modifications became increasingly apparent.

Gerhard Berger was lucky to survive a crash at Tamburello in 1989, as was Rubens Barrichello at the final corner, Variante Bassa, during practice in 1994. Then tragedy struck the following day, as Roland Ratzenberger was killed at the Villeneuve corner during qualifying, and the horror continued on race day with the death of three-times world champion Ayrton Senna, who ploughed into the wall at Tamburello during lap 7.

In 1995, more chicanes were added, existing ones modified, and a wide-ranging review of all Formula One circuits began, and although it has been suggested that Imola and other tracks subsequently lost some of their flow and character, it is widely accepted that this was necessary in order to avert further tragedy at that circuit and within the sport in general.

In the 2000s there was increasing concern over the circuit's deteriorating facilities. With Monza a fixture on the calendar and a clutch of new venues seeking a place at the top table, Imola was seen as expendable. It was dropped in 2007 and has not featured since.

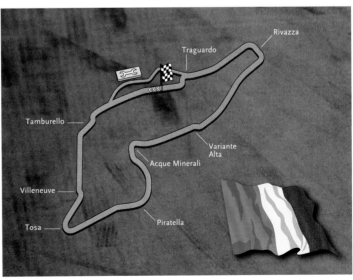

ITALY

Track:	**Autodromo Nazionale di Monza**
Track length:	5793m
Total distance:	306.72km (53 laps)

Despite numerous changes over its long history, Monza, or the Autodromo Nazionale di Monza, remains widely regarded as one of the world's greatest motor-racing circuits, and one of Formula One's spiritual homes. It has played host to every Italian Grand Prix, bar one, since the inception of the world championships in 1950, and the combination of the circuit's history, recent heroes such as Michael Schumacher, and the *tifosi* (fans), makes for an atmosphere that is practically unknown anywhere else in the Formula One calendar, with the possible exception of San Marino before Imola was dropped from the schedule in 2007.

The original circuit, which was constructed in 1922 in a park outside Milan, comprised a road course and a high-speed, banked, oval track, and officially opened to hold the second Italian Grand Prix in September of that year, the first having been held in 1921 at Brescia. The race was dominated by Fiat, who took the top four places.

Sadly, tragedy first struck at Monza in 1928, when Emilio Materassi's steering failed, resulting in one of the worst Grand Prix accidents of all time. Materassi died instantly as his car collided with the barrier, and over 20 spectators were killed by flying debris as his vehicle broke apart. As a result, racing was restricted to the high-speed track until modifications were made during the 1930s.

During WWII, the circuit was used to house military vehicles, and was badly damaged by bombing, and although Formula One racing began in 1950, a full renovation did not occur until 1955. The first race was won by Italian Giuseppe Farina, and the two subsequent races by fellow countryman Alberto Ascari, with Argentine legend Juan Manuel Fangio taking the next three wins. Then for the rest of the decade, Britons dominated the circuit, with three wins by Stirling Moss, and one from Tony Brooks.

In 1960 and 1961, victory went to American Phil Hill for Ferrari, but the 1961 race was marred by another tragedy, when a collision between Jim Clark and Wolfgang von Trips resulted in the death of the latter and 11 spectators.

Improvements were made, including the addition of run-off areas and new safety walls, and chicanes replaced the banked curves. As speeds continued to increase, two further chicanes were added in 1972, but following the deaths of five motorcyclists in 1973, these were reconstructed, and another added in 1976.

Throughout the 1970s and 1980s, improvements continued with safety in mind, and although Monza is still an incredibly fast track, the 1971 race remains the fastest on record, completed at an average of 242.616km/h by Briton Peter Gethin. That race also produced the closest finish of all time, with Gethin beating Ronnie Peterson by 0.01 seconds.

More chicanes were added after the deaths of Ayrton Senna and Roland Ratzenberger at Imola in 1994; and in 2000, the first chicane on the main straight was adjusted with the hope of reducing accidents. However, that same year a marshal was killed after a pile-up at the second chicane.

Despite all the efforts to reduce the overall speed at Monza, the long straights still ensure that drivers are going flat out for much of the race, and in qualifying in 2002, Juan Pablo Montoya completed the fastest-ever lap in Formula One, with an average speed of 259.827km/h. Sebastian Vettel also claimed a record at Monza, becoming Formula One's youngest-ever race winner in 2008. Vettel bagged his second win in 2011, and with Button, Alonso, Hamilton and Schumacher following him home, it meant that the top five spots were occupied by world champions. Schumacher still holds the race record, though, with five Monza victories to his name.

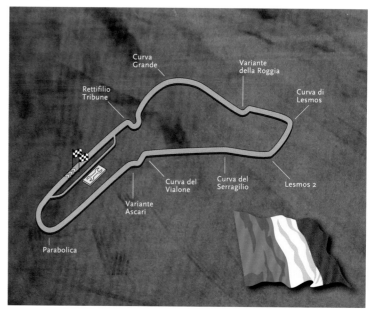

JAPAN

Track:	Suzuka International Racing Course
Track length:	5807m
Total distance:	307.77km (53 laps)

The Japanese Grand Prix was first held at the Fuji Speedway in 1976 but, following a collision between Gilles Villeneuve and Ronnie Peterson in 1977 that resulted in the death of a marshal, the race then moved to Suzuka, where it remained from 1987 to 2006.

The circuit was designed by Dutchman John Hugenholtz in 1962 as a test track for Honda, and is unique in Formula One for its location and layout, consisting of a figure-of-eight contained within a theme park. The course is also amongst the longest in Formula One, and boasts several other challenging features, including a downhill start, a variety of fast, sweeping corners and tight chicanes, and an equal number of left- and right-hand corners, a characteristic that was unique until the construction of the new Shanghai International Circuit in China.

Suzuka is generally regarded as one of the all-time great circuits by both drivers and spectators alike, with plenty of technical challenges for the drivers, but also several opportunities for overtaking, both of which make for exciting racing.

Further excitement is provided by the fact that Suzuka often hosts the last or penultimate race of the calendar, and around half of the encounters at the circuit have been world championship deciders.

The first race at Suzuka was one such affair, with victory being taken by Gerhard Berger for Ferrari, but the championship being handed to Nelson Piquet by Williams team-mate Nigel Mansell, after he crashed during practice.

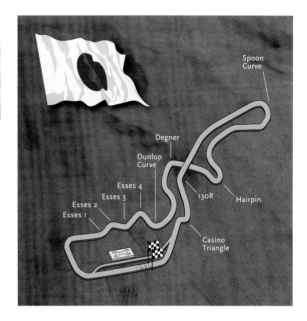

Then in 1989 and 1990 came the highly controversial championship battles between Ayrton Senna and Alain Prost, which witnessed them colliding during both encounters. In 1989 Prost swerved into Senna as he attempted to pass, taking them both out and ensuring Senna would not take the title, then in 1990 Senna forced Prost off the track at the first bend in a move that he later admitted was deliberate, and which had ensured him the championship.

More recently, and certainly more sportingly, much of the entertainment has been provided by the competition between Michael Schumacher and Mika Häkkinen, with Schumacher's win in 2000, in wet conditions, being notable for providing both his third world title and his first for Ferrari. In 2003, first place went to his team-mate Rubens Barrichello, but Schumacher battled to gain the point that gave him his sixth world championship title, beating the record that Argentine legend Juan Manuel Fangio had held since 1957. In 2007 Suzuka lost its place on the schedule as the Japanese GP returned to the rebuilt Fuji Speedway. Suzuka returned to the calendar in 2009 under a deal by which the Japanese Grand Prix will alternate between the two circuits. 2010 should have seen Fuji play host, but track owners Toyota pulled out for economic reasons, thus Suzuka has the race to itself in the short term. In 2011 a podium finish was enough to see Sebastian Vettel clinch his second world championship, adding to the list of title deciders the race has witnessed.

LEFT: **Japanese Grand Prix, 1997, Suzuka, Japan. A view of the Suzuka circuit, on the left showing the Dunlop Curve to the Degner Curve and on the right the notorious Casino Triangle Chicane to 130R.**

MALAYSIA

Track: Sepang International Circuit, Kuala Lumpur	
Track length:	5543m
Total distance:	310.41km (56 laps)

The Sepang International Circuit, which is located near Kuala Lumpur in Malaysia, was the first of the new, ultra-modern Formula One venues to be designed by Hermann Tilke, the architect who has since been responsible for similar projects in China, Bahrain and Turkey, and it made a substantial impression when it opened in 1999 to host the inaugural Malaysian Grand Prix.

Not only are the pit, media and corporate facilities superb, but the track has also been constructed with spectators well in mind. The venue has a capacity of 80,000 fans, some 30,000 of which can be accommodated in a back-to-back grandstand area positioned between the two principal straights, while all the grandstand areas, including the cheaper seats in the Hillstand, provide good viewing opportunities and are well serviced by amenities.

Just as importantly perhaps, the track itself offers the possibility of exciting racing, with a variety of high-speed sections and slower, more tightly twisting areas, five left and ten right-hand turns, and an average width of 16 metres that is designed to encourage overtaking. So although the layout is challenging, it has been well received by both the drivers and spectators alike.

The weather conditions at Sepang add further variety, with the possibilities of blazing heat, high humidity and tropical downpours, but there have been even more unpredictable factors affecting race results, and perhaps none more so than during the first race at Sepang in 1999.

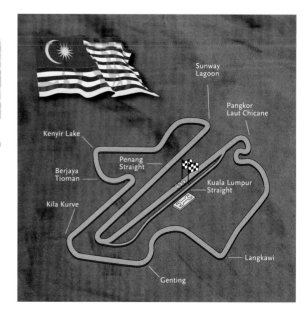

Michael Schumacher made a triumphant return, after sustaining a broken leg at Silverstone earlier in the year, by dominating the race for Ferrari before handing victory to team-mate and championship-hopeful Eddie Irvine, only for both to be disqualified on a technicality, giving Mika Häkkinen the win. However, the decision was later overruled and Irvine was reinstated as the winner.

Then in 2001, the weather came into play, and Schumacher and Rubens Barrichello, both in Ferraris, looked to be out of the race after spinning off in the wet at the same point, but they made miraculous recoveries to end the race in first and second places respectively.

Schumacher secured his third victory at Sepang in 2004, in a race that was also notable for a record lap by Juan Pablo Montoya, who completed the circuit in just 1 min. 34.233 sec. Vettel and Alonso have since notched three wins each in Malaysia, making it a three-way tie for the most successful driver at the circuit.

The creation of the circuit was largely driven in the mid-1990s by the then Malaysian Prime Minister, Dr Mahathir Mohamad, with the specific intention of bringing Formula One to a country whose automotive industry was burgeoning, which had an oil industry that was putting a great deal of investment into Sauber, and which had seen the purchase of Lotus Engineering by Malaysia's Proton. Most would probably agree that in its short history, the Malaysian Grand Prix at the Sepang International Circuit has proved a welcome addition to the Formula One calendar.

LEFT: **Malaysian Grand Prix, Sepang, 2000.**

MONACO

Track:	Monaco
Track length:	3340m
Total distance:	260.52km (78 laps)

No venue on the Formula One calendar captures the glamour, excitement and romance of the sport as much as Monaco. For many years it was the only street circuit in the annual circus, and although the likes of Valencia and Singapore have now joined the schedule, Monaco retains its unique place in the fabric of the championship and in the affection of motor racing fans.

Monte Carlo, home of the super-rich yacht and casino set, staged its first Grand Prix on 14 April 1929. William Grover-Williams took victory in a Bugatti 35B in that inaugural race, the first to be staged in an urban setting. In the 1930s the likes of Achille Varzi and Tazio Nuvolari joined battle around the principality's harbourside streets, while the 1948 race saw Ferrari make its bow as a constructor.

Monaco hosted the second round of the inaugural world championship, on 21 May 1950. Juan Manuel Fangio emerged the victor after a pile-up on the opening lap which took out over half the field.

After a four-year gap, the championship returned to the principality in 1955, and has been a fixture on the calendar ever since. That year is chiefly remembered for double world champion Alberto Ascari's unscheduled dip into the harbour while leading the race. He survived that spectacular crash only to be killed during practice four days later.

Graham Hill's name became forever associated with the circuit after five wins in seven years in the 1960s. It could have been an even better record had he not suffered engine failure while heading the field in 1962.

Despite its reputation as a processional race with overtaking nigh on impossible, Monaco has had more than its share of thrilling encounters. In 1967 Denny Hulme claimed his first GP victory in the street classic en route to the world title. That race saw a fireball accident involving the Ferrari of Lorenzo Bandini, who died from his appalling injuries. Three years later Jack Brabham, with Jochen Rindt hard on his tail, miscalculated the braking at the final bend, handing victory to the Austrian ace. Ronnie Peterson won an accident-littered race for Lotus in 1974, while in 1982 Riccardo Patrese claimed his maiden victory in a spectacular battle which saw the lead change hands four times in the last three laps.

From 1984, Alain Prost and Ayrton Senna divided the Monte Carlo spoils for a decade. When torrential rain caused the 1984 race to be halted at half distance, Senna, from 13th on the grid, was bearing down on leader Prost. This was the race when the Brazilian rookie, driving for Toleman, truly announced himself on the world stage. He might have added another win in 2006, but was ruled to have deliberately stopped his car at La Rascasse during qualifying, thus preventing his rivals from bettering his time, and was relegated to the back of the grid.

Ayrton Senna's six Monaco victories made him the new king of the principality. Michael Schumacher's first win there came just after Senna's death, in 1994, and he racked up four more wins, putting him joint second, with Graham Hill, in the all-time list. Nico Rosberg's victory in 2013 made it a family double, coming 30 years after father Keke won in the Principality.

Monaco may be the slowest of the championship venues – Loews is a sedate 30mph hairpin – but, as Ascari proved in 1955, there is no room for error. This demanding circuit, largely unchanged in the past 70 years, is one in which minor mistakes invariably exact a heavy price.

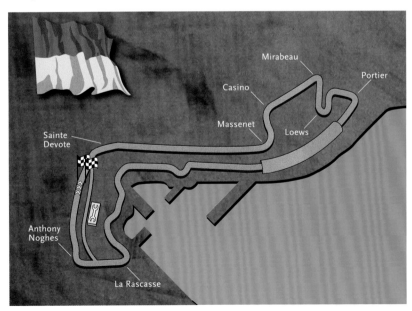

SINGAPORE

Track:	Marina Bay
Track length:	5073m
Total distance:	309.45km (61 laps)

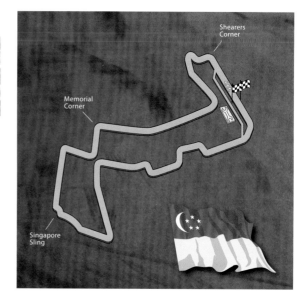

Those responsible for bringing Formula One to Singapore in 2008 must have been heartened by Sir Frank Williams' verdict on Marina Bay: 'It has a good chance of challenging Monaco for being the jewel in the crown of Formula One.' The drivers were also impressed, though all noted how bumpy the track was, which made it highly demanding on both car and driver. Lewis Hamilton, who won there in 2009, said: 'It's a very physical circuit ... I'd say it requires double the energy of Monaco over a single lap. One lap around here is like two laps of Monaco.'

With so many new venues coming on stream in recent years, it helps to have a USP, and Marina Bay did that in style by illuminating the street circuit and giving Formula One its first night race. Bernie Ecclestone was highly receptive to the plan, since it made for a viewer-friendly transmission time in Europe. Naturally, the big concern was visibility, and track bosses insisted that it would be run at night only if safety was not compromised. Those concerns were allayed by the use of some 1600 lighting rigs, capable of flooding the track to the tune of 3000 lux. That is several times brighter than the average football stadium.

Marina Bay runs anti-clockwise, the drivers having to negotiate 61 laps of the 5.07km track. There are 23 turns, 14 left-handers and nine right. There are four high-speed

stretches – top speed is around 300 km/h – and a few spots conducive to overtaking, providing plenty of appeal to the 100,000 spectators, 80,000 of them accommodated in the venue's grandstands. The track winds its way over the man-made harbour via the Anderson Bridge, past the Singapore Flyer – the world's tallest Ferris wheel – and also takes in the famous Raffles Hotel, where the Singapore Sling was invented at the turn of the 20th century. Turn 10 is named after the cocktail, one of three areas of the track to be christened following a competition thrown open to the fans. The others are Sheares Corner and Memorial Corner. The first is situated at Turn 1, which lies in the shadow of the Benjamin Sheares Bridge. Both take their name from a former president of the Republic. Memorial Corner, Turn 7, is so called because of a nearby monument honouring those killed in WWII.

Fernando Alonso has found Marina Bay a happy hunting ground, winning the inaugural 2008 race, and also taking the chequered flag in 2010. The first of those victories was mightily impressive as Alonso started from 15th on the grid. The 2008 Singapore GP was a doubly memorable occasion, for this was the 800th race since the inception of the world championship in 1950. Alonso was on the podium in 2009, too, though on top that day was Lewis Hamilton, who won from pole. Vettel's 2011 win marked the first in a hat-trick of wins that put him top of the circuit's honours board, and in 2013 he crowned victory with a new lap record of 1m 48.574 sec.

Left: Mark Webber, Singapore GP, September 2010.

SOUTH KOREA

Track:	Korea International Circuit, Jeollanam-do
Track length:	5615m
Total distance:	308.63km (55 laps)

It was a desperately close thing as to whether the inaugural Korean Grand Prix would be able to take place at the back end of the 2010 season. Construction of the Korean International Circuit had been delayed by adverse weather conditions in the southwest of the country, and the rain continued to fall on race day. The start was delayed and 26 of the 55 laps were run behind the safety car, which meant that the closing stages took place in murky conditions. But there was excitement aplenty with a spate of accidents, and the title race hotted up as both Red Bulls drew a blank. Championship leader Mark Webber crashed out, while pole-sitter Sebastian Vettel, lying third in the table, suffered engine failure ten laps from home when victory looked assured. Fernando Alonso snaffled up the spoils and took over at the top of the leader board with two races to go, setting up a terrific climax to a season full of twists and turns. Vettel had no such ill fortune in the next three races, scoring a maximum each time during title-winning campaigns.

The track, built on reclaimed swampland adjacent to an artificial seaside lake, is situated in Jeollanam-do, near the port city of Mokpo. The capital, Seoul, lies some 370km to the north. The Korean International Circuit is unique in that it is the first stage of an urban development; eventually, an entire city will rise within its confines. It is another Hermann Tilke creation, and although F1's favourite designer has attracted criticism for some of the tracks he has produced, the early signs were positive regarding this venue. That is partly down to the unusual mix of power straights and street circuit, which demands much of both car and driver. There is 3km of permanent track, with the temporary street section taking in the harbour-side of Jeollanam-do. There are three high-speed stretches. The 1.2km straight between turns 2 and 3 is one of the longest on the calendar, and to see the cars wind up to 320km/h, then tackle the 80 km/h, first-gear hairpin at the end, makes for a spectacular sight. And the potential for even more thrills and spills increased in 2011, with the return of KERS and introduction of a driver-adjustable rear wing offering a high-speed window. The long straight provides just one of several decent overtaking opportunities; there's no excuse for processional races here. The anticlockwise track has 18 turns, 11 left-handers, 7 right. These are unnamed as yet, but there are design features to

add character, not least the 16,000-seat main grandstand, inspired by traditional Hanok-house architecture.

The consensus among the drivers was positive following the inaugural GP, though some concerns were expressed over the pit-lane entry. Sebastian Vettel said: 'It's blind, and someone going into the pits will be going slower than someone who is staying out. If you're trying to pass and they decide to pit, it could be quite difficult.' That didn't stop Vettel winning the 2011 race, and with team-mate Mark Webber taking third, Red Bull wrapped up their second Constructors' title in South Korea. Ironically, it was the only race of the year when Red Bull failed to take pole.

After just four races Korea found itself off the Formula One map. The lengthy trek from Seoul was cited as a key issue, affecting attendance figures and the race-day atmosphere. Sizeable losses prompted the organisers to try and renegotiate their deal with Ecclestone, and when that failed Yeongam's fate was sealed, for now at least.

BELOW: **The safety cars begin their test drive in practice, 2010.**

SPAIN

Track:	Circuit de Catalunya, Barcelona
Track length:	4655m
Total distance:	307.1km (66 laps)

Although Spain, and Catalonia in particular, have a well established tradition of motor racing and a long history of hosting Formula One events, the Circuit de Catalunya in Barcelona, the current home of the Spanish Grand Prix, is a relatively modern venue which was constructed in the early 1990s. While it boasts good facilities and has produced some memorable encounters it has, however, been somewhat eclipsed by the new generation of circuits.

The first major motor racing competition to be held in Spain was probably the Catalan Cup, a road race that was staged in Sitges, close to Barcelona, in 1908, before the first Spanish Grand Prix took place in 1913, near Madrid. A permanent circuit was then constructed at Sitges, the Sitges-Terramar, but Grand Prix racing was to move to Lasarte after 1923.

Between 1936 and 1945, the Spanish Civil War and WWII were to put an end to such events, but the Grand Prix returned to Barcelona at the Pedralbes Circuit in 1946.

In 1951, Pedralbes was to host its first Grand Prix as part of the world championships, an event that was won by the unstoppable Juan Manuel Fangio, but by 1955, the circuit had been removed from the competition due to concerns over safety.

During the 1960s and 1970s, racing alternated between the circuits of Jarama near Madrid, and Montjuic Park in Barcelona, but the latter was dropped after a tragic accident in 1975 which resulted in the deaths of five spectators, and the Spanish Grand Prix moved to Jarama until 1981.

The race then fell from the Formula One calendar, but returned at the new Jerez circuit in southern Spain in 1986, producing the second closest finish of all time, with just 0.050 seconds separating winner Ayrton Senna and Nigel Mansell.

Jerez held its last Spanish Grand Prix in 1990, by which time the construction of the Circuit de Catalunya was well underway and, in 1991, the race returned to make its permanent home in Barcelona.

In a duel reminiscent of the 1986 event, Mansell and Senna battled it out once more, at one point driving side by side down the entire length of the front straight, with Mansell taking the lead, and this time the win.

Mansell triumphed again in 1992, his championship season, and in 1994 another Briton, Damon Hill, would take the win. However, that race was probably most notable for Michael Schumacher's feat of achieving second place with only fourth gear for much of the race.

Schumacher claimed victory in 1995 and 1996, the latter being his first Grand Prix win for Ferrari, and then between 1998 and 2000, Mika Häkkinen scored three consecutive wins. In 2001, Häkkinen again looked set to take first place, but his clutch gave out on the final lap and Schumacher was handed the win, the first of four uninterrupted victories up until 2004.

The circuit itself is quite fast and is varied in terms of its corners, but none are particularly challenging, and there are few opportunities for overtaking, other than at the first, Elf, which has led some to describe the circuit as bland. However, most criticism stems not from the circuit's layout, but from the fact that it is used so often for Formula One testing that the drivers are completely familiar with it so racing at Barcelona has an air of predictability and a lack of atmosphere. However, since the arrival of the young Fernando Alonso onto the Formula One scene, the Spanish, at least, have had a great deal to be excited about. Scenes of wild jubilation greeted his victory in 2006, the first time a Spanish driver had won on home soil. Alonso repeated that achievement in 2013.

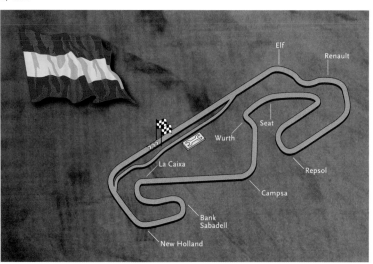

SPAIN

Track:	**Valencia Street Circuit**
Track length:	**5419m**
Total distance:	**308.88km (57 laps)**

Bernie Ecclestone waived the unwritten one-race-per-country rule in 2008, when Valencia joined Barcelona on the schedule in a seven-year deal to host the European Grand Prix. The Spanish port became the fifth venue for this 'nomadic' race, and the sixth from that country to host a world championship event, following Pedralbes, Jarama, Montjuic, Jerez and Catalunya. Not since 1991, when Phoenix was on the list, had there been two street circuits on the calendar. Valencia has a character all of its own, though, and quite different from Monaco or Singapore. Jenson Button describes it thus: 'There are some low-speed corners with some fairly unforgiving walls at the apex, but there are also some high-speed changes of direction and some long straights, so it's quite an interesting place, set-up-wise'.

The circuit completely encompasses the Juan Carlos I Marina – thanks to a Hermann Tilke-designed 140-m swing bridge – while its 25 turns (11 left-handers, 14 right) put it to the top of the F1 list on that score. It is a clockwise track, with top speeds of around 320km/h, comparable to Monza and Spa. Overtaking opportunities, though, are limited, so grid position is key. That view was underlined when Felipe Massa won from pole in the inaugural 2008 race. Lewis Hamilton was the fastest qualifier in 2009, but there was a slight deviation to the script as Rubens Barrichello, who started third, took advantage of a heavier fuel load. The Brazilian was able to keep his Brawn GP 001 out on the track longer and put a major dent in Hamilton's lead after the first round of pit stops. After the second, Barrichello was the front-runner and he went on to claim his first victory in five years. Timo Glock, whose Toyota was well down the field, had the consolation of setting a new fastest lap mark of 1 min. 38.683 sec. No one bettered that in 2010, a race that saw another win for the pole-sitter, this time Sebastian Vettel. His Red Bull team-mate Mark Webber had a memorable day for a very different reason. The Australian was lucky to walk away unscathed from a spectacular airborne spill after tangling with Kovalainen's Lotus on the fastest point on the track.

In autumn 2010, just three years into the seven-race deal, there were reports in the Spanish press that Valencia was facing a cash crisis, casting doubt over its ability to see out the contract. Attendances had dropped off dramatically.

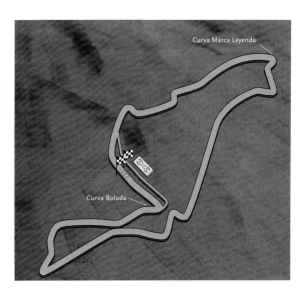

Around 110,000 flocked to the inaugural European GP, reflecting the passion of an F1-mad country where double world champion Fernando Alonso is idolised. But by 2010 that figure had fallen to 75,000 and the alarm bells started to ring. An attempt to add some character by naming a couple of the turns – Curva Marca Leyenda (8) and Curva Boluda (25) – wasn't going to be enough to halt the slide. It was said that the organisers were trying to end the deal before its 2014 due date, or possibly find an alternative venue where the numbers stacked up more favourably. Mark Webber makes no secret of his dislike for the circuit – perhaps for obvious reasons – and wouldn't be sorry to see it go. Another detractor is David Coulthard, who described Valencia as 'a cracking venue but it lacks any challenge'. There was little surprise when Valencia, and the nomadic European GP banner it ran under, disappeared from the schedule after the 2012 race, won by Fernando Alonso.

BELOW: **Fernado Alonso takes part in the 2010 European GP.**

TURKEY

Track:	Istanbul Park
Track length:	5338m
Total distance:	309.4km (58 laps)

The Turkish Grand Prix was added to the Formula One roster in 2005, when the newly built Istanbul Park circuit was unveiled. It is one of the latest of racetrack architect Hermann Tilke's stunning new venues, which also include international circuits at Sepang in Malaysia, Shanghai in China, and in Bahrain.

As with those tracks, Istanbul Park boasts cutting-edge design and technology, and superb facilities, with a capacity of over 155,000, a main grandstand that can house around 25,000 spectators, two seven-storey VIP towers, hospitality areas and excellent facilities for the teams and drivers.

However, the track's layout, and primarily the fact that races are run in an anticlockwise direction, sets Istanbul Park apart, even from Tilke's other recent creations. Only Brazil, Singapore and Abu Dhabi are also run in this direction, presenting drivers with a different physical challenge in terms of G-force. In addition, Istanbul features several changes in elevation, the track having been constructed on four main levels.

Unlike almost all of Tilke's circuits, Istanbul Park lacks a continuous, long straight, and instead the straight is broken by a major kink. This has raised some concerns about overtaking, but overall the circuit has garnered high praise from drivers and fans alike, particularly for its challenging corners, and for Turn 8 specifically, which has already prompted comparisons with parts of the old Nürburgring, Eau Rouge at Spa-Francorchamps and the 130R at Suzuka.

Some drivers, though, have criticised the circuit for being more of a test of machine than man, and have suggested that it is a rather easy track to learn. Nevertheless, Turn 8 caught out a number of drivers during the Inaugural Turkish Grand Prix, which took place on 21 August 2005, with several cars spinning from the track at this point, during both qualifying and racing.

Notably, Juan Pablo Montoya lost control there while attempting to lap Tiago Monteiro with just two laps remaining, enabling Fernando Alonso to take second place, with Kimi Räikkönen, who had begun the race in pole position, securing the win.

Felipe Massa has enjoyed himself at Istanbul Park, notching a hat-trick of wins for Ferrari between 2006 and 2008 on the circuit Bernie Ecclestone once described as 'the best racetrack in the world'. Massa's record looked set to stand for some time as the Turkish GP was dropped from the schedule for 2012.

LEFT: **The Turkish Grand Prix, Istanbul, 21 August 2005.**

UNITED ARAB EMIRATES

Track:	Yas Marina Circuit, Abu Dhabi
Track length:	5554m
Total distance:	305.36km (55 laps)

Oil-rich Abu Dhabi spared no expense in constructing the Yas Marina circuit, which opened its doors to the Formula One circus in 2009. Construction began early in 2007, the circuit's £800 million budget a mere fraction of the overall cost of the development. The 5-star Yas Marina hotel straddles the track, with six others nearby for those with somewhat shallower pockets. There is also a shopping mall, golf course and space to berth your superyacht! Not forgetting Ferrari World, the largest indoor theme park anywhere, boasting a 150-mph rollercoaster ride. The total cost of the entire facility was estimated at £20 billion.

Herman Tilke oversaw the design, the brief being to create a Middle Eastern version of Monaco. The circuit is situated on man-made Yas Island, which lies a short drive – via a 12-lane highway – from Abu Dhabi city. It is one of the few F1 venues that runs anti-clockwise, drivers and cars having to negotiate 21 turns, 12 left and nine right. The championship distance is 55 laps of the 5.5-km circuit, though the design allows for it to be split into two shorter tracks – 3.1km and 2.4km – which can operate independently, even hosting different events simultaneously.

Other points of interest include the distinctive Shams Tower, which rises high above the start-finish straight and operates on solar power – which is in plentiful supply. The tunnel exit to the pit lane also marks Yas Marina out from other circuits. The race itself is unique to Formula One in being a day-night affair, setting it apart from Singapore, which doesn't get under way until after dusk. Fans are well catered for, with covered grandstands that can seat up to 50,000. One of those sits above a run-off area at Turn 8, which means that any driver getting his braking wrong would disappear from view beneath the gallery.

Abu Dhabi was given the honour of hosting the finale to the 2009 season, the first Grand Prix in a seven-year deal that will keep it on the calendar until at least 2015. Unfortunately, there was nothing but pride riding on the outcome, as both the Drivers' and Constructors' titles had already been settled. Sebastian Vettel won, laying down a 1 min. 40.279 sec. marker for others to aim at. The 2010 race, by contrast, was a four-way title shoot-out, Vettel claiming a second victory to leapfrog Fernando Alonso and team-mate Mark Webber and secure his first world championship at the age of 23. Vettel racked up his third win at Yas Marina in 2013, and the circuit's return to the finale slot the following season was lent added interest following the decision to award double points in the last round of the championship.

LEFT: **Vettel at Yas Marina, November 2010.**

UNITED STATES

Track:	Watkins Glen
Track length:	5435m
Total distance:	320.67km (108 laps)

The US has a well-established tradition of motor racing. In recent years, the Indianapolis Motor Speedway circuit has been the home of the United States Grand Prix, but Watkins Glen International in upstate New York also has an illustrious history, and has played host to the United States Grand Prix on 20 consecutive occasions between 1961 and 1980.

Grand Prix racing first began in the area in 1948 with the Watkins Glen Grand Prix which was run on local roads, but after a spectator was killed in 1952 the race was moved out of the town to a wooded hill nearby. The course still used existing roads, but with the foundation of the Watkins Glen Grand Prix Corporation, better organisation and safety were assured.

However, three years later, construction of a permanent racetrack got underway, and in 1957 it began to host the international Formula Libre race, which attracted the likes of Stirling Moss, Jack Brabham, Phil Hill and other great drivers of the day.

In 1959 and 1960 Formula One events took place at Sebring in Florida and Riverside, California, respectively but these were largely unsuccessful, and organisers began to look elsewhere for suitable venues.

So it was that in 1961, Watkins Glen was to stage its first Formula One Grand Prix as part of the World Championships. Following the death of Count Wolfgang von Trips during the previous race at Monza, Ferrari had withdrawn its team from the rest of the season, including the world champion, American Phil Hill, and the race was won by Briton Innes Ireland, who scored the only Grand Prix win of his career, and the first for the Lotus team. Somewhat unexpectedly, however, Ireland was sacked just weeks later and Jim Clark took over as

their top driver, winning the US Grand Prix at Watkins Glen the following year. It was an achievement Clark would repeat in 1966 and 1967, but in the intervening years Graham Hill scored three consecutive wins for BRM. Unfortunately in 1969, Hill was to break both his legs at 'The Glen', in an accident that no doubt foreshortened his career. Jochen Rindt took the win for Lotus that year, and although tragically he would lose his life at Monza the following season, the Lotus team secured another victory at Watkins Glen in 1970 with Emerson Fittipaldi, in what was only his third Grand Prix.

The circuit underwent an extensive modification prior to the 1971 outing, being widened and resurfaced, and extended by just over a mile with the addition of the four-cornered 'Boot' or 'Anvil' section. The win that year was a Grand Prix first for François Cévert, but tragedy befell him two years later when he was killed at the circuit.

As the cars became faster during the 1970s, a series of accidents continued to tarnish the formerly bright reputation of Watkins Glen, and against a backdrop of increasing financial problems the venue was dropped from the Formula One calendar after the 1980 US Grand Prix, which was won by Alan Jones for Williams, their first and only victory at the circuit.

Watkins Glen was closed in 1981; a shame for a historic venue that had on three occasions won the Driver's Association award for the best staged Grand Prix. It was reopened in 1984, and although Formula One has never returned, the circuit continues to host all manner and class of road racing events, including vintage racing and the NASCAR championships.

Left: **Watkins Glen, New York, USA.**

UNITED STATES

Track:	Circuit of the Americas
Track length:	5516m
Total distance:	308.90km (56 laps)

The United States disappeared from the Formula One map for five years following Lewis Hamilton's victory at Indianapolis in 2007. It returned in 2012 with a brand new, purpose-built track in the heart of Texas; and with a street-circuit race in New Jersey in the pipeline for the following year, the US looked set to re-establish a firm foothold in motor-sport's top tier.

The vision to build the grandly named Circuit of the Americas in Austin, capital of a state that alone ranks as the 11th largest economy in the world, was the brainchild of events company boss Tavo Hellmund, a man who had the ear of Bernie Ecclestone as a long-standing family friend. Things turned messy when Hellmund disappeared from the picture and his backers took up the negotiating cudgels. They wanted a signed and sealed deal, since the original ten-year contract was with Hellmund. In November 2011, exactly a year before the US Grand Prix was due to take place, work on the Circuit of the Americas ground to a halt for several weeks in a wrangle over the $25 million sanctioning fee, which the consortium hoped would be met by state funding. Ecclestone, in turn, threatened to pull America from the 2012 schedule, and won the brinkmanship battle as the money was eventually paid.

With the politicking and posturing out of the way, the focus could turn to a track that promised much, the first facility to be built from the ground up to stage a Formula One race in the States. Hermann Tilke's design was an eye-catching layout on the drawing board, running anticlockwise and making full use of the site's natural topography. Full of twists and undulations, it includes a 40-metre incline from the start line-up to a hairpin at Turn 1, the highest point on the circuit, followed by a sweep down to a fast right-hander at Turn 2. Some of the turns were inspired by signature features of other classic tracks, including Silverstone and Hockenheim. The run through Turns 16 to 18 is reminiscent of the multi-apex left-hander at Istanbul Park's Turn 8. The 5.5-km track has 20 turns in all – 12 of them left-handers. The conception was for a fast, challenging circuit that would provide a thrilling spectacle, and it lived up to the billing as the scene of the penultimate round of the 2012 title race. Hamilton prevailed in a battle royal with Vettel, while Austin also saw the constructors' championship settled in Red Bull's favour. 'for the following year'

BELOW: **Former driver David Coulthard pilots a Red Bull show car in Austin, Texas, in August 2011, to promote the US Grand Prix.**

THE WORLD
CHAMPIONSHIPS

1950

Drivers' Championship	1.	Nino Farina	30
	2.	Juan Manuel Fangio	27
	3.	Luigi Fagioli	24

(Constructors' Title not introduced until 1958)

INAUGURAL WORLD CHAMPIONSHIP

The first world championship in motor racing was inaugurated in February 1950. The sport's governing body, the Fédération Internationale de l'Automobile, linked six Grands Prix in one competition. Points were to be awarded based on the results of these six, and the driver with the most would become the 'World Champion'.

Fagiola, Farina and Fangio

This new competition tempted Alfa Romeo to return to the sport – it had been out of racing for a year – and the year was dominated by three star Alfa drivers: Luigi Fagioli, Nino Farina and Juan Manuel Fangio. Alberto Ascari, who drove for Ferrari, was their most notable contender; Ferrari was trying to get its new car up and running, a 4500cc V-12, but it came too late for the 1950 season.

Seven-race championship

Initially the new championship technically involved seven races: six in Europe and the Indianapolis 500. However, the latter was never really fully integrated and though it continued to provide championship points until 1960, only one Formula One driver competed in this US classic.

The first race was on 13 May at Silverstone. Farina won, with Fagioli coming second. Though Fangio had retired eight laps from the end, it was still a triumph for Alfa: third place went to their works driver Reg Parnell.

Monte Carlo pile-up

The next race was at Monte Carlo a week later. A multiple pile-up on the initial lap involved Farina, who had been lying second, and blocked the road. Fangio, who was in the lead and unaware of the incident, managed to weave through the wrecked cars when he came round again; he went on to win. Ascari came second, but a lap behind. This was followed by the Swiss Grand Prix, won by Farina with Fagioli second; Fangio had retired earlier. All three Ferraris had blown up and

a Talbot, driven by Louis Rosier, came in third. Spa hosted the Belgian Grand Prix, and this time Fangio headed Fagioli home, followed again by Rosier. The French Grand Prix was won easily by Fangio, again with Fagioli second. Fangio had 26 points; Fagioli, 24, overhauling Farina.

Farina – first world champion

The last race of the year was at Monza, and Alfa added two more cars, driven by Piero Taruffi and Consalvo Sanesi. On the 24th lap Fangio's gearbox failed and he was able to take over Taruffi's car; unfortunately it then dropped a valve. His chance of the title was gone. Ascari, now driving the full 4500cc Ferrari, was lying second in the early part of the race, hoping to steal the lead from the Alfas which needed two refuelling stops; his Ferrari needed only one. He did manage to take the lead, but his car then failed. He too switched cars, taking over from Dorino Serafini, and managed to get back to second, ahead of Fagioli. He was still a minute behind Farina, whose win put him up to 30 points, ahead of Fangio, making him the first world champion.

1950 clearly belonged to Alfa Romeo. Alfa had won all six European races, and its 'big three' occupied the top places in the Drivers' championship. But there were encouraging signs for Ferrari.

ABOVE: **Alberto Ascari at the wheel of José Froilán González's Ferrari 375, on his way to second position at the 1951 French Grand Prix, Reims-Gueux.**

OPPOSITE: **1950 British Grand Prix, Silverstone, England. Nino Farina leads Luigi Fagioli (both Alfa Romeo 158). They finished in first and second positions respectively in the first ever GP.**

1951

Drivers' Championship	1. Juan Manuel Fangio	31
	2. Alberto Ascari	25
	3. José Froilán González	24
(Constructors' Title not introduced until 1958)		

THE RISE OF FERRARI

Despite the excellent 1950 season, there were already signs that Alfa would not have the same hold in 1951. Ferrari's Ascari had only 12 points in the inaugural year, coming a distant fourth to the three Alfa drivers, but there had been signs that this would change at Monza.

Fangio sets the pace

Switzerland saw the opening round of the 1951 championship, and Fangio won. Ascari finished in sixth place; he had a badly burnt arm, an injury from a Formula Two race. In eighth position was an Englishman driving an HWM – Stirling Moss.

Farina took the honours in the Belgian Grand Prix but Fangio, his Alfa team-mate, had a jammed wheel during a routine pit stop which took nearly 15 minutes to fix, and finished ninth – he did pick up a point for setting the fastest lap, though. Ascari and Villoresi's Ferraris were well adrift of Farina, who led them by 3 minutes.

The next round was on the fast circuit at Reims. Ascari was chasing Fangio when his gearbox failed; a new Ferrari driver, José Froilán González, was called into the pits and Ascari, as senior driver, returned to the race in his car. Fangio, too, needed to switch cars, taking over Fagioli's Alfa early in the race. Fangio crossed the line first, a minute ahead of Ascari, with Villoresi again third. The Ferraris were getting closer to defeating Alfa.

Italian rivals

This finally happened in the next race at Silverstone. Ascari retired with gearbox trouble and when González came in for a routine stop, Ascari realised that his team-mate was in excellent form, so didn't pull rank. Fangio had tried to establish a healthy lead, knowing that his Alfa required two refuelling stops to the Ferraris' one, but he couldn't shake González off. González pulled clear, coming home nearly a minute ahead. There was some British success: Reg Parnell

Drivers' Championship	1.	Alberto Ascari	36
	2.	Nino Farina	24
	3.	Piero Taruffi	22

(Constructors' Title not introduced until 1958)

ASCARI'S SUCCESS

Staging the 1952 championship under Formula Two rules had the desired effect in that it attracted a lot of entries, but it failed to stop Ferrari. The new car, the 4-cylinder Tipo 500, and Ascari's undoubted skill, were irresistible.

Global appeal

The Indianapolis 500 was the eighth round of the championship and clashed with the first European event, the Swiss Grand Prix at Bremgarten. Ferrari and Ascari decided to compete at Indianapolis, but it wasn't a good experience: Ascari was 12th when he was forced to retire. The 500 had originally been included to give the world championship global appeal, attracting American fans, but this was the only time that a driver competing in the European series tried the famous circuit.

Taruffi had a comfortable win in Berne in Ascari's absence, coming home almost 3 minutes ahead of Rudi Fischer, who was driving a privately entered Ferrari. The number of marques competing had increased which was reflected in the minor placings: Jean Behra in a Gordini was third; fourth and fifth places went to Britons Ken Wharton and Alec Brown, driving a Frazer-Nash and Cooper-Bristol respectively. Connaught, HWM and ERA also featured. Stirling Moss pinned his hopes on a new Bristol-engined ERA but crashed out on the first lap when it finally made its debut at Spa in Belgium.

Fangio out for the season

Following Alfa Romeo's withdrawal, Fangio joined Officine Maserati and his former team-mate Farina went to Ferrari. There was a new 6-cylinder car in the pipeline for Fangio at Maserati, where he was the senior driver. He had been competing in Ireland when he received word from Maserati that they wanted him to put the new car through its paces in a non-championship race at Monza. The exhausted Fangio took to the wheel after a frustrating journey and made a mistake at a corner. His neck was broken as he was flung out of the car but he survived.

and Peter Walker's BRMs both completed the 90-lap race, finishing fifth and seventh respectively.

Recognising the threat posed by Ferrari, Alfa Romeo rushed to make last-minute repairs and adjustments to the cars during practice for the German Grand Prix. Fangio realised his car's shortcomings and drove at a fast, regular pace; he led for a time, but fell back to second after his extra stop for fuel. He maintained that position to the end and Ascari won. Fangio beat the other Ferrari drivers, González, Villoresi and Taruffi, who finished in that order after him. His second place, together with the fastest lap, meant that he left Germany with 7 more points. A new, faster version of the Alfetta was introduced at Monza, but Fangio was forced out with mechanical trouble, and Ascari and González finished first and second.

Fangio by 6 points

The last round of the season was at Barcelona. The Ferraris had enough fuel for the entire distance but had changed to smaller-diameter rear wheels than usual, and the rough Pedralbes circuit tore their tyres apart; they needed changing every few laps. Fangio won, giving him the championship by 6 points, and Ascari's chance was gone.

By the end of the season Alfa Romeo knew that the ageing 158 model, dating back to 1938, needed to be replaced. This needed government money, but it was not forthcoming, leaving Alfa with no alternative but to withdraw from Grand Prix racing. This would have resulted in an uncompetitive championship, dominated by Ferrari, and the FIA announced that the 1952 Grand Prix series would be held to 2-litre, Formula Two rules.

Ascari was unstoppable in the six remaining European races; in both France and Belgium he led Farina home. British fans had a new name to cheer in Belgium: Mike Hawthorn, driving a Cooper-Bristol, gave the more powerful Ferraris a run for their money. He was lying third when his petrol tank sprang a leak, and finished fourth. At Silverstone Ascari led from start to finish, followed by Taruffi a full lap adrift. Hawthorn came in third; his performance in Belgium had not been a one-off. He was fast becoming the golden boy of British sport.

Ferrari clean sweep

The German Grand Prix was a walkover for Ferrari, with Farina, Fischer and Taruffi coming in behind the usual leader. It was much the same story at Zandvoort, a new championship venue. Farina and Villoresi took the minor placings in yet another clean sweep for Ferrari.

By the final race at Monza the world title was already settled, but Ascari was finally provided with some serious opposition. González had the new Maserati at last and roared into an early lead, but an overlong refuelling stop lost him the race; Ascari came through for his sixth victory in a row. González was almost a minute behind, but beat the Ferraris of Villoresi and Farina. He also shared the fastest lap with Ascari. But 1952 was Ascari's moment of glory. His 36-point maximum haul was something that not even Fangio would quite match in any of his five title successes.

The new season was keenly anticipated. Ascari had won six times, while his Ferrari team-mate Taruffi had won the remaining European event. But Fangio would be back, fully fit, and in the new Maserati. He was expected to challenge Ascari's supremacy.

1953

Drivers' Championship	1. Alberto Ascari	34.5
	2. Juan Manuel Fangio	28
	3. Nino Farina	26

(Constructors' Title not introduced until 1958)

MASERATI VERSUS FERRARI

As anticipated, the 1953 championship was a battle between Ferrari and Maserati. Fangio made a full recovery and led the Maserati team, supported by González and the man he regarded as his protégé, Onofre Marimon. At Ferrari Ascari, Farina and Villoresi were joined by Hawthorn, who had impressed Enzo Ferrari the previous year. He took his place as the circus moved to Buenos Aires for Argentina's first championship race. As in 1952, the series was a Formula Two competition.

Ascari and Fangio battle it out

The Argentine Grand Prix made it a nine-event championship – eight, if the Indianapolis 500 was discounted – with the best four finishes counting. A new Maserati was in the

BELOW: José Froilán González (Maserati A6GCM), gained second position at the 1952 Italian Grand Prix, Monza, giving Ascari some competition at last.

OPPOSITE: 1952 German Grand Prix at Nürburgring. Alberto Ascari (Ferrari, left) on the podium with Giuseppe Farina (Ferrari) after they finished in first and second positions respectively.

pipeline but not quite ready, so Fangio drove the 1952 model. He was chasing Ascari when his engine blew up, leaving Ascari with an easy win ahead of his team-mate Villoresi. Hawthorn came in fourth, and it was only Marimon's Maserati in third which stopped another Ferrari clean sweep. The race was marred by tragedy; Farina swerved, trying to avoid a boy who ran in front of him and careered into the crowd, killing ten spectators.

In the Dutch Grand Prix Ascari was also a comfortable winner, while Fangio failed to finish again, this time because of an axle problem. Farina made it another one-two for Ferrari, but González's third place was the highlight. When his Maserati's rear axle broke, he took over team-mate Felice Bonetto's car and chased the Ferraris hard.

Superb Hawthorn

Initially it looked as though Spa might see a change. González and Fangio, finally in their new Maseratis, stormed away – then both hit trouble. Gonzalez's accelerator pedal broke and Fangio's engine died, but he continued in the car of one of Maserati's junior drivers. He skidded on a patch of oil and crashed out of the race, escaping with minor injuries. Ascari had yet another success – his ninth win in a row – but he was outpaced at Reims, where he came in fourth. The race turned into a duel between Fangio and Hawthorn, who raced wheel to wheel. Hawthorn squeaked home by a car's length.

At Silverstone things returned to normal; Ascari led the whole way and Fangio had to be content with second. It was becoming clear that the Maseratis' extra power was decisive on faster tracks; on slower ones, like Silverstone, the superior handling of the Ferraris gave them the advantage.

Farina's last victory

Ascari drove one of his finest races at the German Grand Prix. He started well but lost a wheel and made it to the pits on three wheels and a brake drum. He took over Villoresi's car and gave chase, setting a Formula Two record for the Nürburgring circuit; however, this car expired in a pall of smoke. Farina won, keeping up Ferrari's record. It was his final victory.

Ascari and Fangio were vying for the lead in the Swiss Grand Prix at Bremgarten when both were forced into the pits. Fangio took over Bonetto's Maserati and drove the car so hard that it died a death in a cloud of heavy smoke. Ascari had only needed a change of plugs and rejoined in fourth place; he eventually took the lead from team-mates Nino Farina and Mike Hawthorn.

Champion Ascari in a spin

Maserati and Fangio got it right in the final race, at Monza. Fangio battled for the lead with Ascari and Farina, and it was still anybody's race going into the last lap. Then Ascari finally made a mistake, spinning his Ferrari after 313 miles of close slipstreaming. Farina mounted the grass to avoid a collision, but Fangio coolly avoided trouble, winning his only race of the season. He finished runner-up, on 28 points; the championship went to Ascari, with 34.5.

BELOW: **The start of the 1953 German Grand Prix.**

OPPOSITE: **1953 French Grand Prix, Reims, France. Mike Hawthorn (no. 16, Ferrari 500) and Juan Manuel Fangio (Maserati A6GCM) during their battle for the lead. They finished in first and second positions respectively, in what was Hawthorn's maiden Grand Prix victory.**

1954

FANGIO CROWNED

1954 saw the end of the Formula Two era and the introduction of a 2.5-litre limit on engine size. It was already known that Mercedes-Benz would return to Grand Prix. The renowned marque signed Fangio, and it was obvious they would pose a serious threat. Ascari responded, deciding that he needed a stronger team behind him in spite of having spent five successful years with Ferrari; Lancia was also developing a new car, and Ascari put his faith in that. Neither the Mercedes nor the Lancia was ready for the season opener.

Fangio's home soil victory

This was in Argentina. It was initially dry, and González and Farina's Ferraris dominated. When it began raining Fangio took control and went on to win. After the race, the Ferrari team lodged a protest, claiming more than the permitted three mechanics had worked on Fangio's car during a pit stop. This was thrown out.

The new Mercedes was not quite ready and Fangio had needed to borrow a Maserati to compete in Argentina; he had to do likewise in Belgium. He won there, too, despite having to drive in the latter part with a collapsed suspension. Ferrari's Maurice Trintignant came second and Stirling Moss was third. He had begun the new season with no competitive British car available. The patriotic Moss had resisted moving to a foreign team, though he had seen Hawthorn rise by joining Ferrari. The situation became urgent, and Moss bought a Maserati 250F.

Mercedes are back

The Mercedes made its appearance in the next race at Reims. It was a dazzling beginning for the streamlined W196: Fangio and his team-mate, Karl Kling, ran away with it, finishing a lap ahead of Ferrari's Robert Manzon. The third Mercedes driver, Hans Herrmann, returned the fastest lap.

The jubilant German camp came down to earth at Silverstone, however, where flaws in the car's roadholding were exposed. The streamlined bodywork concealed the front wheels and the drivers, Fangio included, found cornering difficult. Fangio's Mercedes was battered by the finish, but he did hold on to fourth place. González and Hawthorn came home first and second, making it an enjoyable day for Ferrari at last.

Tragedy at Nürburgring

For the German Grand Prix at the Nürburgring the Mercedes team produced an unstreamlined version of the W196. Fangio won, despite being deeply upset by the death of Marimon in practice. González, also a close friend of Marimon, was so distraught that he handed over his car to Hawthorn, who finished second.

Fangio was a convincing winner again in the Swiss Grand Prix at Bremgarten. He reverted to the streamlined car at Monza, and even on the fast Italian track the cornering proved suspect. Both González and Ascari, who was driving a

Ferrari, vied with Fangio for the lead, but Moss stole the show. He had been so impressive in his Maserati that he was given a works car to drive, and was leading the race with nine laps to go when his oil-tank ruptured. He restarted, but his engine gave out short of the line – and he pushed the car to the finish. It earned him only tenth place; Fangio won, but later declared it a moral victory for Moss.

Title for Fangio

The final race of the season was at Barcelona, where the Lancia V-8 made its appearance. Both Villoresi and Ascari lasted only a few laps, although Ascari did record the fastest one. Fangio also had trouble after paper was sucked into the Mercedes' air intake. Hawthorn went on to his second Grand Prix victory, and edged out his Ferrari team-mate González for the second spot in the Drivers' Championship, but the crown was Fangio's.

1955

Drivers' Championship	1. Juan Manuel Fangio	40
	2. Stirling Moss	23
	3. Eugenio Castellotti	12

(Constructors' Title not introduced until 1958)

TRAGEDY AND CHANGE

Moss joined Fangio at Mercedes for the 1955 season, and the problems that had dogged the W196 the previous year were resolved. Both the improved car and driver line-up made Mercedes look like the team to beat.

Only two go the distance

The first race, in Argentina, was in such extreme heat that only two drivers, Fangio and Roberto Mieres, were able to

ABOVE: **1954 French Grand Prix, Reims-Gueux. Karl Kling in a streamlined Mercedes-Benz W196. This was the first outing for the cars – with Kling coming second and Fangio winning, making it a one-two for Mercedes.**

OPPOSITE ABOVE: **Race winner Stirling Moss (Mercedes-Benz W196), on the podium at the British Grand Prix, Aintree, England in 1955.**

OPPOSITE BELOW: **1955 Monaco Grand Prix, Monte Carlo. Juan Manuel Fangio leads Stirling Moss (both Mercedes-Benz W196).**

finish without having to hand over to others. Fangio won, and Mieres was fifth in his Maserati, but other than that point allocation was a nightmare. The second-placed Ferrari had been driven by González, Farina and Trintignant; the latter two had also done a turn in the third-placed Ferrari, along with Umberto Magioli. The Mercedes which came in fourth had been shared by Moss, Kling and Herrmann. Fangio's 9 points were his alone; he had also set the fastest lap. Both Ascari and his team-mate Villoresi failed to finish.

Monaco saw the next round. Ascari was leading when his Lancia hit straw bales and headed into the harbour, but he was uninjured. Fangio led for 50 laps, then retired; Moss took over, but also failed to finish. Ferrari's Trintignant moved through the ranks steadily and won.

Ascari killed in practice

Ascari was invited to give his team-mate Eugenio Castellotti's Ferrari a practice run at a deserted Monza a few days later, but took a bend full-speed and went straight on. He was killed. Lancia then withdrew from racing, leaving the potential of the D50 unfulfilled, though Castellotti entered one privately in the next round in Belgium. He was going well but his engine failed on the 16th lap, and the race was a comfortable one-two for Fangio and Moss. Mike Hawthorn's time at Ferrari had made him the most successful British driver, eclipsing Moss, but he had decided to join Vanwall for 1955. Following mechanical problems culminating in an early departure from the Belgian race, Hawthorn returned to Ferrari for the rest of the season.

Tragedy at Le Mans

The next race was at Zandvoort, but before that many drivers competed at Le Mans. Here, on Saturday, 11 June, tragedy struck – on a massive scale. Two and a half hours into the race, Pierre Levegh's Mercedes hit Lance Macklin's Austin Healey and spun over the safety barrier, exploding into the crowd. More than 80 people died, including Levegh. The French, Spanish, German and Swiss Grands Prix were all cancelled following the disaster.

Aintree Grand Prix

There were three more rounds. Fangio and Moss led the rest home again at Zandvoort. Despite his return to Ferrari, Hawthorn suffered gearbox trouble; he did manage to finish, but seventh. Mercedes was outstanding at Aintree, which hosted the British race for the first time. Moss edged Fangio out by a matter of inches, and there was speculation that Fangio had allowed him a home victory. Kling and Taruffi occupied third and fourth places for Mercedes. The race also marked the debut of Jack Brabham, driving a Cooper.

The last round was at Monza, on the high-speed banked circuit. Moss set the fastest lap of more than 134mph but failed to finish; Taruffi followed Fangio home in another one-two for Mercedes. Castellotti finished less than a minute behind Taruffi in third, and that was where he came in the final table. His tally was just 12 points; Moss finished on 25, but Fangio had reached the 40-point mark for a second successive season, giving him his third world title.

Champions to quit

At the end of 1955 Mercedes announced that it was withdrawing from racing, so Fangio and Moss were seeking new teams. Fangio was looking for a car that would keep him at the top, Moss for one that would help him depose Fangio.

1956

Drivers' Championship	1. Juan Manuel Fangio	30
	2. Stirling Moss	27
	3. Peter Collins	25

(Constructors' Title not introduced until 1958)

FANGIO THE UNSTOPPABLE

Fangio and Moss went their separate ways in their search for new teams. Fangio joined Ferrari, though the cars fielded by it in 1956 were modified Lancias. Fangio was always suspicious about the standard of preparation his cars received, and left Ferrari when the season ended. Moss had enjoyed success with Mercedes, but was keen to go for a British car. In the end he settled on Maserati, feeling that would give him the best chance of unseating Fangio.

The rival Italian camps would dominate the 1956 championship. Alongside Fangio, Ferrari had Luigi Musso, Eugenio Castellotti and the young Englishman Peter Collins. Jean Behra and Cesare Perdisa provided strong support to Moss at Maserati.

Fangio sets the pace

The opening round was in Argentina. Fangio's car failed early on, and he took over his team-mate Musso's to win from Behra. Moss had had a spell in front, but his engine also gave out. When Fangio had a problem, he took over the cars of well-placed team-mates; when Moss got into trouble he struggled for points. Monaco was another case in point. Moss gained his second Grand Prix win, while Fangio took over Collins' car to finish second. Fangio had spun his Lancia-Ferrari, then repeatedly hit barriers and kerbs. The car was a mess when he came into the pits, but he still came away from Monte Carlo with 3 useful points for a shared second place.

Behra brought his Maserati home third, while Castellotti had to take over Fangio's battered machine, finishing fourth.

Peter Collins leads the pack

Collins gained back-to-back wins in Belgium and France. Moss and Fangio both had spells in front at Spa, but hit trouble. Fangio's transmission problem was terminal, but Moss did reappear; he took over Perdisa's car and finished third. Collins got home ahead of local favourite Paul Frere, driving a Ferrari. The Ferraris of Fangio, Collins and Castellotti set the pace at Reims. Fangio was delayed by a lengthy pit stop and Collins took the honours, inches ahead of Castellotti. Behra was third, Fangio fourth, and Moss, who again had to take over Perdisa's car, settled for a shared fifth.

Championship all to play for

The works BRMs of Hawthorn and Tony Brooks made an impact early in the British Grand Prix at Silverstone. They led for the first ten laps, but both then had problems. Moss subsequently led in his Maserati; he succumbed to axle trouble. Fangio came through to win; Collins grabbed second, but after he had taken over Alfonso de Portago's Ferrari. The championship was wide open. Collins led on 22 points, but Fangio was close on 21, and Behra was on 18.

Fangio won the German Grand Prix emphatically, with Moss second. Behra was again in the points in third. Collins ran out of luck, lying second when his fuel tank fractured. He took over de Portago's car again, but crashed out of the race. He wasn't hurt, but he was now 8 points adrift of Fangio.

BELOW: **Jean Behra (Maserati 250F) driving to third place in the 1956 French Grand Prix, Reims.**

OPPOSITE ABOVE: **Peter Collins (Ferrari) seen prior to the 1956 Monaco Grand Prix, Monte Carlo.**

OPPOSITE BELOW: **Jack Brabham (Cooper T43-Climax), pictured in action during the 1957 Pescara Grand Prix, Italy. (He finished seventh.)**

Collins' magnanimous gesture

Though Collins and Behra still had a chance of overhauling Fangio, they each needed to win in Italy, and set the fastest lap, in order to do so. Fangio was forced out of the race with steering trouble. Then came an extremely generous gesture. Collins, lying second and with an excellent chance of taking the title himself, pulled into the pits and offered Fangio his car. Fangio accepted, and tore after the leaders Moss and Musso. He couldn't catch Moss, whose victory meant that he finished runner-up for the second year, but a shared second place was enough to secure Fangio's fourth world crown. It was a title that he always acknowledged owed a lot to the magnanimity of Peter Collins.

Two Ferrari drivers killed

Fangio's team-mate Behra and the Ferraris of Castellotti and Collins all had spells in front in Argentina, but Fangio crossed the line ahead of Behra, who was the only other driver to complete the race. It was an excellent day for Maserati: Carlos Menditeguy came third; Harry Schell, who had left Vanwall in 1956, was fourth. A Maserati even took the fastest lap, thanks to Moss driving a borrowed car – Vanwall hadn't travelled to the race. His chances of winning were ended by gearbox trouble, but he came eighth. Ferrari had a terrible time: Collins, Hawthorn and Musso retired while Castellotti lost a wheel. He had a lucky escape then, but was killed a few weeks later testing a Ferrari at Modena. Ferrari soon lost another driver: Alfonso de Portago was killed in the Mille Miglia.

Brabham pushes it for sixth place

Moss hit the barricade at the chicane on the fourth lap at Monaco after taking an early lead. The track became scattered with poles, ending the race for Collins and Hawthorn's Ferraris. Tony Brooks, driving the second Vanwall, was also caught up but managed to escape and went on to finish 20 seconds behind Fangio, the eventual victor. Jack Brabham took his 2-litre Cooper-Climax into third, but his fuel pump failed five laps from the end. He pushed the car half a mile, finishing sixth. There was no race in The Netherlands or Belgium because of financial constraints, so France came next. Moss was ill, missing the race, and Fangio came home 50 seconds ahead of Musso's Ferrari.

Despite early-season setbacks, Vanwall and Moss's star was rising. Moss was leading the home Grand Prix at Aintree, on 20 July, when he swapped his ailing car for Brooks', putting him down to sixth place: he made his way back into the lead. This was the first victory by a British car in a major Grand Prix since 1923.

1957

Drivers' Championship	1. Juan Manuel Fangio	40
	2. Stirling Moss	25
	3. Luigi Musso	16
(Constructors' Title not introduced until 1958)		

FANGIO'S GREATEST RACE

Once again, Fangio and Moss were moving. Fangio rejoined Maserati; Moss had now been impressed by the Vanwall, and another season of development and refinement made that car a serious prospect for the championship.

ABOVE: Action from the first ever Moroccan Grand Prix, Ain Diab, Casablanca, 1958. Stuart Lewis-Evans (Vanwall VW4), before the crash that was to kill him.

OPPOSITE: 1959 United States Grand Prix, Sebring, Florida. Jack Brabham collapsed after pushing his Cooper T51-Climax across the line to finish fourth and clinch the world championship.

Lap record falls ten times

Fangio was not at Aintree, but he was back at the Nürburgring on 4 August. He began the race with a half-full tank, hoping to build up a sizeable lead to compensate for the extra refuelling stop. When he came into the pits he was 28 seconds ahead, but when he left he was more than 60 seconds down on Hawthorn and Collins. He set about catching them, breaking and rebreaking the lap record ten times. He passed both on the penultimate lap, and crossed the line 3.6 seconds ahead of Hawthorn. It was his final Grand Prix success, and his greatest.

Fangio's world crown once again

The Vanwalls were never in the picture in Germany due to suspension problems, but it was different in the last two rounds, both in Italy; Pescara was added to the series to compensate for the absent Belgium and Holland. The 16-mile road circuit was tricky and Enzo Ferrari is said to have banned his cars from participating in Italian road races, so Hawthorn and Collins were left without a drive. Musso still entertained hopes of winning the title, borrowed a car for the race and led in the early stages. Moss soon passed him, and when he retired on the tenth lap, it brought Fangio up to second. At Monza, Moss and Fangio fought an epic battle; Moss won. That gave Moss a final tally of 25 points – for the third year running he was runner-up to Fangio in the Drivers' championship.

Apart from Mercedes in 1954–55, the championship had been dominated by Italian marques. Now Maserati announced its withdrawal from racing and Ferrari was struggling. Maybe a British car could finally win the title.

1958

Drivers' Championship	1.	Mike Hawthorn	42
	2.	Stirling Moss	41
	3.	Tony Brooks	24
Constructors' Title	1.	Vanwall	48
	2.	Ferrari	40
	3.	Cooper-Climax	31

THE BRITISH CHALLENGE

Fangio made some appearances during 1958, but had effectively retired. This opened up the field for other contenders, notably Moss. He remained with Vanwall: its line-up remained unchanged, Tony Brooks and Stuart Lewis-Evans filling the supporting roles.

There were new regulations about fuel; 130-octane aviation fuel became mandatory. The Vanwall team was carrying out adjustments when the season began in Argentina and Moss entered the race in a Rob Walker 2-litre Cooper-Climax. He won, despite the best efforts of Ferrari's Musso. The Vanwalls were ready in time for Monaco, but all three failed to finish. The little Cooper did it again in Monte Carlo, this time with Maurice Trintignant. Faster cars fell by the wayside and Trintignant, driving steadily, emerged the winner; Ferrari's Musso and Collins followed him home. Zandvoort was dominated by British cars. Brooks and Lewis-Evans failed to finish, but Moss won, leading the BRMs of Harry Schell and Jean Behra. Roy Salvadori's Cooper-Climax was fourth, and Cliff Allison finished sixth in the new Lotus. Hawthorn took fifth in his Ferrari.

Another setback for Moss

Moss suffered a setback at Spa; he missed a gear, the revs shot up and the engine blew. It was still a great day for

Vanwall, as Brooks and Lewis-Evans came first and third respectively. Teresa de Filippis became the first woman to compete in a world championship race, driving a Maserati, and finished tenth.

Fangio finished the Reims Grand Prix in fourth; his final bow. This marked a turning point for Ferrari and Hawthorn; he won but any delight was muted by the death of Musso who crashed at Muizon while challenging Hawthorn for the lead. Moss and Hawthorn were tied on 23 points as the circus moved to Silverstone, but Moss's race was over after 24 laps. Hawthorn finished second to his team-mate Collins.

Peter Collins killed at Nürburgring

Magneto trouble put Moss out of the race at the Nürburgring a fortnight later, after only four laps. The Ferraris of Collins and Hawthorn looked like prevailing, but Brooks passed them in his Vanwall. Tragedy then struck. On the 11th lap Peter Collins' Ferrari went off the track at 100mph; he died in the resulting crash. Hawthorn, seeing this, retired almost immediately, devastated by the loss of a team-mate and close friend. Though one big name was lost, another was making an appearance: Bruce McLaren, driving a Cooper, finished first in the Formula Two class, and fifth overall.

At the first Portuguese Grand Prix at Oporto Moss won comfortably, having been on pole. Hawthorn finished second again, maintaining his challenge for the title. At Monza Moss succumbed to gearbox failure; Hawthorn led the race in the latter stages, but a clutch problem allowed Brooks to come through and win. Hawthorn was second, and now had 40 points from six races, the best six finishes counting for championship purposes. Moss had 32, having only finished five times.

Hawthorn by the narrowest of margins

The final round was another new venue, Ain Diab in Casablanca. With an 8-point deficit, Moss had to both win and set the fastest lap. He did exactly that, and took a maximum 9 points, finishing on 41. But for Moss to win the title, Hawthorn had to finish no better than third. The Ferrari team's tactics worked beautifully. Phil Hill, in only his second Formula One drive, held on to second place, then eased off to allow Hawthorn through, giving him a final tally of 42. Hawthorn had won just once, compared with Moss's four, but consistency brought him the championship by a single point. There was even worse news for Vanwall. Lewis-Evans had crashed out of the race, dying before he reached hospital.

Hawthorn killed after retirement

Hawthorn had been considering retiring even before the German Grand Prix; Peter Collins' death made this a certainty. Then, on 22 January 1959, the now-retired Hawthorn was killed when his Jaguar collided with a lorry. He was 29.

1959

Drivers' Championship	1.	Jack Brabham	31
	2.	Tony Brooks	27
	3.	Stirling Moss	25.5
Constructors' Title	1.	Cooper-Climax	40
	2.	Ferrari	32
	3.	BRM	18

SUCCESS FOR COOPER

In January 1959 Vanwall team boss Tony Vandervell withdrew from racing, shocking everyone. Brooks went to Ferrari while Moss hovered between two teams. In some races he drove a Cooper-Climax; in others he struck a deal allowing him to drive a front-engined BRM.

Success for Brabham

The championship began at Monaco; the Argentine Grand Prix was cancelled. Moss fought for the lead with Behra's Ferrari and Brabham's Cooper-Climax, but he and Behra both had to retire, leaving Brabham to score his and Cooper's first victory. Brooks came second, with Brabham's team-mate

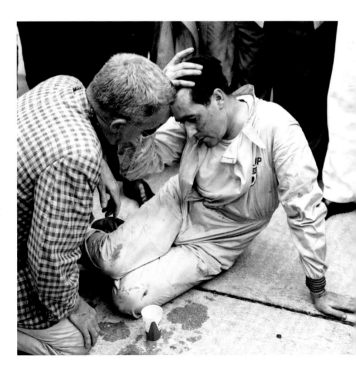

Trintignant third. This Cooper was a much better car than the one in which Moss had won the Argentine Grand Prix the year before. 1958, Cooper's first full season, saw some encouraging results, but 1959 was to be the breakthrough for the impressive rear-engined car, and for Brabham. Since arriving from Australia in 1955, Brabham had been with Cooper. He was the top works driver when it moved to Formula One in 1957.

First win for BRM

Another British marque scored a success at Zandvoort. BRM had been involved in Formula One since 1950, but had never won. Joakim Bonnier changed that, fighting off the Cooper challenge of Brabham, Moss and Masten Gregory. The best Ferrari achieved was Behra's fifth place, but in two of the next three races its speed proved decisive. At Reims Brooks and Phil Hill made it a one-two for Ferrari, with Brabham having to settle for third. However, an Italian strike meant that Ferrari was unable to follow up this success, leaving the British teams to fight it out in the Aintree Grand Prix. Brabham led all the way; Moss chose to drive the front-engined BRM and took second, coming in just ahead of Cooper's up-and-coming McLaren.

Behra killed on 'lethal' circuit

The German Grand Prix was staged for the first time on Berlin's high-speed Avus track, and Ferrari was back. This circuit's steeply-banked section was thought lethal by many drivers, and Behra was killed in the sports car race preceding the main event. The Grand Prix itself was split into two 30-lap heats; Brooks won both, taking overall first place. New Ferrari driver Dan Gurney was second; Hill in third made it a clean sweep.

Moss had driven the Cooper for the two laps he lasted in Germany. Hans Herrmann entered the race in the BRM but crashed out after a brakes failure, destroying the car, and Moss drove Coopers for the rest of the season. He dominated the next race, the Portuguese Grand Prix at Monsanto, where he lapped the entire field. Masten Gregory's Cooper was a distant second, ahead of Gurney's Ferrari.

The Ferraris were expected to dominate at Monza, but Moss was at his best. He sat on Hill's tail, conserving his tyres. Hill, like all the Ferrari drivers, had to stop for new rear tyres; Moss hit the front and finished the race on his original ones. Hill was second, and Brabham was third. There was only one round to go. Brabham had 31 points, Moss 25.5 and Tony Brooks 23, meaning that he, too, could overhaul Brabham by winning the final round and setting the fastest lap.

Brabham's championship at a push

The decider would be on the Sebring airfield track in Florida – the United States' first ever championship event with the exception of the Indianapolis 500 – but not until December, giving the contenders three months to prepare. Moss took pole and was out of the blocks first, but retired with transmission failure after just six laps. Brabham took over and held the lead to the last lap, running out of fuel 500 yards from the line. Again he pushed his Cooper to the finish, earning fourth place. His team-mates McLaren and Trintignant crossed the line first and second. Brooks's third place gave him 4 points, enough to snatch second place from Moss, but not enough to prevent Brabham gaining his first world crown.

Below: **1959 Dutch Grand Prix, Zandvoort. Jack Brabham (Cooper T51-Climax) leads Tony Brooks (Ferrari Dino 246) and Harry Schell (BRM P25). Brabham finished in second place, on his way to the title.**

Opposite: **Willy Mairesse (Ferrari D246) takes a pit stop on the way to third position in the 1960 Italian Grand Prix at Monza.**

1960

Drivers' Championship	1.	Jack Brabham	43
	2.	Bruce McLaren	34
	3.	Stirling Moss	19
Constructors' Title	1.	Cooper-Climax	48
	2.	Lotus-Climax	34
	3.	Ferrari	26

THE END FOR FRONT-ENGINED CARS

1960 would be the final season of the 2.5-litre Formula, and Jack Brabham retired from the opening race in Argentina with transmission trouble. His team-mate Bruce McLaren made the early championship running, winning in Argentina, helped by race leaders Stirling Moss and Jo Bonnier both hitting mechanical trouble. Moss finished third, returning to the race in Maurice Trintignant's Cooper.

Tragedy at Spa

Moss's new rear-engined Lotus 18 appeared at Monaco, and he drove brilliantly in the wet to win from McLaren; Brabham was disqualified for receiving assistance from marshals after he spun off. Moss was also on top form at Zandvoort in the Dutch Grand Prix. Challenging Brabham for the lead, he suffered a puncture; by the time the wheel was changed he found himself in 12th place, but managed to finish in fourth. Brabham, who led from the start, was beginning a run of success; Moss was about to run out of luck in dramatic circumstances.

A series of dreadful accidents marked the Belgian Grand Prix at Spa. A wheel came off Moss's Lotus during practice and he broke both legs; there were deaths in two separate incidents in the race itself, both involving young British drivers. Alan Stacey was hit by a bird and Chris Bristow went off the road. Brabham won, with McLaren second. Jim Clark was in fifth place, gaining his first championship points. He had made an impressive debut at Zandvoort; though he succumbed to gearbox trouble, he tussled for fourth with Graham Hill.

Four in a row for Brabham

Brabham had another win on the fast Reims circuit. Phil Hill and Wolfgang von Trips, driving Ferraris, had been in contention, but both suffered from transmission failure and gave Brabham his third success. He made it four in a row at Silverstone, although Graham Hill got most of the praise. After stalling his BRM on the line, he roared through the field and took the lead, but spun off seven laps short. Brabham received maximum points, and John Surtees, who was in his debut year, took second; the motorcycling champion was driving for Lotus. Silverstone was his best finish, but his best performance probably came in the following race, in Portugal. He built up a ten-second lead over Brabham but was forced out of the race when his radiator split. Brabham profited, and this fifth consecutive victory assured him of another world title with two races still to go. Moss was back at the wheel for the race in Oporto, and was second at one point, but was disqualified for pushing his car in the wrong direction after a spin.

Ferrari's hollow victory at Monza

The championship may have been decided by Monza, but there was still controversy. Many considered the banked sections of the circuit dangerous, and the British teams boycotted the event in protest. Ferrari were left to sweep the board, Phil Hill winning his first championship race. Apart from that somewhat meaningless victory, it had been a wretched year for Ferrari, and the team didn't bother to contest the United States Grand Prix, staged at Riverside. Moss won, ending the series on a high note, and his victory also meant that Climax-engined cars had won every race apart from Monza. Ferrari certainly understood the implications, and their persistence with front-engined cars was about to end.

1961

Drivers' Championship			
	1.	Phil Hill	34
	2.	Wolfgang von Trips	33
	3.	Stirling Moss	21
Constructors' Title	1.	Ferrari	45
	2.	Lotus-Climax	35
	3.	Porsche	22

FERRARI TAKE CONTROL

A 1.5-litre Formula was introduced, and Ferrari's fortunes began to change. It prepared meticulously for the new season and the introduction of the rear-engined V-6 'sharknose' paid off. British teams struggled with cars using dated 4-cylinder units which had a very modest power output.

Ferrari's assault on the championship was spearheaded by Phil Hill, Ritchie Ginther and Wolfgang von Trips, but Moss won the season opener at Monaco and the Ferraris came in second, third and fourth. Dan Gurney was next, with Porsche, a new name in Formula One. The race was a fantastic display by Moss, who went into it with a double handicap: he had to use the old, square-shaped Lotus 18, with the outdated Climax engine under the bonnet. The new model – the 21 – was delayed because of contractual arguments. At Monaco the skill factor compensated for the fact that Moss would be outpaced on faster circuits, and he took the flag just 3.6 seconds in front of Ginther, with Hill and von Trips well behind.

Phil Hill and von Trips neck and neck

Moss was similarly impressive later in the series at the Nürburgring, but the 1961 title race was generally about the battle between Hill and von Trips. At Zandvoort von Trips got home just nine-tenths of a second ahead of his team-mate, giving Germany its first Grand Prix winner for 22 years. Jim Clark was also squeezing out all he could from his outdated Lotus. He took third, and Moss came home ahead of Ginther. This was the first time in a championship event that an entire field – 15-strong that day – completed a race without incident.

ABOVE: **Jim Clark (Lotus 18-Climax) takes third position at the 1960 Portuguese Grand Prix, Porto.**

OPPOSITE ABOVE: **1961 French Grand Prix, Reims-Gueux. Giancarlo Baghetti (Ferrari 156) closely followed by Dan Gurney (Porsche 718), takes the chequered flag for first position and his maiden win on his Grand Prix debut.**

OPPOSITE BELOW: **Wolfgang von Trips (Ferrari). He was killed at the 1961 Italian Grand Prix in Monza, when leading the title race.**

Ferrari had a clean sweep at Spa, occupying the first four places. It was Hill from von Trips this time, with Ginther third and Olivier Gendebien in fourth. Gendebien only had occasional drives during the year and the fact that Ferrari's fourth driver could get into the frame demonstrates the team's dominance. Hill, von Trips and Ginther all retired from the French Grand Prix at Reims, but a Ferrari crossed the line first again. Giancarlo Baghetti, making his Grand Prix debut, was a narrow winner in his privately entered Ferrari, and remains the only man to win a Grand Prix on his first outing. Ferrari had another one-two-three in the British Grand Prix at Aintree: von Trips led Hill and Ginther home in torrential rain.

Black day as championship leader killed

At the Nürburgring Moss broke the Ferrari stranglehold as he had at Monaco – with superb driving and clever tactics. He knew all the intricacies of the difficult 14.2-mile circuit, but he made a gamble in tyre selection that paid off brilliantly. This time there were no objections to the combined road and banked Monza circuit. Von Trips started with 33 points, four ahead of Hill, and looked all set to clinch the title but tragedy struck on the second lap. His Ferrari collided with Clark's Lotus, and both went off at Vedano Corner. Clark emerged unscathed but von Trips was killed, as were several spectators. Phil Hill went on to win, taking the title in unhappy circumstances.

Ferrari withdrew from the Watkins Glen United States Grand Prix. Moss and Brabham vied for the lead, but both retired and Innes Ireland took over and won. It was his first

and only Grand Prix win. Tony Brooks gave BRM their best finish of the year, coming third, and he decided to retire. Brooks had never won the championship itself, but he had six Grand Prix wins to his name and was regarded as a highly accomplished and professional driver.

1962

Drivers' Championship	1.	Graham Hill	42
	2.	Jim Clark	30
	3.	Bruce McLaren	27
Constructors' Title	1.	BRM	42
	2.	Lotus	36
	3.	Cooper	29

GRAHAM HILL TAKES THE CHAMPIONSHIP

This was to be Graham Hill's year. He had made his Grand Prix debut in 1958, but his first two years at Lotus were bedevilled by the unreliability of the cars. Things initially looked no better when he moved to BRM, though there were signs that both team and driver were getting things right in 1960 and 1961. By 1962, BRM's new V-8 unit was ready, but it faced stiff opposition from the rival Climax V-8, which most other teams had adopted.

Moss's career ends in mystery smash

Hill's first Formula One win with BRM came at the Goodwood event, unfortunately overshadowed by a terrible crash involving Moss. Moss had been passing Hill on a fast stretch of the circuit when he left the track and his Lotus piled head-on into a bank. He sustained appalling injuries, and his career was over – though he did make a full recovery. He had done everything except win the world championship; he'd been runner-up four times in succession and had never been out of the top three in the previous seven years.

Ferrari surpassed

After another non-championship victory at Silverstone, an optimistic Hill and BRM went to the Dutch Grand Prix in Zandvoort. Hill led from early in the race and won, giving BRM their second-ever championship win. He was ahead at Monaco before engine trouble forced him out, and Bruce McLaren brought his Cooper home first, ahead of Phil Hill, who was still driving for Ferrari. The car was almost unchanged: Ferrari peaked in 1961 and stood still; the new British V-8s caught them up and overtook. Hill's second place at Monaco was his best in the year, and there was some discontent in the team. He left them at the end of the season.

Clark beset with mechanical problems

Jim Clark took the honours in Belgium. Not only did he benefit from having the new V-8 Climax unit, but he also had a new car: the Lotus 25, whose monocoque chassis was to revolutionise racing car design. Mechanical problems had ruined Clark's chances at both Zandvoort and Monaco but things came right at Spa, and he notched up the first of his 25 Grand Prix wins. Hill had to make do with second. Aintree

BELOW: 1962 Monaco Grand Prix, Monte Carlo. Race winner, Bruce McLaren (Cooper T60-Climax), on the way to gaining 9 points towards his eventual total of 27 and third position in the championship.

OPPOSITE: Jim Clark leads Trevor Taylor (both Lotus 25-Climax), in the final race of the 1963 season, East London, South Africa. Clark finished first but the points were not required to count for his best six results, having won six previously.

was the scene of the British Grand Prix; Clark led from start to finish and set the fastest lap. He was also within a point of Hill in the title race, and he had finished fourth. Hill then scored back-to-back wins at the Nürburgring and Monza. Clark suffered in both. In Germany he stalled on the line but gave chase and brought himself within striking distance of the leaders, then low fuel meant he had to ease off: he came fourth. He had to retire with engine trouble at Monza.

1963

Drivers' Championship	1.	Jim Clark	54
	2.	Graham Hill	29
	3.	Ritchie Ginther	29
Constructors' Title	1.	Lotus	54
	2.	BRM	36
	3.	Brabham	28

JIM CLARK COMES THROUGH

The 1963 championship was a ten-race series, with the best six scores counting towards the title. Jim Clark and Lotus had been beaten into second place in both the Drivers' and the Constructors' Championship in 1962, and there had been a lot of activity since. Both Porsche and Bowmaker-Yeoman decided to withdraw; Porsche's withdrawal left Dan Gurney free to drive for the Brabham team, and the end of Bowmaker-Yeoman meant that John Surtees was open to offers. He joined Ferrari.

It was a period of change for Ferrari. Engineer Carlo Chiti left at the end of the 1962 season and set up his own team,

ATS, and several Ferrari people went with him, including drivers Phil Hill and Giancarlo Baghetti. It wasn't successful; the V-8 cars the team put out were poor and neither Hill nor Baghetti took a single point in the 1963 series. The new team lasted a year.

Seven wins out of ten for Clark

On the track Clark came first in seven of the ten races, and looking at the three races he failed to win shows how his domination could have been even greater. One was the opening race at Monaco, where he was leading from Graham Hill, then spun off with a seized gearbox. Hill went on to win, the first of what would be five Monaco successes in a row. On the other two occasions where Clark missed out he was similarly unlucky. He was hampered by a misfiring engine at the Nürburgring but managed to finish second, behind Surtees. Clark's misfortune helped Surtees to a breakthrough first championship victory, and gave Ferrari its first success since Monza two years earlier. At Watkins Glen Clark lost a lap and a half in the pits with battery trouble, yet still managed to finish third. Graham Hill took the race from his team-mate Ritchie Ginther.

The Flying Scot

After Monaco, Clark recorded four straight wins: Spa, Zandvoort, Reims and Silverstone. The Dutch race possibly best epitomised the level of Clark's performance. He was fastest in practice, led the race from start to finish – lapping the entire field in the process – and became the first man to lap the Zandvoort circuit at over 100mph. He secured the title with three races still to go.

Among the others, Surtees could consider himself rather unlucky. Apart from his win in Germany, he had got a fourth place at Monaco, third at Zandvoort and second at Silverstone – where he passed Hill on the last lap, the 1962 champion running out of fuel desperately close to the finish. However, Surtees failed to finish in any of the last four races, and had to be content with fourth place in the championship, on 22 points.

Best of his era

Hill also had his share of bad luck. He finished in just six races, the two victories at Monaco and Watkins Glen, plus three third places and a fourth in Mexico. BRM introduced their own monocoque design during the season, hoping to emulate the brilliant success of the Lotus 25, but the new car handled badly and Hill was forced to revert to the old model. He ended the year on 29 points, 25 behind Clark's maximum points haul of 54. This was only the second time in the history of the event that such a feat had been achieved, and when Ascari recorded his maximum in 1952, it was the best four finishes out of eight. Clark was well on his way to his reputation as the greatest racing driver of his era.

1964

Drivers' Championship	1.	John Surtees	40
	2.	Graham Hill	39
	3.	Jim Clark	32
Constructors' Title	1.	Ferrari	45
	2.	BRM	42
	3.	Lotus	37

SURTEES, WINNING ON FOUR WHEELS

Ferrari had produced a new V-8 engine for the existing 1963-model chassis for the new season. It was hoped that this hardware, together with Surtees' growing skills, would prove to be a match for the British teams which had dominated the previous two years. John Surtees had won seven motorcycling world titles and, four years after making his Grand Prix debut, was in with a chance of becoming the first man to take world titles on both two and four wheels. 1964 would see the closest championship race for years. Clark and Hill were both hoping to take their second world crown, and Surtees was the third British driver vying for the title as the circus reached its final stop in Mexico.

Mike Hailwood off the mark

In three of the first four rounds of the championship Surtees had to retire; his only success was at Zandvoort, where he finished a distant second behind Clark. Earlier, in the traditional Monaco curtain-raiser, Mike Hailwood, another motorcycling ace, made his mark, finishing sixth to claim his first championship point. At Spa there were several dramatic reversals of fortune. Dan Gurney looked set to give Brabham maximum points, but ran out of fuel; Graham Hill profited from the situation, but only briefly – the BRM's fuel pump failed. Bruce McLaren now found himself in front but he, too, ran out of fuel, spluttering to a halt 100 yards from the finishing line. Jim Clark won – and he too ran out of gas on the slowing-down lap.

British Grand Prix at Brands Hatch

Gurney made up for his disappointment in Belgium by winning the French Grand Prix at Rouen. Hill was second, and Gurney's team boss, Brabham himself, was third. Brabham was now trying to spend more time overseeing the team, but each time he tried to ease himself behind a desk, events conspired to keep him involved. The British Grand Prix was staged at Brands Hatch for the first time. Clark set a new lap record to win the race, chased hard by Hill. Surtees, finishing in third, was back in the points and began a run of solid performances and consistent points. He needed them: at the halfway mark Clark led with 30 points, followed by Hill on 26. Surtees had 10.

1965

Drivers' Championship	1.	Jim Clark	54
	2.	Graham Hill	40
	3.	Jackie Stewart	33
Constructors' Title	1.	Lotus	54
	2.	BRM	45
	3.	Brabham	27

CLARK WINS AGAIN

Lack of reliability undoubtedly cost Jim Clark his second world title in 1964, but things improved radically in 1965. He managed to finish in six races – crucial, because the championship was once again decided on the best six finishes in a ten-event series. The Lotus was fitted with a new and more powerful 32-valve version of the Coventry-Climax engine, and its reliability was much improved.

Stewart the rising star

Taking place on New Year's Day, the South African Grand Prix had been held over to provide the first race of 1965, instead of the last of 1964. Clark immediately set the tone for a series he would dominate to such an extent that races turned into a scramble for minor placings. He started on pole and also set the fastest lap; Surtees and Hill followed him home, the three protagonists who had contested the previous year's title decider. Claiming his first championship point with a sixth place on his debut was Jackie Stewart. Stewart had had offers to join Lotus and Cooper, as well as BRM.

Clark was forced to miss Monaco as the Lotus team was keen to contest the Indianapolis 500. This had not been part of the Formula One championship since 1960, and Clark had no great affection for it. He won, in record speed, having led for 190 of the 200 laps. Clark could now concentrate on his main goal: winning his second Formula One title.

Jochen Rindt debut in Austria

He began by winning on the winding 14.2-mile Nürburgring circuit, a minute clear of Hill. All three title contenders were among the host of retirements in the next race, run on Austria's rough Zeltweg circuit, and Austria's first-ever Grand Prix went to Ferrari's no. 2 driver, Lorenzo Bandini. It also marked the debut of Jochen Rindt.

Surtees on top

Surtees came out on top at Monza, battling with Clark and McLaren. Clark failed to finish, while Hill didn't even get out of the blocks, owing to a jammed clutch. However, Hill led the table on 39 going into the final round in Mexico; Surtees was up to 34 and Clark was still stuck on 30, but with a chance of retaining the title if he won. Third place would have been good enough for Hill, and that was the position he held until an evil-tempered battle with Bandini's Ferrari saw both cars spin off. Hill's departure improved Surtees' hopes, and these were boosted when Clark, leading the race on the penultimate lap, succumbed once again to engine trouble. Surtees moved into third, and was waved through into second by Bandini, where he finished behind Gurney. It gave Surtees the championship by a single point from Hill.

Surtees had become the first man to take world titles on both two wheels and four, a feat which remains unequalled.

OPPOSITE: John Surtees (Ferrari), pictured at the 1964 German Grand Prix, Nürburgring. This was his first win of the series in which he was ultimately triumphant by 1 point.

ABOVE: Dan Gurney (Brabham BT7-Climax) winning the 1964 French Grand Prix, Rouen.

Graham Hill: 'King of Monaco'

In Clark's absence Hill had a hat-trick of wins at Monaco and was dubbed the 'King of Monte Carlo'. In the Belgian Grand Prix Clark returned to the title race with his fourth successive win at Spa; he led all the way in stormy weather, and Stewart came in second. The two drivers repeated the performance at Clermont-Ferrand, for the first time the venue for the French Grand Prix. Stewart was emerging as champion material, and another driver destined to scale the heights quietly gained his first points in this race – Denny Hulme. He was an established Formula Two driver at Brabham, and was regarded so highly that the team occasionally entered a third car for him during the 1965 series. His fourth place in France was followed by a fifth at Zandvoort.

Consecutive wins for Clark

Clark continued his devastating form with wins at Zandvoort and Silverstone. The Dutch race was comfortable, Clark winning once again from Stewart to give him three consecutive wins there. The British Grand Prix was a much closer affair; suffering a loss of oil pressure, Clark nursed his Lotus home barely three seconds ahead of Hill.

Stewart finishes third

Clark claimed his sixth win of the year at the Nürburgring – and this brought him his second world title, though there were still three rounds of the championship to go. It was just as well: he failed to finish at Monza, Watkins Glen and Mexico. Jackie Stewart's win in Italy was the highlight of these final rounds; it came courtesy of a mistake by Graham Hill in the penultimate lap, but was still impressive. He had 33 points in his first season, finishing third, 7 points behind Hill.

Clark's maximum points haul

But 1965, the last year of the 1.5-litre Formula, was all about one man – Clark. His maximum haul of 54 points – repeating his feat of 1963 – established him as the greatest driver of his time. Like Fangio, so dominant throughout the 50s, Clark had all the natural talents.

1966

Drivers' Championship			
	1.	Jack Brabham	42
	2.	John Surtees	28
	3.	Jochen Rindt	22
Constructors' Title	1.	Brabham	42
	2.	Ferrari	31
	3.	Cooper	30

BRABHAM WINS – IN HIS OWN CAR

Jack Brabham planned to form his own racing company even when he was the reigning world champion. He'd won his world titles with Cooper, and his decision to go off and build his own Grand Prix car did not go down very well: the Cooper team felt that Brabham had gained a great deal of knowledge which he would now be using in direct competition. Brabham's new car made its first appearance in 1962 and Dan Gurney joined the team in 1963.

Denny Hulme joins Brabham

Gurney won two Grands Prix in 1964 but, largely because of problems with reliability, 1965 had been a bad year for Brabham. However, the start of the 1966 campaign, which brought with it the new 3-litre Formula, saw the Brabham team better prepared than most. Its cars were powered by an Australian-built V-8 Repco engine that proved to be a model of reliability. Gurney also had thoughts of setting up his own outfit and left Brabham after three years to head up the Eagle team. His place was filled by Denny Hulme.

However, Brabham didn't set the world of racing alight at the start of the season. He had gearbox trouble at Monaco, in a race with a high casualty count. Another early victim was Bruce McLaren, who had decided to branch out on his own like Gurney, and Monaco was the first time he had run a car under his own name. Jackie Stewart won the race, one of only four classified finishers, giving BRM its fourth Monaco success in a row.

Surtees and Rindt battle at Spa

The very wet conditions at Spa reduced the 15-strong field to seven after a series of first-lap incidents. Surtees and Rindt battled it out and finished in that order, with Brabham in the

points, but a distant fourth. At Reims Brabham set a record, averaging over 136mph to win ahead of Ferrari newcomer Mike Parkes. Hulme took third that day, and the team went one better at Brands Hatch, Brabham leading all the way and crossing the line 1.6 seconds in front of his no. 2. He notched up his third win in a row at Zandvoort, taking the race from Graham Hill, while Clark just held on for third place from Stewart.

Next came the Nürburgring. Brabham had never won in Germany, but he did this time, with a magnificent victory in the wet. John Surtees, now driving a Cooper-Maserati, followed him home. Surtees had begun the season with Ferrari, who had produced a very competitive new V-12 unit for the season, but friction between Surtees and the Ferrari team boss Eugenio Dragoni led him to join Cooper after his win at Spa. Surtees was to finish second in the championship, driving the rather less impressive Cooper, and might have gone one better if he had remained with Ferrari.

Three times world champion

As the circus moved on to Monza, however, it was Brabham who had the title within his grasp. He led here before retiring with an oil leak, but those who had a chance of catching him also retired. Ludovico Scarfiotti won the race for Ferrari but, more importantly, Brabham was confirmed as world champion for the third time. There was another retirement for Brabham in the penultimate race at Watkins Glen. Jim Clark won, his Lotus by now fitted with the new H16 engine, his only victory of the series in what was a frustrating year. Surtees took the final honours in Mexico, with Brabham and Hulme occupying second and third places. This left Brabham 14 points clear of Surtees in the final table, and made him the first driver to win in a car bearing his own name.

OPPOSITE: **Graham Hill (BRM P261), driving to third position in the curtain-raiser to the 1965 season – the South African Grand Prix, East London.**

BELOW: **1966 United States Grand Prix, Watkins Glen, New York with Jim Clark (Lotus 43-BRM) on the grid at the start. This was the BRM 75 H16 engine's only Grand Prix win.**

1967

Drivers' Championship	1.	Denny Hulme	51
	2.	Jack Brabham	46
	3.	Jim Clark	41
Constructors' Title	1.	Brabham	67
	2.	Lotus	50
	3.	Cooper	28

BRABHAM'S FIRST AND SECOND

Brabham and Hulme were able to capitalise on the teething trouble suffered by the new Lotus 49, the car of the future. The less sophisticated Repco-Brabham was able to prevail in 1967 because of its reliability: it was a real workhorse, much less temperamental. Unusually, both Brabhams experienced problems in the opening round, on the new Kyalami track in South Africa; however, both limped home in the points. Hulme, who had led for 60 laps, finished fourth, with Brabham sixth. Privateer John Love nearly pulled off a stunning win in an outdated Cooper-Climax but ran out of fuel late in the race and had to content himself with second. Pedro Rodriguez won, giving a flying start to the team he had recently joined, Cooper-Maserati.

Hulme had his first Grand Prix success at Monaco, coming home over a lap ahead of Graham Hill, but the result was overshadowed by a horrific crash in which Lorenzo Bandini was killed. On the 82nd lap Bandini's Ferrari struck some straw bales and burst into flames; he was trapped in the car and died shortly afterwards.

Clark wins at Zandvoort

At Zandvoort Lotus finally showed off the new Ford-powered 49 model which had tempted Graham Hill to leave BRM and join Jim Clark at Lotus. It was immediately clear that the new car was something special. Hill led early on but retired, leaving Brabham in front; Clark then came through to register a brilliant win. Unfortunately for Lotus, Hill's experience, rather than Clark's, was to set the pattern. Brabham and Hulme grabbed the minor placings at Zandvoort, establishing their own pattern of being regularly in the points.

Spa was another example of Lotus's ill-fated year. With Hill already out of the race, Clark was leading, and was forced into the pits with spark-plug trouble. Both Brabham and Hulme had also retired, and Dan Gurney gave his Eagle-Weslake car its first and only success. In the French Grand Prix, run on the Bugatti track at Le Mans, both Clark and Hill were going well until the Lotus 49s gave out again. The Brabhams dominated the race on this occasion, Brabham himself leading, with Hulme second and Jackie Stewart in third.

British Grand Prix – Clark again

Clark enjoyed a trouble-free race at Silverstone and duly won. Hulme and Brabham took second and fourth respectively, with Chris Amon coming third in his Ferrari. But Clark was out at the Nürburgring after just three laps, with a broken suspension. Hill fared even worse: his retirement was his sixth out of the seven races so far. Hulme and Brabham made it another one-two, with Amon third once again. In the Formula Two section of the race, Jacky Ickx drove his Matra brilliantly before suffering suspension trouble. Before that, he actually held overall fourth, ahead of several Formula One cars.

At the inaugural Canadian Grand Prix it was much the same story. Clark left with ignition trouble and Brabham and Hulme took the points again. Monza proved to be the most dramatic race. Clark suffered early problems as usual, but this time pulled back, breaking the lap record repeatedly. This took him into the lead but he ran short of fuel on the final lap. In an exciting final half-lap, Brabham passed Surtees to lead, but the latter retook it and won by just 0.2 seconds. Clark struggled home in third.

Hulme wins world crown with 51 points

It came right for Lotus at Watkins Glen. Clark and Hill came home first and second, though they both had problems late in the race; another solid third place for Hulme enhanced his title hopes still further. There was another win for Clark in the final round in Mexico, but there was also another third place for Hulme which was enough to give him the title with 51 points, 5 ahead of Brabham, who had finished second in the race. This was the first 'team double' since Hill and von Trips in 1961. Clark had accumulated 41 points to finish a frustrating third.

OPPOSITE: **Dan Gurney drives the Eagle T1G Weslake to first place in the 1967 Belgian Grand Prix at Spa-Francorchamps (the car's only success).**

BELOW: **Denny Hulme (Brabham BT24-Repco) in action during the 1967 German Grand Prix, Nürburgring. He went on to win the race in a consistent year that saw him take the title.**

1968

Drivers' Championship	1.	Graham Hill	48
	2.	Jackie Stewart	36
	3.	Denny Hulme	33
Constructors' Title	1.	Lotus	62
	2.	McLaren	51
	3.	Matra-Ford	45

THE LOSS OF CLARK

By this point in the decade, only six drivers had lost their lives; the change to rear-engined cars had brought a slight improvement in safety. However, 1968 saw two further fatalities, and Mike Spence and Ludovico Scarfiotto died in other events on the motor sport calendar.

Jim Clark won the opening round of the series, at Kyalami; this victory – his 25th in just 72 Grands Prix – took him one ahead of the great Fangio. He took part in a Formula Two race at Hockenheim on 7 April and was killed when his Lotus 48 left the track on a gentle right-hand bend and went into trees.

Sponsorship arrives

Lotus then brought in Jackie Oliver to team up with Graham Hill, who had finished second to Clark in South Africa. Kyalami was the last race in which Lotus sported its green and yellow livery; by the next, the outfit had become Gold Leaf Team Lotus, and the car was bedecked in red, white and gold. Sponsorship had arrived.

King of Monte Carlo

For the first time since 1954, Spain was back on the championship calendar. A pre-race accident put Stewart out of contention for several races, and he lost vital ground which was to prove crucial in the latter stages. Hill then scored his fourth Monaco success. After two wins and a second place, he had a run of bad luck which saw him fail to finish in the next four races. The first of these was Spa, where his main rival Stewart looked certain to give Matra their first win in Belgium – he was 25 seconds ahead of Bruce McLaren with just two laps left – but he ran out of fuel. McLaren was able to bring home the car which bore his name for its debut victory. Although it wasn't a successful year for either Ferrari or Brabham, these two were at the forefront of experiments with rear-mounted aerofoils, a trend which would soon become the norm.

Brilliant Stewart at Zandvoort

Stewart drove brilliantly in the wet at Zandvoort. On his way to victory he lapped the entire field, except for Beltoise in the works Matra. The French Grand Prix at Rouen was also run in atrocious conditions, and brought another fatality: Jo Schlesser's Honda crashed out of the race and burst into flames. Stewart was less happy with his Dunlop wets here, and finished third. Ickx gave Ferrari their first win since Monza in 1966.

The Lotuses of Hill and Oliver both led for a time in the British Grand Prix at Brands Hatch, but neither finished. Stewart was desperate for points, but the circuit put too much strain on his injured wrist and he could do no better than sixth. Rob Walker's Lotus, driven by Jo Siffert, won the race, holding off the Ferrari challenge from Amon and Ickx. There was more torrential rain and a heavy mist for the German Grand Prix. Stewart was now happy with the special Dunlop rain tyres fitted to his car. He still had the wrist problem, but was determined to continue. His plan was to get in front so that he could have clear track ahead. It worked brilliantly, and he took the flag four minutes ahead of Hill; he was now within 4 points of Hill in the championship.

Late surge from Hulme

Stewart was forced out at Monza by engine trouble, but Hill's Lotus lost a wheel, so the balance remained unchanged. Hill then slightly extended his lead at the Canadian Grand Prix.

Both drivers were hampered by suspension trouble, but Hill was fourth, while Stewart could only finish sixth. Denny Hulme scored back-to-back wins in these two races, which helped him finish third overall.

Second world crown for Hill

Mario Andretti was given a works Lotus-Ford for the race at Watkins Glen. Andretti and Bobby Unser had practised at the Italian Grand Prix, but were disqualified for taking part in an event in America within a day of Monza. At Watkins Glen Andretti made an immediate impact, setting the fastest lap in practice. He led in the early part of the race, too, but was overhauled by Stewart, who had his third success of the series. Hill finished second, meaning that he would take a 3-point lead into the final race in Mexico.

The Matra and Lotus vied for the lead in the early stages, but Stewart's engine – and his title hopes – fizzled out. He finished seventh. Hill drove impeccably to take the race, and with it his second world title.

1969

ABOVE: Jackie Stewart (Matra MS80-Ford) on his way to his third win from the first four races, at the 1969 Dutch Grand Prix, Zandvoort.

OPPOSITE: 1968 French Grand Prix, Rouen-les-Essarts. Graham Hill (Lotus 49-Ford) who had retired, gives his team-mate Jo Siffert (Lotus 49-Ford) his visor on the trackside.

Drivers' Championship	1.	Jackie Stewart	63
	2.	Jacky Ickx	37
	3.	Bruce McLaren	26
Constructors' Title	1.	Matra-Ford	66
	2.	Brabham	51
	3.	Lotus	47

STEWART'S YEAR

Jackie Stewart's prospects for 1969 looked good and his disappointment at missing out on the 1968 championship soon vanished. He had been runner-up despite losing points through injury and the fuel miscalculation at Spa, and his hopes were further boosted by the fact that he would have a new Ford-powered Matra, the MS80. Matra had withdrawn its works team at the end of 1968, leaving its Formula One involvement in the hands of Ken Tyrrell. Honda, Cooper and Eagle also withdrew.

Hill and Rindt foiled

Stewart dominated the first race at Kyalami in spite of the fact that the new car wasn't ready – the previous year's car was dusted off for the race. His closest challenge came from Mario Andretti, who was contesting the lead with Stewart before his Lotus gave out with transmission trouble. Stewart won again in Barcelona, recovering well after a poor start and clawing back lost ground. His victory was also partly down to some bad luck on the part of those ahead of him: Amon was particularly unfortunate, for he was well ahead when his Ferrari failed. Hill and Rindt's Lotuses both crashed out, with the cause put down to the aerofoils the cars were sporting. Hill was unscathed, but Rindt's injuries forced him to miss the Monaco GP.

The 'wings' debate was one of the contentious issues of the year. Most teams had adopted aerofoils but, following Barcelona, they were banned at Monaco. Stewart again looked well set, sharing the lead with Amon; when both retired, Hill came through to score a fifth Monte Carlo success. It was his only win of the year, and one of the few moments to savour for Lotus, which was an unhappy camp this season. Monaco was also good for the independents: Piers Courage, driving a Frank Williams-entered Brabham-Ford, was second, with Jo Siffert, in a Walker-Durlacher, third.

Stewart back in command

The Belgian Grand Prix was cancelled because of a dispute about safety, and the circus moved to Zandvoort, where Rindt recovered from his injuries to take pole. He led the race until succumbing to driveshaft failure, and Stewart claimed a third win. Several cars sprouted 'wings' again, although they were smaller and less imposing than those

ABOVE: Monaco Grand Prix Monte Carlo. Jochen Rindt (Lotus 49C-Ford) powers to victory for the first of five wins in 1970.

OPPOSITE: Ken Tyrrell confers with Jackie Stewart in the pit lane during the 1971 season.

which had attracted criticism. Stewart was in commanding form again in France. His latest triumph contrasted with the situation at BRM, whose slow and unreliable V-12 gave John Surtees and Jackie Oliver a miserable season. They didn't bother to enter at Clermont-Ferrand.

Stewart had a high-speed crash in practice at Silverstone and was forced to take over team-mate Jean-Pierre Beltoise's car in the race; he and Rindt were involved in a battle until Rindt was forced into the pits with a loose wing. Both Lotus and McLaren showed off their innovative four-wheel-drive cars, with mixed results. John Miles had a smooth ride and brought his Lotus home in tenth, while Derek Bell's McLaren lasted just five laps.

Civic reception for champion Stewart

Stewart was beaten into second place at the Nürburgring, hampered by gearbox trouble. Jacky Ickx gave Brabham its first win of the season; he had been signed after Rindt decided to go to Lotus the previous year. Brabham himself had an indifferent, injury-hit year but Ickx was impressive, lying second in the championship with 22 points. Stewart was almost unreachable on 51, and removed any further doubt at Monza where he headed home Rindt, Beltoise and McLaren. The title was definitely his.

Stewart's last three races saw him retire twice, and manage only fourth in Mexico. Ickx won in Canada, and Rindt finally had his first win at Watkins Glen in the United States. Graham Hill was badly injured after a tyre blew on the straight as he was heading for the pits; long convalescence looked likely, but Hill was determined to be back for the start of the 1970 season. He made it, but there were to be no more Grand Prix successes in his career.

1970

Drivers' Championship	1.	Jochen Rindt	45
	2.	Jacky Ickx	40
	3.	Clay Regazzoni	33
Constructors' Title	1.	Lotus	59
	2.	Ferrari	55
	3.	March	48

TRAGEDY FOR RINDT

In 1970 things began to look favourable for Jochen Rindt, whose five years in the sport had been frustrating. Following his accident in 1969, Graham Hill vowed to race on, but not with Lotus, so Rindt was now their no. 1. There was also a new car, the Lotus 72, with which Rindt could mount a serious challenge.

Stewart races with March

At Kyalami, in the opening round, Rindt received a bump from Brabham early in the race. He continued, but engine trouble put paid to his chances. Brabham, now in his 23rd year of racing, won in his new Brabham-Ford BT33; Graham Hill claimed a point by finishing sixth. The new Lotus made its appearance in Spain, sporting many technical advances. There were early glitches, however, and Rindt retired with ignition trouble. Stewart won; he was driving the new March 701 as the Tyrrell outfit and Matra had parted at the end of 1969.

McLaren killed while testing

There was a sensational finish at Monaco. Brabham was well ahead in the latter stages. Rindt, who had been forced to revert to the old Lotus 49, was driving increasingly quickly in an attempt to catch him. Brabham got the danger signal from the pits and responded but Rindt was on his tail going into the final lap. Brabham overshot his braking on the last bend; Rindt swept through and won.

He had to retire at Spa. This race saw BRM – now sponsored by Yardley – back on top: Pedro Rodriguez gave it its first success since 1966. The McLarens had withdrawn from the race as a mark of respect for Bruce McLaren, who had been killed a few days earlier testing his CanAm car.

The revised Lotus 72 made a brilliant reappearance at Zandvoort; Rindt took the lead on the third lap and held it to the end. His victory was marred by the death of his friend Piers Courage, whose de Tomaso had crashed and exploded early in the race. Rindt considered retiring from the sport but decided that a mid-season withdrawal was out.

Three in a row for Rindt

He now led the championship and consolidated by winning the next three races. The first was in France, where he came through after Ickx's Ferrari and Beltoise's Matra both hit trouble. At Brands Hatch, Brabham shadowed Rindt and succeeded in passing him, but ran out of fuel on the final lap. There was more to come: a protest regarding the height of the Lotus's aerofoil was upheld, and Brabham was declared the winner. That decision was later reversed and Rindt was reinstated. This was John Surtees' first season running his own team and he showed off his new car, the TS7, at Brands Hatch; it made a promising start before succumbing to engine trouble. Another feature of that race was the performance of the young Emerson Fittipaldi. He had been given Team Lotus's old 49C car and finished eighth.

Safety issues at the Nürburgring meant that the German Grand Prix moved to Hockenheim for the first time. Rindt again came out on top, a narrow winner over Ickx. Ickx was on form again in Austria, and made it a Ferrari one-two with his team-mate Clay Regazzoni. Ickx was now a clear threat, but the Lotus camp knew that a win at Monza would give Rindt an unassailable lead. However, in final practice on 5 September, Rindt was killed when his Lotus lurched into a crash barrier. He was 28.

Rindt posthumous champion

Lotus withdrew from the race, which was won by Regazzoni in his first season in Formula One. It also scratched from the Canadian Grand Prix, the first of a trio of trans-Atlantic races ending the series. Ickx was the only driver who could top Rindt's 45 points, and only if he won all three final rounds. He succeeded in Canada, and in the final race in Mexico, but he was fourth at Watkins Glen. Rindt was the first posthumous winner of the Drivers' championship.

1971

Drivers' Championship	1.	Jackie Stewart	62
	2.	Ronnie Peterson	33
	3.	François Cévert	26
Constructors' Title	1.	Tyrrell	73
	2.	BRM	36
	3.	March	34

TYRRELL ON THE MARCH

Early in 1970 Jackie Stewart realised that the March was inferior to his 1969 Matra. Ken Tyrrell had a new car under development, and Stewart drove it in the final three rounds of the 1970 series. It was further refined by the time the 1971 championship began, and a second was prepared for Stewart's team-mate, François Cévert. The ubiquitous Ford Cosworth engines should have made all the teams using them fairly even, but Stewart's Tyrrell-Ford proved to be more powerful and reliable than its rivals.

Ferrari threat

Ferrari were a threat to all the Ford powered cars. Mario Andretti won the opener, at Kyalami. It was Andretti's first Grand Prix success – he had been a star of American racing for some time – and it marked a step on the way to fulfilling a lifelong ambition. He was champion material, but after this he came back to earth; his day was still several years away.

At the Spanish Grand Prix Stewart began to steamroll his way to the title. He took over the lead from Jacky Ickx's Ferrari on the sixth lap and stayed there, crossing the line 3.4 seconds ahead, giving the Tyrrell team its maiden success. He was on form at Monaco, dominating the race from start to finish. There were many plaudits for Ronnie Peterson, who came in second; Ickx took third after Siffert retired.

Rodriguez killed in Germany

The Tyrrell had engine problems during practice at Zandvoort, and there was no time to set it up for the wet conditions; Stewart went through the motions and trailed home 11th. Ickx, by contrast, gave a masterclass in wet-weather driving and came out on top after a battle with Pedro Rodriguez in the BRM. The French Grand Prix was at the new Paul Ricard circuit, near Marseilles. Stewart won again, and Cévert followed him home; Emerson Fittipaldi put up a great show in third. Before the British Grand Prix Pedro Rodriguez was killed in a minor sports car event in Germany. He had won only twice in his eight-year career in Formula One, but was regularly in the points. Clay Regazzoni took pole at Silverstone, and led in the early stages. Stewart then took over and dominated from the front. Peterson gave another fine showing to finish second, half a minute behind Stewart. Fittipaldi was third again.

The Nürburgring brought another top two finishes for Tyrrell. Stewart won, but Cévert set the fastest lap. Ickx was Stewart's closest rival, but he still only had a theoretical chance of catching him, and though Stewart crashed out of the Austrian Grand Prix, Ickx also failed to finish. Jo Siffert won the race for BRM. Two Austrians made their first Formula One appearance here: one was Helmut Marko who finished 11th. The other fared worse, retiring in his rented March-Ford after 20 laps: Niki Lauda.

Thrilling duel

Stewart was also unlucky at Monza. Just 0.61 seconds covered the first five cars across the line, the tightest Grand Prix finish ever; Peter Gethin squeaked home first. He had begun the season with McLaren but had moved to BRM. Peterson, Cévert and Howden Ganley were three of the others in the shake-up, finishing second, third and fifth respectively. Stewart's season seemed to be petering out, though the title was settled. In Canada, however, he got the

better of a duel with Peterson, who came second. Conditions were bad and the race was halted after 64 of the 80 laps.

Stewart had enjoyed six wins. The final race, at Watkins Glen, added icing to the cake for Tyrrell. Cévert took the lead from Stewart on the 14th lap and held on, winning from Siffert and Peterson; Tyrrell had won seven of the eleven championship rounds. Peterson and Cévert finished second and third in the final table, with 33 and 26 points respectively. Stewart's 62 points underlines just how far ahead of the field he was.

The season finished on a tragic note. Jo Siffert was killed in a specially arranged race at Brands Hatch when his BRM crashed and caught fire.

1972

Drivers' Championship	1.	Emerson Fittipaldi	61
	2.	Jackie Stewart	45
	3.	Denny Hulme	39
Constructors' Title	1.	Lotus	61
	2.	Tyrrell	51
	3.	McLaren	47

FITTIPALDI'S YEAR

Lotus had an unsuccessful 1971; the Lotus 72 proved no match for the Tyrrells, Ferraris and March 711. Fittipaldi had done well, despite being injured for part of the season, and having numerous mechanical troubles: he managed a second place and two thirds, finishing sixth overall. Lotus undertook a lot of work in the close season, and the car was reborn as the John Player Special in black and gold colours. It was now as quick and reliable as any other.

Jackie Stewart won the opening race in Argentina, suggesting that Tyrrell was going to sweep the board again, but his year was blighted by a stomach ulcer. He still recorded four victories, but this time that wouldn't quite be enough. Fittipaldi had retired with suspension trouble. He took second in South Africa, behind Denny Hulme. Hulme had got off to a good start in the title race, the South African win following his second behind Stewart in Argentina. This was a great change for McLaren, who hadn't won a race in three years, instead concentrating on the Indianapolis 500 and the CanAm races the previous year. Now, with Yardley's sponsorship, the focus was back on Formula One.

Appalling conditions for Monaco

The Spanish Grand Prix at Jarama was the first 1971 victory for Fittipaldi. Monaco followed, where there were many slides in appalling conditions; Jean-Pierre Beltoise won in his BRM – the marque's last success. Fittipaldi had a far from happy race, but he stayed in contention and avoided errors; his efforts were rewarded by a third place. Stewart's Tyrrell fell back with wet electrics.

The Belgian Grand Prix at the new Nivelles circuit, a race which Stewart's ulcer caused him to miss, gave Fittipaldi his next win. Stewart was back in time for the French race at Clermont-Ferrand; he won, with Fittipaldi second. They contested the British Grand Prix at Brands Hatch, but Fittipaldi came out on top: the championship was looking like a two-horse race. As they headed for the next round at the Nürburgring, Fittipaldi led with 43 points to Stewart's 27.

Jacky Ickx notches eighth victory

Fittipaldi was chasing Ickx's Ferrari in the German Grand Prix when oil leaking from his gearbox ignited. Ickx had his eighth Grand Prix victory, also his last. His team-mate Clay Regazzoni was second, giving Ferrari their first one-two since the duo

had finished in that order two years before, in Canada. Stewart failed to finish and was unable to make up any ground on Fittipaldi in the championship.

In Austria Fittipaldi bounced back, taking the lead from Stewart at around the half-distance mark. He was pressed all the way to the line by Denny Hulme, not Stewart – who finished seventh and out of the points. Hulme's team-mate Peter Revson finished third, giving him his third podium finish of the year.

Fittipaldi now led Stewart by 52 points to 27. The title was nearly safe. The next race was Monza, and Fittipaldi took up the running after the Ferraris of Ickx and Regazzoni both retired. Easing off, he crossed the line 14 seconds clear of Hailwood. His 61 points was now unassailable; Denny Hulme was his nearest challenger on 31 with just two races to go. Fittipaldi didn't add to his tally in those, in Canada and the United States; Stewart finished strongly to win both. That was enough to take second place from Hulme, but he was still 15 points below Fittipaldi. The new champion also put himself into the record books by becoming the youngest ever holder of the title – at 25 years, 8 months and 29 days.

BELOW: **Emerson Fittipaldi (Lotus-Ford) pictured prior to the start of the 1972 German Grand Prix, Nürburgring.**

1973

Drivers' Championship	1.	Jackie Stewart	71
	2.	Emerson Fittipaldi	55
	3.	Ronnie Peterson	52
Constructors' Title	1.	JPS/Lotus	92
	2.	Tyrrell	82
	3.	McLaren	58

STEWART AND TYRRELL VICTORIOUS FOR A SECOND TIME

Once again, Fittipaldi and Stewart were the main features for Lotus and Tyrrell respectively; Ronnie Peterson and François Cévert were able supporting acts for the same teams. The season started well for Fittipaldi; he won both South American races. Cévert had led for much of the race in Argentina, but Fittipaldi took over, and Cévert and Stewart settled for the minor placings. In Brazil he led all the way, though he hadn't taken pole; Peterson had, but he failed to finish, as he had in Argentina.

South Africa gave Jackie Stewart his first win; he was already considering retiring and wanted to leave at the top. Revson pipped Fittipaldi for second. Revson's team-mate Denny Hulme gave the new McLaren M23 its first outing; he had taken pole in a machine that was to be very successful for McLaren over the next few years. He could finish only fifth, but Revson got his second in the old M19. Both would race the new machine from this point.

James Hunt debuts at Monaco

Fittipaldi got his third win out of four in Spain. Cévert came a distant second and Stewart succumbed to brake problems. Peterson also failed to finish. He had taken pole, and set the fastest lap; he led for most of the race but gearbox trouble allowed Fittipaldi to take the lead. Stewart now had back-to-back victories in Belgium and Monaco. Cévert was second at Zolder, giving Tyrrell their first one-two of the year and Fittipaldi finished a distant third. They were the only drivers to complete the full 70 laps. Stewart won narrowly from Fittipaldi at Monaco; Peterson finally had some luck and finished third, ahead of Cévert. Revson and Hulme's McLarens came fifth and sixth. In ninth was James Hunt, making his debut in a March 731 for Hesketh Racing, the team of the eccentric Lord Alexander Hesketh.

Denny Hulme won for only the second time in four years as the Formula One circus went to Sweden for the first time. A puncture allowed Hulme to win but Peterson held on to take second place from Cévert. It finally came right for Peterson at the French Grand Prix. Jody Scheckter was an occasional third driver for McLaren, and France was only his third Grand Prix outing; he crashed out, having led to the three-quarter mark, and Peterson won.

Impulsive Scheckter

Scheckter went off on the first lap and took out 13 other cars in the next race at Silverstone. Revson won after a restart, with Peterson edging out Hulme for second. Hunt was in the points for the second time, at fourth. There were no major casualties in the Silverstone pile-up, but that was not so at Zandvoort. Roger Williamson's March crashed; he was killed. Stewart and Cévert finished first and second, and repeated the feat at the Nürburgring.

Monza decides the championship

Peterson led in the opening stages in Austria, then allowed Fittipaldi through. Peterson won in spite of the ploy as a broken fuel line ended Fittipaldi's hopes a few laps from the end. Monza turned out to be the championship decider, and tactics employed there had wider implications. Again Peterson and Fittipaldi were first and second, but this time Peterson didn't allow his team-mate through. Though they finished in those positions, it wasn't enough to prevent the title going to Stewart. His fourth place put him on 71 points: his third world championship.

Revson won the penultimate round in Canada. Stewart had finished fifth, his 99th race. He then withdrew, after François Cévert was killed in practice, never racing again. His five wins made a total of 27, putting him two ahead of Jim Clark on the all-time list, a record that would stand for 14 years.

Peterson won the final round, and finished the season on 52 points. He had won four races, but he had taken nine poles and led in 11 of the 15 races. He finished just 3 points behind Fittipaldi in the final table.

1974

Drivers' Championship	1.	Emerson Fittipaldi	55
	2.	Clay Regazzoni	52
	3.	Jody Scheckter	45
Constructors' Title	1.	McLaren	73
	2.	Ferrari	65
	3.	Tyrrell	52

McLAREN, FOR THE FIRST TIME

There were many changes. Fittipaldi moved to McLaren, now backed by Texaco and Marlboro. He was replaced at Lotus by Jacky Ickx; Ronnie Peterson remained. Clay Regazzoni had spent three seasons with Ferrari before joining BRM where he teamed up with Niki Lauda; between them they accumulated only 5 points. Ferrari had not done much better with Jacky Ickx and Arturo Merzario and was keen for Regazzoni to return. Lauda decided to go with him.

Denny Hulme's swansong

Hulme took the opening race in Argentina, his final win; Carlos Reutemann led virtually all the way in the Brabham BT44, but ran out of fuel two laps from the finish. Fittipaldi prevailed in Brazil, also having a stroke of luck: a mid-race tussle ended when Peterson had a puncture. In South Africa, Reutemann held the lead in both of the first two races, and claimed his maiden Grand Prix victory at Kyalami; it was overshadowed by Peter Revson's death in practice. Lauda and Regazzoni scored a one-two success for Ferrari in the Spanish Grand Prix.

Quiet start for Scheckter

Regazzoni led for the first half of the Belgian Grand Prix, having taken pole. But Fittipaldi won, marginally ahead of Lauda, with Regazzoni fourth. Jody Scheckter was third. He had made a quiet start – his third place in Belgium followed a fifth in Spain – but was to play a part in the final shake-up for the title.

Ronnie Peterson came out on top at Monaco. His victory there coincided with Lotus's decision to revert to the 72 model; the new 76 had been trialled in the previous three races, but had been disappointing. Scheckter took second, while Regazzoni came fourth. The see-sawing continued in Sweden, as Scheckter and Depailler gave Tyrrell their first win. Neither Ferrari finished that day, but Lauda once again led Regazzoni home in the Dutch Grand Prix.

Third pole in a row for Lauda

In the French Grand Prix Lauda took pole and led in the early stages; Peterson took over on lap 17 and stayed in front for the remainder of the 80-lap race. Lauda then took his third pole in a row at Brands Hatch. He led for 69 of the 75 laps, but delayed coming into the pits for a tyre change and suffered a puncture. Scheckter profited from Lauda's miscalculation, holding off Fittipaldi for the remaining six laps. Lauda was gaining the reputation of being the quickest driver; of the 15 championship races he would take pole position no less than nine times. His rise had been relatively swift, however, and he tended to make mistakes. The next came at the Nürburgring where he failed to warm up his tyres; his race ended on the first lap in a bump involving Scheckter who went on to finish second. The winner was Ferrari's Regazzoni.

Regazzoni in the lead

Regazzoni led the table with 44 points to Lauda's 38, with four races to go. Lauda retired from the Austrian Grand Prix; Regazzoni finished fifth. Carlos Reutemann gave the Brabham another success at Osterreichring, dominating the race. At Monza Ferrari went into self-destruct mode. Lauda led for 30 laps, then Regazzoni for 10. Regazzoni felt that Lauda was in a position to cover him and give him the best possible chance of picking up maximum points, but both drivers went all out to win and both retired with engine trouble. Three of their chief rivals took the top honours: Peterson, Fittipaldi and Scheckter, finishing in that order.

Fittipaldi wins the title in the final race

Lauda made another mistake in Canada. He shot into the lead and held it to the three-quarter distance, but skidded out, allowing Fittipaldi to win. Regazzoni was again critical of Lauda's tactics; as a result Fittipaldi had now drawn level with him going into the final round at Watkins Glen. Scheckter also had a slender chance of taking the title which disappeared when he failed to finish: it was thus a straight fight between Fittipaldi and Regazzoni. Regazzoni experienced terrible handling problems. Reutemann won, but Fittipaldi's fourth place was enough to bring him his second championship, and McLaren their first.

1975

Drivers' Championship	1.	Niki Lauda	64.5
	2.	Emerson Fittipaldi	45
	3.	Carlos Reutemann	37
Constructors' Title	1.	Ferrari	72.5
	2.	Brabham	54
	3.	McLaren	53

LAUDA FROM FITTIPALDI

Both Lauda and Regazzoni stayed at Ferrari for 1975, though the latter was now the clear no. 2. Lauda was determined to learn from his mistakes and was focused on winning the title.

Fittipaldi made a strong start, winning in Argentina, and followed it up with a second place in Brazil. Ferrari's start was quieter. Lauda and Regazzoni squeezed into the points in both South American races, but were behind Fittipaldi. However, for the third race of the series, at Kyalami, Ferrari played its ace: the new 312T model. It didn't win in South Africa – that honour went to Scheckter – but it was the crucial turning point. Its teething problems were relatively minor and Lauda enthused over its handling.

Both Ferraris were on the front row in Spain, but Lauda's race was quickly over, following a shunt from Mario Andretti; Regazzoni got caught up in the ensuing chaos. Accidents took out many cars, and Embassy Racing's Rolf Stommelen found himself an unlikely leader. Then, on the 25th lap, his car somersaulted over a barrier, killing four spectators – practice had earlier been disrupted when the Grand Prix Drivers Association lodged a protest about the safety of the

circuit, particularly the barriers. The race was halted soon afterwards and half points were awarded. Jochen Mass had been leading, from Ickx and Reutemann.

Lauda makes a charge

Lauda's challenge seriously began at Monaco. He enjoyed a 3-second win over Fittipaldi, and followed it up with more comfortable winning margins over Scheckter and Reutemann in Belgium and Sweden respectively. In the Dutch Grand Prix he had to settle for second place; James Hunt made a brave decision with his Hesketh's tyres, earning him a narrow 1-second win over the Austrian. Hesketh's triumph was short-lived; running a team without a major sponsor was impossible and Hesketh had to quit at the end of the year. Although the name carried on, it wasn't such a force.

Lauda avenged that defeat in France, edging out Hunt. There were only a couple of seconds in it at the finish, but Lauda had dominated, having taken pole and led from the start to lap 54. Silverstone was the next venue, a race which was also curtailed when a downpour caused a dozen cars to slide off. Of the top six finishers, only two were still running when the red flag was waved. Fittipaldi was ahead at the time.

Williams' team in the points

Lauda suffered a puncture in Germany, which meant only a third-place finish, well behind Reutemann and Jacques Laffite in the Williams. Laffite's second place provided a welcome boost to Frank Williams' outfit, striving to keep going at the time. There was more bad weather for the Austrian Grand Prix; Mark Donohue, of the Penske team, lost his life in the warm-up. Vittorio Brambilla won, although he too crashed over the line in his works March. Half points were again awarded for the curtailed event.

Single-minded Lauda takes the title

Regazzoni got the better of his team-mate for only the third time in the season at Monza, the penultimate race. But Lauda's third place was enough to put him out of sight as far as the championship was concerned. He capped it with another victory at Watkins Glen, putting him 19.5 points clear of Fittipaldi.

1975 ended sadly, with the death of Graham Hill and several members of his Embassy Racing team. Hill had run the team for two years, and had announced that he was retiring in order to concentrate on management. In November, he was piloting the light aircraft bringing the team home from Paul Ricard. The plane crashed in fog near Elstree airfield. Hill and several members of the crew died, including the talented young driver Tony Brise.

1976

Drivers' Championship	1.	James Hunt	69
	2.	Niki Lauda	68
	3.	Jody Scheckter	49
Constructors' Title	1.	Ferrari	83
	2.	McLaren	74
	3.	Tyrrell	71

HUNT: BY ONE POINT

There was drama on the track this year, and controversy off it. Lauda won in Brazil and South Africa, followed by a second behind team-mate Regazzoni in the US West Grand Prix at Long Beach. Hunt had two retirements, and ran second to Lauda at Kyalami. He was now fronting for McLaren.

The first drama came in the fourth round, at Jarama. Lauda was the early leader, despite recovering from two broken ribs. Hunt overtook him on lap 32 of the 75-lap race, and crossed the line first. He was disqualified after it was discovered that his car was 1.8cm too wide; Lauda was awarded first place, and increased his lead. McLaren appealed, but it took weeks to resolve – in favour of Hunt, whose win was reinstated.

Tyrrell's six-wheel wonder

In Belgium, Lauda and Regazzoni finished well ahead of the field. They were now driving the Ferrari 312T2, a revised version of the car in which they had enjoyed so much success. Tyrrell was giving the six-wheeled P34 its second outing at Zolder; Scheckter brought it into a respectable fourth place. Lauda beat off the challenge of both Jody Scheckter and Patrick Depailler in the six-wheelers in Mexico, but Tyrrell then took first and second in Sweden. However, the innovative P34 never won another race.

Lauda well ahead

Lauda was third in Sweden. Hunt picked up a point in sixth, having retired in both Belgium and Monaco; Lauda's lead stood at 47 points. The next race, in France, was the final round in the first half of the championship. Hunt won at Paul Ricard, while Lauda had his first bad luck of the year, retiring with mechanical trouble. Immediately after this came the news about the result of the Spanish Grand Prix. Lauda's lead was reduced to 27 points.

ABOVE: **1976 Japanese Grand Prix, Fuji. James Hunt (McLaren M23-Ford) leads away from the front row, in atrocious weather conditions, at the start. Hunt came third to gain the points required to win the Drivers' Championship.**

OPPOSITE: **James Hunt (Hesketh-Ford) pictured prior to the 1975 Dutch Grand Prix, Zandvoort. This was his and the team's maiden Grand Prix win. It was also Hesketh's only Grand Prix victory.**

Since 1968 the championship had been split into halves, with drivers having to derive points from a stipulated number of races in each half. In 1976 Brands Hatch began the second phase, with more controversy. Regazzoni tried to get a flyer at the start, and there was a collision involving Hunt and Lauda. Hunt won the restarted race, with Lauda second. However Hunt had some repairs done to his car before the restart and another inquiry was instigated. It went against Hunt, who was disqualified; maximum points were awarded to Lauda.

Lauda badly burned

1 August 1976 was the day Lauda nearly died. On the second lap at the Nürburgring he cut a corner, ran over a kerb and tried to keep control of the Ferrari, but it went into a full spin. It hit a bank, bouncing back onto the track, where it burst into flames. It was hit by at least two more drivers with Lauda unconscious inside. Others managed to stop, helping until the ambulance arrived. Lauda was not expected to survive, but was soon off the danger list. Amazingly, he reappeared in his Ferrari just five weeks later.

Hunt won the restarted race to put himself within 14 points of Lauda. He was in the points in the two races Lauda missed, taking fourth at Osterreichring and winning at Zandvoort. Lauda returned for Monza on 12 September, his championship lead now down to just 2 points. He was still recovering, but took fourth. As Hunt had retired from the race, he increased his lead.

Hunt stripped of points

McLaren now received the news that Hunt would be stripped of the points from Brands Hatch, but he took back-to-back victories in Canada and the United States. Lauda was out of the points at Mosport Park, and third at Watkins Glen. Going into the last race, the first Japanese Grand Prix, he led – by 3 points. Conditions were appalling and Lauda returned to the pits after two laps. If Hunt finished in the first three the championship would be his. He led for 61 of the 73 laps, but a tyre change put him back in fifth. He managed to claw his way up to third, and took the title by a single point.

1977

Drivers' Championship	1.	Niki Lauda	72
	2.	Jody Scheckter	55
	3.	Mario Andretti	47
Constructors' Title	1.	Ferrari	95
	2.	Lotus	62
	3.	McLaren	60

LAUDA REPAYS FERRARI'S TRUST

Enzo Ferrari had doubts about Lauda's future, but gave him the benefit of the doubt and confirmed him as lead driver. His partner for the new season was Carlos Reutemann, now in his sixth Formula One season, with four Grand Prix wins.

Scheckter the Wolf

After three years at Tyrrell, Jody Scheckter decided to join the new Wolf team. This concern became only the third in the event's 28-year history to win at the first outing. Watson, Hunt and Carlos Pace had all led in Argentina, but Scheckter took over five laps from home to win from Pace's Brabham. Watson and Hunt both retired, as did Lauda, and Reutemann flew the Ferrari flag in third.

Ferrari's newcomer did even better at Interlagos, having a 10-second lead over Hunt at the finish. Lauda was third, and went on to win at Kyalami, his first victory since his crash. The race was overshadowed by another tragedy: Tom Pryce crested a rise in his Shadow and hit a marshal who was crossing the track. Pryce had no time to react and both men were killed.

Mario Andretti edged out Lauda by a second at Long Beach, marking a resurgence in Lotus's fortunes. The Lotus 77 had now given way to the 78. Sidepods on either side of the cockpit channelled air under the car to create huge amounts of downforce. 'Ground effect' wasn't a new idea, but the Lotus put the theory into very successful practice.

Lauda mystery in Spain

Lauda was missing from the Spanish Grand Prix. There were rumours of an injury, but relations between driver and team were cooling and an argument was possible. Lauda could not afford to miss many races; the Ferrari 312/T2 was no longer dominant. Andretti was on target again in Spain, taking pole and leading for the entire 75 laps. Scheckter gave Wolf its second win of the season at Monaco; Lauda was second once again.

The Lotus eclipsed the Ferrari again at Zolder, but this time it was Andretti's team-mate Gunnar Nilsson who won. Andretti took pole at the next race in Sweden, and led for 67 of the 72 laps, setting the fastest lap. Five cars overhauled him in the dying stages, and he emerged with just 1 point to show for his efforts. The French Grand Prix was one of his good days. John Watson had led virtually all the way, only to have the lead snatched from him on the 80th and final lap.

ABOVE: **1977 Monaco Grand Prix, Monte Carlo. Jody Scheckter (Wolf WR1-Ford) powers away at the start of the race. He went on to take the chequered flag in first position.**

OPPOSITE: **Alan Jones (Shadow DN8-Ford) takes his maiden Grand Prix win and the Shadow Racing Team's last at the 1977 Austrian Grand Prix, Osterreichring, Zeltweg.**

1978

Drivers' Championship	1.	Mario Andretti	64
	2.	Ronnie Peterson	51
	3.	Carlos Reutemann	48
Constructors' Title	1.	Lotus	86
	2.	Ferrari	58
	3.	Brabham	53

Hunt wins at Silverstone

James Hunt had been having an awful time, but improvement began at Silverstone. He was involved in a close tussle with Watson for two-thirds of the race, until the latter's Brabham developed a fuel injection problem. Lauda finished second to Hunt, but even a big improvement wasn't going to put Hunt in the final frame. One of those who failed to finish at Silverstone was Jean-Pierre Jabouille, driving a Renault. Renault, returning to racing after 70 years, was showing off the 1.5-litre RS01, the first turbo-charged car in a Formula One race.

Lauda won only his second race of the year at Hockenheim, then took his fifth second in Austria. That race provided the Shadow team with their only win, for Alan Jones; welcome news after the Kyalami crash. Another win followed for Lauda at Zandvoort, but success was barely masking discontent within the team. Before Monza – where he finished second yet again, this time to Andretti – he made it clear that his days at Ferrari were numbered. The next round, at Watkins Glen, gave Lauda a fourth, and an unassailable lead in the championship. Lauda walked away from Ferrari and signed for Bernie Ecclestone's Brabham team.

Jody Scheckter won the penultimate race in Canada, and Hunt won in Japan. Scheckter was runner-up to Lauda in the championship, but it was Andretti who might easily have got closer. He had scored four wins to Lauda's three, but lost valuable points through a spate of collisions and engine failures.

LOTUS ONE-TWO

With Lauda's move to Brabham, Carlos Reutemann was promoted to Ferrari's no. 1 driver, with Gilles Villeneuve filling the other slot. The team Ferrari had to beat was going to be Lotus. They, too, had a change: Andretti remained, while Gunnar Nilsson left to join the new Arrows team, but cancer prevented him ever contesting a race for Arrows. Ronnie Peterson took over at Lotus; he knew he would be running as second-string to Andretti in 1978, but rejoining Lotus put him back on top, where he belonged.

In Argentina, Andretti led from start to finish. Lauda followed him home, but the Brabham's Alfa Romeo engine was to be a bone of contention for the entire season. Reutemann then won the Brazilian Grand Prix for Ferrari. Back came Lotus at Kyalami, Peterson this time edging out Patrick Depailler's Tyrrell on the last lap. Battle lines were being drawn up between Lotus and Ferrari. Reutemann won from Andretti in the US West Grand Prix at Long Beach, but the next race, Monaco, was the only one in the series in which neither Ferrari nor Lotus registered a single point. Peterson and Villeneuve retired, and Reutemann and Andretti finished out of the points. Patrick Depailler eased home ahead of Lauda.

More improvements by Chapman

That was a turning point for Lotus, it was the last time that both Andretti and Peterson featured in the 78 model. In the following round, at Zolder, Andretti drove the 79, an improved version of an already impressive car. He duly won in Belgium, with Peterson following him home in the old 78 model. They followed this with another one-two in Spain, although both drivers were in 79s.

The last round in the first half of the championship season saw Lauda score his first win. His Brabham was fitted with a controversial rear-mounted fan in an attempt to create the kind of downforce that Lotus was working on. Lauda's victory at Anderstorp prompted immediate outcry from rival teams. The innovation was immediately banned by the FIA, although the Swedish result was allowed to stand. The 'fan car' never raced again.

High Court ban for Arrows

Andretti and Peterson had yet another one-two at Paul Ricard. Reutemann won the British Grand Prix at Brands Hatch, helped by the fact that neither Andretti nor Peterson finished. Peterson was performing in an exemplary manner as no. 2 to Andretti. Sometimes he was quicker, but respected the terms of his contract. Andretti crashed out at the start in atrocious conditions in Austria, however, and Peterson came home ahead of Depailler and Villeneuve. The race at Osterreichring was notable for the introduction of the new Arrows car, the A1. The car with which the fledgling team started the season had been banned, the High Court ruling that it was similar enough to the Shadow DN9 to constitute breaking copyright.

Ronnie Peterson dies from crash injuries

Andretti was back on form at Zandvoort, so Peterson reverted to his usual role of second-place man. As the circus moved to Monza, the title was between the two Lotus men. Peterson crashed in the warm-up and had to start the race in the old 78 model, but was then involved in a huge pile-up at the start. Andretti won from Villeneuve in the restarted race, but they were both penalised for jumping the start and Lauda inherited his second win of the year. Andretti was now confirmed as champion, but this was overshadowed: Peterson, a close friend as well as team-mate, had died. His injuries had not been considered life-threatening, but a fatal embolism developed.

Reutemann scored his fourth win of the year at Watkins Glen on his way to third place in the title race. Villeneuve was a popular winner in the final race of the season in Canada. 1978 was all about Lotus. Peterson, the quickest driver of his time, had fulfilled his contract and finished runner-up as a result. For Andretti, meanwhile, the title was the culmination of a ten-year dream.

1979

Drivers' Championship	1.	Jody Scheckter	51
	2.	Gilles Villeneuve	47
	3.	Alan Jones	40
Constructors' Title	1.	Ferrari	113
	2.	Williams	75
	3.	Ligier	61

SCHECKTER EDGES OUT VILLENEUVE

Ferrari believed that Carlos Reutemann was talented but prone to the occasional expensive mistake. He bore the consequences of failure, and was shown the door. Reutemann asserted that the Lotuses were, quite simply, better cars – and joined the team, where he teamed up with Andretti. Ferrari went into the new season with Jody Scheckter partnering the mercurial Villeneuve.

However, it had a disappointing start: Scheckter had an accident in Argentina and was only sixth in Brazil. Villeneuve fared little better, with just 2 points for finishing ahead of his team-mate at Interlagos. The star of these opening races was Jacques Laffite and Ligier. Laffite won both, with his team-mate Patrick Depailler following him home in Brazil. Ferrari took one-two in the next two races, at Kyalami and Long Beach, Villeneuve taking the top honours. Ferrari's new car, the 312-T4, was introduced at Kyalami; it wasn't without problems, but they were ironed out as the season went on. It was powerful and reliable, and it needed to be. As the early challenge from Ligier faded, strong opposition was provided by Williams and the turbo-powered Renault.

James Hunt bows out

The Ligier came back in Spain, Depailler leading from start to finish. Lotus took first and second at Jarama, a rare good day for Reutemann and Andretti. The Lotus 80, the successor to the 79, was plagued by problems. Scheckter won the next two races, in Belgium and Monaco: significantly, for Ferrari was considering putting all the team's efforts behind Villeneuve's title bid. More significant was the debut of the Williams FW07, which took the ground-effect principle to a different level. Williams, now backed by Saudi money, was firmly on the way. Monaco also saw James Hunt decide that it was time to call it a day.

Turbo-charged Renault

At the French Grand Prix it was the other looming threat to Ferrari that took centre stage. Renault's perseverance with turbo-charged cars paid off as Jabouille crossed the line first in the RS10. His team-mate René Arnoux lost out to Villeneuve for second place in a ding-dong battle, their cars often touching as they passed each other repeatedly. Villeneuve squeaked home a quarter of a second ahead.

Opposition to Ferrari became more intense. Regazzoni and Arnoux came home first and second at Silverstone. Regazzoni, now 39, brought Williams its maiden victory. His team-mate Alan Jones then built on that success; he had taken pole and led for 38 of the 68 laps in the British Grand Prix at Silverstone

before retiring with water-pump trouble. He won four of the next five races, dominating the latter half of the season.

However, Scheckter was in the points in every one of these races: second behind Jones at Zandvoort, and fourth in Germany, Austria and Canada – vital in terms of the championship. As the championship was to be decided on the best four finishes from the first seven races, plus the best four finishes from the final eight rounds, Jones's superb run wasn't going to be enough. By Monza only Scheckter and Villeneuve could take the crown. Team orders were issued; Villeneuve followed them and protected race leader Scheckter, who won the race and with it the championship.

Comfortable first and second for Ferrari

Jones won the penultimate round in Canada. In practice there, Niki Lauda decided he'd had enough after a frustrating season at Brabham. Villeneuve rounded off his season with a win in the US East Grand Prix at Watkins Glen, putting him 4 points behind Scheckter in the final table. Ferrari had emulated Lotus's 1978 achievement, taking first and second in the Drivers' Championship and comfortably winning the Constructors' title (the points system for the latter changed in 1979 to include each car from a constructor that finished in the top six in any race).

BELOW: **Alan Jones pictured in the cockpit of his Williams FW07B Ford Cosworth, prior to the 1980 Canadian Grand Prix, Montreal. He clinched a win thanks to a 60-second penalty against Pironi for jumping the start.**

OPPOSITE: **1978 Spanish Grand Prix, Jarama. Mario Andretti leads team-mate Ronnie Peterson (both Lotus 79-Fords). They finished first and second respectively.**

1980

A CLEAN SWEEP FOR WILLIAMS

Alan Jones featured in Williams' new campaign: predictably, after his performances in 1979. Less predictable was the rise of Nelson Piquet, Brabham's second driver behind Lauda; following Lauda's departure he became Brabham's no.1. 1979 had been his first full season. Brabham reverted to Ford power in the BT49, and that, together with Piquet's skill, gave Brabham its best season for a decade.

The first race was in Argentina; Jones won from Piquet and third was Keke Rosberg who had signed with Fittipaldi for 1979. In Brazil and South Africa, René Arnoux scored back-to-back wins in the new Renault, the RE20. Piquet scored his first win in the US West Grand Prix at Long Beach; he took pole, led from laps 1 to 80 and set the fastest lap. This race was marred by a career-ending accident for Clay Regazzoni. He had been replaced at Williams by Carlos Reutemann and had rejoined Ensign. The throttle of his car jammed open and he hit a concrete wall. He survived, but was confined to a wheelchair. Coming fifth at Long Beach was Jody Scheckter in the latest Ferrari, the 312-T5. The 2 points were to be his season total, and Villeneuve only gained 6 – a turn in Ferrari's fortunes.

Didier Pironi headed the rostrum in the Belgian Grand Prix at Zolder. He joined the Ligier team for the 1980 campaign after two successful Formula One seasons with Tyrrell. Jacques Laffite was the team leader but Pironi matched him throughout the season; 2 points separated them by the end, though they both finished well adrift of Jones and Piquet.

Arnoux – the new French talent

Williams took the honours in the next three races. Reutemann had his first success at Monaco, after Pironi crashed. Then Jones won the French and British Grands Prix to give him three victories plus a second and third from the first eight races. The Williams team was performing well, but there was still a threat from the Ligiers, Arnoux's Renault and, particularly, Piquet in the Brabham.

Spanish Grand Prix declared void

In-fighting between FISA and FOCA (the governing body and the constructors' association) meant the Spanish Grand Prix – won by Jones – was declared void for championship purposes. Next came the German Grand Prix, and Jones suffered a puncture while leading, allowing Laffite to come through and give Ligier their second success. Reutemann took second, while Jones came third. Piquet was fourth: out of the nine races so far, he had been in the points seven times, and had retired in Brazil and Belgium. The sport's latest tragedy came in practice: Patrick Depailler was killed after a crash in his Alfa Romeo.

him, even if he won in the final race at Watkins Glen. In fact Jones won, with team-mate Reutemann second. Williams had become the latest team to celebrate a clean sweep of the honours, following Lotus in 1978 and Ferrari in 1979.

1981

Drivers' Championship	1. Nelson Piquet	50
	2. Carlos Reutemann	49
	3. Alan Jones	46
Constructors' Title	1. Williams	95
	2. Brabham	61
	3. Renault	54

BRABHAM AND PIQUET'S CHALLENGE

FISA and FOCA were in dispute again, over the decision to ban side skirts for the new season. The ruling had huge implications for the 'ground effect' cars, which were predominantly British, and Lotus had to field the old 87 model as a result. Jones and Reutemann were still at Williams, and Piquet remained at Brabham. Laffite continued as Ligier's no. 1, with the team reverting to Matra power.

Reutemann in team orders row

Jones and Reutemann began the season at Long Beach the way they had finished in 1980. When Jones took the lead from his team-mate on lap 32, the race was all but over, because Reutemann's contract specified that he could only go for a win if he was 7 seconds ahead of Jones; otherwise he had to let him through. This fell apart in Brazil. Reutemann led the whole way but was signalled to let second-placed Jones pass with four laps to go; he disregarded the order and won. There was a huge row afterwards and Reutemann's race fee was withheld; the relationship between the two drivers broke down.

Mansell's first podium finish

In Argentina and San Marino Piquet scored successive victories. In Buenos Aires he had led the whole way and won by nearly half a minute from Reutemann. Villeneuve took pole and led in the early stages at Imola, but Piquet came through to win from Patrese and Reutemann. Jones went off the track at Zolder as he tried to impose himself on Reutemann; with Jones out of contention his team-mate went on to win the

OPPOSITE: **Nelson Piquet (Brabham BT49C-Ford), on the way to winning the 1981 German Grand Prix, Hockenheim. This was his last win of the season – therefore the points gained were vitally important to Piquet's quest for the title.**

ABOVE: **Nigel Mansell made the first of many podium appearances by coming third at the 1981 Monaco Grand Prix, Monte Carlo.**

Piquet challenging hard for Brabham

In the Austrian Grand Prix, Jabouille in the Renault held off Williams, leading from the halfway mark and crossing the line just ahead of Jones. Reutemann took third. With four races to go, Jones had an 11-point lead. At Zandvoort Arnoux took pole but Jones shot into a first-lap lead; he then had to pit with damaged bodywork and was out of the points. Piquet won, bringing him to within 2 points of Jones, whose slender advantage became a 1-point deficit after Monza. Piquet took up the running on lap 4 and held it to the end. Jones was second.

Piquet took pole in Montreal, with Jones in the other front row spot. Both hurtled out of the blocks and neither backed off as they approached the first corner; there was a pileup. Jones led in the restart, but was passed by Piquet on the third lap. On the 24th, Piquet's engine blew. Jones followed Pironi home, but he received a 60-second penalty for jumping the start and Jones had maximum points. Piquet couldn't overhaul

Silverstone gave him a 17-point lead, but the man who had been trying to win the title for nine years could only score 2 points in the next three races, a fifth in Austria sandwiched between retirements at Hockenheim and Zandvoort. In Germany Piquet won his third race of the year, taking the lead from Jones, who had fuel feed problems again. Laffite became the year's seventh different winner when he won from Arnoux and Piquet in Austria. Piquet was second behind Prost at Zandvoort, giving him 19 points for the three races and edging him ahead of Reutemann with three races to go.

Piquet by a single point

Prost joined Piquet with three wins by leading all the way at Monza. Jones and Reutemann finished behind him; Piquet picked up just 1 point in sixth. Laffite won in Montreal from tenth place on the grid; Piquet scored 2 points in fifth, while Reutemann was out of the top six.

Going into the final round Reutemann still led with 49 points, despite the latter half of the season. Piquet was 1 behind, with Laffite on 43. In Nevada, Reutemann was superb in practice and took pole; in the race itself, however, he put in a lacklustre performance and finished eighth. Laffite, sixth, scored 1 point, and was overhauled by Jones, who stormed to victory. Piquet's fifth place proved decisive: it was enough to give him his first championship by a single point from Reutemann.

ABOVE: **1982 Detroit Grand Prix, Detroit, USA. Eddie Cheever (Ligier JS17B-Matra), leads René Arnoux (Renault RE30B) and Niki Lauda (McLaren MP4/1B-Ford Cosworth), into a hairpin, on the way to second place.**

OPPOSITE: **Alain Prost leading his team-mate René Arnoux (both Renault RE30B), at the 1982 South African Grand Prix, Kyalami. They finished in first and third positions respectively.**

rain-shortened race. Nigel Mansell was third in his Lotus, his first podium finish in his first full season in Formula One.

Jones was leading at Monaco when a fuel feed problem hampered him with just four laps to go. Villeneuve came through, giving Ferrari their first win for two years. He then crossed the line first in a tight finish in Spain. Laffite, Watson, Reutemann and de Angelis were hot on his heels: less than 1.5 seconds separated all five.

Dennis and Barnard in control at McLaren

Like Mansell, another future champion had his first taste of success in 1981. Alain Prost did even better, winning at Dijon two seconds ahead of Watson's McLaren.

Watson came out on top at Silverstone in a win for the MP4 – an early sign of the huge success that McLaren would enjoy during the 1980s. Reutemann's second place at

1982

Drivers' Championship	1.	Keke Rosberg	44
	2.	Didier Pironi	39
	3.	John Watson	39
Constructors' Title	1.	Ferrari	74
	2.	McLaren	69
	3.	Renault	62

A TRAGIC YEAR

Williams was obviously a team on the up, but both Jones and Reutemann decided to call it a day: Jones at the end of 1981 and Reutemann after the 1982 opener in South Africa. Williams signed Keke Rosberg, who had experienced a disastrous couple of years with Fittipaldi. The only potential problem at Williams was that the team was still running the normally aspirated V-8 Cosworth engine, bucking the turbo trend.

Piquet and Rosberg disqualified

Prost recovered from a puncture to win the South African Grand Prix. Reutemann came second, in his last completed race for Williams, and Rosberg was fifth. Prost also won in Brazil: an inherited victory after Piquet and Rosberg were disqualified for running underweight cars.

After being out of the sport for two years, Niki Lauda returned to Formula One in 1982. His first win came at Long Beach, his third race. Andrea de Cesaris took pole and led until the 14th lap, when an accident put him out of the race; Lauda remained in front for the remaining 60 laps, with Rosberg second. Villeneuve crossed the line third, but his Ferrari was found to have an illegal wing and Patrese moved up from fourth to take the 4 points.

Villeneuve killed in practice

The Brazilian disqualifications led to a mass withdrawal from the San Marino race by the FOCA teams. There were only 14 starters, and just 5 finishers. The lead changed hands several times between Villeneuve and Pironi's Ferraris, and Arnoux in the Renault. He retired with engine trouble, and Pironi passed Villeneuve on the last lap to win. This infuriated Villeneuve, who vowed not to speak to him again. Tragically, this feud

lasted just two weeks as Villeneuve was killed in practice for the Belgian Grand Prix at Zolder. There Rosberg had victory in his sights when he locked his brakes, and John Watson came through.

At Monaco the lead changed hands four times in the last three laps, and Riccardo Patrese claimed his first Formula One win, giving Brabham their first win of the season. Watson won a restarted race at Detroit, after which another tragedy occurred at Montreal: Riccardo Paletti was killed in a start-line accident when his Osella collided with Pironi's Ferrari. At the restart Mansell was involved in a nasty spill, his car overshooting Bruno Giacomelli's Alfa. Piquet and Patrese made it a one-two for Brabham. Their cars were differently powered: Piquet had the BMW turbo, Patrese the normally aspirated Cosworth engine.

Pironi's career over

The Dutch Grand Prix was dominated by Pironi, who next took second at Brands Hatch behind Lauda. After a third at Paul Ricard, he led the championship on 39 points, 9 clear of his nearest rival. Hockenheim was next, and the dreadful season got worse: Pironi broke both legs in a crash during practice, ending his career. Patrick Tambay, also driving for Ferrari, won.

ABOVE: **Action from the 1983 Brazilian Grand Prix, Rio de Janeiro. Nelson Piquet (Brabham BT52-BMW) won the opening race of the 1983 season. His next win was six months later at Monza in Italy.**

OPPOSITE: **Both Ayrton Senna and Martin Brundle made their mark in F3 in 1983. The following season Senna moved up to F1, driving for Toleman-Hart, and Brundle joined Tyrrell-Ford.**

Lotus was now in decline. The new 91 model performed well on fast circuits, but struggled against the turbos. The Osterreichring was one of the few tracks which suited it, and Elio de Angelis won narrowly from Rosberg, but only after much of the turbo-powered opposition was out of the race. After a string of finishes in the points, Rosberg finally scored a win in the Swiss Grand Prix – held at Dijon because of Switzerland's ban on circuit racing. He passed Prost, who had gearbox trouble, on the last lap.

Only one win for champion Rosberg

At Monza, Arnoux led from start to finish and Rosberg finished out of the points, while Watson picked up 3 in fourth place. Rosberg went into the final round at Caesar's Palace with 42 points from his nine finishes. Watson, on 33, needed a win to have a chance of snatching the title but came second, behind Alboreto's Tyrrell. Rosberg finished fifth, taking the crown by 5 points. He had won only once, but his consistent run of ten finishes was the decisive factor.

1983

Drivers' Championship	1.	Nelson Piquet	59
	2.	Alain Prost	57
	3.	René Arnoux	49
Constructors' Title	1.	Ferrari	89
	2.	Renault	79
	3.	Brabham	72

PIQUET AND PROST HEAD-TO-HEAD

Nelson Piquet remained at Brabham for 1983, with Patrese. The famous Cosworth engine, with over 150 wins to its credit, finally had to give way as one by one the teams turned to turbo power. Brabham had hedged its bets by running a turbo and normally aspirated car side by side in 1982. They concentrated on the turbo in 1983.

Williams wait for Honda

Piquet won the opening race in Brazil. Williams had an unfortunate start: Rosberg crossed the line second but was disqualified for receiving a push start in the pits. The team had done an engine deal with Honda, but was continuing with Ford until the new unit was ready. Lauda had been third in Brazil, but came home second in a McLaren one-two at Long Beach, behind Watson. Prost won his sixth race for Renault at Paul Ricard, and followed it up with a second behind Tambay at Imola. It was the beginning of a consistent run which would put the title within his grasp.

Keke Rosberg, driving a flat-bottomed version of the FW08 to comply with the new regulations, scored a win over Piquet and Prost at Monaco. Prost had his third pole and second win of the year at Spa. The seventh round was at Detroit, and provided a landmark in sports history: Michele Alboreto's win in his Tyrrell was the 155th – and last – for the famous Cosworth engine, which had made its debut in 1967. Montreal saw René Arnoux score his first win for Ferrari since his move from Renault, and Eddie Cheever, his replacement, was behind him.

Mansell gets competitive

Nigel Mansell finally got his hands on the Renault-turbo car at Silverstone. After a dismal beginning to the season, he finished fourth, some 40 seconds behind race winner Prost. Arnoux kept up his title hopes by winning at Hockenheim. It had been a Ferrari front row, with Arnoux's team-mate Tambay on pole and Arnoux should have let Tambay have a clear run – he trailed Tambay by 12 points in the championship. As it was, Tambay retired with engine trouble. Despite that, the Ferraris were now enjoying a good run. Tambay was on pole again in Austria, and led for the first 21 laps. After an oil problem put him out, his team-mate took over. Arnoux held the lead until six laps from home, when Prost overtook. They finished in that order, with Piquet third. Ferrari then had a one-two at Zandvoort. Piquet had led up to lap 41, when an incident involving Prost put them both out. Arnoux took over and won by 20 seconds from Tambay.

Prost's four wins had helped him to an 8-point advantage over Arnoux, with Piquet and Tambay a further 6 points behind, but Monza was disastrous for Prost. His turbo went at the halfway mark, while Piquet, Arnoux and Tambay finished first, second and fourth respectively. Prost was second in the European Grand Prix, staged at Brands Hatch. But Piquet dominated this race too, crossing the line 7 seconds ahead.

Piquet overhauls Prost for second title

Neither Ferrari was in the points, so it was a straight fight between Prost and Piquet in the final round, Prost's lead now down to 2 points. Piquet was on the front row, with Tambay on pole. Piquet got the better start and led for the first 59 laps of the 77-lap race, but Prost could only qualify fifth and his race ended with a turbo failure on the 35th lap. He now had to hope that Piquet finished no better than fifth. Though Piquet did relinquish the lead, being passed by both Patrese

and de Cesaris, his 4 points for third place were enough to give him his second title. Prost was criticised for letting the championship slip from his grasp, one of the factors leading to a parting of the ways between him and Renault.

1984

Drivers' Championship	1.	Niki Lauda	72
	2.	Alain Prost	71.5
	3.	Elio De Angelis	34
Constructors' Title	1.	McLaren	143.5
	2.	Ferrari	57.5
	3.	Lotus	47

McLAREN, WITH LAUDA AND PROST

Towards the end of 1983, when Piquet and Prost were battling for the title, McLaren drivers Watson and Lauda gave their new TAG Porsche engine a quiet start. Lauda stayed with the team and was joined by Prost. McLaren was ready: there was an impressive new turbo unit fitted to the MP4, and two top drivers.

The opening race was in Brazil. Elio de Angelis took pole in the Lotus-Renault, but Alboreto, beside him on the front row, got the better start. Lauda took over in front; when his car succumbed to an electrical fault, the race turned into a fight between Prost and Derek Warwick, who had replaced him at Renault. Warwick's suspension gave out and Prost scored the first in a succession of McLaren successes.

First points for Senna

At Kyalami, Prost and Lauda qualified in only fifth and eighth places respectively, but had a one-two success, with Lauda more than a minute clear of Prost. Warwick was third, more than a lap behind. Here, gaining his first championship point in sixth, was Ayrton Senna. He had tested for both Williams and McLaren but decided that he was better off being a bigger fish in a smaller pond, and joined Toleman.

Mansell loses grip

Both Lauda and Prost retired at Zolder, one of just two 1984 races when neither finished in the points. Alboreto took pole and enjoyed a start-to-finish victory. Piquet had suffered three retirements in a row, and had another at Imola: he took pole, but his turbo failed 12 laps from the line when he was second. Prost won, having led for the entire distance. Lauda's engine blew in the early stages at San Marino, but he won the French Grand Prix at Dijon. Second was Patrick Tambay, who, along with Warwick, made up Renault's partnership for 1984. Nigel Mansell scored his first points of the year by finishing third; he had stayed with Lotus. Monaco was run in torrential rain. Mansell should have won; he passed Prost to take the lead, but lost grip on the painted white lines and slid into the Armco; frustratingly, the race was stopped shortly after. Prost was ahead again by then and was declared the winner. Senna drove brilliantly: ninth on the opening lap, he was within 8 seconds of Prost when the race was halted.

Piquet finally had some luck in Montreal, relegating the McLarens to the minor placings. He repeated this at Detroit, in a race that was restarted after a first-lap shunt. Martin Brundle finished within a second of him, but his achievement was short-lived: he was disqualified for a weight irregularity in his Tyrrell. In Dallas, Mansell and de Angelis occupied the front row, the first time Lotus had done so for six years. Mansell led up to halfway, when Rosberg passed him in the Williams-Honda. Rosberg went on to win, while Mansell had transmission failure on the last lap. He fainted while he pushed his car to the line, but earned a point – he was classified sixth. Lauda won at Brands Hatch, leading after Prost hit gearbox trouble. At Hockenheim it was Prost's turn to benefit from others' misfortune: he headed Lauda home after de Angelis and Piquet both fell by the wayside.

Lauda joins the exclusive club

In Austria the entire field was made up of turbo-powered cars for the first time. Lauda crossed the line 24 seconds ahead of Piquet; Prost spun off. Zandvoort saw the third McLaren one-two of the year. Piquet was again first away, but retired on the tenth lap with an oil leak. Prost took over and won, 10 seconds ahead of Lauda.

Lauda won again at Monza, and Prost won the European Grand Prix at the new Nürburgring. Prost had retired in Italy, and Lauda took 3 points for fourth in Germany. The decider was at Estoril, and Lauda led Prost 66 to 62.5. Prost took the lead and held on to win, but Lauda moved through to finish second. Prost had won seven races to Lauda's five, but Lauda had a half-point advantage. He joined Fangio, Brabham and Stewart as one of the few three-times winners.

1985

Drivers' Championship	1.	Alain Prost	73
	2.	Michele Alboreto	53
	3.	Keke Rosberg	40
Constructors' Title	1.	McLaren	90
	2.	Ferrari	82
	3.	Williams	71

FIRST TITLE FOR PROST

Lauda stayed with McLaren for one more season, alongside Prost. At Williams, Rosberg had a new no. 2, Nigel Mansell moving from Lotus to replace Laffite.

Prost won the opener in Brazil from sixth on the grid. Alboreto and Rosberg had occupied the front row; both had spells in the lead but Alboreto finished in second place, while Rosberg went out early with a failed turbo. Mansell also retired in Brazil, but he was in the points at Estoril. He had to start in the pit lane because of a bump on the warm-up lap, but recovered and finished fifth. Ayrton Senna won; he had joined Lotus to replace Mansell. Senna took the first pole of his career and led all the way in terrible conditions, finishing more than a minute clear of Alboreto.

It ought to have been two in a row for Senna at Imola, where he took pole and led for most of the 60-lap race, but he ran out of fuel. Prost crossed the line first, only to be disqualified after his McLaren was found to be underweight. Elio de Angelis profited, gaining only his second win in six years of Formula One. Senna was quickest in Monaco, and led until his engine failed on lap 13. Prost then traded the lead with Alboreto for 20 laps, before establishing an advantage that he held to the line.

Rosberg sets 160mph record

Alboreto ended a barren spell for Ferrari at Montreal; Stefan Johansson followed him home, giving Ferrari their first one-two since Zandvoort two years earlier. Both drivers were on the podium in Detroit, though well adrift of winner Keke Rosberg. Both he and Mansell had experienced handling problems with the Williams-Honda, but things improved with the arrival of the new Honda engine. It looked good for Williams at Paul Ricard, too. Mansell was out after a 200mph spill in practice, but Rosberg took pole. He led early on, and set the fastest lap. He had to settle for six points; Piquet passed him on the 11th lap and kept the lead to the end. Rosberg was on pole again at Silverstone, becoming the first man to lap at more than 160mph in a Grand Prix. Both he

and Mansell, who hadn't really recovered from his crash, had to retire; they needed more reliability. Senna led for 57 of the 65 laps, when he ran out of fuel. Prost took over and won, a lap ahead of Alboreto and Laffite.

Alboreto qualified eighth at the Nürburgring, but led for the last 20 laps, winning from Prost after Rosberg and Senna retired. He now headed the championship on 46 points, 5 ahead of Prost, who brought the two drivers level by winning in Austria, with Alboreto third. Lauda led in the middle part of the race, then had his eighth retirement in ten races; he was about to retire for good. He had the 25th and final win of his illustrious career at Zandvoort.

Prost, second in the Netherlands, went one better at Monza; Alboreto's season dried up. The Williams-Honda was now more reliable and Mansell and Rosberg were second and fourth at Spa. Senna won his second Grand Prix there, giving him five podium finishes in the five races he'd completed. Prost was third, racking up the points.

First win in 72 outings for Mansell

The European Grand Prix was at Brands Hatch. It was Nigel Mansell's 72nd Grand Prix and he finally won; Rosberg gave Williams further cause for optimism by coming third. He recovered from a spat with the fiercely competitive Senna on lap 7, the two cars touching; Senna finished second. Prost picked up 3 points for fourth place. He now had 73 points from the required 11 finishes, becoming the first Frenchman to win the title.

Williams dominated the last two rounds. Mansell had another success after taking pole at Kyalami; Rosberg, second that day, won in Adelaide. The Williams-Honda was obviously a car with a future, and Senna could be a threat in the right machine. There would be no comfortable 20-point margin for Prost and McLaren the next season.

1986

Drivers' Championship	1.	Alain Prost	72
	2.	Nigel Mansell	70
	3.	Nelson Piquet	69
Constructors' Title	1.	Williams	141
	2.	McLaren	96
	3.	Lotus-Renault	58

END OF THE ALL-POWERFUL TURBOS

1986 was the last full year in which the unfettered turbo engines were allowed to dominate Formula One. Prost, Mansell and Senna remained with their teams from 1985. Piquet had been with Bernie Ecclestone's Brabham team since 1978, but teamed up with Mansell at Williams, the team with the car of the year.

Senna on pole eight times

Senna took pole in Brazil, and he, Piquet and Prost all enjoyed time in front. Piquet took over and held on to win; Prost retired, and an accident meant that Mansell's race was over before it started. Senna was on pole again in Spain and won by a whisker from Mansell, his third Grand Prix victory. At Imola he took his third successive pole, an honour he would hold in eight of the 16 races though he won only twice. His Lotus-Renault was up against the formidable Williams and McLaren cars, but he showed his worth.

He retired at Imola, and Prost scored his first win of the year. Piquet, the only other man to complete the distance, came in second. Prost also won at Monaco; his McLaren team-mate Rosberg followed him home. Rosberg soon discovered that he had left Williams just as they were coming up with a superb car.

Mansell dominates

Mansell won four of the next five races, in Belgium, Canada, France and Britain; Piquet got within six seconds of him at Brands Hatch. In the middle of this winning streak, Senna came out on top in Detroit, a race where the lead changed several times. The next two races saw a return to Hockenheim for the German Grand Prix and a new venue, Hungary's Hungaroring, providing Williams with their sixth and seventh wins of the season, but this time it was Piquet who crossed the line first. Senna was second both times. The inaugural race in Hungary was the first time Formula One had gone

beyond the Iron Curtain. Piquet and Senna traded the lead, surprisingly – overtaking opportunities were limited on the winding circuit, later voted Course of the Year.

Senna, Mansell and Piquet all retired in Austria. Prost didn't, and won. Some of the other drivers had a chance to get in the frame: the Ferraris of Alboreto and Johansson, together with the Lolas of Jones and Tambay, followed Prost home, though none got to within a lap of him. Teo Fabi took pole at Monza, as he had in Austria. His BMW-engined Benetton had awesome power in short bursts, but he regularly failed to finish. This was another one-two for Williams, Piquet taking the flag 10 seconds ahead of Mansell, who hit back at Estoril: his fifth win of the season.

BELOW: The inaugural Hungarian Grand Prix was staged at the Hungaroring, Budapest in 1986. It was won by Nelson Piquet (Williams FW11-Honda), seen here during the race.

OPPOSITE: 1986 German Grand Prix, Hockenheim. Alain Prost (McLaren MP4/2C TAG Porsche) ran out of fuel on the last lap and dropped from third to sixth position, as he pushed his car across the finish line.

Mansell's tyre agony

The penultimate round saw a return to Mexico. Gerhard Berger got his first Grand Prix success as the Benetton lasted the full distance. Benetton had taken over the Toleman team only this year; the change from being sponsors to running a team had thus brought an early reward.

Nigel Mansell was in the box seat going into the final race at Adelaide. Third place would be enough to give him the title, whatever happened, but a tyre on his Williams blew on lap 63 and his race ended. Piquet lost ground, making a precautionary pit stop, and Prost came through to take the race and the title, the first to win successive championships since Brabham in 1959–60. Piquet and Mansell had been scoring off each other all season, splitting points, making Williams victims of their own success; the car had won nine of the 16 races and took the Constructors' title by a mile. But Prost had won four races and been consistent; he added to his reputation for being the most complete driver of his time.

1986 also had its share of tragedy. Elio de Angelis was killed testing his Brabham at Paul Ricard; a crash at Brands Hatch ended Jacques Laffite's career. Off the track Frank Williams was involved in a car crash which confined him to a wheelchair.

1987

Drivers' Championship	1.	Nelson Piquet	73
	2.	Nigel Mansell	61
	3.	Ayrton Senna	57
Constructors' Title	1.	Williams	137
	2.	McLaren	76
	3.	Lotus	64

MANSELL EDGED OUT BY PIQUET

The 1987 season was almost a rerun of the year before. Prost, Senna, Piquet and Mansell were the main focus.

Prost, in an all-new car, got off to a good start, winning two of the first three races and surprising everybody; Piquet and Mansell were still using the tried and tested Williams-Honda. They were quickest in practice in Brazil, but Prost won from Piquet. It was a Williams front row in Belgium, too. Early on there was a huge shunt involving both Tyrrells, and Senna and Mansell's cars touched in the restart; both went off.

Piquet profited briefly, but he, too, failed to finish and Prost went on to win. This was his 27th win, equalling Jackie Stewart's record.

Japan's Nakajima and Honda join Lotus

Between these Prost victories Mansell won at Imola. Prost's alternator failed, while Piquet had been involved in a crash in practice. Senna took pole and led early on, but Mansell took over, winning easily. Senna won the next two, Monaco and Detroit. It was his third year at Lotus and he saw it as a make-or-break season. Lotus had switched to Honda power; Renault had withdrawn from Formula One and Lotus clinched the Honda deal by taking on Satoru Nakajima, Japan's first Formula One driver. Senna's wins in Monte Carlo and the United States were not without some good fortune. At Monaco he inherited the lead from Mansell, who retired on lap 29. Mansell had pit-lane trouble while leading in Detroit, and Senna took advantage. Mansell had scored just 2 points from three races, all of which he might have won.

Mansell's heroics at Stowe

In France Mansell was on pole again and eased home 8 seconds ahead of team-mate Piquet. It was another one-two for Williams at Silverstone. Mansell won, passing Piquet on the 63rd lap out of 65 at Stowe. He'd been almost half a minute down on Piquet, following an unscheduled wheel change. He took his sixth pole of the year at Hockenheim, but a seized engine ended his hopes. The McLaren team had ironed out a technical problem that blighted the cars in the two previous races and the race looked to be going Prost's way when his alternator failed five laps from home. Piquet, who had seemed resigned to his sixth second place of the year, came through for his first win instead.

Senna was third at Hockenheim, though a lap down. Around this time he decided that Lotus wasn't competitive enough, and began negotiations with McLaren. He and Piquet fought for top spot in Hungary; Piquet won, taking the lead from Mansell six laps from the line. Mansell had led for 70 laps, then lost a wheel nut. Senna was second, Prost third. However, Mansell won from Piquet in Austria; only the Williams duo went the full distance. By this point Senna, on 43 points, was still 4 ahead of Mansell – but couldn't see his Lotus reproducing the form of Monaco and Detroit in the final races. Prost had 31; Piquet led with 54 points and extended this by winning at Monza. Senna may have been unhappy with his Lotus but drove a superb race, finishing in second place.

Derek Warwick's 160mph smash

Prost won for a record-breaking 28th time at Estoril, but Piquet's third place was critical. Senna and Mansell failed to score. Mansell won in Spain and Mexico, putting himself back in contention. He led all the way at Jerez, while he came out on top in Mexico on aggregate; the race was split into two halves as the result of Derek Warwick going into the tyre wall at 160mph. Neither Prost nor Senna finished, and their title hopes were over. The championship was decided in practice for Suzuka: Mansell went off and was ruled out of the race.

Piquet's honour

The honour was now Piquet's, whatever happened in the last two rounds. He failed to score – both were won by Gerhard Berger for Ferrari, and Senna crossed the line second in each, but was disqualified at Adelaide over a brake irregularity. This cost him second place in the championship, but he still had 57 points to put him third behind the Williams pair.

OPPOSITE: **Alain Prost (McLaren MP4/3 TAG Porsche) leads Nelson Piquet and Nigel Mansell (both Williams FW11B Hondas) into Copse at the start of the 1987 British Grand Prix, Silverstone.**

RIGHT: **Ayrton Senna (McLaren-Honda) celebrates on the podium after winning the 1988 Japanese Grand Prix, Suzuka. The result also delivered him the championship.**

1988

Drivers' Championship	1.	Ayrton Senna	90
	2.	Alain Prost	87
	3.	Gerhard Berger	41
Constructors' Title	1.	McLaren	199
	2.	Ferrari	65
	3.	Benetton	46

PROST AND SENNA

By the end of 1987, it was known that Senna was joining Prost at McLaren. Senna took pole in Brazil but gestured that he had a gear selection problem and was forced to start from the pit lane; he cut his way through to lie second behind Prost. He was disqualified for switching cars after the light had gone green.

Senna slip lets Prost in at Monaco

At Imola Senna won from Prost, though there was a problem with his car which ground to a halt just over the line. At Monaco he made an expensive mistake, hitting the Armco before the tunnel. He had been well clear of Prost, who moved into the lead, with Ferrari's Berger and Alboreto following him home. The Ferraris continued well in Mexico,

Berger and Alboreto finishing third and fourth; McLaren were dominant again, however. The pair occupied the front row and Prost led the whole way. In Canada, Prost led from his team-mate until the 19th lap; Senna then took over for the remaining 50. Detroit saw Senna take his sixth successive pole, equalling a record set by Moss and Lauda. The race was another McLaren procession, although there was a gap of some 40 seconds between Senna and second-placed Prost.

ABOVE: **1988 Italian Grand Prix, Monza. Gerhard Berger won the race in his Ferrari F187/88C, the only driver, other than Senna or Prost, to win that year.**

OPPOSITE: **1989 Brazilian Grand Prix, Jacarepagua, Rio de Janeiro. Ayrton Senna (McLaren MP4/5 Honda) in the pits having a new front wing fitted after the original one was lost in a collision with Berger and Patrese at the start.**

Berger takes pole at Silverstone

Prost broke Senna's run by taking pole at Paul Ricard. He set the pace, then lost the lead to Senna when he came into the pits with tyre trouble, re-emerging 3 seconds behind his team-mate. He regained the lead at the three-quarter distance. At Silverstone Gerhard Berger took pole, with Alboreto's Ferrari beside him on the front row, and led for 13 laps. It was the halfway mark in the championship and the first time that anyone other than Prost or Senna had led at any stage in any race. Senna passed him on lap 13 and held the lead to the end. Mansell finally had some success in his Williams-Judd by finishing second. Prost retired with handling problems, declaring the rain-soaked track a safety risk. He led Senna by 54 points to 48, and was criticised in some quarters for his withdrawal. Conditions were similar at Hockenheim but he went the distance, finishing second behind Senna, who led all the way. His lead was cut to 3 points.

Two weeks later, at the Hungaroring, the result was just the same, although this was a much closer affair, Senna edging Prost out by half a second. Senna had yet another start-to-finish win at Spa. It was his fourth in a row, and seventh of the season. This put him ahead of Prost for the first time: 75 to 72. There were five rounds to go.

Ferrari break McLaren's hold

The 12th race of the year broke McLaren's stranglehold. All looked well as Senna took a record-breaking ninth pole and led for 49 of the 51 laps. He then hit Jean-Louis Schlesser's Williams, and his race was over. Prost had retired, and the way was left clear for a Ferrari one-two, Berger heading Alboreto home. McLaren came back at Estoril. Running level with each other, Prost and Senna vied to gain the upper hand on the first lap, coming close to touching. Prost pressed on to take the advantage, and the race; Senna trailed home sixth. Prost won again in Spain. He and Senna were next to each other on the front row; Prost got his nose in front and led all the way. Senna, getting a negative reading from his fuel gauge, eased his car home in fourth.

The best 11 finishes counted towards the title, which favoured Senna. After Suzuka, Prost had another 6 points, while Senna's win enabled him to swap 9 points for the single one gained in Portugal. The title was now his. He had been left at the start, and was 14th by the time his engine caught. Prost was then leading, with clear track in front of him. Senna's charge through the field was extraordinary and he took a decisive lead on lap 27. Prost won the final, academic race in Australia, followed home by the new world champion.

1989

Drivers' Championship	1.	Alain Prost	76
	2.	Ayrton Senna	60
	3.	Riccardo Patrese	40
Constructors' Title	1.	McLaren	141
	2.	Williams	77
	3.	Ferrari	59

ANOTHER FOR PROST

The unrest between Senna and Prost turned to open hostility in 1989, the start of the new non-turbo era. Both remained with McLaren, but it became clear that they could not continue in the same team for long.

As early as the first race, Brazil, Senna was involved in controversy – this time with Gerhard Berger. He, Senna and Patrese approached the first corner abreast, and there wasn't room for three cars. Senna would never give ground in such circumstances, and he and Berger touched. Mansell won; he was now driving for Ferrari. He was determined to win the title, and Ferrari offered him the best chance. His victory first time out meant jubilation in the Ferrari camp.

The race at Imola was restarted after Berger had a spill early on; he escaped with minor injuries. Senna slipped past Prost on the first corner and stayed in front all the way. Prost claimed a breach of the agreement that the leading McLaren at the first corner wouldn't be challenged by the other. Senna claimed his manoeuvre began before the corner. Senna also took pole and led all the way at Monaco. There was no argument here; he was on form and finished nearly a minute ahead of Prost. He got his third start-to-finish win in Mexico, and this provided another landmark: it gave him his 33rd pole, equalling Jim Clark's record. The next race, a first-time visit to Phoenix, saw Senna break the record. He was out of luck in the race, though, retiring after leading for ten laps. Prost took over, winning his first race of the year.

Boutsen wins in the Montreal rain

Stormy conditions followed by a drying track made tyre selection difficult in Montreal. Repeated pit stops meant that the lead changed hands several times. Senna made up the time he'd lost and was ahead with 3 laps to go when his engine failed. With Prost also out of the race, victory went to Boutsen. Patrese made it a one-two for Williams.

Senna retired in both France and Britain; Prost won both races, with Mansell second each time. At Hockenheim, Prost lost top gear with three laps to go and Senna powered past to win. Mansell had his fourth podium finish that day, but the best was to come in Hungary. He started 12th on the grid, carved his way through the field, overtook Senna on lap 58 and was nearly half a minute clear at the flag. At Spa less than 2 seconds covered Senna, Prost and Mansell as they crossed the line in that order.

Race ban for ignoring black flag

Before Monza, Prost revealed that he had had enough and was moving to Ferrari the following year. In the race Senna led for 44 laps when his engine blew up; Prost stepped in to increase his lead in the championship. At Estoril Mansell overshot the pits and reversed, breaching regulations: he rejoined the race, ignoring the black flag, and collided with Senna on the 48th lap. Mansell was fined $50,000 and given a one-race ban, but that was little consolation to Senna, who believed Mansell might have cost him the title.

Senna won comfortably in Spain, ahead of Berger and Prost. He now needed to win at Suzuka and Adelaide to retain his title. He took his 12th pole of the year in Japan, but Prost got the better start. Senna made his move at the chicane on lap 47, Prost closed him off, the cars touched and both spun off. Prost headed back to the pits, and Senna rejoined the race with the help of a push start. He won but disqualification was inevitable because he'd received assistance, and Alessandro Nannini scored his debut victory for Benetton.

Prost saw no reason to risk competing on a very wet Adelaide circuit. Senna's season fizzled out with a shunt involving Martin Brundle, whose Brabham he was trying to lap. Prost joined the club of drivers who had won three world titles.

1990

Drivers' Championship	1.	Ayrton Senna	78
	2.	Alain Prost	71
	3.	Nelson Piquet	43
		Gerhard Berger	43
Constructors' Title	1.	McLaren	121
	2.	Ferrari	110
	3.	Benetton	71

PROST AND SENNA – WAR CONTINUES

During the close season Senna was told to retract allegations he had made about FISA's handling of the Japanese incident. Senna grudgingly accepted that FISA hadn't acted unduly, McLaren paid his fine and he was welcomed back into the fold for 1990.

The first race was at Phoenix. Senna lost the lead to Jean Alesi's Tyrrell, but retook it, winning by 10 seconds. He didn't win in Brazil, colliding with Nakajima while lapping him, but

the fire was back. His car needed a new nosecone and he finished third, behind Prost's Ferrari and Senna's new McLaren team-mate, Gerhard Berger. Senna was on pole at Imola, but his race was over after three laps, when a stone damaged his brakes. Riccardo Patrese, in his third season with the Williams team and his 14th in Formula One, scored the third win of his long career.

Ferrari back on form

Senna won the next two races, at Monaco and Montreal. He led the whole way in the former, but owed his victory in Canada to a 60-second penalty given to Berger, who had jumped the start – a mistake relegating him to fourth. Piquet, now with Benetton, finished second, with Mansell's Ferrari third. Senna led for 60 of the 69 laps in Mexico, then had a puncture. Prost won, Mansell was second: a good day for Ferrari.

The lead changed hands no fewer than six times at Paul Ricard. One leader was Senna, but a 16-second pit stop for tyres spoiled his chances. Ivan Capelli held the lead for 44 laps, but was passed by Prost three laps from home. He had to be content with second. Prost scored his fourth win for the rejuvenated Ferrari team at Silverstone. Boutsen was a distant second; Senna, who had had a spin, came third. Mansell retired with gearbox trouble, tossed his gloves into the crowd and announced his retirement; he believed Prost was getting preferential treatment.

Senna won at Hockenheim, then became embroiled in another controversy at the Hungaroring. Boutsen led for the entire race. Behind him was a four-way fight involving Senna, Mansell, Berger and Nannini. Senna attempted to pass Nannini's Benetton at a corner on lap 64; their cars touched. Nannini's car was pitched into the air, while Senna carried on and finished second. Senna had appeared to infringe the rule stating that a driver had to draw alongside a rival to claim a corner.

ABOVE: **1990 Japanese Grand Prix, Suzuka. The wrecked car of Ayrton Senna (McLaren MP4/5B Honda), after the collision with Alain Prost (Ferrari 641) at the start of the race.**

OPPOSITE: **1989 Monaco Grand Prix, Monte Carlo. Andrea de Cesaris (Dallara 189-Ford) pictured at Loews Hairpin.**

Arch-rivals fight it out

Senna won from Prost in the next two outings, at Spa and Monza. With Senna now on 72 points to Prost's 56, and just four races to go, the sport's top two would be fighting for the spoils for the third year running. Senna increased his lead to 18 points at Estoril, where he came second and Prost was third. Mansell cut across Prost at the start, which dropped Prost several places down the field. Prost all but conceded the title before the Spanish Grand Prix, then won. A damaged radiator meant that Senna failed to finish. He still led by 9 points, but if Prost could score well in the last two races he had a fifth and fourth place to discard. Senna, by contrast, had fared no worse than third in the 11 finishes he had racked up. Prost could still take the title but Senna could prevent that with a win in the penultimate round, Suzuka. He took pole, but Prost got a better start. However, both ended up in the run-off area after Senna drove into Prost by the first corner.

Tactical crash

The collision gave Senna the title. Even if Prost won at Adelaide and Senna failed to score, it wouldn't be enough. As it happened, Prost came third in Australia, behind Piquet and Mansell. Senna went off the track while holding a comfortable lead. Prost suspected foul play at Suzuka, and Ferrari waded in, complaining about 'tactical crashes'. FISA set up an inquiry, but only one man could know for sure. Later, Senna admitted that it had been deliberate.

1991

Drivers' Championship	1.	Ayrton Senna	96
	2.	Nigel Mansell	72
	3.	Riccardo Patrese	53
Constructors' Title	1.	McLaren-Honda	139
	2.	Williams-Renault	125
	3.	Ferrari	55.5

FOUR IN A ROW FOR McLAREN

Prost took a back seat in 1991; by the end he'd failed to register a single win. Minor placings put him on 34 points: respectable, but only good enough to give him fifth place. Even before the season was out, it was announced that he and Ferrari were parting company.

Four straight wins for Senna

However, Senna and McLaren didn't have everything their own way, though it looked like it at the beginning. Senna had four straight victories. Patrese was close at Interlagos, as was Berger at Imola. There were more generous margins over Prost and Mansell, at Phoenix and Monaco respectively. Senna's haul for these efforts was 40 points – a new points structure meant 10 for a win. All 16 races now counted towards the championship, too.

Williams' success

Piquet ended Senna's run in Montreal. Mansell led all the way but suffered engine failure with victory in sight; Piquet nipped through and Mansell trailed in a disconsolate sixth. Senna had retired with alternator trouble. In Mexico he had his first defeat in a race where he went the full distance. The two Williams cars came home first and second, with Senna third. Mansell finished behind his team-mate Patrese in Mexico, but at the French Grand Prix, at Magny-Cours for the first time, he won – starting a great mid-season run. He and Prost traded the lead several times, but Mansell was in front when it mattered. A start-to-finish triumph at Silverstone was a far cry from his frustrating experience of 1990; Senna was unlucky on this occasion, running out of fuel just before the finish. He dropped from second to fourth, his McLaren team-mate Berger and Prost slipping by him to finish second and third. Mansell made it three in a row at Hockenheim, and Patrese gave Williams a second one-two. Again Senna ran out of fuel on the penultimate lap, finishing out of the points in seventh. His lead was cut to just 8 points.

Jordan picking up points

It was becoming a McLaren–Williams battle. Senna got back to form in Hungary, leading all the way with Mansell 5 seconds behind him. Patrese was third, ahead of Berger. The fastest lap was set by Bertrand Gachot, driving the new Team 7-Up Jordan. It was the latest in a fine first season for the team: Gachot and team-mate de Cesaris had both finished in the points in Canada and Germany, and one of the Jordans had finished in the top six in three other rounds.

In the next race, Spa, de Cesaris's engine overheated when he was running second. His fine effort was overshadowed by the man driving the other Jordan that day – not Gachot, but a new and temporary team-mate: Mercedes sports car driver Michael Schumacher. Schumacher amazed everyone by qualifying seventh on an unfamiliar circuit. A clutch problem meant that he didn't complete one lap of the race, but he'd done more than enough to make people take notice. Senna and Berger enjoyed a McLaren one-two in the race; Mansell failed to finish. The top of the table was opening up again.

Enter Michael Schumacher

The next race was Monza. Benetton had swooped to sign Schumacher, who outscored his new team-mate Piquet, finishing fifth, one place ahead of the three-times champion. Mansell scored his fourth win, but Senna took second, so Mansell only pegged back 4 points. Senna was second again at Estoril, behind Patrese; Mansell was disqualified after a pit lane error.

Senna clinches second title for McLaren

Mansell had his fifth win in Spain, while Senna managed just 2 points back in fifth place. However, he had a lead of 16 points, and there were only two races left. He clinched the title at Suzuka, sacrificing first place on the final lap and allowing Berger to come through for his sixth career win. Senna and Mansell finished first and second in the academic final round in Adelaide. It was McLaren's year, but the team's four-year winning streak was about to end.

1992

Drivers' Championship	1.	Nigel Mansell	108
	2.	Riccardo Patrese	56
	3.	Michael Schumacher	53
Constructors' Title	1.	Williams-Renault	164
	2.	McLaren-Honda	99
	3.	Benetton-Ford	31

MANSELL BREAKS RECORDS

Senna had blown the opposition away in the early rounds of 1991; Mansell was even more dominant as 1992 began. The Williams he was driving was basically the same as the preceding year's model, but with active suspension. The team had flirted with this several years earlier but got it right in 1992.

Mansell wins the first five Grands Prix

Mansell won the first five races, starting on pole each time. In four of them – South Africa, Mexico, Spain and San Marino – he was never headed. This was a record in itself, and there was even more good news for Williams as Patrese followed Mansell home in four of the races, giving an awesome display of early-season domination. Michael Schumacher, the new sensation, prevented a clean sweep of the first five rounds: he finished second to Mansell in Spain. Patrese fell by the wayside after an early spin.

Fifth Monaco success for Senna

Senna had just two third places at this point; even the introduction of the new MP4/7 didn't make much difference. He did end Mansell's run at Monaco, but had to put in a superhuman effort. He also needed Mansell to have an off day, and that manifested itself in a delay with a tyre problem. Mansell finished the race just 0.2 seconds behind Senna despite losing time, and Senna was shattered at the end of the race. His first win of the season enabled him to equal Graham Hill's record of five Monaco wins.

OPPOSITE: **Michael Schumacher (Jordan 191-Ford) made his Formula One debut in the 1991 Belgian Grand Prix at the Spa-Francorchamps circuit. It ended on the first lap with clutch failure.**

LEFT: **Nigel Mansell (Williams FW14-Renault) takes the chequered flag, for his fourth win of the season, at the 1991 Italian Grand Prix, Monza.**

Both Williams cars missed out in Canada. Mansell spun out of the race, later blaming Senna. Gearbox trouble did for Patrese. Gerhard Berger won, a welcome boost for McLaren and the new car. It was yet another Williams one-two in France, a race that was restarted due to rain. Patrese was the early leader but Mansell passed him just after the restart. That took Mansell to Silverstone and a fervent, 200,000-strong home crowd. He didn't disappoint them, and victory that day brought another record: his 28th win, taking him past Jackie Stewart's British record of 27.

Mansell champion by August

There were rumblings of discontent behind the scenes at Williams, however: Frank Williams was sounding out Mansell on the prospect of Prost joining the team for 1993. Mansell had felt undermined by Prost's presence at Ferrari in 1990, and wanted to block the move, but it was already settled. On the track, meanwhile, the Williams bandwagon continued. Mansell beat Senna into second place at Hockenheim. Even though there were six rounds still to go, a win or second place in the next race would give him an unassailable lead.

The place was Hungary; the date, 16 August. There were no team orders, and Patrese was out of the blocks quickest; he spun off at the halfway mark and, though he rejoined the race, he was out of contention. That left Mansell tracking Senna; he only needed to hold his place to take the greater prize. A puncture forced him into the pits, putting him back

to sixth, but Schumacher spun out, and Mansell passed Häkkinen, Brundle and Berger to reclaim second. He held the position to the end, and was champion at last.

Controversy to the bitter end

Mansell scored one more win, at Estoril, giving him a record-breaking nine victories for the season. Another season highlight was Michael Schumacher's debut win, in Belgium: he had finished in 12 races, scoring points in all but one and stepping onto the podium eight times.

There were dramatic events off the track. Mansell reluctantly agreed to team up with Prost for 1993, but Senna then let it be known that he would drive for Williams on almost any terms. Williams made Mansell an unfavourable offer, which he promptly refused, deciding that if Williams didn't want him – and if he couldn't defend his title in a competitive car – then he would retire. Williams relented, putting the original deal back on the table, but the damage was done. Mansell turned his back on Formula One.

BELOW: **Ayrton Senna (McLaren MP4/7A Honda), pictured at Ste. Devote, during the Monaco Grand Prix, Monte Carlo. His win broke the run of five consecutive victories for Nigel Mansell at the start of the 1992 season.**

OPPOSITE: **1992 Hungarian Grand Prix, Hungaroring, Budapest. Nigel Mansell (Williams FW14B-Renault) took second place and also clinched the Drivers' World Championship.**

1993

Drivers' Championship	1.	Alain Prost	99
	2.	Ayrton Senna	73
	3.	Damon Hill	69
Constructors' Title	1.	Williams-Renault	168
	2.	McLaren-Ford	84
	3.	Benetton-Ford	72

PROST IS BACK

Alain Prost returned after a year's sabbatical, stepping into Mansell's shoes as the Williams no. 1. Patrese wasn't retained, and moved to Benetton, lining up with rising star Michael Schumacher. Senna remained with McLaren. Prost's team-mate came from within the Williams camp: Damon Hill was promoted from test driver.

The first race was in South Africa. Prost won, with only second-placed Senna on the same lap when he crossed the line. Senna faced an additional handicap in taking on the mighty Williams cars: Honda had withdrawn, and the latest MP4 was powered by an unspectacular Ford V-8 unit. However, he followed up his second place at Kyalami with a win in Brazil. Prost and Hill had occupied the front row at Interlagos; Prost spun off, Senna picked off new leader Hill, then held the advantage to the end.

Senna flying in the rain

Senna was impressive at the European Grand Prix at Donington Park. The Williams pair were quickest in practice, but were beaten in wet conditions. Senna, who had been so desperate to get inside a Williams that he had allegedly offered to drive for nothing, now had two wins and a second place in the McLaren-Ford. He was apprehensive, though: he had a race-by-race deal. He was running second at Imola when his hydraulics went. Hill led, but spun off; Prost took over, holding the lead for the last 50 laps to win from Schumacher, with Martin Brundle's Ligier third. Spain was almost a repeat: Prost took pole, but Hill was quickest away and led for the first ten laps. This time Hill's race ended with engine failure, and Prost again took over to win from Schumacher.

At Monaco, Senna took maximum points; race leader Schumacher was forced out with hydraulics problems. Senna led the title race but Prost then had four straight wins, in Canada, France, Britain and Germany. The only driver who headed him in any of these races was his team-mate Hill. He was away first in all of them, but Prost hit the front, and stayed there, each time. Prost had seven wins from ten starts but, like Mansell, found that critics tended to put his stunning victories down to the car, while defeats were down to the driver.

Hill's run of bad luck

During Prost's run, Hill was delayed in the pits at Magny-Cours, his engine blew up at Silverstone, and he suffered a puncture while leading at Hockenheim with just two laps to

Häkkinen, whose gamble to leave Lotus and become a McLaren test driver had paid off; he'd replaced Andretti as McLaren's no. 2. There was also some off-track drama; Senna and Jordan driver Eddie Irvine came to blows because Senna felt that the lapped Irvine had blocked him.

Prost had a record of 51 wins from his 199 Grands Prix. His four championships put him second only to Fangio in the all-time rankings.

1994

Drivers' Championship	1. Michael Schumacher	92
	2. Damon Hill	91
	3. Gerhard Berger	41
Constructors' Title	1. Williams-Renault	118
	2. Benetton-Ford	103
	3. Ferrari	71

ABOVE: **1993 Hungarian Grand Prix, Hungaroring, Budapest. Damon Hill (Williams FW15C-Renault) holds his fist aloft as he takes the chequered flag for his maiden Grand Prix win.**

OPPOSITE: **Ayrton Senna (Williams FW16-Renault) leads at the start of the 1994 San Marino Grand Prix, Imola, Italy. Senna was killed after the fifth lap when he left the track and crashed into a wall.**

go. He now reeled off three wins. He was on the front row of the grid behind Prost in Hungary, Belgium and Italy. At the Hungaroring he led all the way, Prost being relegated to the back of the grid after stalling on the parade lap. Schumacher pushed him hard all the way to the line at Spa, while at Monza he inherited the lead from Prost after his engine gave out five laps from home. The Williams pair were beaten into the minor placings by Schumacher at Estoril, his best race in a season which would see him on the podium nine times. This would have received greater attention had he not been up against the dominant Williams.

51 wins recorded by Prost

Prost's second place behind Schumacher in Portugal secured his fourth world title. He then announced that he was retiring from the sport, a decision influenced, at least partly, by the fact that Senna was to join Williams in 1994. Senna won both of the remaining races, in Japan and Australia, beating Prost into second each time. In third place at Suzuka was Mika

SENNA KILLED

Now it was Senna's turn at the wheel of the Williams. There were a few niggling problems with the FW16 – the latest Williams – in the early part of the year; it performed well in practice, but struggled in the opening two races.

Williams slow off the mark

Senna took pole in Brazil, with Schumacher beside him. He led in the early stages, but Schumacher's Benetton took over after the first pit stop and Senna spun out on lap 55. Schumacher won, with Damon Hill in the other Williams second, though a lap down. The second race was in Japan, the first of two visits. This round, called the Pacific Grand Prix, was held on the narrow TI circuit. Senna was again on pole, but a nudge from Häkkinen's McLaren ended his interest in the race on the first lap. Schumacher led all the way. Only Berger's Ferrari finished on the same lap, over a minute behind.

Horror at Imola

Next came Imola, where Senna had won three times. The weekend of 29 April–1 May was one of the worst for the sport. Rubens Barrichello had a lucky escape after a major spill during the Friday practice session; prompt action from Formula One's renowned doctor Sid Watkins prevented him from swallowing his tongue. The following day Roland

Ratzenberger lost his life when his Simtek crashed into a wall. The next day Senna was on pole again. He got away first, with Schumacher close behind. After five laps Senna's Williams went into a concrete wall at Tamburello Corner. It was a huge impact, but Senna might have survived had not part of the suspension become dislodged and struck his head.

Schumacher won the shortened, restarted race, and made it four out of four with a victory at Monaco two weeks later. With pole position, fastest lap, a start-to-finish win and Senna lost to the sport, Schumacher was suddenly looking unstoppable. Damon Hill, now Williams' no. 1, won in Spain, profiting from Schumacher's gearbox problems. Schumacher still finished second, less than half a minute behind. At Montreal Schumacher won again; Hill was a distant second.

David Coulthard promoted at Williams

David Coulthard was promoted internally, becoming no. 2 at Williams. He was in the points second time out, in Montreal, where he came fifth. For the next race the team brought back Nigel Mansell but transmission problems ended his race at Magny-Cours after 45 laps, when he was running third. Schumacher won and Hill followed him home.

Silverstone marked the halfway point. Hill won, and Schumacher, who crossed the line second, was dramatically disqualified; he had broken ranks on the parade lap, then ignored the black flag. He forfeited his 6 points, and received a two-race suspension. Neither scored at Hockenheim: Schumacher retired with engine trouble, while Hill finished out of the points. A first-lap accident took ten cars out of the race, which was won by Berger, giving Ferrari their first win for four years. Schumacher won from Hill in Hungary, the fourth time they had finished in that order. Third was Schumacher's Benetton team-mate Jos Verstappen, who had had a miraculous escape in Germany when he'd been engulfed in a fireball during refuelling.

At Spa Schumacher crossed the line ahead of Hill, but he was disqualified again, for illegal skidblock wear. Hill inherited first place, and turned up the heat by winning in Italy and Portugal, the two races for which Schumacher was suspended. It was very nearly a Williams one-two in both of these rounds. Coulthard was second at Estoril, as he was when he ran out of fuel close to home at Monza.

Schumacher by one point from Hill

Hill's 30-point haul, with Schumacher failing to register, put him only one point behind. They each took a first and second in the next two races, so Schumacher carried his advantage into the final race at Adelaide. He led until lap 35, when he hit a wall and rebounded into Hill's path; Mansell won. It was an unsatisfactory ending to the championship, but Schumacher had become the first German to hold the title.

1995

Drivers' Championship	1. Michael Schumacher	102
	2. Damon Hill	69
	3. David Coulthard	49
Constructors' Title	1. Benetton-Renault	137
	2. Williams-Renault	112
	3. Ferrari	73

SCHUMACHER AGAIN

Michael Schumacher set the pace with a win at Interlagos. Damon Hill was unlucky; he took pole in Brazil and was leading when his suspension failed. He then scored back-to-back wins in Argentina and San Marino, with Alesi bringing his Ferrari home second in both. Schumacher was third in Buenos Aires, and crashed out in the early stages at Imola. The San Marino Grand Prix was also notable for Nigel Mansell's first outing in the McLaren Mercedes. An

undersized cockpit caused him to miss the first two rounds; now he discovered that though the cockpit was improved the car was still unimpressive. He finished tenth at Imola, retired in the next race in Spain, and told McLaren that he had had enough.

Early exit for big two at Silverstone

Schumacher was back on form in the Spanish Grand Prix, and Johnny Herbert made it a one-two for Benetton. The team had switched from Ford engines to the same Renault unit that powered the Williams cars; with evenly matched hardware Schumacher looked unbeatable. Damon Hill was on pole at Monaco, but lost out to Schumacher: Williams opted to run a two-stop race to Benetton's one. They occupied the front row again at Montreal, but with Hill out of the race, Schumacher seemed set for yet another win. An unscheduled pit stop allowed Alesi, Barrichello, Irvine and Panis to come through, giving Alesi his first victory in his eighth year. Magny-Cours was a repeat of Monaco; Hill got the better of Schumacher in practice, with the roles reversed when it mattered. Benetton bested Williams when it came to pit-stop strategy, and that played a crucial part. The big two departed the Silverstone scene after clashing at Priory Corner on the 46th lap. The race still centred on Benetton and Williams, though; their no. 2 drivers vied for victory. Johnny Herbert came out on top for Benetton, after Coulthard, who had taken the lead, was penalised for speeding in the pit lane. Hill took his third successive pole at Hockenheim, but crashed out again, this time on the first lap. Schumacher crossed the line 6 seconds ahead of Coulthard, extending his championship lead over Hill to 23 points.

Schumacher's stunning victory

Williams enjoyed their only one-two success of the season in Hungary. Hill and Coulthard were first and second on the grid, and finished the race in that order, Hill leading the whole way while Schumacher succumbed to a fuel pump problem. Incredibly, Schumacher qualified only 16th at Spa, but drove one of the races of his life to win from Hill. Coulthard was unlucky, suffering gearbox trouble while leading on lap 13; at Monza he was again blighted while leading, also on the 13th lap, but by a wheel bearing. Hill and Schumacher collided on lap 23. Johnny Herbert came through to win his second race of the year, ahead of Häkkinen and Frentzen. After two unlucky races, it came right for Coulthard at Estoril where he dominated: he took pole, set the fastest lap, and led for 66 of the 71 laps. Schumacher held off Hill for second place.

Tenth pole for Williams

The European Grand Prix was at the Nürburgring. Coulthard was on pole once more, but Schumacher again produced the goods. He passed Alesi, who had dominated the race, 3 laps from home, crossing the line less than three seconds ahead. Damon Hill crashed out in Germany for the fourth time in seven races, meaning that he trailed Schumacher by 29 points with just three races to go. Schumacher won at the TI circuit. Again the Williams duo occupied the front row; again Schumacher came out on top. He eased past Coulthard on the 50th lap and finished the race 15 seconds clear. The title was in the bag.

Schumacher out on his own

Schumacher scored his ninth win at Suzuka; Hill won by two laps in the final race at Adelaide. A string of retirements took out many big names, and only eight cars were running when Hill crossed the line. Despite this, Hill finished the season 33 points behind Schumacher.

1996

Drivers' Championship	1. Damon Hill	97
	2. Jacques Villeneuve	78
	3. Michael Schumacher	59
Constructors' Title	1. Williams-Renault	175
	2. Ferrari	70
	3. Benetton-Renault	68

HILL'S CHANCE

When Schumacher joined Ferrari for 1996, it hadn't won the championship since 1979. Williams still looked like the team to beat. Hill won the first three races, at Melbourne, Interlagos and Buenos Aires. His main rival was his new Williams team-mate Jacques Villeneuve, replacing David Coulthard, who had moved to McLaren. Not even Schumacher could work miracles at Ferrari; after those three rounds he had registered just one third place, in Brazil, and two retirements.

Brundle's spectacular crash

Melbourne staged the Australian Grand Prix for the first time, and Villeneuve took pole in his very first outing. He clipped a kerb on lap 33, damaging an oil-line, then eased off to ensure a finish and took a creditable 6 points on his debut, coming second behind Hill. The race was memorable for a spectacular spill: Martin Brundle's Jordan barrel-rolled through the air, landing on Johnny Herbert's Sauber before coming to rest in the sand. Brundle dusted himself off, obtained the necessary medical clearance and climbed into his spare car for the restart. Villeneuve spun off in Brazil, and was second to Hill again in Argentina. His maiden victory came in only his fourth race, the European Grand Prix, held at the new Nürburgring. From second on the grid, behind Hill, he led all the way, crossing the line less than a second ahead of Schumacher. With Coulthard and Hill half a minute back, followed by Barrichello, Brundle, Herbert, Häkkinen and Berger, Villeneuve had outgunned all the big names very early on.

Only four finish in Monaco

Schumacher hadn't taken long to squeeze the best out of the Ferrari 310 and took pole at Imola; Hill edged him into second place in the race. Gerhard Berger brought his Benetton home in third. A spate of accidents swept the field at Monaco and only four cars were running at the end of the race, which was won by Olivier Panis. He was in his third Formula One season, all with Ligier.

Ferrari on the march

The seventh race of the year saw Michael Schumacher put Ferrari back on top of the podium. Hill retired, but Schumacher relegated Alesi and Villeneuve to the minor placings. Schumacher's car didn't allow him to build on this success, failing him in each of the next three races, all won by Williams. Villeneuve followed Hill home at Montreal and Magny-Cours. Villeneuve lost out to Hill in Canada, and returned the favour by winning at Silverstone. With six races to go, Hill's championship lead was down to 15 points. The margin went back up to 21 after Hockenheim, where Hill won and Villeneuve finished third. It was a lucky win for Hill; he inherited the lead two laps from home when Berger's car suffered a blown engine. His Benetton team-mate Jean Alesi split the Williams duo, coming second.

Williams pair battle it out

The championship was now a two-horse race. Villeneuve clawed 4 points back by crossing the line a whisker ahead of Hill at the Hungaroring. At least one issue was now settled: Williams had a record-equalling eighth Constructors' Championship.

The next two races, Spa and Monza, were Schumacher's, the latter giving Ferrari its first home success since 1988. Villeneuve was second to Schumacher at Spa, while Hill could finish only fifth. Neither scored in Italy, so with two races to go Hill led Villeneuve by 13 points. Estoril was the scene of the penultimate round. The pressure was on, though Hill was still hot favourite. The heat was turned up when it was announced that Heinz-Harald Frentzen would replace Hill the following year.

The Williams pair slugged it out in fine style in Portugal. Villeneuve gained a vital edge after the third of their pit stops and pressed home to win by 20 seconds. A 9-point lead for Hill going into Suzuka meant that just one point would be enough. Villeneuve took pole, but Hill got away first. He led for the entire race, although the championship was settled even before he took the flag: Villeneuve lost a wheel and crashed out on the 37th lap.

1997

Drivers' Championship	1. Jacques Villeneuve	81
	2. Heinz-Harald Frentzen	42
	3. Jean Alesi	36
	David Coulthard	36
Constructors' Title	1. Williams-Renault	123
	2. Ferrari	102
	3. Benetton-Renault	67

VILLENEUVE'S CROWN

Marlboro and McLaren parted company after 23 years; the sponsor now supported Ferrari. The new car, the 310B, was unveiled in January; Schumacher and Irvine remained. Hill was now with Arrows. Villeneuve had lost to Hill in 1996; his new Williams team-mate, Heinz-Harald Frentzen, was under pressure, having displaced the reigning champion.

At Melbourne Irvine took out Villeneuve and Herbert as he tried to overtake. Frentzen and Coulthard traded the lead, but Frentzen suffered a brake disc failure three laps from home, leaving Coulthard and McLaren to take the honours. Villeneuve then won in Brazil and Argentina. At Interlagos he crossed the line less than five seconds ahead of Gerhard Berger's Benetton. His Buenos Aires win was tighter: he staved off a Ferrari challenge by less than a second.

Stewart team make the podium

Frentzen had his first win at Imola, emerging from the final pit stop just ahead of Schumacher. They finished in that order; Irvine was third. A wet Monaco saw the race curtailed but Schumacher dominated, winning by nearly a minute from Barrichello in second, whose performance meant a podium finish for the Stewart team. Villeneuve, failing to finish at Imola and Monte Carlo, hit back in Spain. He led for 62 of the 64 laps and took the flag ahead of Prost's Olivier Panis, who drove superbly. Next, the Montreal race was stopped after an accident involving Panis, who broke both legs. Schumacher was declared the winner; Coulthard had been leading but a pit-stop delay had relegated him to seventh when the race was halted.

Berger's final victory

Schumacher came out on top at Magny-Cours, his Ferrari sporting the new 046/2 engine. Villeneuve won at Silverstone, although a pit stop nearly proved expensive: Schumacher had built up a lead, but a wheel-bearing failure ended his chances. Gerhard Berger had missed the last three races but returned at Hockenheim, putting his Benetton on pole and

winning the race from Schumacher and Häkkinen. He retired at the end of the season.

In Hungary, Schumacher looked like increasing his 10-point lead. He took pole and led for the opening laps, but had to pit as the team had chosen the wrong tyres. Hill took up the running; victory was in sight when clutch problems slowed him right down. Villeneuve passed him on the last lap, denying Arrows their maiden success.

Before the race at Spa it poured; the safety car was deployed until lap 4. Schumacher had opted for intermediates – most of his rivals had wets – and stormed to victory. There was great pressure on him to win at Monza, but he qualified only ninth on the grid, his worst position of the year. He crossed the line sixth; Villeneuve finished only one place ahead. Coulthard scored his and McLaren's second win; Alesi and Frentzen occupied the minor placings.

10-second penalty setback for Schumacher

In Austria Schumacher was lying third when Irvine and Alesi were involved in an accident that brought out the yellow flag. He didn't see it, overtook Frentzen and incurred a mandatory 10-second penalty, putting him back to ninth. He got back to sixth, and a point, by the end of the race. Villeneuve won,

1998

Drivers' Championship	1. Mika Häkkinen	100
	2. Michael Schumacher	86
	3. David Coulthard	56
Constructors' Title	1. McLaren-Mercedes	156
	2. Ferrari	133
	3. Williams-Mecachrome	38

HÄKKINEN WINS BATTLE

1998 saw the introduction of new tyre regulations to improve safety, the departure of Renault and a battle royal between Schumacher and Häkkinen for the title.

New engine deal for Williams

Jacques Villeneuve's immediate concern was trying to keep Williams on top now that Renault had departed the scene; a deal with BMW had been done, but wouldn't come into effect until 2000. The McLaren-Mercedes looked like the car to beat and dominated the opening race in Melbourne, Coulthard leading from Häkkinen with no one else in sight. Coulthard stuck to the pre-race agreement and allowed his team-mate through to win. Another one-two for McLaren followed in Brazil, Häkkinen again crossing the line first. It was already looking ominous for the other teams but Schumacher, third that day, could not be written off. He won the very next race, Argentina; Irvine finished third, making it a good day for Ferrari. Häkkinen's second place meant that he had 26 points from three races as the circus headed for Europe.

Häkkinen was out of the race at Imola; Coulthard held off Schumacher to take what would be his only win of the year. Häkkinen was back in form at Barcelona, where he notched his fourth win; Coulthard and Schumacher took the minor placings. Monaco was even better for Häkkinen. Not only did he win, but his closest rivals failed to score. Schumacher clashed with one of Benetton's new young drivers, Alexander Wurz, and was classified tenth, then scored his second win of the year in a restarted race at Montreal, with the advantage of having no McLaren to push him. Häkkinen's car failed on the grid; Coulthard suffered his second successive retirement after holding the lead. Fisichella took 6 points.

Schumacher took maximum points at Magny-Cours and Silverstone. The French Grand Prix also had to be restarted; Schumacher and Irvine managed to get the Ferraris ahead,

cutting Schumacher's championship lead to a single point. Next came the Luxembourg Grand Prix. Schumacher's race ended early; he was thumped by his brother Ralf. Häkkinen and Coulthard were first and second, then both hit trouble, clearing the way for Villeneuve. At Suzuka, he was disqualified for a yellow flag infringement during practice; Schumacher won and led by one point going into the decider, the European Grand Prix at Jerez. They occupied the front row, with Villeneuve on pole. By lap 48 Schumacher held the advantage. Villeneuve dived through on the inside; Schumacher tried to shut him out, clipping the side pod of the Williams and putting himself out. Villeneuve nursed his car over the remaining 21 laps; both McLarens passed him, but third was enough for him to take the title by 3 points.

Schumacher stripped of all points

The FIA held an inquiry into the race's decisive moment; Schumacher was stripped of all the points he had gained over the season.

then staved off the challengers. The safety car at a waterlogged Silverstone held up Häkkinen, eating into his sizeable lead, and a spin allowed Schumacher to come through for victory. Häkkinen and Coulthard hit back with successive one-two finishes in Austria and Germany. Schumacher was in the points in both – finishing third and fifth – but he lost ground. Third place at Hockenheim went to the reigning champion. Villeneuve gave it his best shot in the FW20, and often put the car further up the field than it had any right to be. Williams' success this year came from scrambling for points; the occasional podium win was a bonus.

Häkkinen and Schumacher tied on points

Schumacher was on top form in Hungary, where the team ran a three-stop race that worked to perfection. Häkkinen gained just 1 point: Häkkinen 77 points, Schumacher 70. That position was unaltered after a dramatic race in the wet at Spa, where neither driver finished. Damon Hill seized the opportunity and brought his Jordan through, giving the team a first victory. After Monza, Schumacher and Häkkinen were tied on 80 points. Schumacher won after Coulthard, who had been leading, retired; Häkkinen dropped back to fourth with

brake problems. Häkkinen's win over Schumacher in the Luxembourg Grand Prix was probably his best performance of the year. It gave him a 4-point advantage going into the final round at Suzuka.

Häkkinen worthy winner

Schumacher stalled on the grid in Japan and, in accordance with regulations, had to start from the back of the field. A brilliant drive took him up to third, when some track debris punctured a tyre. Häkkinen went on to score his eighth win of the year, giving him a round 100 points for the season. Schumacher had excelled himself, but Häkkinen was a worthy champion. Of the 16 races he had completed 13, scoring in every one. He had nine poles, six fastest laps – and 11 podium finishes, including eight victories.

BELOW: **Jarno Trulli (Prost AP01-Peugeot) runs away from his crashed car during the 1998 Canadian Grand Prix, Montreal, Quebec.**

OPPOSITE: **Pedro Diniz (Arrows A18-Yamaha) leads Olivier Panis (Prost JS45 Mugen Honda), in the 1997 Luxembourg Grand Prix, Nürburgring, Germany.**

1999

Drivers' Championship	1. Mika Häkkinen	76
	2. Eddie Irvine	74
	3. Heinz-Harald Frentzen	55
Constructors' Title	1. Ferrari	128
	2. McLaren-Mercedes	124
	3. Jordan-Mugen-Honda	61

TWO IN A ROW FOR HÄKKINEN

The 1999 opener was in Australia. The McLarens dominated practice, but both Häkkinen and Coulthard were out of the race by the halfway mark. Irvine held the lead to the end: his first Grand Prix victory. Frentzen pushed him hard all the way, finishing just 1 second behind in his first outing for Jordan.

Barrichello off to a flyer

Rubens Barrichello was first away at Interlagos but Michael Schumacher took up the running after he pitted; Häkkinen passed him and led to the line. He had a comfortable lead in the early stages at Imola, but crashed out; Coulthard, who had been in the front row alongside his team-mate in all three races, took over in front. After a pit stop he emerged in traffic and lost vital time; Schumacher finished 5 seconds ahead. Schumacher split the two McLarens at the front row of the grid in Monaco, and dominated the race. A mistake by Häkkinen let Irvine come through for a Ferrari one-two. Häkkinen had to settle for third, while Coulthard failed to finish.

The McLarens took first and second in Barcelona where they were followed home by the two Ferraris; the season was shaping up into a battle between the giants. Montreal saw Schumacher break Häkkinen's run of five successive poles, but his race ended after he made a mistake on lap 29 and crashed into a wall, one in a spate of accidents. Häkkinen scored his third win and edged ahead of Schumacher by 4 points in the championship.

Schumacher breaks leg at Silverstone

Difficult qualifying conditions made for an odd grid at Magny-Cours: Barrichello took pole; Häkkinen and Irvine were back in 14th and 17th. Häkkinen stormed through to lead with 7 laps to go, but a pit stop pushed him down to second, where he finished. Frentzen scored his and Jordan's second Grand Prix victory: remarkably, as he was nursing a fractured leg from Montreal. Silverstone was both the halfway point and the turning point. Schumacher's first-lap crash resulted in a broken leg and an enforced lay-off that lasted for six races. The race changed hands several times and Coulthard came out on top.

Irvine is Ferrari's new no. 1

Irvine rose to the challenge of becoming Ferrari's no. 1 by winning in Austria. Coulthard was the early leader, nudging his team-mate into a spin on the opening lap. Irvine took over when he pitted, and built up enough of a lead to hold first place when he in turn made his stop. He crossed the line less than 0.1 seconds before Coulthard.

Irvine won narrowly again at Hockenheim, this time over his stand-in Ferrari team-mate Mika Salo. Häkkinen was on pole but lost his lead because of a lengthy refuelling stop; a tyre then blew, putting him out. Salo could have won, but team orders prevailed and he waved Irvine through. Irvine now led the championship by 8 points, but McLaren responded with a one-two in Hungary. The result looked as if it would mirror the grid positions: Häkkinen, Irvine, then

Coulthard. A mistake by Irvine in the latter stages allowed Coulthard to swap places.

Häkkinen spun out while leading at Monza; Coulthard and Irvine could finish only fifth and sixth respectively. Frentzen's second win put him on 50 points, 10 behind joint leaders Häkkinen and Irvine. In the European Grand Prix at the Nürburgring, Frentzen went out of the race halfway with an electrical problem. Coulthard spun out a few laps later and Johnny Herbert came through, giving the Stewart team its first success. Häkkinen crossed the line in fifth, with Irvine seventh, meaning that Häkkinen had a 2-point advantage.

Schumacher returned for the Malaysian Grand Prix. He took pole, but had to provide support for Irvine. He did so,

ABOVE: **1999 French Grand Prix, Magny-Cours. Heinz-Harald Frentzen (Jordan-Mugen-Honda) celebrates his first position on the podium. The result was remarkable in the fact that he had a fractured leg.**

OPPOSITE: **1999 European Grand Prix, Nürburgring. Johnny Herbert (Stewart-Ford) first position, celebrates the Stewart Grand Prix team's first victory, on the podium with Stewart Grand Prix chairman Jackie Stewart.**

lying second and acting as a buffer between Irvine ahead and Häkkinen behind. Irvine had a 4-point lead going into the final race at Suzuka. Häkkinen was on peerless form and won the race comfortably, with Schumacher in second. Irvine was a distant third, finishing 2 points behind Häkkinen in the final table.

2000

Drivers' Championship	1. Michael Schumacher	108
	2. Mika Häkkinen	89
	3. David Coulthard	73
Constructors' Title	1. Ferrari	170
	2. McLaren-Mercedes	152
	3. Williams	36

FERRARI, AFTER 21 YEARS

McLaren and Ferrari once again engaged in a long struggle for supremacy in 2000. There was one driver change at the top: Barrichello moved from Stewart-Ford to Ferrari, replacing Eddie Irvine.

Ferrari was the first to succeed, despite the McLarens having the edge in qualifying. At Interlagos the McLarens ran with one heavy load, but Ferrari opted for an extra stop – and extra speed. Both Schumacher and Barrichello started from the second row and passed their McLaren rivals. Barrichello's engine blew, but Schumacher built up a sizeable lead. Jenson Button crossed the line in seventh in the Williams-BMW, gaining his first championship point.

Häkkinen and Coulthard finally got into their stride at Imola, but Schumacher relegated them to the minor placings. Then Coulthard had an excellent win at Silverstone, despite gearbox problems, and a flawless performance by Häkkinen at Barcelona saw him take the flag 16 seconds ahead of Coulthard.

ABOVE: Rubens Barrichello (Ferrari F1-2000) took first position for his maiden Formula One victory in 2000 German Grand Prix, Hockenheim.

OPPOSITE: Mika Häkkinen (West McLaren-Mercedes MP4/16), winner of the 2001 British Grand Prix, Silverstone, on a pit-stop.

Schumacher won convincingly at the Nürburgring with only Häkkinen finishing on the same lap; Coulthard was the best of the rest. At Monaco he looked like having a fifth win of the year, but a cracked exhaust caused the rear suspension to overheat and fail. Coulthard won, with Barrichello and Fisichella following him. Eddie Irvine was fourth, bringing Jaguar their first points. At the next race, Coulthard, Schumacher's only serious challenger, received a 10-second stop-go penalty for an infringement at the start of the parade lap. Schumacher got his fifth win.

Barrichello's joy as long wait ends

Then Coulthard won again at Magny-Cours, despite Schumacher's blatant attempts to block him – a tactic prompting Coulthard to gesticulate at his rival. He eventually managed to get by, and Häkkinen made it a McLaren one-two after Schumacher's car failed to finish. In the Austrian Grand Prix, BAR-Honda driver Ricardo Zonta pitched Schumacher out at the first corner, turning the race into a walk-over for McLaren: Häkkinen won, with Coulthard second. Barrichello finally won at Hockenheim: his maiden success, after seven years and 123 races. No other Grand Prix winner had waited so long.

Schumacher was back in the points in Hungary where he started on pole, ahead of Coulthard and Häkkinen. He had to settle for splitting them and taking 6 points; Häkkinen scored his third win of the season, and followed it up with a victory at Spa. Schumacher was now 6 points adrift of the top spot.

However, he did brilliantly in the last four rounds. At Monza, his victory over Häkkinen put him to within 2 points, and he cruised to victory at Indianapolis, swinging the balance back towards Ferrari. It was his 42nd win, taking him ahead of Senna, whose record he had equalled at Monza. After the Japanese Grand Prix his 8-point lead became an unassailable 12. The big two again slugged it out in front; Ferrari judged pit-stop strategy brilliantly, Schumacher did the rest – and delivered the prize the team had sought for 21 years. Schumacher's ninth victory followed in the final race at Kuala Lumpur, a win which also sealed the Constructors' Title for Ferrari. The season's statistics show the extent of McLaren and Ferrari's domination: 442 points were available in the 17-race series; they scored 332 between them.

2001

Drivers' Championship	1. Michael Schumacher	123
	2. David Coulthard	65
	3. Rubens Barrichello	56
Constructors' Title	1. Ferrari	179
	2. McLaren-Mercedes	102
	3. Williams	80

SCHUMACHER OVERHAULS 'PROFESSOR'

Michael Schumacher's 19-point margin of victory in 2000 became a 58-point chasm as he retained the crown, repeating his mid-90s achievement with Benetton. Schumacher dominated the series, edging ever closer to becoming the most successful driver in F1 history by any yardstick the sport had to offer. Victory at Spa – his eighth of the year and 52nd in total – took him past Alain Prost's all-time mark. By the end of the season he had also passed 800 points, once again relegating the 'Professor' into second place in the record books.

Schumacher shrugged off a spill during practice at Melbourne to cruise to victory from pole, the first of 11 races in which he would head the grid. Coulthard, who qualified sixth, did well to split the Ferraris in a race that was marred by the latest F1 fatality: a marshal was killed by a flying wheel from Villeneuve's BAR-Honda after the Canadian's high-speed shunt into the back of Ralf Schumacher's Williams on lap 4.

Pit-stop debacle

Not even a pitstop debacle could prevent a Ferrari one-two at Sepang. In monsoon conditions, the safety car was out by early on. The Ferraris were parked up together, Schumacher having to wait over a minute before being attended to. They emerged 10th and 11th, though the decision to run with intermediates rather than wets proved a canny choice. The Rainmaster clinched his sixth successive victory, with Barrichello picking up 6 points.

Coulthard won at Interlagos, but Juan Pablo Montoya stole the show. The former CART star, in his debut season with Williams, performed a stunning overtaking manoeuvre on the champion to take the lead but was bumped out of the race by the lapped Arrows of Jos Verstappen.

Ralf completes record family double

There was no such misfortune for Williams at Imola. Ralf Schumacher scored his maiden victory, the first in four years for the Didcot outfit. Michelin celebrated their return to F1; it was the first time since 1984 that a Michelin-shod car had won a race. Michael Schumacher suffered the first of his two retirements of the year but joined in the celebrations as he and Ralf became the first brothers to stand atop a Formula One podium.

Barcelona saw the return of traction control, ending an eight-year ban. It was back to business as usual for Michael Schumacher, though he had the gremlins in Häkkinen's engine to thank, the McLaren expiring on the final lap. Montoya followed the champion home for his first podium finish.

Barrichello profited from a gladiatorial joust between Schumacher and Montoya in Austria, but was ordered to give way to the champion, who finished second to Coulthard. In fourth place was 21-year-old Kimi Räikkönen, who had signed for Sauber-Petronas with just 23 races behind him. The Finn fared better than another young tyro making his first steps in the sport. At 19 years and seven months, Minardi recruit Fernando Alonso had been the third youngest driver in history when he qualified for Melbourne.

First podium for Jaguar

It was another scarlet one-two at Monaco, with Eddie Irvine giving Jaguar its first podium. Ralf got the better of Michael in Canada, and might have done so again as they battled for the lead at the European GP. Ralf infringed regulations emerging from the pit lane, the stop-go penalty ending his chances. The champion dominated in France, while McLaren had a miserable day. Häkkinen stalled on the grid, while Coulthard's penalty for speeding in the pit lane meant that fourth place was a disappointment.

Häkkinen ended his run of cruel luck with a superb win at Silverstone, leading the Ferraris home. At Hockenheim Schumacher survived a spectacular lap-1 crash involving Prost's Luciano Burti, but retired at mid-distance. Brother Ralf claimed his second win. Ferrari sealed both the Drivers' and Constructors' championships with another one-two in Hungary. It was the 11th win in each category for Maranello.

The champion added two more wins to his haul, at Spa and Suzuka, but at Monza he was clearly affected by the recent terrorist outrage in America. The Italian GP saw Montoya become only the seventh man to win in his rookie season. At Indianapolis a fortnight later Häkkinen notched his

20th career victory, having already announced he would be taking a sabbatical from F1 in 2002. But this was Schumacher's year. Of the 15 races he completed, the German was first or second in all but one. His sights were now set on Fangio's five titles, and Senna's record 65 times on pole.

2002

Drivers' Championship	1. Michael Schumacher	144
	2. Rubens Barrichello	77
	3. Juan-Pablo Montoya	50
Constructors' Title	1. Ferrari	221
	2. Williams	92
	3. McLaren-Mercedes	65

SCHUMACHER EQUALS FANGIO'S RECORD

Ferrari was even more dominant in 2002, Schumacher and Barrichello's aggregate 221 points eclipsing the previous year's emphatic mark by 33. The rest of the field combined just managed to accumulate the same points total. A scarlet car crossed the line first in 15 of the 17 races, though the way in which Maranello manufactured the finishing order brought forth cries of 'foul' from many quarters. Austria was the most blatant example, Barrichello handing victory to his team-mate at the final corner. There was no infringement of the rules, but it seemed to contravene the spirit of racing, and at the end of the year the FIA acted to bring an end to team orders.

Schumacher avoided a pile-up at the start to win the Melbourne curtain-raiser. Barrichello was among the casualties, Montoya and Räikkönen filling the minor placings. Montoya would not add to his tally of victories this campaign, but seven poles, following the three in his debut season, showed that Williams had on their books a driver of immense potential. Räikkönen, meanwhile, had wasted no time in getting on the podium with McLaren, having taken Häkkinen's berth. The Finn also claimed the fastest lap. Home fans were able to cheer a fine debut for Mark Webber, who took fifth for Minardi on his debut. Unfortunately, that was to be the high watermark of the year for Paul Stoddart's outfit.

Penalty leaves Montoya fuming

Williams enjoyed a one-two at Sepang, though the order should have been reversed. Second-placed Montoya was left fuming at the drive-through penalty imposed for his early clash with the reigning champion. Michael Schumacher recovered from 21st place to get on the podium, easing past Jenson Button's ailing Renault on the last lap.

The new Ferrari was unveiled in Brazil, which saw the first of four successive wins for Schumacher. There was another first-lap spat with Montoya, but at least the Colombian recovered to finish fifth; home favourite Barrichello had yet another Interlagos nightmare, his car failing after Schumacher allowed him to take the lead. Imola was a processional Ferrari clean sweep which left even aficionados bemoaning the lack of excitement – not that Jean Todt or the tifosi would have agreed with the doom-mongers.

Montoya took 6 points in Spain, though more than half a minute behind Schumacher and only after Barrichello suffered yet another retirement. When things did finally go well for the Brazilian, as they did in Austria, he had to contend with his bosses, who told him to let the champion through. Schumacher's first victory on the A1-Ring meant he completed the set for the championship circuits, but it left an unpleasant taste in the mouth and the crowd showed their displeasure. Schumacher turned PR man by allowing Barrichello to join him on top of the podium, but the damage was done.

David Coulthard wins in Monaco

Montoya and Coulthard occupied the front row at Monaco, but the superior launch and traction control of the McLaren saw those positions reversed by the first corner. The Colombian's engine eventually gave out, and Coulthard held off Schumacher's challenge for the last 27 laps of the street classic. Coulthard managed to split the Ferraris in Montreal, but forthwith the season turned into a Maranello juggernaut. Canada had been Ferrari's 150th Grand Prix victory; after the remaining nine rounds that figure stood at 159.

A rare Schumacher error at the European GP left him tracking Barrichello, with the spectre of another Austria looming. In the event Todt chose not ruffle any more feathers – or antagonize the FIA three days before a hearing

OPPOSITE: **Juan Pablo Montoya (BMW-Williams FW23) leads at the start of the 2001 Italian Grand Prix, Monza, as Jenson Button (Benetton-Renault B201) and Jarno Trulli (Jordan-Honda EJ11) collide. Montoya went on to win, the Colombian's maiden Grand prix victory in his first F1 season.**

LEFT: **2002 Monaco Grand Prix, Monte Carlo. A view of the Grand Hairpin with David Coulthard (McLaren MP4/17-Mercedes) on course to victory.**

concerning events at the A1-Ring – and the Brazilian took maximum points. Räikkönen again showed his promise with another podium for McLaren.

Records tumble

Schumacher clocked up his 60th career win at Silverstone, but Ferrari's dominance was best exemplified by Barrichello, who started from the back of the field after stalling on the formation lap, had a spin during the race, yet still carved his way through the field to finish second. It was Montoya's turn to pick up the podium scraps. Victory at Magny-Cours gave Schumacher a record-equalling fifth crown, and with three wins garnered from the last six rounds, he made it a record 11 victories for the season, beating the nine maximums that he had held jointly with Nigel Mansell. Third place in Sepang had been Schumacher's 'worst' return, making him the first man to record a podium finish in every race.

BELOW: **2002 British Grand Prix, Silverstone, England. Michael Schumacher (Ferrari F2002) takes the chequered flag for the 60th Grand Prix win of his career.**

OPPOSITE: **2003 British Grand Prix, Silverstone, England. Race winner Rubens Barrichello, (Ferrari F2003 GA), lifts his trophy aloft, applauded by second-placed Juan-Pablo Montoya (BMW-Williams FW25).**

2003

Drivers' Championship	1. Michael Schumacher	93
	2. Kimi Räikkönen	91
	3. Juan-Pablo Montoya	82
Constructors' Title	1. Ferrari	158
	2. Williams	144
	3. McLaren-Mercedes	142

FERRARI AGAIN – BUT IT GOES TO THE WIRE

The prospect of the F1 roadshow becoming increasingly predictable and sterile – and thus less attractive televisually – galvanised the sport's bosses into action in the winter of 2002. They came up with a back-to-basics package aimed at levelling the playing field and making their product a more exciting spectacle. Unsurprisingly, this was received more favourably by the teams with lesser budgets than by the Big Three. Out went team orders and telemetry; in came a revised qualifying

procedure, consisting of two single-lap sessions; points were now awarded to the top eight; and cars had to go into the race with the fuel load left after qualifying – no topping up the tank. The changes certainly livened things up: eight drivers topped the podium, and although Ferrari eventually came up trumps again, it was only after an absorbing battle that went to the wire.

First podium for Alonso

In Melbourne it looked like business as usual as the Ferraris scorched away. But Barrichello crashed out, and Michael Schumacher lost time after running over a kerb and damaging the F2002's bargeboards. That meant a Ferrari-free podium, David Coulthard's consistency winning the day in an error-strewn race. New Renault recruit Fernando Alonso was immediately in the points, finishing seventh, and in Malaysia the Spaniard claimed his first pole, the youngest driver to take that honour. He converted that into a first podium, despite suffering gearbox trouble. Schumacher made another mistake, penalised for running into the back of Alonso's team-mate Jarno Trulli on lap one. Kimi Räikkönen won, finishing some 40 seconds ahead of Barrichello.

The drama was cranked up even further at rain-soaked Interlagos, where the race was red-flagged after Mark Webber totalled his Jaguar, then Alonso struck the debris. Räikkönen was awarded victory, but Jordan successfully appealed on the grounds of a timing error and Giancarlo Fisichella got the decision, receiving his trophy from the Iceman a week later.

Michael Schumacher now stood 16 points behind Räikkönen in the championship, Ferrari 23 behind McLaren in the Constructors' race. That picture changed to a more familiar one as the champion won four of the next five rounds. In San Marino, Spain and Austria, Schumacher converted poles into victories. There were muted celebrations following the win at Imola as it came within hours of the death of Schumacher's mother, a tribute to his professionalism, dedication and concentration. Spain saw the unveiling of the 2003 Ferrari, Schumacher's victory made all the sweeter as Räikkönen left Barcelona empty-handed. The German brushed aside a pit-lane fire to notch another win at the A1-Ring. Kimi took second, but his championship lead was now down to just 2 points.

Spa dropped from championship

When the stops unwound at Monaco, Montoya held off Räikkönen and Schumacher to claim his second F1 victory, less than 2 seconds covering all three cars. Montreal – the season's halfway mark following the dropping of Spa over a tobacco advertising row – saw Schumacher top the table for the first time. He nursed his ailing tyres and brakes to victory, superbly fending off the Williams duo in the process.

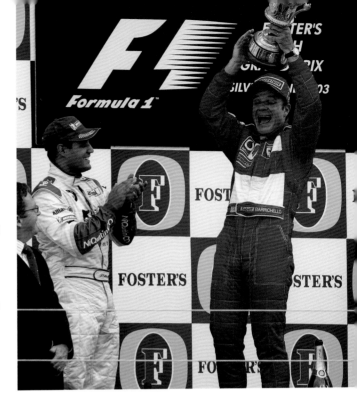

Ralf Schumacher led a Williams one-two at the European GP, though it surely would have been Räikkönen's race had his engine not expired. It was the same story in France, though there was no luck this time; the FW25 and new Michelins were proving a formidable package. Barrichello took the full set at Silverstone – pole, fastest lap and 10 points – in a race remembered for a kilted spectator dicing with death on the track. Montoya did likewise at Hockenheim. He was away and clear of a first-lap shunt involving Räikkönen, Barrichello and team-mate Ralf, which helped his cause, but even so, finishing the race over a minute ahead of Coulthard was impressive.

Alonso breaks McLaren's record

Fernando Alonso, aged 22 years 26 days, took over from Bruce McLaren as the youngest ever GP winner with a start-to-finish victory in Hungary. Renault's first win for 20 years came in their second season back in F1. Schumacher now led Montoya by a single point, Räikkönen just a point further back. Back-to-back wins for the champion, at Monza and Indianapolis, made the situation a lot rosier for Ferrari: Schumacher 92, Räikkönen 83, Montoya 82. Schumacher won in Italy at an average speed of 153.814 mph, setting yet another F1 record.

In order to pip Schumacher for the title, Kimi needed to win at Suzuka with the champion failing to score. In the event the Finn only managed second, and a point for eighth place was enough for Schumacher to clinch his sixth crown, beating Fangio's 46-year-old record.

ABOVE: **2004 Bahrain Grand Prix, Bahrain International Circuit, Manama. The field head into turn one at the start of the inaugural race, as leader Michael Schumacher (Ferrari F2004) locks a brake.**

OPPOSITE: **Fernando Alonso (Renault R25) during the 2005 Malaysian Grand Prix, Sepang. This was his first win of the season, on the way to becoming the youngest ever F1 champion.**

2004

Drivers' Championship	1. Michael Schumacher	148
	2. Rubens Barrichello	114
	3. Jenson Button	85
Constructors' Title	1. Ferrari	262
	2. BAR-Honda	119
	3. Renault	105

SCARLET JUGGERNAUT ROLLS ON

Going into the 2004 season, all the signs suggested that if McLaren and Williams could manage one more heave, Ferrari could finally be toppled from their perch. What transpired was the very opposite, the prancing horse looking as frisky and uncatchable as ever in a devastatingly consistent display. Round 13, Hungary, saw Michael Schumacher notch his 12th win. With five races to go only the champion's Ferrari team-mate could catch him, a mathematical possibility that soon evaporated.

Schumacher and Barrichello rocketed into the distance in Australia. Alonso, in third, never had a prayer of catching them. The signs were already ominous as the McLarens were running 2 seconds a lap down on the scarlet cars.

The Ferraris invariably ran well in Australia, and the cool temperatures suited the Bridgestones. Perhaps, some thought, Sepang would be a different matter. It wasn't. Schumacher took pole and came home 5 seconds clear of Montoya, setting the fastest lap in the process. Jenson Button, in his second season with BAR-Honda, grinned from ear to ear as he climbed onto the podium for the first time; he would repeat the achievement on nine further occasions, the surprise winner of the 'best of the rest' category as the season unfolded.

F1 goes to Bahrain

At the inaugural Bahrain GP, the chasing pack found that even the climate was favouring the Maranello cars. Stifling heat during qualifying turned into a relative cold snap on race day, once again suiting the Bridgestones more than the Michelin-shod teams. A Ferrari one-two duly followed. Räikkönen's latest engine failure meant that the man who narrowly lost out to Schumacher six months earlier now trailed 30-0. Coulthard had given McLaren their 4 points to date; Ferrari already had 51 on the board.

Button took his first pole in San Marino and got away well, but when he peeled off into the pits Schumacher streaked away and the result was never in doubt. Button had the consolation of a career-best second place, crossing the finish line comfortably clear of Montoya. Schumacher battled to victory in Spain despite a damaged exhaust, which could easily have halted his perfect start to the season. It seemed that everything was conspiring to Ferrari's advantage as the champion chalked up win number 75.

First retirement in 19 races

Monaco brought temporary solace to those who found Ferrari's metronomic performances uninspiring. Schumacher and Montoya tangled, and the former was out of the running for the first time in 19 races. Schumacher had been leading, having stayed out when the safety car was deployed. Ross

Brawn hoped having a clear track ahead would have enabled Schumacher to put daylight between him and the field. The clash with the Colombian's Williams made that academic. At the business end of the race Jarno Trulli had Button breathing down his neck hoping for a mistake but the Italian held firm to score his maiden victory.

McLaren's nightmare continued with another brace of engine failures at the European GP. Even worse for the race, second-placed Räikkönen stayed out long enough to hold up those who might at least have made a fight of it. Schumacher established a 17-second advantage in eight laps, and by the time the Finn pitted no one was going to reel him in.

Schumacher won for the seventh time in Montreal, setting another record for victories in an individual race. He qualified only sixth, having run with a heavy fuel load, but the two-stop strategy worked perfectly. It was a frustrating day for Williams, for whom Ralf Schumacher and Montoya finished second and fifth but had their points expunged for a technical infringement. A home victory for Renault at Magny-Cours was craftily prevented by Ferrari's clever four-stop strategy. Schumacher was stuck in second behind Alonso anyway, so Brawn calculated that it was worth a try in order to give the champion a clear track. It worked perfectly. Alonso at least had the consolation of splitting the Maranello pair and taking 8 points.

Replacement engine costs Button

McLaren finally had something to cheer about as Räikkönen finished second to Schumacher at Silverstone. Button took the supporting role at Hockenheim, though it could have been 10 points had he not fallen foul of the new rule which dropped a driver ten places down the grid if the car needed a replacement engine. Hungary provided Ferrari with their seventh one-two of the year, and although McLaren at last made the MP4-19 a winner, at Spa, Schumacher's second place sealed his seventh title. A 13th win followed at Suzuka, meaning that Schumacher dropped just 32 points in another crushing campaign.

2005

Drivers' Championship	1.	Fernando Alonso	133
	2.	Kimi Räikkönen	112
	3.	Michael Schumacher	62
Constructors' Title	1.	Renault	191
	2.	McLaren-Mercedes	182
	3.	Ferrari	100

ALONSO BECOMES YOUNGEST CHAMPION

Following Michael Schumacher's leisurely stroll to a fifth successive crown in 2004, F1 was sorely in need of a title race that extended beyond the summer holidays in order to stave off the widespread murmurings that the championship was becoming a predictable procession. If that was the wish, it was granted in thrilling style. The record 19-race series produced a battle royal between Fernando Alonso and Kimi Räikkönen, the Spaniard clinching the title with two rounds to

spare to become the youngest champion in the event's 56-year history.

Double for Renault

Renault and McLaren dominated, between them winning every race apart from the farcical US GP, where the Michelin-shod teams withdrew on safety grounds, leaving the way clear for Schumacher to clock up victory number 84. The Constructors' title went right to the wire. When Alonso took his seventh chequered flag of the year in Shanghai, it put the icing on a marvellous year for Renault, while the Iceman and McLaren were no doubt left to ponder what might have been if the car had been less temperamental.

Renault were out of the blocks first, the much-vaunted new R25 chassis giving the team a maximum return from the first four races. Giancarlo Fisichella dominated from pole in the Melbourne curtain-raiser, but a hat-trick of wins for Alonso followed, sending an early signal to Schumacher, Räikkönen et al that this might be the breakthrough year for Spain's rising star.

Ferrari's indifferent start to the season prompted the team to hasten the introduction of the new car, at Bahrain. Schumacher's race ended in hydraulics failure, the first time in four years that a mechanical problem had caused the seven-times champion to retire.

Iceman dogged by bad luck

If Räikkönen thought his ill-luck was behind him when he scored successive wins, in Barcelona and Monaco, he was to be sadly mistaken. At the European GP, staged at the Nürburgring, the McLaren's suspension failed within sight of victory. The fact that Alonso snatched his fourth win of the year made it even harder to take. The Finn did win an error-strewn Montreal GP, but with three blown engines in the next six rounds, his luck was definitely out. Those engine changes dropped him 10 places down the grid at Magny-Cours, Silverstone and Monza, Räikkönen performing miracles to finish in the top four in each race.

Alonso's win in France gave Renault their first home victory since Alain Prost's victory at Paul Ricard in 1983. Jenson Button's fourth place was his and BAR's first points of the year. It was a welcome boost for the team which had seen Button's third place at Imola chalked off for a technical infringement, then been hit with a two-race ban.

About-turn by Button

It would be a disappointing year for BAR, after finishing second to Ferrari in 2004. Yet before the season was out, Button nailed his long-term colours firmly to the team's mast. His dramatic about-turn came at a heavy cost: Button was

reported to have stumped up over £10 million to buy himself out of the contract which tied him to Williams in 2006.

Juan Pablo Montoya scored his maiden victory for McLaren at Silverstone, heading Alonso and Räikkönen. Another 10 points for Alonso at Hockenheim – after Räikkönen ground to a halt while leading – gave the Spaniard a 36-point cushion going to the Hungaroring. That was cut to 26 when the Iceman scored a maximum while Alonso failed to score for only the third time in 13 races.

Istanbul, a new venue for the F1 circus, proved a happy hunting ground for Kimi, but Alonso capitalised on a Montoya mistake to snatch second and limit the damage. Another Räikkönen–Alonso one-two at Spa meant that the Finn had only shaved 2 points off the Spaniard's lead with races running out. Alonso's third place at Interlagos made the title secure, taking the edge off a McLaren clean sweep. The Spaniard had realised his dream in the back yard of Emerson Fittipaldi, whose record as the youngest F1 champion he had broken.

Alonso dominated from pole as the curtain on the season came down at Shanghai. He had thus mounted the podium 15 times in 18 starts – discounting the US fiasco – and stood atop it on seven occasions. He was undoubtedly a worthy champion, though if Räikkönen kept away from ladders in the close season, 2006 had all the makings of another titanic battle.

2006

Drivers' Championship		
1. Fernando Alonso		134
2. Michael Schumacher		121
3. Felipe Massa		80
Constructors' Title	1. Renault	206
	2. Ferrari	201
	3. McLaren-Mercedes	110

SCHUMACHER CALLS TIME

The defining event of the 2006 season was certainly the announcement after the Italian Grand Prix that Michael Schumacher was to retire from F1.

A slow start to the season made Shumacher's chances of a final victory unlikely, but the Ferrari team returned to form as the season progressed and Schumacher celebrated three

consecutive wins in America, France and Germany in July. Renault's fortunes began to change at the same time as Ferrari's, albeit in the opposite direction. Fernando Alonso had started well, winning the first race in Bahrain and securing a run of victories, beginning on his home ground at the Spanish Grand Prix in May and ending in Montreal three races later. However, several FIA rulings went against Renault and Alonso faced a dry spell, finishing fifth in Indianapolis and Hochenheim and retiring altogether from the Hungaroring.

A two-horse race

Schumacher began to close the gap in the Drivers' Championship, which Alonso continued to dominate in spite of his bad run. The young Spaniard was beset by further difficulties, most notably he was penalised for obstructing Massa in qualifying for the Italian Grand Prix. The penalty, which saw him demoted from fifth to tenth position on the starting grid, was the subject of some controversy, but serious protest was averted when he was forced to retire with engine trouble. Schumacher won the race and was by then trailing Alonso by just two points. His victory had also allowed Ferrari to nudge ahead of Renault in the Constructors' Championship for the first time that season.

The next meeting in Shanghai three weeks later saw Alonso gain pole position with Schumacher starting back in sixth. However, Schumacher turned the race around and

ABOVE: **2006 Chinese Grand Prix, Shanghai. Fernando Alonso, (Renault R26), 2nd, Michael Schumacher, (Ferrari 248F1) winner, and Giancarlo Fisichella, (Renault R26), 3rd.**

pushed Alonso into second place. Schumacher's victory meant the two titans were level on points, with Schumacher clinching first place owing to a greater number of wins. With just two races to go, Schumacher's last season was proving to be one of the most nail biting. At the Suzuka Circuit in Japan the following week, Schumacher's engine trouble forced him to retire and handed Alonso victory.

Alonso seals victory

Going into the final race in Brazil with 10 points clear, Alonso would have taken some beating; Schumacher needed to win and for his rival to score no points whatsoever. In the event, neither of them won, Felipe Massa was victorious, the first native to take the Brazilian Grand Prix since Ayrton Senna in 1993. Schumacher could not even hope for second place after suffering a puncture and losing considerable ground. However, confirming his place as the world's greatest driver, he pulled back from nineteenth to finish a respectable fourth. It was not good enough to pry the Drivers' Championship from Alonso, who finished in second place. No other driver came close to challenging Alonso or Schumacher for the Drivers' Champion-ship. Of the three other drivers to win a race during the season, only Jenson Button was not in a Ferrari or Renault. Button's victory in Hungary for the Honda Racing Team was his first ever. The other two winners were Massa in Turkey and Brazil and Fisichella in Malaysia.

Constructors' Championship

If the Drivers' Championship had been all but won by Alonso before any competitors arrived in São Paulo, the race for the Constructors' Championship was still to play for. Ferrari was just 11 points adrift of Renault going into the race and Massa's surprise victory handed Ferrari 10 points. Despite Schumacher's best efforts to storm his way around the Autodromo Carlos Pace, Renault was unbeatable once Alonso had secured second place and Fisichella's 3 points merely sealed the victory.

An exit for Villeneuve

The 2006 season also marked the exit of former Champion Jacques Villeneuve. The Canadian suffered from injuries after a crash in Hochenheim and BMW Sauber replaced him with the young Polish driver Robert Kubica in the next race at Hungaroring.

Underperforming Juan Pablo Montoya also departed F1 in July 2006 and headed for NASCAR. After a lacklustre season, Montoya decided to leave McLaren, who had already snapped up Alonso for the 2007 season and had not yet settled upon a second driver. Two months later, Kimi Räikkönen also left McLaren to fill the void left by Schumacher at Ferrari. It was later announced that Lewis Hamilton, a rising British driver, would become Alonso's team-mate at McLaren.

A season of change

The season heralded lots of changes in the sport. 2006 was to be the last season that Michelin would supply tyres for F1. The FIA had wanted to have just one tyre supplier in the interests of fairness and safety. However, Michelin believed the move went against the interests of competition and innovation in the tyre industry and withdrew from the sport, leaving Bridgestone as the sole supplier.

Several established teams disappeared in 2006 following a series of buy-outs. Peter Sauber sold up to the German car giant BMW, Jordan became Spyker and BAR changed to Honda, after the Japanese colossus assumed total control of the team. Minardi was bought by Red Bull to develop rookie drivers. As well as changes to exiting teams, a new team also made its debut in 2006, albeit with strong support from Honda. Super Aguri was introduced at the last minute by Aguri Suzuki, the former F1 driver and served to give the Japanese driver, Takuma Sato, a new lease of life after being left out of the Honda team in favour of Button and Barrichello.

2007

Drivers' Championship	1. Kimi Räikkönen	110
	2. Lewis Hamilton	109
	Fernando Alonso	109
Constructors' Title	1. Ferrari	204
	2. BMW Sauber	101
	3. Renault	51

'ICEMAN' WINS THREE-WAY SHOOT-OUT

Formula One adjusted to life after Schumacher by hailing the arrival on the scene of a 22-year-old from Stevenage who made an even bigger impact than the German ace managed in his rookie year. Lewis Hamilton may have been off the radar for many fans, but insiders were well aware that here was a rising star who regarded F1 as his dream and his destiny, and had been working tirelessly towards fulfilling both for over a decade.

Hamilton's debut season didn't include a trip to Imola, as San Marino was dropped from the schedule after a quarter of a century on the F1 roster. There was no German Grand Prix, either, though that country maintained its representation in the circus via the European GP. Spa, meanwhile, had had a facelift and was restored to the circuit line-up, making 2007 a 17-round extravaganza.

Record rookie performance

Hamilton quickly showed he was in no mood to play the part of understudy to double world champion Fernando Alonso, recruited from Renault to spearhead McLaren's bid for honours. He followed up a third-place finish at the Melbourne curtain-raiser with eight consecutive podium finishes, a record performance by a rookie in the 58-year history of the championship. One person who remained aloof as the Hamilton bandwagon rolled on was Alonso. The frosty relationship between the two McLaren drivers never thawed.

The season turned into a virtual duopoly and a four-horse race for the title, such was the dominance of McLaren and Ferrari. If one didn't take the chequered flag, the other did. Ferrari, who had lost the services of technical wizard Ross Brawn, as well as Schumacher, recorded nine wins to McLaren's eight. It was also pretty much a two-way carve-up

of the minor placings. Of the 51 podium spots up for grabs during the course of the season, Ferrari and McLaren bagged 46, and with a little more luck that figure could have been even higher.

Nick Heidfeld and Alexander Wurz took the minor placings in Canada, the scene of Hamilton's maiden triumph. They were helped by the fact that Alonso was handed a 10-second penalty for pitting when the safety car was out, and Massa was disqualified for leaving the pits when the exit was closed. Wurz had been promoted to the Williams team following Mark Webber's departure to Red Bull. He didn't even see the season out, retiring from F1 before Interlagos, but he had the honour of giving the team its first podium of the new Toyota-powered era.

Heidfeld was the only driver outside the big four to claim a top-three spot in two races, bringing his BMW Sauber home behind Hamilton and Räikkönen in Hungary. Once again, things might have been different had Alonso not been bumped back five places on the grid, to sixth, for impeding his team-mate during qualifying. Even so, BMW Sauber was the surprise package of the year, outpacing reigning champions Renault in the race for the Constructors' title.

Mark Webber took third at the European Grand Prix, after Räikkönen retired and Hamilton slid off in a downpour that claimed several victims. Hamilton finished ninth after being craned back onto the track, the last driver to be afforded that assistance before the FIA ruled against it.

Kovalainen impresses

The only other man to loosen the Ferrari-McLaren grip on the podium was another impressive rookie, Heikki Kovalainen, who had taken Alonso's seat at Renault. He finished second to Hamilton in Japan from 11th on the grid, keeping his head as a string of drivers hit trouble. The Finn held off his compatriot, 'Iceman' Räikkönen, to secure his first podium in F1.

Hamilton was joint leader after Bahrain, and out on his own by Round Four, Barcelona. There were setbacks along the way, notably a disastrous Shanghai sortie, where the Briton beached his MP4-22, but he clung to his lead until the final round. Massa had fallen by the wayside by then, making it a dramatic three-way shoot-out involving Alonso and Räikkönen: the current McLaren duo battling with the man who had left the team to step into Schumacher's shoes.

And so to Brazil, with Hamilton holding a 4 point lead over Alonso and a seven-point advantage over Räikkönen. Pole-sitter Felipe Massa would have sent his legions of fans delirious with a home victory, but after leading for much of the race, he made way for his Ferrari team-mate. Alonso needed second place to pip the Finn but never looked like threatening the Ferraris and had to settle for third. Fate was against Hamilton, who recovered from an off-road excursion, only to suffer a gearbox problem and slip to 18th – 16 places down on his grid position. Many an eyebrow was raised at the three-stop strategy, which backfired badly. Hamilton battled on gamely to finish seventh, when fifth would have been enough to give him the title. McLaren's appeal over a fuel temperature irregularity involving the Williams and BMW Sauber cars that finished ahead of their man came to naught, and Hamilton was gracious enough to say he didn't want to win by default.

Räikkönen became the third Finnish driver to don the crown, following in the footsteps of Keke Rosberg and Mika Häkkinen, and by taking the title from third place going into the final round, he emulated the achievement of Nino Farina in the inaugural championship.

'Spygate'

The 'Spygate' scandal turned the Constructors' Championship from a tight, two-horse race into a stroll for Ferrari. The FIA slapped a £50 million fine on McLaren and expunged the team's points from the records when it was revealed that chief designer Mike Coughlan had been found in possession of a dossier detailing Ferrari F1 update 2007 technical data.

2008

Drivers' Championship	1. Lewis Hamilton	98
	2. Felipe Massa	97
	3. Kimi Räikkönen	75
Constructors' Title	1. Ferrari	172
	2. McLaren-Mercedes	151
	3. BMW Sauber	135

HAMILTON SNATCHES THE TITLE

How could the 2008 season possibly match a three-way shoot-out in the deciding race and a final table that saw the top trio separated by a single point? Simple. Have the title won and lost in the last corners of the eight-month-long battle; and witness the shortest victory party on record as the team first across the line realised that the chequered flag had not delivered the championship. 2008 had an emotional wringer of a finale, one that Hollywood scriptwriters might have thought twice about serving up.

Räikkönen and Massa again spearheaded Ferrari's challenge, but the frosty relations between Hamilton and Alonso meant that something had to give at McLaren. Alonso returned to Renault, swapping places with Heikki Kovalainen, who had impressed in his debut season. Nelson Piquet Jr was promoted from test driver to partner Alonso, which left no room for Giancarlo Fisichella. He joined Force India, the new incarnation for Spyker, which had billionaire businessman Vijay Mallya at its helm. Cash-strapped Super Aguri had no such benefactor and folded after four races. David Coulthard announced that 2008 would be his final lap, while Ralf Schumacher departed to join the DTM Touring Cars series. Schumacher's replacement at Toyota was compatriot Timo Glock, the 2007 GP2 champion who had enjoyed a brief spell in the limelight with Jordan in 2004.

New street circuits

Indianapolis lost its place on the schedule, but two new street circuits were added, Valencia and Singapore. The former took over the European Grand Prix slot, leaving the Nürburgring to alternate with Hockenheim when the circus visited Germany. The Singapore GP, staged at the Marina Bay harbourside circuit, heralded the elite division's first ever night race.

Lewis Hamilton got off to a flier in the post-traction control era, avoiding a first-lap pile-up on his way to taking maximum points from pole in Melbourne. Nick Heidfeld gave BMW Sauber second place, while Nico Rosberg brought his Williams home third to record his first podium finish. Ferrari had a forgettable day; neither car made it home and the team registered a solitary point as Räikkönen was classified seventh.

Ferrari hit back at Sepang. Pole-sitter Massa again failed to finish, but Räikkönen scored maximum points to get his title defence well under way. Robert Kubica took a career-best second, while Kovalainen, who had outqualified Hamilton, bagged 6 points and his first podium. Lewis crossed the line fifth, an acceptable return for McLaren considering both drivers were demoted five grid places for qualifying misdemeanours.

Ferrari took one-two in Bahrain, but it was a black day for Hamilton, who dropped six places in a disastrous first lap, then tangled with Alonso's Renault to effectively end his interest. Kovalainen gave McLaren a consolation fifth as he trailed home the BMW Sauber duo. Kubica and Heidfeld put their team atop the constructors' pile after three rounds, but when Räikkönen won from pole in Barcelona, and Massa matched that achievement in Istanbul, the picture assumed a more familiar hue. Hamilton picked up minor placings in those two races, then struck a major blow by winning from third on the grid behind the Ferraris in Monaco. An early puncture worked in his favour, allowing the MP4-23 to be fully fuelled so that he could stay out on a drying track. He became the first Englishman to win in Monaco since Graham Hill in 1969.

Maiden win for Kubica

There was high drama in Montreal. Hamilton got away well from pole, but when the safety car came out and the leading cars dived into the pits, he failed to spot a red light at the exit and rear-ended Räikkönen, taking them both out of the race.

Kubica claimed his and BMW Sauber's maiden victory, with Heidfeld following him home. Hamilton was docked ten grid places at Magny-Cours for his indiscretion, and the Ferraris made hay with another one-two. Massa profited from Räikkönen's exhaust problem to take the flag and with it the championship lead for the first time in his career.

Hamilton cruised home a minute ahead of the field at Silverstone, and followed it up with another 10-point haul at Hockenheim. If anyone had a bigger grin on his face than Lewis after the German GP it was second-placed Piquet Jr, who led eight laps from home after qualifying 17th. A puncture ended Hamilton's chance of making it a hat-trick in Hungary, but McLaren celebrated a maiden win for Kovalainen, while Glock

took second to give him his first experience of spraying the champagne.

Räikkönen was third at the Hungaroring, but his campaign faltered with blanks in his next four outings. Massa won two of those, Valencia and Spa, to become the Ferrari front-runner. He inherited the victory in Belgium after race winner Hamilton was penalised for cutting a chicane, enough to drop him to third. Massa pegged another point back on Hamilton at Monza in a scrap for the minor placings. Top honours went to Toro Rosso and Sebastian Vettel, who replaced Fernando Alonso in the record books as F1's youngest winner.

Alonso himself won the next two races, in Singapore and Japan, though it was somewhat late for a third championship bid. Massa had a forgettable race in Singapore, incurring a drive-through penalty for taking off down the pitlane with the fuel hose attached. He finished well down the field while Hamilton garnered 6 points. Both men were penalised for infringements at

BELOW: **Rival drivers Felipe Massa (l) of Brazil (Ferrari) and Lewis Hamilton (r) of Great Britain (McLaren-Mercedes) pictured prior to the Brazilian Grand Prix. The race, at the Interlagos Circuit in São Paulo, would decide the destination of the Drivers' Championship.**

Fuji Speedway, but Massa recovered to take seventh, Hamilton finishing out of the points.

Two-way battle

Hamilton stretched his lead to 7 points with a win in China. Räikkönen, now out of contention, ceded second place to his team-mate, while Kubica's slim hopes of taking the title disappeared. It was now a straight fight between the top two going into Massa's home race.

The Brazilian could have done no more at Interlagos. He took pole, set the fastest lap and scored maximum points, knowing that it counted only if Hamilton finished out of the top five. That looked a distinct possibility as a cloudburst made the track treacherous in the latter stages. All the front-runners dived into the pits for intermediates, except for Glock. He inherited fourth place in the shake-up, hoping to nurse his Toyota home on dry tyres. Behind him, Vettel seized upon a Hamilton mistake to take the all-important fifth spot two laps out. The Ferrari camp began celebrating, prematurely, for both Vettel and Hamilton passed Glock at the death. It was a desperately close-run thing but Hamilton had done just enough to be crowned the youngest ever champion, while Ferrari had the consolation of landing a 16th Constructors' Title.

2009

Drivers' Championship	1	Jenson Button	95
	2	Sebastian Vettel	84
	3	Rubens Barrichello	77
Constructors' Title	1	Brawn-Mercedes	172
	2	RBR-Renault	153.5
	3	McLaren-Mercedes	71

BUTTON ANSWERS CRITICS AS BRAWN STRIKES GOLD

2009 provided one of sport's great fairytales, when the long-time talented nearly-man finally had his day. At the start of the year, Jenson Button's stats made unimpressive reading: one win in 152 starts over nine years. At 29 he was often pigeon-holed as a playboy midfield runner rather than serious contender. Button would have argued that luck had been against him, that he had backed his share of uncompetitive

horses. While Lewis Hamilton came from nowhere to lift the title in only his second season with McLaren, Jenson had been having a miserable time at Honda, scoring just 9 points in those two campaigns. Team-mate Rubens Barrichello lifted that aggregate tally to a mere 20.

Points-scoring was the last thing on the duo's mind when Honda pulled out in December 2008. They were unsure of a drive until a Ross Brawn-led buy-out saved the day at Brackley just three weeks before the Melbourne curtain-raiser. Mercedes provided the power, and it soon became clear that the new team was not there just to make up the numbers. Brawn studied the new regulations and produced a stunningly quick BGP 001, which proceeded to steal a march on the rival outfits in the first half of the season.

Rule changes

There was a raft of rule changes, all designed to promote more wheel-to-wheel racing. Slick tyres were back for the first time since 1998, while many pieces of kit that increased aerodynamic downforce – including barge boards, turning vanes and chimneys – were outlawed. Front wings were fitted with driver-adjustable flaps that could be used twice per lap, and cars had the option of using KERS – Kinetic Energy Recovery System – which used batteries to harness the energy lost during braking. An extra 80 horsepower was available for six seconds per lap, though the kit did weigh in at 35kg. The big talking point surrounded the rear diffuser, which was moved to a position where it caused less dirty air. Brawn's design in that department helped the fledgling team score a dramatic one-two in Melbourne. Button took pole and strolled home ahead of Barrichello under safety car conditions, a result that had statisticians trawling through the record books. They had to go back to 1954 and Fangio and Kling's double for Mercedes at the French GP to find a similar triumphant entry into the sport.

Controversy surrounded the final podium place in Australia. Jarno Trulli crossed the line third, only to be accused of passing Lewis Hamilton when the safety car was out. He was handed a penalty and bumped down to 12th place, but reinstated after audio recordings revealed that Hamilton had conceded the position following consultation with his team. McLaren and Hamilton were found to have misled the stewards and the reigning champion was disqualified.

A protest lodged over Brawn's diffuser design (and that of Toyota and Williams) was dismissed by the FIA, a ruling that helped set the pattern for the next half dozen races. Button won five of those, early-season dominance that put him in the hallowed company of Jim Clark and Michael Schumacher. One of those victories came in a downpour at Sepang, which had to be abandoned before the three-quarter mark was reached. Half-points were awarded for the first time since 1991.

Maiden win for Red Bull

The man who broke Button's run was Sebastian Vettel. The 'new Schuey', promoted to Red Bull to replace the retiring Coulthard, gave the team its first pole and race win on a wet Shanghai circuit. That was also a milestone for Adrian Newey, the former Williams and McLaren ace designer who had now elevated Red Bull to the top of the rostrum. Mark Webber crossed the line second to make it a red-letter day for the team.

Red Bull would battle it out with Brawn in both championships, McLaren and Ferrari having little their own way. Räikkönen's sixth place in Bahrain, Round Four, gave Ferrari their first points of the year and prevented the team from suffering its worst ever start to a season.

Button chose his home Grand Prix for his worst showing of the year. He qualified sixth, though his disappointment must have been as nothing compared with reigning champion Lewis Hamilton: 19th place on the back row was the low point in his F1 career thus far. McLaren boss Martin Whitmarsh admitted that they were struggling for downforce, and that the team hadn't supplied Hamilton with the tools to defend his title. By mid-season, their thoughts were already turning to 2010.

Vettel dominated from pole at Silverstone to score his first win in the dry, disappearing into the distance from the off and only briefly relinquishing the lead to Webber during a pit stop round. His team-mate took second, repeating Red Bull's China result, with Barrichello third. Button finished in sixth. He struggled for grip in the early stages, unable to get heat into the hard tyres. His championship lead was still a healthy 23 points over Barrichello, but Vettel was now within 2 points of the Brazilian.

Reprieve for Silverstone

Vettel's win was to have marked the swansong for Silverstone, home to the British GP since 1987. Negotiations to bring much-needed improvements to the Northamptonshire circuit had stalled, and Bernie Ecclestone's patience with the owners, British Racing Drivers' Club, had finally run out. To keep the British race on the calendar it was deemed necessary to find a circuit that ticked more boxes, and Donington Park – which had last played host to a F1 race in 1983 – presented a development programme that provided just that. A ten-year deal starting in 2010 was in place, but it fell through when the East Midlands circuit suffered a cash crisis. Silverstone was back in pole position.

Back on the track, things got twitchier for Button as the season progressed. The gap closed as rival teams literally got up to speed, and Button's best result in the back half of the year came at Monza, where he ran second to Barrichello. The wins were being shared round: two for Rubens, another for

ABOVE: **Jenson Button led Rubens Barrichello to a Brawn one-two in the Monaco Grand Prix. Button celebrated his fifth victory in six races.**

Vettel, one for Räikkönen. And Hamilton belatedly came to the party with victories in Hungary and Singapore. Any good cheer at Maranello was dented during qualifying at the Hungaroring, when Massa was the victim of a freak accident. His season ended after he was struck in the helmet by a flying spring, sustaining head injuries that required a titanium plate to be fitted. There was talk of Michael Schumacher taking his seat, but he had injury worries of his own and Luca Badoer, then Giancarlo Fisichella, filled in for the Brazilian.

Ecclestone plan stalls

With six wins under his belt, Button wouldn't have needed to look over his shoulder had Bernie Ecclestone's idea to award the title on chequered flags instead of points been adopted. But that proposal found little favour with Fota (Formula One Teams Association) and every points finish was invaluable as the season approached its climax. McLaren and Ferrari's revival came too late to have an impact on the standings; Red Bull, by contrast, had their eyes on the prize. Vettel pulled a point back on Button under the lights in Singapore – and could have made bigger inroads had he not incurred a drive-through penalty for speeding in the pitlane – then gave himself an outside chance of the title with a win in Japan.

The championship was settled in the penultimate race, São Paulo. Button had a 14-point cushion over Barrichello, with Vettel 2 points further adrift. By now some press reports were criticising Jenson for limping towards the line instead of taking the crown in style. He answered them with a storming drive, taking fifth after qualifying a disappointing 14th. Vettel and Barrichello swapped places, but Button's lead was now unassailable, and Brawn made it a double celebration as they also clinched the Constructors' Title. It meant no final-race showdown on the new Yas Marina circuit in Abu Dhabi. F1's newest venue, constructed on a man-made island, was the work of the doyen of race circuit architects, Hermann Tilke. Vettel bagged his fourth win of the year, though Button and his team had already celebrated a remarkable double. Button became Britain's tenth champion in his tenth season among the elite, silencing the doubters and rendering unimportant the £5 million pay cut he had agreed at the start of the season to help put the BGP 001 on the grid. For Ross Brawn – the man known as 'The Big Bear' – it meant an eighth world title to add to the seven he won as technical director with Benetton and Ferrari, though this was his first wearing a team principal's hat.

2010

Drivers' Championship	1.	Sebastian Vettel	256
	2.	Fernando Alonso	252
	3.	Mark Webber	242
Constructors' Title	1.	RBR-Renault	498
	2.	McLaren-Mercedes	454
	3.	Ferrari	396

VETTEL SNATCHES CROWN TO BECOME YOUNGEST WORLD CHAMPION

2010 offered the mouthwatering prospect of four world champions going head to head, Button, Hamilton and Alonso pitting themselves against Michael Schumacher, who was back on the grid after three years on the sidelines. 'It's not need, it's want,' said the seven-time champion of his return to the fray. The prospect of driving for Mercedes GP,

which had taken over the all-conquering Brawn team at the end of 2009, was enough to induce the 41-year-old to sign a three-year-deal. It also reunited him with the man who masterminded his glory days at Benetton and Ferrari as Ross Brawn stayed on to orchestrate the Mercedes challenge. Nico Rosberg ended his four-year spell at Williams to join his compatriot, while the driver merry-go-round saw world champion Jenson Button move to McLaren, and Alonso head to Ferrari. Toyota's withdrawal left Trulli and Glock free agents, and they hooked up with new entrants Lotus and Virgin respectively. Hispania was the other new name on the grid, Bruno Senna – Ayrton's nephew – spearheading their foray into the big league. Peter Sauber bought his old team back after BMW decided to end their interest in the sport. Meanwhile, it was as-you-were at Red Bull, Vettel and Webber hoping to carry their fine late-season form of 2009 into the new season.

Refuelling was outlawed, the first time since 1993 that the teams had to grapple with that regulation. The big change, though, was the amended points system, extended to reward the top ten finishers. With 25, 18 and 15 points now on offer for the first three home, the incentive to push for a win was greater than ever.

Lead changes hands

The Bahrain curtain-raiser was something of a damp squib, Alonso making a winning debut for Ferrari after pole-sitter Vettel suffered mechanical problems. It set the season-long pattern for qualifying. Red Bull would head the grid in 15 of the 19 races – Vettel took pole on 10 occasions – but he and Webber couldn't replicate that dominance on race day with any regularity. Five drivers topped the podium in the first seven races – Alonso, Button, Vettel, Webber and Hamilton. All had their moments during the campaign, the lead changing hands nine times in the 19-race marathon. As the year progressed the only safe bet was that the championship was heading to Red Bull, Ferrari or McLaren.

Button put in a great performance in Melbourne to win second time out for his new team, and also scored a maximum in the wet in Shanghai after Alonso was penalised for jumping the start. Vettel led his team-mate home in Malaysia, and Webber took back-to-back wins in Spain and Monaco. The latter victory put the Australian on top of the leader board, and the entire Red Bull team celebrated with a dip in the swimming pool, trophy and all. Mercedes took their first podium at Sepang, and another in China, but both third places were courtesy of Rosberg; Schumi would do no better than fourth in the entire campaign, and the most vivid memory of his season would be almost ramming former team-mate Barrichello into a wall in Hungary.

LEFT: **Race winner Sebastian Vettel celebrates on the podium following the Japanese Grand Prix at Suzuka on 10 October.**

Webber and Vettel had a costly coming together in Turkey. Hamilton and Button profited with a one-two, though some of their jousting suggested they might have suffered the same fate as the Red Bulls. Hamilton took pole in Round Eight, Montreal, which broke Red Bull's early-season stranglehold on qualifying, temporarily, at least. Lewis crossed the line ahead of Button for another McLaren one-two, a result that put them in the same order in the overall standings – 109 to 106 – with Webber a further 3 points adrift.

Webber escaped unscathed from a horrifying spill in Valencia, and watched his team-mate take maximum points from pole, ahead of the McLaren duo. The Australian felt that Vettel was getting preferential treatment at Red Bull, a sentiment that spilled into the public arena at the British GP, staged at a remodelled Silverstone. The updated nose fitted to Vettel's car came off during practice, and the team appropriated Webber's front-end kit to fix the German's problem. Webber prevailed on race day, and he let his feelings be known as he took the congratulations of the backroom staff over the intercom. 'Not bad for a number two driver.' Christian Horner admitted the situation could have been handled better.

Team orders row

The Red Bull spat was followed by another at Hockenheim, this time involving Ferrari. Felipe Massa was the odd-man-out in what was turning into a three-team fight for honours. He

had just two podiums to show for his first ten starts, and Alonso was looking the likelier challenger to Red Bull and McLaren. The point was driven home in Germany, where race leader Massa was 'advised' to allow his team-mate through. The ban on team orders meant the message had to be transmitted in coded form, but no one was in any doubt as to the true meaning of the words 'Fernando is faster than you'. Massa duly moved aside, Ferrari took the $100,000 fine – and, more importantly, Alonso bagged 25 points. At the end of the year the FIA would abolish the team orders rule that had been introduced in the wake of the 2002 Austrian GP, where Barrichello handed victory to Schumacher on a plate.

Alonso managed to split the Red Bulls in Hungary, but it was clear that the RB6 was the class act of the field. Adrian Newey channelled exhaust gases through the diffuser to provide extra downforce, an idea others belatedly latched onto, though not in time to challenge for the accolade of 'car of the season', as David Coulthard hailed it.

Button clashed with Vettel at Spa, and Alonso spun out, making it a good day for Hamilton, who himself survived an off-track moment in the wet. He now led the title race from Webber, who finished second on the day. Alonso was lying fifth, 41 points adrift of Lewis, but the picture changed dramatically as the Spaniard won at Monza and Singapore, while collisions in both meant Hamilton failed to add to his tally. Vettel led Webber home at Suzuka, maintaining their grid positions, and it was the Australian who held a handy 14-point championship lead going into the final three rounds. That advantage evaporated in monsoon conditions at the inaugural South Korean GP. Webber failed to finish, while Vettel's engine gave out when he looked set for victory. Alonso pounced. Button, out of the points, was now effectively out of contention.

Tactical error by Ferrari

Nico Hulkenberg took his first F1 pole in Brazil – Williams' first in over five years – though it wouldn't be enough for him to retain his seat for 2011. A fourth Red Bull one-two sealed the Constructors' Title, but third-placed Alonso still held an 8-point lead over Webber – 15 over Vettel – going into the Abu Dhabi decider. Hamilton, 24 points adrift, needed victory and a lot more besides. Christian Horner insisted he would let his men fight it out on even terms, when swinging behind Webber might have offered the best means of preventing the laurels going to Ferrari. It could have backfired, but it was Vettel's day, and year. His third win in the last four races meant that he led the championship for the first time, when it mattered most. Even as he took the chequered flag, there were a few anxious moments before it was confirmed that neither Alonso nor Webber had done enough. Alonso paid a heavy price for pitting early to shadow Webber, then getting stuck behind Vitaly Petrov's Renault. At 23 years 134 days, Vettel also took over from Hamilton as Formula One's youngest champion. It also meant a remarkable double for Red Bull, just six years after taking their bow in the sport.

2011

Drivers' Championship	1. Sebastian Vettel	392
	2. Jenson Button	270
	3. Mark Webber	258
Constructors' Title	1. RBR-Renault	650
	2. McLaren-Mercedes	497
	3. Ferrari	375

VETTEL CONQUERS ALL

2011 saw a raft of new regulations ushered in, with the aim of increasing overtaking opportunities and enhancing the race-day spectacle. For some those twin objectives were opposite sides of the same coin. They welcomed the return of KERS, the introduction of the Drag Reduction System and the arrival of fast-degrading Pirelli tyres. DRS, like KERS, provided a time-limited performance boost. The wing could be opened up only in designated sectors of the track, and only if a car was within a second of the one it had in its sights. But perhaps the biggest challenge for drivers and team strategists was the way the Pirelli rubber handled. Never was the exhortation for drivers to 'look after the tyres' more keenly uttered. The changes contributed to over 800 overtaking manoeuvres during the 19-race season.

The shuffling of the driver pack was restricted to the midfield and lower-ranked outfits. An unwanted change was forced on Renault when Robert Kubica suffered career-threatening injuries while competing in an off-season rally. The Pole's former BMW Sauber team-mate Nick Heidfeld was recruited to partner Vitaly Petrov. He peaked with a third-place finish in Malaysia before departing mid-term, replaced by Bruno Senna, who garnered just two points from eight starts. The loss of Kubica was a crushing blow, and Renault were further hampered by the failure of the R31's front-exit exhaust to live up to expectations.

Di Resta scores on debut

DTM champion Paul di Resta made an eye-catching start to his F1 career with Force India, the Scot in the points in his first two starts and consistently outqualifying his Force India team-mate Adrian Sutil in the first half of the season. His best return came in Singapore, where he claimed eight points for a fine sixth place. Mexico's Sergio Pérez, who joined Sauber on the back of finishing runner-up in the GP2 championship, was another rookie who could feel well pleased with his debut season. Employing a bold one-stop strategy, Pérez crossed the line seventh in Melbourne, only to be robbed by a technical infringement. Australia became the curtain-raiser after political instability saw Bahrain scratched from the schedule. The Mexican had a better time of it than Pastor Maldonado, the man who beat him to the GP2 title. The Venezuelan notched just one point for a Williams team that had its worst ever year, though that was one more than the eight drivers who turned out for Lotus, HRT and Virgin over the course of the campaign.

At the business end of the grid, the top five teams of 2010 – Red Bull, McLaren, Ferrari, Mercedes and Renault – finished in the same order 12 months on. This time, however, the spread was significantly wider. Red Bull ended the year over 150 points clear of McLaren, who in turn finished over 100 points ahead of Ferrari. Vettel and Webber's 650-point aggregate haul reflected the dominance of the RB7, which carried the team to victory in both Drivers' and Constructor Championships for the second year running.

Vettel imperious

If Webber had been irked at his no. 2 status in 2010, he could have had no complaints this time round. Vettel was imperious and relentless in capturing his second crown, taking pole in 15 of the 19 rounds – eclipsing Nigel Mansell's 1992 record – and the chequered flag 11 times. His win from pole in Melbourne set the template for the year. He headed the grid in every race until Spain, and even there he bagged maximum points. Vettel showed he was not merely a devastating front runner but could also joust with the pack, most memorably in a daring, high-speed pass on the outside of Alonso at Monza. Nor was there a chink in the armour in terms of race craft, the German cannily opting for a one-stopper at Monaco and holding off Alonso and Button, both on fresher rubber. An accident brought the safety car out and he led them home. His one noteworthy mistake came on the final lap of a rain-lashed Canadian GP, on which Button gleefully pounced. But the errors that blotted his copybook in 2010 were rare during this campaign.

At Silverstone a row blew up over off-throttle blown diffusers, which channel exhaust gases onto the aerodynamic

ABOVE: **Sebastian Vettel celebrates in Brazil after qualifying in pole position for the 15th time of the season.**

rear to provide extra downforce. The RB7 system was the best of the bunch, thus it was felt limiting off-throttle blowing would hit Red Bull hardest. In the event, Vettel fell victim to a sloppy pit stop, and the regulation change was soon reversed.

Youngest double winner

Victory under the lights at Singapore – where Vettel set another personal landmark by leading every lap, including those where he pitted – all but sealed his retention of the crown. With five races to go, he needed just one point to put himself beyond the reach of Button, the only man with a mathematical chance of catching him. Third place behind Jenson at Suzuka confirmed Vettel as only the ninth man in history to retain the title, and at 24 the youngest double winner. Red Bull wrapped up the Constructors' title next time out in Korea, with three races to spare. It meant there was

nothing riding on the inaugural Indian Grand Prix, staged at the new Buddh International Circuit. That marked victory no. 11, at a canter, for the man who had already secured the crown. He also took Mansell's record for the number of laps led in a season.

There were a couple of late-season glitches for Vettel, notably a first-lap puncture in Abu Dhabi, but those came long after the prizes had been handed out. And even with engine problems in Brazil he nursed the car home in second place behind his Aussie partner. Webber fronted the grid on three occasions – Korea was the only race in which Red Bull failed to take pole – but had to wait until that Interlagos finale to record his sole win of the campaign. The fact that he led home a team-mate with an ailing car capped a frustrating year for Webber, desperate to prove himself on equal terms. But 2011 showed the gulf between the two, revealed in the 134-point gap between them. While Vettel quickly got to grips with the way the Pirellis performed, Webber struggled to adapt to the challenges posed by the rubber. There were flashes of brilliance, such as carving through the field to take third in China and executing a stunning pass on Alonso at Spa, but Webber was generally outgunned. In short, even though the RB7 was the car to beat, Vettel wrung every ounce from it in confirming his top-dog status.

Hamilton woes

Button split the Red Bulls, stepping onto the podium 12 times. From the Hungarian GP on, the Frome Flyer scored just 15 points fewer than the champion. The highlight was Montreal, where he came from the back of the pack to pressure Vettel into that late error. Button's performances left egg on the faces of those who thought he was walking into the lion's den in signing for McLaren and taking on Hamilton. Lewis added three wins to his tally, the same as his McLaren team-mate in a season of mixed fortunes. He won in fine style in China and Germany, and acclaimed his Abu Dhabi victory as one of his best. On the downside, the year was littered with crashes – six involving Massa – and penalties. After a storming drive to finish second in Korea, a performance that left Martin Whitmarsh purring, Hamilton took the glass-half-empty view: 'One good race does not redeem a whole year of negative races.' His mood would not have been improved by the fact that he lost out to a team-mate for the first time in his career.

Fernando Alonso extracted all he could from Ferrari's underwhelming F150°, getting on the podium ten times – the same as Webber – and topping it at a remodelled Silverstone. Fourth in the title race, a point behind the Aussie, represented a solid achievement, with the promise of better hardware to come. Team-mate Felipe Massa's future at Ferrari was thrown into doubt as the Brazilian finished no higher than fifth all season. Michael Schumacher celebrated his 20th anniversary in F1 at Spa, the track he calls his 'living room' on the strength of six victories there. It was fifth this term, from the back of the grid. He also notched ten points at Monza, but with Vettel, Button, Alonso and Hamilton ahead of him.

But 2011 was all about Red Bull, with the promise of more to come from a team boasting the talents of Vettel and Adrian Newey. Newey's solution to the ban on double diffusers was the envy of the paddock. He also left others to try to milk every last ounce from KERS; his design allowed for a smaller battery unit than the regulations permitted, and even that proved to be temperamental. The performance of the ultra-reliable RB7 showed that, as ever, he got it spot-on, and left commentators pontificating on the possibility of the Red Bull-Vettel axis dominating Formula One in a way reminiscent of the Ferrari-Schumacher years.

2012

Drivers' Championship	1. Sebastian Vettel	281
	2. Fernando Alonso	278
	3. Kimi Räikkönen	207
Constructors' Title	1. RBR-Renault	460
	2. Ferrari	400
	3. McLaren-Mercedes	378

VETTEL JOINS THE HAT-TRICK CLUB

On the eve of the 2012 season the question on everyone's lips was simple: who can stop Sebastian Vettel? The reigning champion was a short-priced favourite to collect a third world title, and Christian Horner's assertion that his star performer was still improving meant Red Bull's rivals would have to be on their mettle to wrest the crown.

Many thought the rule changes might be a leveller. Blown diffusers were out, exhaust gases now rerouted so that they could no longer be deployed to aerodynamic advantage. Prior to the ban, no team had got the system to work better than Red Bull, hence it was thought the new regulations would impact RBR most. Then there were the personnel changes that presented a potential threat, notably the return of a recharged Kimi Räikkönen after a two-year sabbatical. It was undoubtedly a coup for Lotus F1 – the former Lotus Renault midfielders – to sign the 2007 champion, whose presence on the grid meant an unprecedented six title-winning drivers were gunning for glory in 2012.

Lotus squabble settled

The arrival of Lotus F1 coincided with the rebranding of Team Lotus, who would now take to the track as Caterham. Thus ended the long-running naming-rights battle which had been played out in the law courts. Caterham welcomed Vitaly Petrov into the fold, a move that almost certainly drew the curtain on Jarno Trulli's long career in the premier class. It was all change at Lotus as Bruno Senna also departed, paving the way for Romain Grosjean's promotion to the seat alongside Räikkönen. Senna's move to Williams was overlaid with emotion, coming 18 years after his uncle signed for the then-front-running outfit. Ayrton's nephew, in contrast, was heading for a Grove team in the doldrums following its worst-ever season.

Nico Hulkenberg impressed Force India enough in his season occupying the test-reserve slot to land the race drive for 2012. Daniel Ricciardo, the young Aussie who had long been on Red Bull's radar, took a seat at Toro Rosso, having cut his teeth in a loan deal with HRT. Joining him at STR was rookie Frenchman Jean-Eric Vergne, one-time member of Red Bull's young driver programme and former British F3 champion. Vergne's compatriot Charles Pic was also getting his first taste of the big time, signing for Marussia after impressing in GP2. The Russian sportscar manufacturer and former Virgin title sponsor entered the fray under its own name, having acquired a majority stake. With a Russian grand prix in the pipeline, it was a clear signal of intent that the East European heavyweight was keen to make its presence felt in motorsport's elite division.

Early spoils shared

The early-season skirmishes suggested that no driver or team was going to disappear into the distance. The first seven rounds saw a different man on top of the podium – a first for the sport – while five teams occupied the 25-point position. It was no surprise to see the Red Bull and McLaren quartet claim an early maximum, perhaps more so to see Fernando Alonso win second time out in Malaysia in an F2012 widely derided as a dud. There was already talk of Ferrari looking to its next-generation car when Alonso took the flag in Sepang. It was a rain-lashed race, however, and the Spaniard cautioned that he would not go overboard about his chances until the car performed well in good conditions. The way Alonso wrung the neck out of indifferent hardware would be a feature of the season.

Pressing the Ferrari all the way to the line in Malaysia was Sergio Pérez, his second place in his sophomore year the best showing by a Mexican driver since the days of Pedro Rodríguez in the early 70s. Talk of the hotshot tyro taking the underperforming Massa's seat at Maranello proved unfounded, but Pérez was indeed in line for a substantial career uplift in a year which saw him bag two more podiums for Sauber.

The other early winners were Nico Rosberg and Pastor Maldonado, in Shanghai and Barcelona respectively. Rosberg claimed his maiden win in race number 111 – only four other men had hung around longer for their first victory. His lights-to-flag victory gave Mercedes their first success as a works team since Fangio prevailed at Monza in 1955.

Williams hadn't waited quite that long, but Maldonado's Spanish triumph was the team's first since Brazil 2004. It was a welcome 70th birthday present for Sir Frank, and a sweet success for Maldonado, who became Venezuela's first F1 race-winning driver. It was an emphatic riposte to critics who suggested his chief asset was the oil company sponsorship money he brought to the party. Williams wouldn't trouble the podium again, but the return to Renault power – the combination that delivered so much past glory – yielded an aggregate 76 points, 71 more than that accrued in 2011.

LEFT: **Fernando Alonso, Pastor Maldonado and Kimi Räikkönen celebrate on the podium at the Circuit de Catalunya on 13 May.**

Catalogue of woe for McLaren

Maldonado inherited pole from Hamilton in Barcelona, the latter relegated for being underfuelled during qualifying. It was but one of a catalogue of mishaps to befall McLaren, the team dogged by ill luck, pit lane blunders and reliability issues. Jenson Button's fortunes fluctuated wildly after his season-opening win in Australia, while Lewis had to wait till Canada – Round Seven – before driver, car and strategy combined to winning effect. Such was the division of the spoils in the first third of the season – or 'lottery', as Webber termed it – that Hamilton's Montreal victory gave him a narrow leaderboard advantage over Alonso and Vettel, who prevailed in the controversial return to Bahrain. The reigning champion was far from having it all his own way, yet many cited his second place at Albert Park – splitting the McLarens from sixth on the grid – as evidence that he could mix it in the pack. There followed more dramatic proof that he was much more than just an outstanding front-runner.

Alonso added two more wins before the summer break, on the streets of Valencia and Hockenheim. In Germany Ferrari had the added bonus of seeing Vettel bumped down from second to fifth for an illegal pass on Button on the penultimate lap. Indeed it was Mark Webber, with a Silverstone success to add to his Monaco triumph, who was running Alonso closest. The Northamptonshire circuit was a quagmire in the run-up to race day, but the sun came out as Webber reversed the grid positions, overhauling the pole-sitting Spaniard four laps from home.

The home grand prix was a day to forget for the Brits, Button ruefully remarking that the MP4-27 was battling with the midfield runners. Hopes were pinned on an upgrade package to salvage the season, and it worked straight out of the box in Germany, where Jenson took second to end a dismal run. Then Hamilton dominated from pole in Hungary to reignite his championship challenge. At the August hiatus Alonso had a 40-point cushion over Webber, with Vettel, Hamilton and Räikkönen in close contention.

Alonso and Vettel pull clear

Alonso had scored in every race thus far, and in the remaining nine rounds would stand on the podium in each of the seven races he finished. It was a remarkable level of consistency, yet those retirements in Belgium and Japan would prove costly for Sebastian Vettel hit his stride as the title race heated up, helped by the double-DRS system now fitted to the RB8. Monza apart, he put together a scintillating late-season set of results, including four wins on the spin. And as he did so the contenders fell away one by one to leave a Red Bull-Ferrari shoot-out.

Button followed Vettel home on the Singapore streets, third-placed Alonso ceding 10 points to the German. Pole-sitter Hamilton's gearbox failure – his fourth retirement in seven races, with a couple still to come – heaped further misery on his year. Speculation that he was on his way to Mercedes was soon confirmed.

Vettel cruised home at Suzuka, an excellent day for Red Bull as it was Massa's Ferrari that followed him home – the under-fire Brazilian's first podium in two years – while Kobayashi held off Button to become only the third Japanese driver to step onto the podium. Japan was another bad day at the office for Grosjean, instigator of a huge pile-up at Spa and now involved in his seventh opening-lap incident.

Victory in Korea put Vettel in the box seat, and he edged further ahead of Alonso as they crossed the line first and second in India. Vettel's lights-to-flag victory meant he had led over 200 laps since inheriting the lead from Hamilton at Singapore. The run was halted at Abu Dhabi, where Vettel was bumped to the back of the grid for running too light on fuel, opted to start from the pit lane and was soon nursing a damaged front wing. Colliding with a marker board didn't help his cause, either, but as Räikkönen profited from yet another Hamilton hardware failure out in front, all eyes were on the relative positions of Vettel and Alonso. Aided by a couple of safety car appearances, Vettel clawed his way up to third, just one place behind Alonso. The Iceman celebrated the first win of his second stint in F1 – the eighth different winner of the year – but the smiles were equally big in the Red Bull garage, for their man had mitigated sizeable potential losses.

BELOW: **The start of the US Grand Prix at Austin on 18 November.**

America returns to the calendar

For the penultimate race the circus rumbled into Austin, Texas. With Turkey off the menu, America returned to the roster for the first time since 2007, the only addition to the schedule save for the return to Bahrain. Vettel took to the Circuit of the Americas quickly, securing his sixth pole of the year, with Alonso back in ninth. The Spaniard was promoted one place courtesy of a Grosjean penalty, and that became seventh as Ferrari broke the seal on Massa's gearbox, relegating him down the grid. Having started to show some of his old form, Felipe effectively took one for the team, but at least had a contract extension to show for it.

The extra position was valuable in putting Alonso on the clean side of the £250 million track, especially important as the new surface was not 'rubbered in'. And Alonso made the most of it, making his way up to third with the help of Webber's first mechanical failure since Japan 2009. Hamilton won the jousting match with Vettel for top spot on the podium, his fourth win of the year. Vettel's 18 points was more than enough to clinch Red Bull's third straight constructors' title. Alonso's third place meant yet another Interlagos decider, with Vettel holding a 13-point lead.

A top-four finish in Brazil and the title was Vettel's; Alonso had to get on the podium to stand any chance. Before the action there was a valedictory lap for Michael Schumacher, who might have added to his 91 career victories had a penalty not robbed him of pole at Monaco. He signed off for the second time with a single podium from his three-year stint at Mercedes, a handful of races short of Barrichello's record for the number of starts.

Vettel and Alonso began the race fourth and seventh respectively, but the German's advantage vanished immediately as he was tagged and relegated to the back of the pack. Conditions were changeable, tyre changes numerous, and with a safety car thrown in there was plenty of positional see-sawing. Button was away and clear, and the

best Alonso could do was accept Massa's invitation to take second nine laps from home. A couple of laps later Vettel eased past an uncomplaining Schumacher into sixth, and a late safety car reappearance meant a procession to the line, a sedate end to an incident-packed race and eventful season. Vettel had squeaked home by three points, becoming the youngest triple world champion. With three successive wins he joined the exclusive hat-trick club, whose only other members were Fangio and Schumacher, and at 25 there is ample opportunity for other records to come his way.

2013

Drivers' Championship	1. Sebastian Vettel	397
	2. Fernando Alonso	242
	3. Mark Webber	199
Constructors' Title	1. RBR-Renault	596
	2. Mercedes	360
	3. Ferrari	354

VETTEL EQUALS 60-YEAR-OLD RECORD

A year that began with no discernible pattern, where the prizes were shared out among the top teams and drivers, ended in all too familiar style. It took a mid-season row and a tweak in the regulations, but as summer turned to autumn Sebastian Vettel and Red Bull exerted a grip that no other contender could live with.

The big news going into the season was Lewis Hamilton's severing of the McLaren apron strings, the first driver change among the front-running outfits for three years. His switch to Mercedes was a gamble, his new employers having won just once in 58 races since returning to the sport in 2010. Doubtless he was attracted by the prospect of collaborating with Ross Brawn, the man who master-minded Michael Schumacher's seven world titles and former team-mate Jenson Button's victorious 2009 campaign. It was a move clearly born of frustration. 'Should I have had more championships?' he said, reflecting on his time at Woking. 'Absolutely.'

McLaren plumped for hard-charging tyro Sergio Pérez to fill Lewis's boots. 'The most exciting young talent in Formula One,' according to team boss Martin Whitmarsh, though the Mexican's form ebbed dramatically in the back half of 2012

after the deal was done. Pérez brought with him a sackful of sponsorship money, yet another example of the pay-driver phenomenon. Max Chilton fell into the same category, though he had been a winner in GP2. His unseating of Glock at Marussia meant four Britons would take to the grid in 2013. The pursuit of backers' cash as well as talent, increasingly prevalent in teams with tighter budgets, brought home the financial reality of running a Formula One team. It proved too rich for HRT's blood, the Spain-based outfit becoming the latest to head for the exit. But it was a trend bucked by Williams. The money following Bruno Senna didn't save him from being ousted in favour of new flying Finn Valterri Bottas. Esteban Gutiérrez at Sauber, Giedo van der Garde at Caterham and Jules Bianchi – Chilton's Marussia team-mate – meant there were five new faces out to grab their opportunity.

First blood to Lotus

It was one of the old hands who drew first blood. Kimi Räikkönen gave Lotus the perfect start in Australia, bagging 25 points from a lowly seventh starting slot. Second-placed Alonso also made up ground on his grid position, while the Red Bulls that locked out the front row delivered only third and sixth respectively for Vettel and Webber. If that was disappointing, the aggregate two points McLaren took from Albert Park – courtesy of Button's squeezing into the top 10, was a miserable return for a team that had ended 2012 so strongly. These were 'difficult days,' said Jenson. Indeed. The decision to go with an all-new MP4-28 rather than develop the old car backfired badly in the final year of the 2.4-litre V8s, McLaren's worst showing for a generation. Neither driver would step on the podium all year, which would have consequences both for Pérez and Whitmarsh.

Lotus, by contrast, would add 13 more top-three finishes to Kimi's Melbourne opener, without quite managing to find the top step again. Solid points accumulation, from the Finn in the first half of the year and Romain Grosjean in the second, masked a different kind of problem at Enstone. The team that went on to take fourth in the constructors' battle and amass over 300 points faced a cash crisis that had Räikkönen complaining about unpaid salary and making it known that he was upping sticks long before the season was out.

The 10 races up to the mid-term break left a muddy picture. Yes, Vettel looked in decent shape with four victories to his name. But Alonso and Rosberg had also each won twice, and Lewis's win at the Hungaroring gave Mercedes a third success just before the month-long hiatus. Vettel had a 38-point buffer over his main rivals, Räikkönen, Alonso and Hamilton, who were tightly bunched. The German showed that three championships had not quenched his thirst for more, notably in Malaysia, where he rode roughshod over team orders to pass Webber. He apologised, while Mark said he would enjoy protection 'as usual'. The latest spat in a fractious relationship came as the Aussie announced this would be his last year in the elite class. As for Seb, the desire he had shown with his 'Hungry Heidi' RB9 won him few friends. His action contrasted with that of Rosberg, who acquiesced to intercom instructions when lying fourth behind Hamilton and eyeing up a pass. Nico's restraint had its reward at Monaco, where he converted the third of a hat-trick of poles into a maximum. It came 30 years after father Keke won in the Principality. Two rounds later, at Silverstone, Rosberg topped the podium again, this time from second on the grid. He outgunned Lewis on that score, for the Briton's win in Hungary was his only 25-pointer. But Hamilton had been far more consistent: qualifying only once outside the top four in those first 10 rounds and crossing the line no worse than fifth on nine occasions.

What of Fernando Alonso, the man with 'the best toolkit mentally of all the drivers' according to Sir Jackie Stewart? Victories in China and Spain, plus three more podium finishes, saw him handily placed at the summer break, albeit 39 points adrift of Vettel. As ever, he wrung every ounce from his hardware, but it was asking a lot even of a driver of his stature to drag the F138 beyond its capabilities over a 19-race marathon. His frustration boiled over as he realised that another year had slipped by with the crown still out reach. After finishing fifth in Hungary, the two-time champion, asked what he wanted for his 32nd birthday, joked: 'A different car.' It didn't go down well with the Ferrari suits. Soundings were taken over a possible move to Red Bull, and though those came to nought, Ferrari covered themselves by re-signing Räikkönen for 2014. Having had little competition from Felipe Massa in recent years, Alonso had a heavyweight rival on his way to Maranello.

Safety row erupts at Silverstone

And so to the row that exploded – quite literally – post-Silverstone and the game-changing effect it had on the championship. Webber had predicted that 2013 would be shaped by 'tyres, tyres, tyres'. The knife-edge balance between flat-out racing and conserving the Pirelli rubber was key. Mercedes' W04 was particularly hard on tyres, evidenced by the Barcelona race, where Rosberg's sixth place was scant return for a front row lock-out. 'This has nothing to do with racing anymore,' opined Red Bull boss Dietrich Mateschitz, the performance of the RB9 having also been adversely affected by the new compounds. Lotus, Ferrari and Force

BELOW: **Sebastian Vettel leads Nico Rosberg and Fernando Alonso during the 2013 Singapore Grand Prix.**

India, by contrast, were reasonably content with the 2014 specification. The teams' perspective was driven by self-interest, which was overridden in the wake of a spate of spectacular tyre failures at Silverstone. The race director said he came 'quite close' to aborting the contest, after which the inquest began in earnest. Fast-degrading rubber to spice up races was one thing; compromising safety was another altogether. Beleaguered Pirelli was caught between a rock and hard place: trying to fulfil its brief while addressing safety concerns. But when the problem materialised, its hands were tied by a ban on in-season testing. A private arrangement between Pirelli and Mercedes to get to the root of the problem merely landed both parties in hot water. The upshot, from Hungary on, was a return to the more resilient, Kevlar-based 2012 compounds, which Red Bull had been angling for all along, knowing they would suit the RB9 perfectly.

And so it proved – almost. Events conspired against Vettel in Hungary, but thereafter he was unstoppable. Nine races on the spin turned a handy lead in August into a gulf by the time the circus pitched up in São Paulo in late November. Both championships were wrapped up long before then, Red Bull's fourth double in nine years since entering the sport. It was design genius Adrian Newey's 10th success in the constructors' stakes, achieved with three different teams.

Weighing the quality of the triumph was not straightforward, though. At Spa, the race that began the remorseless run to the line, Vettel reeled in pole-sitting Hamilton and disappeared into the distance. How to compare that with Alonso's charge from ninth on the grid to take second? Some fans had already begun to make their feelings known regarding Vettel's dominance. At Silverstone, where he ground to a halt while leading, sections of the crowd greeted what would be his sole retirement of the year with unconcealed delight. The boo boys were out in force as Vettel closed in on his fourth title, clinched in India with another precision drive. He joined the quadruple club – Fangio, Prost and Schumacher were the only other members – with three rounds to spare. The 'Professor' was 38 when he lifted his fourth crown, eight years after the first. At 26, Vettel had time on his side to eclipse Fangio and even his compatriot – with five and seven titles respectively. If he prevailed in 2014 he would stand apart; no one had ever won five back-to-back championships. Vettel was also nudging up other lists: now fourth in the all-time standings for race wins on 39, just two short of Senna; and third behind Michael and Ayrton in terms of pole positions.

Consistency reaps rewards

It was almost inevitable that one man and the same team scooping all the prizes would bring as many brickbats as bouquets. David Coulthard was one who had no time for the doubters, urging that the 'Is Vettel a true great?' debate had to be put to bed. Irrespective of how good the car was, becoming a four-time champion at such a tender age was 'simply astonishing', said DC. The nine-race winning streak matched Alberto Ascari's achievement spread over the 1952–53 seasons. Thirteen wins for the year equalled Schumacher's record 2004 haul. It was a bravura display of metronomic consistency, rendered all the more impressive by the fact that Webber – setting aside the unfortunate events in Malaysia – did not add to his victory tally as he bowed out after 215 races. 'What we've witnessed this year is something very, very special,' said team boss Christian Horner.

Those who wanted to see how Seb fared in a less dominant car looked as if they might get their wish as Red Bull found themselves well off the pace going into the new era. The biggest shake-up in the sport's history saw the introduction of 1.6-litre V6 engines, with turbos back for the first time since the late 1980s. It was a hybrid powertrain that went well beyond KERS, harvesting energy from both the brakes and exhaust gases. Add in the reduced 100kg fuel allowance, changes to the nose, front and rear wings, along with a different aerodynamic picture thanks to new regulations governing the exhaust position, and it made the backroom boffins' job more taxing than usual. The most controversial amendment, however, was the introduction of double points for the final race – Abu Dhabi this year – a transparent attempt to prevent dead rubbers that attracted plenty of criticism for its arbitrariness. Before then there are two new stops on the calendar. Austria is back for the first time since 2003, and the circus is also set to roll into Russia for the first time, at the Black Sea resort of Sochi that had just hosted the Winter Olympics.

There are plenty of individuals with a lot to prove in 2014. Kevin Magnussen, fresh from his success in Formula Renault, heads the rookie contingent, taking Pérez's McLaren seat. Ron Dennis returns to an executive position, vowing the team would bounce back after slipping to fifth in the 2013 constructors' race, almost 200 points shy of fourth-placed Lotus. Pérez and Massa are out to prove that their old teams were wrong to let them go; Ricciardo that he was worth promotion to Webber's seat; Hulkenberg that he should have been snapped up by one of the top teams; and even Vettel, that he could exert his influence in a car that might not be the class act of the field. Add in the Alonso-Räikkönen intra-team face-off, and potential fireworks between Hamilton and Rosberg if Mercedes lives up to its favourites' tag, and it promises to be the most intriguing season for many a long year.

STATISTICS

Drivers' Championship

1950

	Driver	Country	Car	Points
1	Nino Farina	Italy	Alfa Romeo	30
2	Juan Manuel Fangio	Argentina	Alfa Romeo	27
3	Luigi Fagioli	Italy	Alfa Romeo	24
4	Louis Rosier	France	Lago-Talbot	13
5	Alberto Ascari	Italy	Ferrari	11
6	Johnnie Parsons	USA	Kurtis Offenhauser	8
7	Bill Holland	USA	Deidt Offenhauser	6
8	Prince Bira	Thailand	Maserati	5
9	Mauri Rose	USA	Deidt Offenhauser	4
	Reg Parnell	Great Britain	Alfa Romeo, Maserati	4
	Louis Chiron	Monaco	Maserati	4
	Peter Whitehead	Great Britain	Ferrari	4

1951

	Driver	Country	Car	Points
1	Juan Manuel Fangio	Argentina	Alfa Romeo	31
2	Alberto Ascari	Italy	Ferrari	25
3	José Froilán González	Argentina	Lago-Talbot and Ferrari	24
4	Nino Farina	Italy	Alfa Romeo Alfetta	19
5	Luigi Villoresi	Italy	Ferrari	15
6	Piero Taruffi	Italy	Ferrari	10
7	Lee Wallard	USA	Kurtis Offenhauser	9
8	Felice Bonetto	Italy	Alfa Romeo	7
9	Mike Nazaruk	USA	Kurtis Offenhauser	6
10	Reg Parnell	Great Britain	Ferrari, BRM	5

1952

	Driver	Country	Car	Points
1	Alberto Ascari	Italy	Ferrari	36
2	Nino Farina	Italy	Ferrari	24
3	Piero Taruffi	Italy	Ferrari	22
4	Rudi Fischer	Switzerland	Ferrari	10
	Mike Hawthorn	Great Britain	Cooper Bristol	10
6	Robert Manzon	France	Gordini	9
7	Troy Ruttman	USA	Kuzma Offenhauser	8
	Luigi Villoresi	Italy	Ferrari	8
9	José Froilán González	Argentina	Maserati	6
10	Jim Rathmann	USA	Kurtis Offenhauser	6

1953

	Driver	Country	Car	Points
1	Alberto Ascari	Italy	Ferrari	34.5
2	Juan Manuel Fangio	Argentina	Maserati	28
3	Nino Farina	Italy	Ferrari	26
4	Mike Hawthorn	Great Britain	Ferrari	19
5	Luigi Villoresi	Italy	Ferrari	17
6	José Froilán González	Argentina	Maserati	13.5
7	Bill Vukovich	USA	Kurtis Offenhauser	9
8	Emanuel de Graffenried	Switzerland	Maserati	7
9	Felice Bonetto	Italy	Maserati	6.5
10	Art Cross	USA	Kurtis Offenhauser	6

1954

	Driver	Country	Car	Points
1	Juan Manuel Fangio	Argentina	Maserati, Mercedes-Benz	42
2	José Froilán González	Argentina	Ferrari	25.14
3	Mike Hawthorn	Great Britain	Ferrari	24.64
4	Maurice Trintignant	France	Ferrari	17
5	Karl Kling	Germany	Mercedez-Benz	12
6	Bill Vukovich	USA	Kurtis Offenhauser	8
	Hans Herrmann	Germany	Mercedes-Benz	8
8	Jimmy Bryan	USA	Kuzma Offenhauser	6
	Nino Farina	Italy	Ferrari	6
	Luigi Musso	Italy	Maserati	6
	Roberto Mieres	Argentina	Maserati	6

1955

	Driver	Country	Car	Points
1	Juan Manuel Fangio	Argentina	Mercedes-Benz	40
2	Stirling Moss	Great Britain	Mercedes-Benz	23
3	Eugenio Castellotti	Italy	Lancia, Ferrari	12
4	Maurice Trintignant	France	Ferrari	11.33
5	Nino Farina	Italy	Ferrari, Lancia-Ferrari	10.33
6	Piero Taruffi	Italy	Ferrari, Mercedes-Benz	9
7	Bob Sweikert	USA	Kurtis Offenhauser	8
8	Roberto Mieres	Argentina	Maserati	7
9	Tony Bettenhausen	USA	Kurtis Offenhauser	6
	Jean Behra	France	Maserati	6
	Luigi Musso	Italy	Maserati	6

1956

	Driver	Country	Car	Points
1	Juan Manuel Fangio	Argentina	Lancia-Ferrari	30
2	Stirling Moss	Great Britain	Maserati	27
3	Peter Collins	Great Britain	Ferrari, Lancia-Ferrari	25
4	Jean Behra	France	Maserati	22
5	Pat Flaherty	USA	Watson Offenhauser	8
6	Eugenio Castellotti	Italy	Lancia-Ferrari	7.5
7	Sam Hanks	USA	Kurtis Offenhauser	6
	Paul Frere	Belgium	Lancia-Ferrari	6
	Francesco Godia	Spain	Maserati	6
10	Jack Fairman	Great Britain	Connaught-Alta	5

1957

	Driver	Country	Car	Points
1	Juan Manuel Fangio	Argentina	Maserati	40
2	Stirling Moss	Great Britain	Maserati, Vanwall	25
3	Luigi Musso	Italy	Lancia-Ferrari	16
4	Mike Hawthorn	Great Britain	Lancia-Ferrari	13
5	Tony Brooks	Great Britain	Vanwall	11
6	Harry Schell	USA	Maserati	10
	Masten Gregory	USA	Maserati	10
8	Peter Collins	Great Britain	Lancia-Ferrari	8
	Sam Hanks	USA	Epperly Offenhauser	8
10	Jean Behra	France	Maserati	6

1958

	Driver	Country	Car	Points
1	Mike Hawthorn	Great Britain	Ferrari Dino	42
2	Stirling Moss	Great Britain	Cooper, Vanwall	41
3	Tony Brooks	Great Britain	Vanwall	24
4	Roy Salvadori	Great Britain	Cooper	15
5	Peter Collins	Great Britain	Ferrari Dino	14
	Harry Schell	USA	Maserati	14
7	Luigi Musso	Italy	Ferrari Dino	12
	Maurice Trintignant	France	Cooper, Maserati	12
9	Stuart Lewis-Evans	Great Britain	Vanwall	11
10	Phil Hill	USA	Maserati, Ferrari	9
	Taffi von Trips	Germany	Ferrari, Porsche	9
	Jean Behra	France	Maserati	9

1959

	Driver	Country	Car	Points
1	Jack Brabham	Australia	Cooper	31
2	Tony Brooks	Great Britain	Ferrari Dino, Vanwall	27
3	Stirling Moss	Great Britain	Cooper, BRM	25.5
4	Phil Hill	USA	Ferrari Dino	20
5	Maurice Trintignant	France	Cooper	19
6	Bruce McLaren	New Zealand	Cooper	16.5
7	Dan Gurney	USA	Ferrari Dino	13
8	Jo Bonnier	Sweden	BRM	10
	Masten Gregory	USA	Cooper	10
10	Rodger Ward	USA	Watson Offenhauser	8

1960

	Driver	Country	Car	Points
1	Jack Brabham	Australia	Cooper	43
2	Bruce McLaren	New Zealand	Cooper	34
3	Stirling Moss	Great Britain	Cooper, Lotus	19
4	Innes Ireland	Great Britain	Lotus	18
5	Phil Hill	USA	Ferrari Dino	16
6	Olivier Gendebien	Belgium	Cooper	10
	Taffi von Trips	Germany	Ferrari Dino, Cooper	10
8	Jimmy Clark	Great Britain	Lotus	8
	Richie Ginther	USA	Ferrari Dino, Scarab	8
	Jim Rathmann	USA	Watson Offenhauser	8

Juan Manuel Fangio

1961

	Driver	Country	Car	Points
1	Phil Hill	USA	Ferrari Dino	34
2	Taffi von Trips	Germany	Ferrari Dino	33
3	Stirling Moss	Great Britain	Lotus, Ferguson	21
	Dan Gurney	USA	Porsche	21
5	Richie Ginther	USA	Ferrari Dino	16
6	Innes Ireland	Great Britain	Lotus	12
7	Jimmy Clark	Great Britain	Lotus	11
	Bruce McLaren	New Zealand	Cooper	11
9	Giancarlo Baghetti	Italy	Ferrari Dino	9
10	Tony Brooks	Great Britain	BRM	6

1962

1	Graham Hill	Great Britain	BRM	42
2	Jimmy Clark	Great Britain	Lotus	30
3	Bruce McLaren	New Zealand	Cooper	27
4	John Surtees	Great Britain	Lotus	19
5	Dan Gurney	USA	Porsche	15
6	Phil Hill	USA	Ferrari, Porsche	14
7	Tony Maggs	South Africa	Cooper	13
8	Richie Ginther	USA	BRM	10
9	Jack Brabham	Australia	Lotus, Brabham	9
10	Trevor Taylor	Great Britain	Lotus	6

1963

1	Jimmy Clark	Great Britain	Lotus	54
2	Graham Hill	Great Britain	BRM	29
	Richie Ginther	USA	BRM	29
4	John Surtees	Great Britain	Ferrari	22
5	Dan Gurney	USA	Brabham	19
6	Bruce McLaren	New Zealand	Cooper	17
7	Jack Brabham	Australia	Brabham	14
8	Tony Maggs	South Africa	Cooper	9
9	Innes Ireland	Great Britain	Lotus, RP	6
	Lorenzo Bandini	Italy	BRM, Ferrari-Aero	6
	Jo Bonnier	Sweden	Cooper	6

1964

1	John Surtees	Great Britain	Ferrari	40
2	Graham Hill	Great Britain	BRM	39
3	Jimmy Clark	Great Britain	Lotus	32
4	Lorenzo Bandini	Italy	Ferrari-Aero	23
	Richie Ginther	USA	BRM	23
6	Dan Gurney	USA	Brabham	19
7	Bruce McLaren	New Zealand	Cooper	13
8	Jack Brabham	Australia	Brabham	11
	Peter Arundell	Great Britain	Lotus	11
10	Jo Siffert	Switzerland	Lotus, Brabham	7

1965

1	Jimmy Clark	Great Britain	Lotus	54
2	Graham Hill	Great Britain	BRM	40
3	Jackie Stewart	Great Britain	BRM	33
4	Dan Gurney	USA	Brabham	25
5	John Surtees	Great Britain	Ferrari	17
6	Lorenzo Bandini	Italy	Ferrari	13
7	Richie Ginther	USA	Honda	11
8	Bruce McLaren	New Zealand	Cooper	10
	Mike Spence	Great Britain	Lotus	10
10	Jack Brabham	Australia	Brabham	9

1966

	Driver	Country	Car	Points
1	Jack Brabham	Australia	Brabham	42
2	John Surtees	Great Britain	Ferrari, Cooper	28
3	Jochen Rindt	Austria	Cooper	22
4	Denny Hulme	New Zealand	Brabham	18
5	Graham Hill	Great Britain	BRM	17
6	Jimmy Clark	Great Britain	Lotus	16
7	Jackie Stewart	Great Britain	BRM	14
8	Lorenzo Bandini	Italy	Ferrari Dino	12
	Mike Parkes	Great Britain	Ferrari	12
10	Lodovico Scarfiotti	Italy	Ferrari	9

1967

1	Denny Hulme	New Zealand	Brabham	51
2	Jack Brabham	Australia	Brabham	46
3	Jimmy Clark	Great Britain	Lotus	41
4	John Surtees	Great Britain	Honda	20
	Chris Amon	New Zealand	Ferrari	20
6	Pedro Rodriguez	Mexico	Cooper	15
	Graham Hill	Great Britain	Lotus	15
8	Dan Gurney	USA	Eagle-Climax	13
9	Jackie Stewart	Great Britain	BRM	10
10	Mike Spence	Great Britain	BRM	9

1968

1	Graham Hill	Great Britain	Lotus	48
2	Jackie Stewart	Great Britain	Matra	36
3	Denny Hulme	New Zealand	McLaren	33
4	Jacky Ickx	Belgium	Ferrari	27
5	Bruce McLaren	New Zealand	McLaren	22
6	Pedro Rodriguez	Mexico	BRM	18
7	Jo Siffert	Switzerland	Cooper, Lotus	12
	John Surtees	Great Britain	Honda	12
9	John-Pierre Beltoise	France	Matra	11
10	Chris Amon	New Zealand	Ferrari	10

1969

1	Jackie Stewart	Great Britain	Matra	63
2	Jacky Ickx	Belgium	Brabham	37
3	Bruce McLaren	New Zealand	McLaren	26
4	Jochen Rindt	Austria	Lotus	22
5	Jean-Pierre Beltoise	France	Matra	21
6	Denny Hulme	New Zealand	McLaren	20
7	Graham Hill	Great Britain	Lotus	19
8	Piers Courage	Great Britain	Brabham	16
9	Jo Siffert	Switzerland	Lotus	15
10	Jack Brabham	Australia	Brabham	14

1970

1	Jochen Rindt	Austria	Lotus	45
2	Jacky Ickx	Belgium	Ferrari	40
3	Clay Regazzoni	Switzerland	Ferrari	33
4	Denny Hulme	New Zealand	McLaren	27
5	Jack Brabham	Australia	Brabham	25
	Jackie Stewart	Great Britain	March, Tyrrell	25
7	Chris Amon	New Zealand	March	23
	Pedro Rodriguez	Mexico	BRM	23
9	Jean-Pierre Beltoise	France	Matra-Simca	16
10	Emerson Fittipaldi	Brazil	Lotus	12

Jackie Stewart

1971

	Driver	Country	Car	Points
1	Jackie Stewart	Great Britain	Tyrrell	62
2	Ronnie Peterson	Sweden	March	33
3	François Cévert	France	Tyrrell	26
4	Jacky Ickx	Belgium	Ferrari	19
5	Jo Siffert	Switzerland	BRM	19
6	Emerson Fittipaldi	Brazil	Lotus-Turbine	16
7	Clay Regazzoni	Switzerland	Ferrari	13
8	Mario Andretti	USA	Ferrari	12
9	Chris Amon	New Zealand	Matra-Simca	9
	Peter Gethin	Great Britain	McLaren	9
	Denny Hulme	New Zealand	McLaren	9
	Pedro Rodriguez	Mexico	BRM	9
	Reine Wisell	Sweden	Lotus-Turbine	9

1972

1	Emerson Fittipaldi	Brazil	Lotus	61
2	Jackie Stewart	Great Britain	Tyrrell	45
3	Denny Hulme	New Zealand	McLaren	39
4	Jacky Ickx	Belgium	Ferrari	27
5	Peter Revson	USA	McLaren	23
6	François Cévert	France	Tyrrell	15
	Clay Regazzoni	Switzerland	Ferrari	15
8	Mike Hailwood	Great Britain	Surtees	13
9	Chris Amon	New Zealand	Matra-Simca	12
	Ronnie Peterson	Sweden	March	12

1973

1	Jackie Stewart	Great Britain	Tyrrell	71
2	Emerson Fittipaldi	Brazil	JPS-Lotus	55
3	Ronnie Peterson	Sweden	JPS-Lotus	52
4	François Cévert	France	Tyrrell	47
5	Peter Revson	USA	McLaren	38
6	Denny Hulme	New Zealand	McLaren	26
7	Carlos Reutemann	Argentina	Brabham	16
8	James Hunt	Great Britain	March	14
9	Jacky Ickx	Belgium	Ferrari, McLaren Iso Williams/Marlboro	12
10	Jean-Pierre Beltoise	France	BRM	9

1974

	Driver	Country	Car	Points
1	Emerson Fittipaldi	Brazil	McLaren	55
2	Clay Regazzoni	Switzerland	Ferrari	52
3	Jody Scheckter	South Africa	Tyrrell	45
4	Niki Lauda	Austria	Ferrari	38
5	Ronnie Peterson	Sweden	Lotus	35
6	Carlos Reutemann	Argentina	Brabham	32
7	Denny Hulme	New Zealand	McLaren	20
8	James Hunt	Great Britain	March-Hesketh	15
9	Patrick Depailler	France	Tyrrell	14
10	Mike Hailwood	Great Britain	McLaren	12
	Jacky Ickx	Belgium	Lotus	12

1975

	Driver	Country	Car	Points
1	Niki Lauda	Austria	Ferrari	64.5
2	Emerson Fittipaldi	Brazil	McLaren	45
3	Carlos Reutemann	Argentina	Brabham	37
4	James Hunt	Great Britain	Hesketh	33
5	Clay Regazzoni	Switzerland	Ferrari	25
6	Carlos Pace	Brazil	Brabham	24
7	Jochen Mass	Germany	McLaren	20
	Jody Scheckter	South Africa	Tyrrell	20
9	Patrick Depailler	France	Tyrrell	12
10	Tom Pryce	Great Britain	Shadow	8

1976

	Driver	Country	Car	Points
1	James Hunt	Great Britain	McLaren	69
2	Niki Lauda	Austria	Ferrari	68
3	Jody Scheckter	South Africa	Tyrrell	49
4	Patrick Depailler	France	Tyrrell	39
5	Clay Regazzoni	Switzerland	Ferrari	31
6	Mario Andretti	USA	Lotus, Parnell	22
7	Jacques Laffite	France	Ligier	20
	John Watson	Great Britain	Penske	20
9	Jochen Mass	Germany	McLaren	19
10	Gunnar Nilsson	Sweden	Lotus	11

1977

	Driver	Country	Car	Points
1	Niki Lauda	Austria	Ferrari	72
2	Jody Scheckter	South Africa	Wolf	55
3	Mario Andretti	USA	Lotus	47
4	Carlos Reutemann	Argentina	Ferrari	42
5	James Hunt	Great Britain	McLaren	40
6	Jochen Mass	Germany	McLaren	25
7	Alan Jones	Australia	Shadow	22
8	Gunnar Nilsson	Sweden	Lotus	20
	Patrick Depailler	France	Tyrrell	20
10	Jacques Laffite	France	Ligier	18

1978

	Driver	Country	Car	Points
1	Mario Andretti	USA	Lotus	64
2	Ronnie Peterson	Sweden	Lotus	51
3	Carlos Reutemann	Argentina	Ferrari	48
4	Niki Lauda	Austria	Brabham	44
5	Patrick Depailler	France	Tyrrell	34
6	John Watson	Great Britain	Brabham	25
7	Jody Scheckter	South Africa	Wolf	24
8	Jacques Laffite	France	Ligier	19
9	Gilles Villeneuve	Canada	Ferrari	17
	Emerson Fittipaldi	Brazil	Copersucar	17

1979

	Driver	Country	Car	Points
1	Jody Scheckter	South Africa	Ferrari	51
2	Gilles Villeneuve	Canada	Ferrari	47
3	Alan Jones	Australia	Williams	40
4	Jacques Laffite	France	Ligier	36
5	Clay Regazzoni	Switzerland	Williams	29
6	Carlos Reutemann	Argentina	Lotus	20
	Patrick Depailler	France	Ligier	20
8	René Arnoux	France	Renault	17
9	John Watson	Great Britain	McLaren	15
10	Mario Andretti	USA	Lotus	14

1980

	Driver	Country	Car	Points
1	Alan Jones	Australia	Williams	67
2	Nelson Piquet	Brazil	Brabham	54
3	Carlos Reutemann	Argentina	Williams	42
4	Jacques Laffite	France	Ligier	34
5	Didier Pironi	France	Ligier	32
6	René Arnoux	France	Renault	29
7	Elio de Angelis	Italy	Lotus	13
8	Jean-Pierre Jabouille	France	Renault	9
9	Riccardo Patrese	Italy	Arrows	7
10	Derek Daly	Ireland	Tyrrell	6

1981

	Driver	Country	Car	Points
1	Nelson Piquet	Brazil	Brabham	50
2	Carlos Reutemann	Argentina	Williams	49
3	Alan Jones	Australia	Williams	46
4	Jacques Laffite	France	Talbot-Ligier	44
5	Alain Prost	France	Renault	43
6	John Watson	Great Britain	McLaren	27
7	Gilles Villeneuve	Canada	Ferrari, Arrows	25
8	Elio de Angelis	Italy	Lotus	14
9	René Arnoux	France	Renault	11
	Hector Rebaque	Mexico	Brabham	11

1982

	Driver	Country	Car	Points
1	Keke Rosberg	Finland	Williams	44
2	Didier Pironi	France	Ferrari	39
	John Watson	Great Britain	McLaren	39
4	Alain Prost	France	Renault	34
5	Niki Lauda	Austria	McLaren	30
6	René Arnoux	France	Renault	28
7	Patrick Tambay	France	Arrows, Ferrari	25
	Michele Alboreto	Italy	Tyrrell	25
9	Elio de Angelis	Italy	Lotus	23
10	Riccardo Patrese	Italy	Brabham	21

1983

	Driver	Country	Car	Points
1	Nelson Piquet	Brazil	Brabham	59
2	Alain Prost	France	Renault	57
3	René Arnoux	France	Ferrari	49
4	Patrick Tambay	France	Ferrari	40
5	Keke Rosberg	Finland	Williams	27
6	John Watson	Great Britain	McLaren	22
	Eddie Cheever	USA	Renault	22
8	Andrea de Cesaris	Italy	Alfa Romeo	15
9	Riccardo Patrese	Italy	Brabham	13
10	Niki Lauda	Austria	McLaren	12

1984

Driver	Country	Car	Points
1 Niki Lauda	Austria	McLaren	72
2 Alain Prost	France	McLaren	71.5
3 Elio de Angelis	Italy	Lotus	34
4 Michele Alboreto	Italy	Ferrari	30.5
5 Nelson Piquet	Brazil	Brabham	29
6 René Arnoux	France	Ferrari	27
7 Derek Warwick	Great Britain	Renault	23
8 Keke Rosberg	Finland	Williams	20.5
9 Nigel Mansell	Great Britain	Lotus	13
Ayrton Senna	Brazil	Toleman	13

1985

Driver	Country	Car	Points
1 Alain Prost	France	McLaren	73
2 Michele Alboreto	Italy	Ferrari	53
3 Keke Rosberg	Finland	Williams	40
4 Ayrton Senna	Brazil	Lotus	38
5 Elio de Angelis	Italy	Lotus, Brabham	33
6 Nigel Mansell	Great Britain	Williams	31
7 Stefan Johansson	Sweden	Tyrrell, Ferrari	26
8 Nelson Piquet	Brazil	Brabham	21
9 Jacques Laffite	France	Ligier	16
10 Niki Lauda	Austria	McLaren	14

1986

Driver	Country	Car	Points
1 Alain Prost	France	McLaren	72
2 Nigel Mansell	Great Britain	Williams	70
3 Nelson Piquet	Brazil	Williams	69
4 Ayrton Senna	Brazil	JPS/Lotus	55
5 Stefan Johansson	Sweden	Ferrari	23
6 Keke Rosberg	Finland	McLaren	22
7 Gerhard Berger	Austria	Benetton	17
8 Jacques Laffite	France	Ligier	14
René Arnoux	France	Ligier	14
Michele Alboreto	Italy	Ferrari	14

1987

Driver	Country	Car	Points
1 Nelson Piquet	Brazil	Williams	73
2 Nigel Mansell	Great Britain	Williams	61
3 Ayrton Senna	Brazil	JPS/Lotus	57
4 Alain Prost	France	McLaren	46
5 Gerhard Berger	Austria	Ferrari	36
6 Stefan Johansson	Sweden	McLaren	30
7 Michele Alboreto	Italy	Ferrari	17
8 Thierry Boutsen	Belgium	Benetton	16
9 Teo Fabi	Italy	Benetton	12
10 Eddie Cheever	USA	Arrows	8

1988

Driver	Country	Car	Points
1 Ayrton Senna	Brazil	McLaren	90
2 Alain Prost	France	McLaren	87
3 Gerhard Berger	Austria	Ferrari	41
4 Thierry Boutsen	Belgium	Benetton	27
5 Michele Alboreto	Italy	Ferrari	24
6 Nelson Piquet	Brazil	Lotus	22
7 Ivan Capelli	Italy	March	17
Derek Warwick	Great Britain	Arrows	17
9 Alessandro Nannini	Italy	Benetton	12
Nigel Mansell	Great Britain	Williams	12

1989

Driver	Country	Car	Points
1 Alain Prost	France	McLaren	76
2 Ayrton Senna	Brazil	McLaren	60
3 Riccardo Patrese	Italy	Williams	40
4 Nigel Mansell	Great Britain	Ferrari	38
5 Thierry Boutsen	Belgium	Williams	37
6 Alessandro Nannini	Italy	Benetton	32
7 Gerhard Berger	Austria	Ferrari	21
8 Nelson Piquet	Brabham	Lotus	12
9 Jean Alesi	France	Tyrrell	8
10 Derek Warwick	Great Britain	Arrows	7

1990

Driver	Country	Car	Points
1 Ayrton Senna	Brazil	McLaren	78
2 Alain Prost	France	Ferrari	71
3 Nelson Piquet	Brazil	Benetton	43
Gerhard Berger	Austria	McLaren	43
5 Nigel Mansell	Great Britain	Ferrari	37
6 Thierry Boutsen	Belgium	Williams	34
7 Riccardo Patrese	Italy	Williams	23
8 Alessandro Nannini	Italy	Benetton	21
9 Jean Alesi	France	Tyrrell	13
10 Roberto Moreno	Brazil	EuroBrun, Benetton	6
Ivan Capelli	Italy	March	6
Aguri Suzuki	Japan	Lola-Larrousse	6

1991

Driver	Country	Car	Points
1 Ayrton Senna	Brazil	McLaren	96
2 Nigel Mansell	Great Britain	Williams	72
3 Riccardo Patrese	Italy	Williams	53
4 Gerhard Berger	Austria	McLaren	43
5 Alain Prost	France	Ferrari	34
6 Nelson Piquet	Brazil	Benetton	26.5
7 Jean Alesi	France	Ferrari	21
8 Stefano Modena	Italy	Tyrrell	10
9 Andrea de Cesaris	Italy	Jordan	9
10 Roberto Moreno	Brazil	Benetton, Jordan	8

1992

Driver	Country	Car	Points
1 Nigel Mansell	Great Britain	Williams	108
2 Riccardo Patrese	Italy	Williams	56
3 Michael Schumacher	Germany	Benetton	53
4 Ayrton Senna	Brazil	McLaren	50
5 Gerhard Berger	Austria	McLaren	49
6 Martin Brundle	Great Britain	Benetton	38
7 Jean Alesi	France	Ferrari	18
8 Mika Häkkinen	Finland	Lotus	11
9 Andrea de Cesaris	Italy	Tyrrell	8
10 Michele Alboreto	Italy	Footwork	6

1993

Driver	Country	Car	Points
1 Alain Prost	France	Williams	99
2 Ayrton Senna	Brazil	McLaren	73
3 Damon Hill	Great Britain	Williams	69
4 Michael Schumacher	Germany	Benetton	52
5 Riccardo Patrese	Italy	Benetton	20
6 Jean Alesi	France	Ferrari	16
7 Martin Brundle	Great Britain	Ligier	13
8 Gerhard Berger	Austria	Ferrari	12
9 Johnny Herbert	Great Britain	Lotus	11
10 Mark Blundell	Great Britain	Ligier	10

1994

	Driver	Country	Car	Points
1	Michael Schumacher	Germany	Benetton	92
2	Damon Hill	Great Britain	Williams	91
3	Gerhard Berger	Austria	Ferrari	41
4	Mika Häkkinen	Finland	McLaren	26
5	Jean Alesi	France	Ferrari	24
6	Rubens Barrichello	Brazil	Jordan	19
7	Martin Brundle	Great Britain	McLaren	16
8	David Coulthard	Great Britain	Williams	14
9	Nigel Mansell	Great Britain	Williams	13
10	Jos Verstappen	Netherlands	Benetton	10

1995

	Driver	Country	Car	Points
1	Michael Schumacher	Germany	Benetton	102
2	Damon Hill	Great Britain	Williams	69
3	David Coulthard	Great Britain	Williams	49
4	Johnny Herbert	Great Britain	Benetton	45
5	Jean Alesi	France	Ferrari	42
6	Gerhard Berger	Austria	Ferrari	31
7	Mika Häkkinen	Finland	McLaren	17
8	Olivier Panis	France	Ligier	16
9	Heinz-Harald Frentzen	Germany	Sauber	15
10	Mark Blundell	Great Britain	McLaren	13

1996

	Driver	Country	Car	Points
1	Damon Hill	Great Britain	Williams	97
2	Jacques Villeneuve	Canada	Williams	78
3	Michael Schumacher	Germany	Ferrari	59
4	Jean Alesi	France	Benetton	47
5	Mika Häkkinen	Finland	McLaren	31
6	Gerhard Berger	Austria	Benetton	21
7	David Coulthard	Great Britain	McLaren	18
8	Rubens Barrichello	Brazil	Jordan	14
9	Olivier Panis	France	Ligier	13
10	Eddie Irvine	Ireland	Ferrari	1

1997

	Driver	Country	Car	Points
1	Jacques Villeneuve	Canada	Williams	81
2	Heinz-Harald Frentzen	Germany	Williams	42
3	David Coulthard	Great Britain	McLaren	36
	Jean Alesi	France	Benetton	36
5	Gerhard Berger	Austria	Benetton	27
	Mika Häkkinen	Finland	McLaren	27
7	Eddie Irvine	Ireland	Ferrari	24
8	Giancarlo Fisichella	Italy	Jordan	20
9	Olivier Panis	France	Prost	16
10	Johnny Herbert	Great Britain	Sauber	15

1998

	Driver	Country	Car	Points
1	Mika Häkkinen	Finland	McLaren-Mercedes	100
2	Michael Schumacher	Germany	Ferrari	86
3	David Coulthard	Great Britain	McLaren-Mercedes	56
4	Eddie Irvine	Ireland	Ferrari	47
5	Jacques Villeneuve	Canada	Williams-Mecachrome	21
6	Damon Hill	Great Britain	Jordan-Mugen Honda	20
7	Heinz-Harald Frentzen	Austria	Williams-Mecachrome	17
	Alexander Wurz	Austria	Benetton-Playlife	17
9	Giancarlo Fisichella	Italy	Benetton-Playlife	16
10	Ralf Schumacher	Germany	Jordan-Mugen Honda	14

1999

	Driver	Country	Car	Points
1	Mika Häkkinen	Finland	McLaren-Mercedes	76
2	Eddie Irvine	Ireland	Ferrari	74
3	Heinz-Harald Frentzen	Germany	Jordan-Mugen Honda	55
4	David Coulthard	Great Britain	McLaren-Mercedes	48
5	Michael Schumacher	Germany	Ferrari	44
6	Ralf Schumacher	Germany	Williams-Supertec	35
7	Rubens Barrichello	Brazil	Stewart-Ford	21
8	Johnny Herbert	Great Britain	Stewart-Ford	15
9	Giancarlo Fisichella	Italy	Benetton-Playlife	13
10	Mika Salo	Finland	Ferrari	10

2000

	Driver	Country	Car	Points
1	Michael Schumacher	Germany	Ferrari	108
2	Mika Häkkinen	Finland	McLaren-Mercedes	89
3	David Coulthard	Great Britain	McLaren-Mercedes	73
4	Rubens Barrichello	Brazil	Ferrari	62
5	Ralf Schumacher	Germany	Williams-BMW	24
6	Giancarlo Fisichella	Italy	Benetton-Playlife	18
7	Jacques Villeneuve	Canada	BAR-Honda	17
8	Jenson Button	Great Britain	Williams-BMW	12
9	Heinz-Harald Frentzen	Germany	Jordan-Mugen Honda	11
10	Jarno Trulli	Italy	Jordan-Mugen Honda	6

2001

	Driver	Country	Car	Points
1	Michael Schumacher	Germany	Ferrari	123
2	David Coulthard	Great Britain	McLaren-Mercedes	65
3	Rubens Barrichello	Brazil	Ferrari	56
4	Ralf Schumacher	Germany	Williams-BMW	49
5	Mika Häkkinen	Finland	McLaren-Mercedes	37
6	Juan Pablo Montoya	Colombia	Williams-BMW	31
7	Jacques Villeneuve	Canada	BAR-Honda	12
	Nick Heidfeld	Germany	Sauber-Petronas	12
	Jarno Trulli	Italy	Jordan-Honda	12
10	Kimi Räikkönen	Finland	Sauber-Petronas	9

2002

	Driver	Country	Car	Points
1	Michael Schumacher	Germany	Ferrari	144
2	Rubens Barrichello	Brazil	Ferrari	77
3	Juan Pablo Montoya	Colombia	Williams-BMW	50
4	Ralf Schumacher	Germany	Williams-BMW	42
5	David Coulthard	Great Britain	McLaren-Mercedes	41
6	Kimi Räikkönen	Finland	McLaren-Mercedes	24
7	Jenson Button	Great Britain	Renault	14
8	Jarno Trulli	Italy	Renault	9
9	Eddie Irvine	Ireland	Jaguar-Ford	8
10	Nick Heidfeld	Germany	Sauber, Petronas	7
	Giancarlo Fisichella	Italy	Jordan-Honda	7

2003

	Driver	Country	Car	Points
1	Michael Schumacher	Germany	Ferrari	93
2	Kimi Räikkönen	Finland	McLaren-Mercedes	91
3	Juan Pablo Montoya	Colombia	Williams-BMW	82
4	Rubens Barrichello	Brazil	Ferrari	65
5	Ralf Schumacher	Germany	Williams-BMW	58
6	Fernando Alonso	Spain	Renault	55
7	David Coulthard	Great Britain	McLaren-Mercedes	51
8	Jarno Trulli	Italy	Renault	33
9	Jenson Button	Great Britain	BAR-Honda	17
	Mark Webber	Australia	Jaguar-Ford	17

2004

	Driver	Country	Car	Points
1	Michael Schumacher	Germany	Ferrari	148
2	Rubens Barrichello	Brazil	Ferrari	114
3	Jenson Button	Great Britain	BAR-Honda	85
4	Fernando Alonso	Spain	Renault	59
5	Juan Pablo Montoya	Colombia	Williams-BMW	58
6	Jarno Trulli	Italy	Renault, Toyota	46
7	Kimi Räikkönen	Finland	McLaren-Mercedes	45
8	Takuma Sato	Japan	BAR-Honda	34
9	Ralf Schumacher	Germany	Williams-BMW	24
	David Coulthard	Great Britain	McLaren-Mercedes	24

2005

1	Fernando Alonso	Spain	Renault	133
2	Kimi Räikkönen	Finland	McLaren-Mercedes	112
3	Michael Schumacher	Germany	Ferrari	62
4	Juan Pablo Montoya	Colombia	McLaren-Mercedes	60
5	Giancarlo Fisichella	Italy	Renault	58
6	Ralf Schumacher	Germany	Toyota	45
7	Jarno Trulli	Italy	Toyota	43
8	Rubens Barrichello	Brazil	Ferrari	38
9	Jenson Button	Great Britain	BAR-Honda	37
10	Mark Webber	Australia	Williams-BMW	36

2006

1	Fernando Alonso	Spain	Renault	134
2	Michael Schumacher	Germany	Ferrari	121
3	Felipe Massa	Brazil	Ferrari	80
4	Giancarlo Fisichella	Italy	Renault	72
5	Kimi Räikkönen	Finland	McLaren-Mercedes	65
6	Jenson Button	Great Britain	Honda	56
7	Rubens Barrichello	Brazil	Honda	30
8	Juan Pablo Montoya	Colombia	McLaren-Mercedes	26
9	Nick Heidfeld	Germany	BMW Sauber	23
10	Ralf Schumacher	Germany	Toyota	20

2007

1	Kimi Räikkönen	Finland	Ferrari	110
2	Lewis Hamilton	Great Britain	McLaren-Mercedes	109
	Fernando Alonso	Spain	McLaren-Mercedes	109
4	Felipe Massa	Brazil	Ferrari	94
5	Nick Heidfeld	Germany	BMW Sauber	61
6	Robert Kubica	Poland	BMW Sauber	39
7	Heikki Kovalainen	Finland	Renault	30
8	Giancarlo Fisichella	Italy	Renault	21
9	Nico Rosberg	Germany	Williams	20
10	David Coulthard	Great Britain	Red Bull	14

2008

1	Lewis Hamilton	Great Britain	McLaren-Mercedes	98
2	Felipe Massa	Brazil	Ferrari	97
3	Kimi Räikkönen	Finland	Ferrari	75
	Robert Kubica	Poland	BMW Sauber	75
5	Fernando Alonso	Spain	Renault	61
6	Nick Heidfeld	Germany	BMW Sauber	60
7	Heikki Kovalainen	Finland	McLaren-Mercedes	53
8	Sebastian Vettel	Germany	Toro Rosso	35
9	Jarno Trulli	Italy	Toyota	31
10	Timo Glock	Germany	Toyota	25

2009

	Driver	Country	Car	Points
1	Jenson Button	Great Britain	Brawn GP	95
2	Sebastian Vettel	Germany	Red Bull	84
3	Rubens Barrichello	Brazil	Brawn GP	77
4	Mark Webber	Australia	Red Bull	69.5
5	Lewis Hamilton	Great Britain	McLaren-Mercedes	49
6	Kimi Räikkönen	Finland	Ferrari	48
7	Nico Rosberg	Germany	Williams	34.5
8	Jarno Trulli	Italy	Toyota	32.5
9	Fernando Alonso	Spain	Renault	26
10	Timo Glock	Germany	Toyota	24

2010

1	Sebastian Vettel	Germany	RBR-Renault	256
2	Fernando Alonso	Spain	Ferrari	252
3	Mark Webber	Australia	RBR-Renault	242
4	Lewis Hamilton	Great Britain	McLaren-Mercedes	240
5	Jenson Button	Great Britain	McLaren-Mercedes	214
6	Felipe Massa	Brazil	Ferrari	144
7	Nico Rosberg	Germany	Mercedes	142
8	Robert Kubica	Poland	Renault	136
9	Michael Schumacher	Germany	Mercedes	72
10	Rubens Barrichello	Brazil	Williams-Cosworth	47

2011

1	Sebastian Vettel	Germany	RBR-Renault	392
2	Jenson Button	Great Britain	McLaren-Mercedes	270
3	Mark Webber	Australia	RBR-Renault	258
4	Fernando Alonso	Spain	Ferrari	257
5	Lewis Hamilton	Great Britain	McLaren-Mercedes	227
6	Felipe Massa	Brazil	Ferrari	118
7	Nico Rosberg	Germany	Mercedes	89
8	Michael Schumacher	Germany	Mercedes	76
9	Adrian Sutil	Germany	Force India-Mercedes	42
10	Vitaly Petrov	Russia	Renault	37

2012

1	Sebastian Vettel	Germany	RBR-Renault	281
2	Fernando Alonso	Spain	Ferrari	278
3	Kimi Räikkönen	Finland	Lotus-Renault	207
4	Lewis Hamilton	Great Britain	McLaren-Mercedes	190
5	Jenson Button	Great Britain	McLaren-Mercedes	188
6	Mark Webber	Australia	RBR-Renault	179
7	Felipe Massa	Brazil	Ferrari	122
8	Romain Grosjean	France	Lotus-Renault	96
9	Nico Rosberg	Germany	Mercedes	93
10	Sergio Pérez	Mexico	Sauber-Ferrari	66

2013

1	Sebastian Vettel	Germany	RBR-Renault	397
2	Fernando Alonso	Spain	Ferrari	242
3	Mark Webber	Australia	RBR-Renault	199
4	Lewis Hamilton	Great Britain	Mercedes	189
5	Kimi Räikkönen	Finland	Lotus-Renault	183
6	Nico Rosberg	Germany	Mercedes	171
7	Romain Grosjean	France	Lotus-Renault	132
8	Felipe Massa	Brazil	Ferrari	112
9	Jenson Button	Great Britain	McLaren-Mercedes	73
10	Nico Hulkenberg	Germany	Sauber-Ferrari	51

Constructors' Championship

1958

	Car	Country	Points
1	Vanwall	Great Britain	48
2	Ferrari Dino	Italy	40
3	Cooper	Great Britain	31

1959

	Car	Country	Points
1	Cooper	Great Britain	40
2	Ferrari Dino	Italy	34
3	BRM	Great Britain	26

1960

	Car	Country	Points
1	Cooper	Great Britain	48
2	Lotus	Great Britain	32
3	Ferrari Dino	Italy	24

1961

	Car	Country	Points
1	Ferrari Dino	Italy	45
2	Lotus	Great Britain	35
3	Porsche	Germany	22

1962

	Car	Country	Points
1	BRM	Great Britain	42
2	Lotus	Great Britain	36
3	Cooper	Great Britain	29

1963

	Car	Country	Points
1	Lotus	Great Britain	54
2	BRM	Great Britain	36
3	Brabham	Australia	28

1964

	Car	Country	Points
1	Ferrari	Italy	45
2	BRM	Great Britain	42
3	Lotus	Great Britain	37

1965

	Car	Country	Points
1	Lotus	Great Britain	54
2	BRM	Great Britain	45
3	Brabham	Australia	27

1966

	Car	Country	Points
1	Brabham	Australia	42
2	Ferrari	Italy	31
3	Cooper	Great Britain	30

1967

	Car	Country	Points
1	Brabham	Australia	67
2	Lotus	Great Britain	50
3	Cooper	Great Britain	28

1968

	Car	Country	Points
1	Lotus	Great Britain	62
2	McLaren	New Zealand	51
3	Matra Ford	France	45

1969

	Car	Country	Points
1	Matra	France	66
2	Brabham	Australia	51
3	Lotus	Great Britain	47

1970

	Car	Country	Points
1	Lotus	Great Britain	59
2	Ferrari	Italy	55
3	March	Great Britain	48

1971

	Car	Country	Points
1	Tyrrell	Great Britain	73
2	BRM	Great Britain	36
3	March	Great Britain	34

1972

	Car	Country	Points
1	Lotus	Great Britain	61
2	Tyrrell	Great Britain	51
3	McLaren	New Zealand	47

Luigi Villoresi (Ferrari 375) in 1951.

1973

	Car	Country	Points
1	JPS/Lotus	Great Britain	92
2	Tyrrell	Great Britain	82
3	McLaren	New Zealand	58

1974

1	McLaren	New Zealand	73
2	Ferrari	Italy	65
3	Tyrrell	Great Britain	52

1975

1	Ferrari	Italy	72.5
2	Brabham	Australia	54
3	McLaren	New Zealand	53

1976

1	Ferrari	Italy	83
2	McLaren	New Zealand	74
3	Tyrrell	Great Britain	71

1977

1	Ferrari	Italy	95
2	Lotus	Great Britain	62
3	McLaren	New Zealand	60

1978

1	Lotus	Great Britain	86
2	Ferrari	Italy	58
3	Brabham	Australia	53

1979

1	Ferrari	Italy	113
2	Williams	Great Britain	75
3	Ligier	France	61

1980

	Car	Country	Points
1	Williams	Great Britain	120
2	Ligier	France	66
3	Brabham	Australia	55

1981

1	Williams	Great Britain	95
2	Brabham	Australia	61
3	Renault	France	54

1982

1	Ferrari	Italy	74
2	McLaren	New Zealand	69
3	Renault	France	62

1983

1	Ferrari	Italy	89
2	Renault	France	79
3	Brabham	Australia	72

1984

1	McLaren	New Zealand	143.5
2	Ferrari	Italy	57.5
3	Lotus	Great Britain	47

1985

1	McLaren	New Zealand	90
2	Ferrari	Italy	82
3	Williams	Great Britain	71

1986

1	Williams	Great Britain	141
2	McLaren	New Zealand	96
3	Lotus-Renault	Great Britain	58

1987

	Car	Country	Points
1	Williams	Great Britain	137
2	McLaren	New Zealand	76
3	Lotus	Lotus	64

1988

1	McLaren	New Zealand	199
2	Ferrari	Italy	65
3	Benetton	Italy	46

1989

1	McLaren	New Zealand	141
2	Williams	Great Britain	77
3	Ferrari	Italy	59

1990

1	McLaren	New Zealand	121
2	Ferrari	Italy	110
3	Benetton	Italy	71

1991

1	McLaren-Honda	New Zealand	139
2	Williams-Renault	Great Britain	125
3	Ferrari	Italy	55.5

1992

1	Williams-Renault	Great Britain	164
2	McLaren-Honda	New Zealand	99
3	Benetton-Ford	Italy	31

1993

1	Williams-Renault	Great Britain	168
2	McLaren-Ford	New Zealand	84
3	Benetton-Ford	Italy	72

Mario Andretti (Lotus 79 Ford) in 1978.

Right: David Coulthard,
Red Bull Racing Cosworth RB1 in 2005.

1994

Car	Country	Points
1 Williams-Renault	Great Britain	118
2 Benetton-Ford	Italy	103
3 Ferrari	Italy	71

1995

1 Benetton-Renault	Italy	137
2 Williams-Renault	Great Britain	112
3 Ferrari	Italy	73

1996

1 Williams-Renault	Great Britain	175
2 Ferrari	Italy	70
3 Benetton-Renault	Italy	68

1997

1 Williams-Renault	Great Britain	123
2 Ferrari	Italy	102
3 Benetton-Renault	Italy	67

1998

1 McLaren-Mercedes	Great Britain	156
2 Ferrari	Italy	133
3 Williams-Mecachrome	Great Britain	38

1999

1 Ferrari	Italy	128
2 McLaren-Mercedes	Great Britain	124
3 Jordan-Mugen Honda	Great Britain	61

2000

1 Ferrari	Italy	170
2 McLaren-Mercedes	Great Britain	152
3 Williams	Great Britain	36

2001

Car	Country	Points
1 Ferrari	Italy	179
2 McLaren-Mercedes	Great Britain	102
3 Williams	Great Britain	80

2002

1 Ferrari	Italy	221
2 Williams	Great Britain	92
3 McLaren-Mercedes	Great Britain	65

2003

1 Ferrari	Italy	158
2 Williams	Great Britain	144
3 McLaren-Mercedes	Great Britain	142

2004

1 Ferrari	Italy	262
2 BAR	Great Britain	119
3 Renault	France	105

2005

1 Renault	France	191
2 McLaren-Mercedes	Great Britain	182
3 Ferrari	Italy	100

2006

1 Renault	France	206
2 Ferrari	Italy	201
3 McLaren-Mercedes	Great Britain	110

2007

1 Ferrari	Italy	204
2 BMW Sauber	Germany	101
3 Renault	France	51

2008

Car	Country	Points
1 Ferrari	Italy	172
2 McLaren-Mercedes	Great Britain	151
3 BMW Sauber	Germany	135

2009

1 Brawn–Mercedes	Great Britain	172
2 RBR–Renault	Great Britain	153.5
3 McLaren-Mercedes	Great Britain	71

2010

1 RBR-Renault	Great Britain	498
2 McLaren-Mercedes	Great Britain	454
3 Ferrari	Italy	396

2011

1 RBR-Renault	Great Britain	650
2 McLaren-Mercedes	Great Britain	497
3 Ferrari	Italy	375

2012

1 RBR-Renault	Great Britain	460
2 Ferrari	Italy	400
3 McLaren-Mercedes	Great Britain	378

2013

1 RBR-Renault	Great Britain	596
2 Mercedes	Great Britain	360
3 Ferrari	Italy	354

ACKNOWLEDGEMENTS

Thanks to everyone at LAT especially Peter Higham, Tim Wright,
Kevin Wood, Zoë Mayho and the digital team John Tingle,
Tim Clarke and Alastair Staley.

Thanks also to Oliver Higgs, Kate Truman, Cliff Salter and John Dunne.